Damien Lewis
BLOODY
HEROES

arrow books

1 3 5 7 9 10 8 6 4 2

Arrow Books
20 Vauxhall Bridge Road
London SW1V 2SA

Arrow Books is part of the Penguin Random House group of companies
whose addresses can be found at global.penguinrandomhouse.com.

Penguin
Random House
UK

First published in the United Kingdom by Century in 2006
First published in paperback by Arrow Books in 2007
This edition published by Arrow Books in 2020

www.penguin.co.uk

A CIP catalogue record for this book is available from the British Library.

ISBN 9781787461475

Printed and bound in Great Britain by Clays Ltd, Elcograf S.p.A.

Penguin Random House is committed to a sustainable future
for our business, our readers and our planet. This book is made
from Forest Stewardship Council® certified paper.

MIX
Paper from
responsible sources
FSC® C018179

For David, aka Chubbs, who as I write is one year old;
and for Jess, aka Nana, who has just
passed her ninetieth birthday.

'Dat, Dat-Dat, Dat, Dat … there was fire coming from all directions. It felt like WW3 had broken out all around us – you could just feel the air expanding and contracting with all the explosions.' **Jamie Bryan, SBS soldier,** on the Qala-I-Janghi uprising

'I'm glad the story for the battle for Qala-I-Janghi has been told – and especially how those heroic British soldiers tried to rescue my son, Mike Spann. My son could have turned and ran, but he elected to step forward and take a stand. If he'd run that day he'd not have been able to live with himself.' **Johnny Spann Senior** (father of CIA Agent Johnny Mike Spann, killed in action at Qala-I-Janghi, November 2001)

'A graphic account of an amazing mission and an utterly gripping story. Misses nothing in the detail. Heroes – every one of them!' **C/Inspector Kevin Smith,** PSNI and former UN Police Commander

BLOODY HEROES

CONTENTS

ACKNOWLEDGEMENTS

Special thanks are due to the following without whom this book would not have been possible: my literary agent, Andrew Lownie, a consummate operator in the world of literary affairs and a fearless warrior on behalf of his authors; my editors, Mark Booth and Tim Andrews, for their enthusiasm and unstinting support for this story; Kate Watkins, Ron Beard, Robert Nichols, Neil Bradford et al., who make writing for Random House such an enjoyable and edifying experience; SAS Mike, for first bringing the story to my attention and alerting me to its potential as a book – cheers, mate, again; Doughnut, thanks a million, you are one of the Bloody Heroes; his wife and little one, for the hospitality and putting up with our beery antics; his father-in-law, not least for the jokes; Big J, Little T and the other lads – thanks a million for the obvious; my very special thanks to Johnny Spann (Sr), for sharing your son's story with me; once again Hannah Lewis, for research and all-round support, and for bravely overcoming your injuries from the 7/7 terror attacks on London; once again my father, for his comments on early drafts and for the wonderful Quinsat discovery; Keir Lewis, my big bro, for timely translations from the French; Don McClen, your comments on the manuscript and your encouragement have again been invaluable; A. J. Hogan, for casting a sharp eye over early drafts and for the constant words of support; Michael Kargbo, for the background research materials; Colonel Richard and Barbara Price, of ASA Analysis, for the insight into chemical weapons issues; Julian Perry-Robinson, of SPRU, for his expert opinion on producing a poor man's chemical weapon; Rachel Maletnlema, for being there when we needed you; my mother, for being here when you could be and your care for others allowed; Stephen O'Keeffe, for finding me a place to work in peace on the edge of the world; Tim and Ellen, for 'the scoops', the chilli and great company during the writing; Steve Clarke, for the beer, the mountain walks, the laughs and a reader's comments from the ground up; his father, John Clarke, for the military history on Afghanistan; his son, Billy Clarke, for a wildly precocious critique of the early drafts; Geoff, ex-lighthouse keeper and literary wizard, for your comments on the early drafts; Kevin – yachtsman, philosopher and landlord extraordinaire, for comments on the early drafts; Sinead and Adrian, for such perceptive feedback on the early drafts and your wonderful company; Mohammed and KA, for sharing your experience of fighting in Afghanistan with me; my good friend Zeinal Abdeen, for your comments from an Arabic and Islamic perspective; and finally, Eva, my very special loving thanks to you.

Picture Credits

All photographs copyright John Smith, excepting the following:

1. British, US, Aussie and New Zealand special forces deployed by Chinook on low level flights. One hit from an enemy stinger and this chopper would be blasted out of the sky – Courtesy Royal Marines Commando.

2. Flying in line astern, MH47 Chinooks deployed special forces teams deep into hostile Afghan terrain – Courtesy Royal Marines Commando.

The artist's impressions used in this book showing scenes of British special forces in action at Qala-i-Janghi fort are by Niall Arden, himself an SAS officer (reserves, now retired). Niall served in 21 SAS for many years and, more recently, on clandestine operations in Iraq and elsewhere. Due to his artistic skill, Niall became one of the Regiment's main informal artists painting scenes from various SAS missions – including those in Sierra Leone, the Balkans and East Timor. Due to his work producing paintings commemorating those who had died in action, Niall became known by the nickname 'Death Pilgrim' to his fellow SAS officers and men.

To see more of Niall's artwork of the events portrayed in this book go to: www.damienlewis.com

Graphics by Fast.net Business Services, www.myfast.ie

AUTHOR'S NOTE

THIS book tells of British and US special forces in action in the war in Afghanistan. Its timescale covers the first eight weeks of that conflict, and the narrative follows the exploits of a dozen British and American soldiers. The war in Afghanistan was fought largely by British and American special forces (aided by their Aussie and Kiwi counterparts), working alongside the Afghan resistance. This band of brothers consisted of British SBS and SAS troops and their US counterparts in Delta Force, the SEALs, the Special Operations Forces and the CIA. They operated in close-knit units the likes of which have rarely been seen since the Second World War. This is a story of elite forces in action in a secret conflict, a war fought in the shadows.

While fighting the al-Qaeda and Taliban (AQT) threat in the Afghan wildlands, the British and American special forces soldiers became involved in action and drama that go far beyond the ordinary. War is certainly hell, and there are hellish events portrayed in these pages. But war also has the ability to draw out extremes of human action

– whether that manifests itself in bestiality and mass murder, or the heroism, selflessness and the epic will to survive as portrayed in these pages. As the author of this book, I have double- and triple-checked these stories from many different sources, and I know them to be truthful and accurate portrayals of the events as they took place.

Very little has been written about the actions of the SBS and SAS in Afghanistan. Of the written accounts that do exist, much is pure fiction masquerading as fact – resulting in part from the culture of secrecy that surrounds the operations of our elite units. Consequently, books of this nature are written almost exclusively from the verbal accounts of those who have taken part in the events portrayed. In this book, where there are significant sections of dialogue, this is largely recreated from the memories of those present at the time. Certain incidents written about were recorded on tape, and I have had access to those tapes during the course of researching the stories recounted herein.

Nothing that I have written should threaten the security of our special forces, or their ability to operate in all theatres of war. Had there been anything in the events portrayed that might have done so, I would have been asked to remove it and would have done so. However, I have been assisted in its writing by those whose identities must remain secret. Because of this I have changed some of the names, dates and locations of this story. But I have done so only where necessary and at the request of the personnel involved. For example, the names of the British and American special forces soldiers and intelligence agents have been altered.

Excessive secrecy surrounding SAS and SBS operations acts as a licence for sensationalised stories to appear in the media. Is this detrimental to the ability of those units to function properly? Possibly. It certainly creates unrealistic expectations concerning what those units are capable of. I also believe that those unique individuals drawn to a career within Britain's elite units deserve to be free, within limits, to tell their stories. These are important, instructional areas of our recent military history, and they need to be told. I have several special forces soldiers whom I count as close friends, and they are by their nature intelligent, thinking individuals. It is perhaps unrealistic to expect them to remain forever silent, and a little more openness might not be such a bad thing.

I have also attempted in this book to tell the 'other side of the story' – that of the al-Qaeda and Taliban elements. I have spoken to several of the foreign (non-Afghan) Taliban fighters and the foreign mujahidin – including those who claim to have fought against allied forces in the battles portrayed in this book. The siege of Afghanistan's Qala-i-Janghi fort – the central narrative – has attained a mythical status among AQT forces. It is seen as something of a Custer's Last Stand for them. I have no way of absolutely verifying their stories, but they do fit with the accounts of these events as told to me by others, most importantly the special forces soldiers and intelligence agents present during the battle.

A percentage of the royalties from this book will be donated to the UK's Veterans Agency.

The President of the United States Takes Pleasure in Presenting the Navy Cross to:

Sam Brown, United States Navy
For Services as Set Forth in the Following:

FOR extraordinary heroism while serving with the British Special Boat Service (SBS) during combat operations in Afghanistan. Chief Petty Officer Sam Brown deployed to the area as a member of a Joint American and British Special Forces Team to locate and recover two American citizens, one presumed to be seriously injured or dead, after al-Qaeda and Taliban prisoners at the Qala-i-Janghi fortress in Mazar-e-Sharif overpowered them and gained access to large quantities of arms and ammunition stored at the fort. Once inside, Chief Petty Officer Sam Brown was engaged continuously by direct small-arms fire, indirect mortar fire and rocket-propelled grenade fire. He was forced to advance through an active anti-personnel minefield in order to gain entry to the fortress. After establishing the possible location of both American citizens, under heavy fire and without concern for his own personal safety, he made two attempts to rescue the uninjured citizen by crawling toward the fortress interior to reach him. Forced to withdraw due to large volumes of fire falling on his position he was undeterred . . . As darkness began to fall, no attempt was going to be made to locate the injured American citizen. Chief Petty Officer Sam Brown then took matters into his own hands. Without regard for his own personal safety, he moved forward another 300–400 meters into the heart of the fortress by himself under constant enemy fire in an attempt to locate the injured citizen. Running low on ammunition, he utilized weapons from the deceased Afghans to continue his rescue attempt. Upon verifying the condition and location of the American citizen, he withdrew from the fortress. By his outstanding display of decisive leadership, unlimited courage in the face of enemy fire, and utmost devotion to duty, Chief Petty Officer Sam Brown reflected great credit upon himself and upheld the highest traditions of the United States Naval Services.

Statement from George J. Tenet, Director of the Central Intelligence Agency (CIA)

It is my sad duty to announce that one of our officers at the Central Intelligence Agency has died in the line of duty in Afghanistan. Johnny Michael 'Mike' Spann, who worked in the Directorate of Operations, was where he wanted to be: on the front line serving his country. Mike was in the Qala-i-Janghi fortress in Mazar-e-Sharif, where Taliban prisoners were being held and questioned. Although these captives had given themselves up, their pledge of surrender – like so many other pledges from the vicious group they represent – proved worthless. Their prison uprising – which had murder as its goal – claimed many lives, among them that of a very brave American, whose body was recovered just hours ago. Mike joined the CIA in June 1999. A young man – only thirty-two years old – he was no stranger to challenge or daring. He came to us from the United States Marine Corps, whose traditions he loved and whose values of courage and commitment he carried with him to the end. Quiet, serious, and absolutely unflappable, Mike's stoicism concealed a dry sense of humor and a heart of gold. His brand of leadership was founded not on words, but on deeds – deeds performed in conditions of hazard and hardship. His was a careeer of promise in a life of energy and achievement. A precious life given in a noble cause. Mike fell bringing freedom to a distant people while defending freedom for all of us at home. Mike Spann was an American hero, a man who showed passion for his country and his Agency through his selfless courage. Mike Spann will live forever in our memories. May God grant him eternal peace and give his wonderful family the strength to carry on. His CIA family, too, is in mourning. But just as we grieve together, we work together to continue the mission that Mike Spann held sacred. And so we will continue our battle against evil – with renewed strength and spirit. We owe that to Mike and to every man and woman who dreams of a future free from the menace of terrorism. Johnny Michael Spann was the husband of Sharon Spann, and is survived by his infant son, two young daughters, and two sisters. He was the son of Johnny and Gail Spann, of Winfield, Alabama.

Go as a pilgrim and seek out danger
Far from the comfort and the well lit avenues of life,
Pit your very soul against the unknown
And seek stimulation in the company of the brave.
Experience cold and hunger, heat and thirst,
And survive to see another challenge and another
    dawn.
Only then will you be at peace with yourself,
And be able to know and say
I looked down on the farthest side of the mountain
And fulfilled, and understanding all, and truly content
I lived a life that was my own.
We are the pilgrims, master: we shall go
Always a little further: it may be
Beyond the last blue mountain barred with snow,
Across that angry or that glimmering sea.

UK Special Forces poem (anon)
The last four lines are extracted
from James Elroy Flecker,
'The Golden Journey to Samarkand'

They fight in Allah's cause, so they kill and are killed.
                                    – Koran, 9:111

A note on security: a number of the military figures who have read this book during draft stages have commented on the fact that the local Afghans who assisted Allied special forces in this war and are described herein as doing such may be open to reprisals by al-Qaeda and Taliban elements. For the record, the identities of those local Afghans portrayed as doing so in this book have been changed, as have the names of the locations where such events took place. That caveat aside, the events themselves are described completely accurately and entirely as they took place on the ground.

I

SURPRISE, SURPRISE

It was 22 December 2001, just over three months after the 9/11 terror attacks on America, and the ultimate nightmare scenario was unfolding before the eyes of Her Majesty's security services. A cargo ship believed to be carrying a massive chemical weapon was steaming its way towards London. For days now, British intelligence agents had been tracking the vessel as she made her way up the coast of Europe. They suspected that she was crewed by terrorists and on a mission to hit London. If the attack went ahead, thousands could be poisoned and a huge swathe of the city left a devastated wasteland. As the ship steamed into the English Channel only Britain's elite special forces were seen as being capable of stopping her. The men of the SBS (Special Boat Service) and SAS (Special Air Service) were about to be called into action yet again.

At 6.45 a.m. on that cold December morning the men of the SBS were rousing themselves from their beds in preparation for heading into their Poole base, on the Dorset coast. Or at least those who were still on active duty were. Having just spent two hard months in the hostile wild lands of Afghanistan hunting down al-Qaeda and Taliban terrorists, many of the SBS lads had already left Poole for a well-earned Christmas break and were still wrapped up warmly with their wives or girlfriends at home in their beds. Nothing could have been further from their minds than a terrorist strike on London. And few could have imagined that they were about to be thrust into action yet again – on a life-or-death mission.

Earlier that morning SBS Company Sergeant Major (CSM) Gav Tinker, had been woken by a surprise telephone call. It came from the Cabinet Office Briefing Room (COBR), Britain's national crisis control centre in London, staffed by key ministers and top military officials.

The CSM had been given a 'gypsy warning', an officers-only alert to a potential SBS operation. Gav Tinker had immediately driven over to the SBS's deserted base and started working the phones. With few of the soldiers around, the CSM was deeply worried about who the hell he could call in to man the forthcoming mission.

By 8.30 those SBS lads still on duty were rolling up at their Poole base, a series of dull grey hangars and prefab buildings clustering along the shoreline of Poole harbour. They were pitifully few in numbers. For the first time ever in the SBS's long and quietly distinguished history, the regiment's headquarters element (its command and control structure) had been deployed overseas, to the war in Afghanistan. And two of the SBS's three combat squadrons – M and Z, each consisting of some sixty-odd men – were still operationally deployed there. Only a handful of the men from C Squadron – the on-call counter-terrorism force based in the UK – were still on duty at Poole.

Route of the MV Nisha Cargo Ship

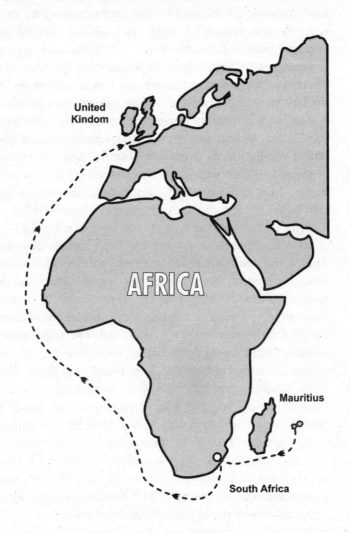

United Kindom

AFRICA

Mauritius

South Africa

CSM Gav Tinker's short-cropped grey hair betrayed his age, as he was pushing fifty. But his lean frame and quick movements reflected the fact that he kept himself very much in shape. A forceful leader, used to getting his own way, he still believed himself as tough as any of the younger boys. At around 8.45 a.m. he headed over to C Squadron's 'den', where he found SBS Trooper Mat Morrisey just firing up the tea urn to get a brew on. In his late twenties, Mat was a short, stocky tree trunk of a man, with a shock of unruly dark hair. Originally from Lancashire, he had a gruff, northern manner, and he also had a reputation as a maverick in the SBS, an unconventional soldier with a willingness to try anything in battle. Mat still carried the scars from the recent hell that he'd been through in Afghanistan, where he'd fought a series of battles that had all but cost him his life.

Mat had immense respect for Gav Tinker. Gav was one of the 'old and bold', a career soldier who'd seen action with the SBS all over the world. More importantly, as far as Mat and the rest of the lads were concerned, he was a conscientious leader who cared deeply for the men under his command. The CSM treated them as thinking individuals, all too often a neglected aspect of command in the British military these days. Mat would have followed Gav Tinker anywhere if ordered to do so, and had already done as much in Afghanistan (or 'the Stan', as the lads like to call it).

C Squadron's 'den' – a makeshift bar-cum-canteen – was a product of the CSM's concern for the well-being of his men. Gav Tinker had recently decided that each troop needed an on-site caff-boozer – somewhere informal where they could wind down and chew the fat at the end of training sessions or operations. So he'd found three old huts on the base that the lads could rip to shreds and refurnish and rename as they wished. In keeping with the maritime traditions of the SBS – who specialise in fighting over, on or under the water – C Squadron's den had been christened the Toad, M Squadron's, the Frog, and Z Squadron's, the Newt. As soon as Mat caught sight of the CSM on this bleak winter's morning he knew that something was up.

'Look like you've just seen a bloody ghost,' Mat remarked. 'What's eating you, mate?'

'Mat! Thank fuck you're 'ere at least,' the CSM said, as he closed the door to the Toad. 'See you've still got that sweet tooth then, lad,' he commented, pointing at the bag of doughnuts that Mat had picked up on his way into work. 'I've told you before to lay off the lard. You'll be turning into a tubby fucker. Fat lot of good you'll be to the girls then, knowing how partial you are to 'em an' all.'

It was typical of the CSM that when the going got tough, he'd start cracking the jokes. It was all part of the SBS's way of doing things – to remain cool and to keep your sense of humour under pressure.

'It's me breakfast, mate,' Mat shot back at him. 'Anyhow, what's wrong with you? You look like death. Your old lady forgotten it's Christmas or something?'

'Very funny, lad,' the CSM grunted in reply. 'Well, if you thought you'd had enough action in the Stan, you don't know the half of it. Get a bloody load of this. We've been warned off for an immediate DAA [direct action assault] against a terrorist target. Ship it is. Steaming up the bloody English Channel right now she is, and stuffed full of God only knows what nasty shite.'

'Holy fuck, you're taking the piss, aren't you, mate?' Mat replied, a doughnut frozen halfway to his mouth in amazement. 'I mean, three days before Christmas an' all. Is nowt sacred?'

''Fraid I'm serious, lad. Just got the call from Whitehall. Look, al-Qaeda ain't going to put a freeze on ops just cos of Christmas, are they? Santa Claus and sleigh bells don't mean bugger all to them, do they? More 'n likely to go for a festive bonus, aren't they? And from everything I've been told about this one, it'll make 9/11 look like a bloody picnic.'

The CSM paused for a moment to let his words sink in. 'I want you to get on the blower and get every man and his dog back into base,' he continued. 'I don't care who they are, where they are, whether they've been in admin or stores or whatever for the last five years – I don't care if they've forgotten how to fire a bloody weapon even – just get the fuckers in. Cos what've we got around Poole at the moment, lad? Me, you, the cleaner and the regimental cat. And we ain't going to stop al-Qaeda's terror ship with that, are we? So get on the blower, smartish. Wake 'em up, drag 'em out of their beds, haul 'em in from their holidays – I don't care how you do it. Just get 'em in here quickly – cos this one's more 'n likely going to kick off tonight.'

'Holy fuck, *tonight*? *Tonight*? How many blokes d'you reckon we'll need? I mean, how many do we need to stop the bastards?'

'Look, it's a container ship, MV *Nisha*, or some such half-arsed name, steaming up the Channel bound for London she is. She's got some sort of improvised chemical weapon on board. Evil. Crew of sixteen or so. You do the maths. We need to hit it with overwhelming fire-power. Swamp the fuckers with enough men so they don't know what's hit them – and before they can wake up to us being on to them and detonate the bloody bomb.

Reckon we need sixty to seventy of us, minimum. I've got twenty-three SAS lads promised from Hereford who'll soon be on their way down to us. That leaves forty-seven blokes to find our end. Minus me, you, the cat and the cleaner, that leaves forty-three. OK? So get to it, lad.'

'Twenty-three SAS lads, did you say? They'll be about as much use as an ashtray on a motorbike. I'll just finish me breakfast and then I'll get the real boys in. This is a job for us lot, and no mistake.'

'That's the spirit, lad. And while you're at it, I'll be breaking out the stores. We'll be needing some serious hardware if we're going to mallet this lot good an' proper.'

'What d'you reckon the chances are of it getting the green light, boss?' Mat asked, just as Gav Tinker was turning to leave.

'From what I've been hearing, I'd say we're 90 per cent on already. Make no mistake, lad – this one's going down.'

During Mat's seven years in the SBS they had done several phantom call-ins – where the men were rushed back to base for a mock counter-terrorism operation. So the mechanics of getting the lads in were well known. What made this different was the timing – three days before Christmas and with two-thirds of the SBS still deployed in Afghanistan. As he worked the phones, one half of Mat's brain was dealing with the requirements of the call-in, while the other half was drawing up a mental checklist of everything that would have to be done before they hit that ship.

At the same time, a thousand questions were running through his mind. From where would the mission be launched? Would they hit the ship by boat from the sea, or by air in the choppers? Exactly what sort of explosive device was on board? And how would the SAS lads going into action alongside them perform? The SAS were brilliant when it came to airborne and land-based missions, but seaborne assaults weren't their speciality. This was the SBS's terrain.

The SBS is arguably the most elite and the most secretive special forces unit in the world. In contrast to the SAS, their exploits receive little, if any, publicity. Their motto is 'By Strength and by Guile' and in contrast to the SAS the unit prefers to operate wholly in the shadows. They specialise in fighting over, on or under the water. While they are experts in water-borne operations, they are trained to operate in any conditions. Their combat record has caused a great deal of rivalry with the SAS. In spite of this the two units regularly train together, with practically every exercise having both SBS and SAS teams present. And they deploy together in joint combat missions.

The SBS and SAS train all the time for attacking an enemy vessel. Most of this training is done on HMS *Rame Head*, a ship anchored in Portsmouth harbour. The *Rame Head* was first built to serve as an escort ship during the Second World War. In recent years she was turned into a giant firing range, having a huge steel box resembling an aircraft hangar bolted on to her deck. This is where the SBS carry out their ship-assault exercises, using live bullets and explosives. They rehearse hostage-rescue scenarios, close-quarter battles (CQB), ladder ascents and anchor-chain climbs. They practise the explosive method of entry, where shaped charges are used to take off doors and windows, and they even blow entry holes through a ship's bulkheads.

While HMS *Rame Head* is perfect for practising assaults on a stationary target, it can't be used to rehearse a direct action assault on a moving target at sea. For this, the SBS run two main exercises every year, code-named Exercise Bitter Fruit and Exercise Sea Harvest. These are carried out jointly with the SAS and are made as realistic and lifelike as possible. The exercise takes place on a fast, hydrofoil Seacat ferry when the ship is closed to passengers and has a minimum crew on board. The SBS and SAS use their helicopters and rigid inflatable boats to assault the ship from the sea and air. The exercise takes place just before Christmas, when the weather can be guaranteed to be at its most atrocious, so testing the men to their very limits.

But training apart, the men of the SBS and SAS had never carried out a DAA against a hostile ship in the whole history of British special forces. The MV *Nisha* operation was going to be a first – a baptism of fire for those mounting the attack.

By 5 p.m. on that grey December day a mixed squadron of SAS and SBS men had been assembled at the SBS's Poole base. Twenty-six were from the SAS and the rest were 'Shakyboats', as the SBS jokingly call themselves (SBS=Shaky Boat Service=Shakyboats). Normally, there would have been at least twenty-four hours put aside prior to launching an attack for assault planning, rehearsals and intelligence gathering. But with the MV *Nisha* making a steady sixteen knots she was now no more than two hundred miles away from her intended target. In less than thirteen hours the ship would be in London, primed to launch a catastrophic and deadly attack. The threat assessment was so severe that it was decided to take her out as soon as possible, before she had the chance to get any closer to the British coastline. And so the assault force was told that they would be hitting the vessel at dawn the following morning.

The SBS and SAS soldiers loaded their specialist assault kit, weapons, ammunition and boats on to twenty

Mercedes-Benz vans, which were fitted with two-way radios and souped-up engines. With blue lights flashing they set off at top speed, a police escort leading the way. As the traffic was forced to the roadside, the convoy of elite special forces sped past. They made the forty-mile drive to RAF Yeovilton – a helicopter base from which they would launch their attack – in record time.

The convoy pulled into Yeovilton at 5.45 p.m., and the men began slinging their camp beds in one of the giant aircraft hangars. Scant information had been given out about the forthcoming mission but, somehow, word had got around about the basic nature of what they were up against. As the men waited for the mission briefings to begin, the atmosphere was electric, buzzing with excitement in anticipation of the coming assault. By now, the mission to take down the MV *Nisha* had been given its code name: Ocean Strike.

In the makeshift ops room the officers and NCOs (non-commissioned officers) were establishing the nerve centre of the assault. Banks of computers, whiteboards and projector screens were being set up, and aerial photographs and sea charts pinned on to noticeboards. Experts from MI5 and MI6 were present, as this had by now become both a foreign and domestic terrorist incident. The SBS and SAS lads called these intelligence agents the 'Green Slime'. The Green Slime had managed to rustle up some ship's plans showing the layout of the MV *Nisha*, and these would be used to plan the ship assault.

The special forces soldiers would be operating in four-man units, called 'fire teams'. As the leader of his fire team, Mat set about checking over all the gear that they would need for the assault. Different levels of force are authorised before any SBS/SAS operation goes ahead. The normal method of entry is manual, using crowbars and sledgehammers to break down doors and windows. Very rarely is the explosive method of entry given the green light, but on this mission the men had been cleared to use every means available to them.

With the briefing still seeming a long way off, Mat set about making up the explosive charges that he'd need for the assault. Without Mat having had to say a word, the lads in his fire team had followed suit – each of them making up the half-dozen explosive charges that they'd need for the assault.

Mat glanced at his watch: it was 6.45 p.m. Surely the mission briefings would be starting soon? He was more than a little anxious to learn exactly what they were up against. He looked around at the men in his team. Whatever role they were given on the assault, it was a great bunch of guys to be going in with. They'd been together now for approaching two years, operating as a close-knit unit, an instinctive band of brothers.

Jamie 'Bomber' Bryan – in his late twenties and a gentle giant of a guy – was one of Mat's closest mates. Like Mat, he was a northerner and shared the same dour sense of humour. A six foot two, dark-haired Yorkshireman, Jamie had a quiet, almost shy manner. He rarely swore, and always thought about what he wanted to say before he opened his mouth. He had kind eyes ringed with laughter lines, and used his hands a lot when trying to explain things. Also like Mat, he had a massive capacity for beer drinking and was known to get all emotional when drunk. But underneath his quiet exterior Bomber Bryan was known to be an absolute killer when the red mist of combat went down. Jamie was Mat's right-hand man – the one person he would trust more than any other. If Mat ever had to choose someone to fight back to back with, Bomber was his man.

Tom 'Scrapper' Knight, also in his late twenties, was a complete contrast to Jamie. He was a little, stocky, punchy lad from the East End of London, with a sharp tongue and a quick eye. He had close-cropped sandy hair, which was going thin on top. Mat had always found Tom a difficult guy to get to know or feel close to. Even when they'd been out on the lash together, Scrapper gave little away about his family or other personal details. A lot of the blokes reckoned Tom was on a mission to prove himself, but in spite of his aloofness, Mat knew he was a good operator and played well in the team. In fact, there were aspects of Tom's character that reminded Mat of himself. Tom was a rebel without a cause. He had a massive disrespect for authority, believing most of the 'ruperts' (officers) were 'total wankers'. He made no bones about how he felt about them, and the officers in turn gave Tom a wide berth whenever they could. And this was no bad thing, as far as Mat was concerned, because it generally kept them off his back, too.

Then there was the last member of the team, Donald 'Mucker' Jones, the real joker in the pack. Mucker, a Scot, was about the same height and build as Mat – five foot eight and solid, going on overweight. They both shared an incurable sweet tooth, although Mucker seemed to pile the weight on far more easily than Mat. With his wild brown hair, pudgy face and bulbous stomach, Mucker's alternative nickname was 'the Hobbit'. While Mucker saw himself as the team joker, often as not the joke would be on him. None of the lads could quite understand how Mucker had made it into the SBS in the first place. But, for Mat at least, his incurable good humour made him a great asset on the team.

Having been in the SBS for several years now, Jamie, Tom and Donald had been through enough with Mat to know that they trusted his leadership implicitly. Mat 'Doughnut' Morrisey was a solid, rugged northern soul, and an excellent all-round sportsman, despite his short, tree-trunk-like figure, playing in several military teams. From as early as he could remember Mat had always wanted to be a 'commando', so he'd left school at sixteen and joined the Royal Marines. He'd spent the next ten years of his life drinking and fighting, burning every penny of his monthly wages on booze, women and his mates. Mat put a huge value on loyalty – to his mates first and foremost. If any of them ever got into trouble – a fight over a woman or a spilled pint of beer – Mat would be the first to wade in, fists flying in support of his pals.

Joining the SBS had really helped straighten Mat out. It had made him grow up fast and realise his true talents and intellect. He soon curtailed the fighting and the boozing, and he chose to train as a medic as his SBS specialist skill. As an added bonus he'd been sent to work for three months in an accident and emergency unit at a hospital – to gain real-life experience of treating medical trauma. He'd got to stay in the nurses' accommodation. Never inclined to be overly modest, Mat would often joke about how he'd managed to seduce every one of the nurses on the ward – all except the male ones. Mat was calm under pressure and inspired natural trust and confidence in the men in his team. The only time he ever seemed to lose his rag when anyone called him 'Doughnut' – a nickname the lads had coined just to wind him up.

Just as Mat's team were finishing making up the last of the explosives charges, a call went out for all the men to attend the mission briefing. The seventy soldiers of the SBS and SAS crowded into one of the deserted helicopter hangars, and silence quickly settled as the SBS

CSM, Gav Tinker, stood out front to speak. With the commanding officer of the SBS away in Afghanistan, it had fallen to the CSM to give the overall mission briefing. And even though he was one of the old and the bold, Gav Tinker was not used to speaking to such a large, crowded room. As a result, when he began the briefing, he was feeling decidedly nervous.

'Right, as you lot probably know already you're deploying on a bona fide marine counter-terrorism operation. This is not, I repeat not, a rehearsal,' the CSM announced, pausing for a second to let his words sink in and to help get over his nerves. 'You are to hit the MV *Nisha*, a merchant ship suspected of carrying a chemical weapon and bound for London. Your priority is to stop the ship, keep it on a heading, search her and apprehend any terrorists on board.

'The assault will take place in international waters, off the Sussex coast. We're still trying to clarify exactly what time you're going to hit the ship, but expect it to be under cover of darkness, most likely just before first light. At all costs that vessel must be stopped before she reaches the Thames estuary. Every available man of the SBS together with twenty-six of our SAS colleagues will be going in on this one. I want you to swamp her with maximum firepower so as to prevent the ship's crew triggering any device that may be on board. Make no mistake, you are to use all necessary measures – whatever it takes – to stop that ship.

'Right, that's the formal mission brief over with. Now to the specifics. You are to hit the MV *Nisha* simultaneously from the air and the ocean – roping down from Chinooks, and using RIBs and hook-and-pole ladders to scale her from the sea. Obviously, no one's diving on this one. The *Nisha*'s underway and likely to remain that way until we stop her, so there's no way we can hit her from under the water. You'll have two Lynx attack helicopters in support, and four Sea Kings coming in directly behind them. Now, this is a recent photo of the *Nisha* taken by some of our intel people.' The CSM pulled up an aerial photo of the MV *Nisha* on the projector screen. The ship consisted of a long hull packed full of cargo holds, with a towering white superstructure at the rear. For the assembled SBS and SAS soldiers this was the first image they'd seen of the target. It looked like a bog-standard cargo ship as far as they could tell.

'I'll leave it to the intel boys to give you the whole how's your father on the make-up of the ship,' the CSM continued. 'But the overall assault plan works like this. There'll be four RIBs [rigid inflatable boats] launched from HMS *Sutherland*, out of visual range of the ship, each with one fire team on board. That force will take the starboard bow, then work through the cargo holds from the bow to the stern. There'll be two Chinooks with the rest of you on board. You lot'll rope down from the choppers on to the rear of the ship, here.' He indicated two flat areas on the roof of the ship's bridge. 'Now, this part of the assault is bleedin' critical. If we're hitting the ship at night – as I presume we will be – the majority of the crew should still be asleep. So, it's crucial you hit them hard in their beds before they have time to wake up to the attack. If you are spotted by any watchmen when you hit the ship, the snipers on board the Lynx choppers will be tasked with taking them out. The two Chinooks and the four RIBs will be hitting the ship at exactly the same time.'

The CSM then ran through the specifics of the operation peculiar to this particular assault. Each four-man team would have one member of the Explosives Ordnance

Disposal (EOD) unit on hand, so if they came across any bombs then the EOD men could disable them. Royal Engineers from 49 Field Squadron would also be present and tasked with disabling any complex and/or non-conventional explosive devices. A reception/handover cell for prisoners would be established at Thorny Island, in Chichester harbour – the nearest secure landfall to the intended location of the ship interception and assault. There, sixteen members of CSMR – chemical and biological warfare specialists attached to the SBS/SAS – would be on standby with a full nuclear, biological and chemical decontamination unit. The four Sea King choppers would carry the command and control elements of the assault, plus teams from HM Customs & Excise and Special Branch.

'I'll leave your troop leaders to brief each of you on your team-specific roles,' the CSM said, rounding off his brief. 'You all know the drill, cos you've rehearsed this more times than I can remember. I have every confidence in you all. So go in and take down that ship. Any questions?'

'Who's first on to the target, boss?' one of the SBS lads asked.

'Mat Morrisey's team will take the lead role – first down the fast ropes and on to the bridge.'

A groan went up from the rest of the SBS teams, who'd all wanted the honour of taking the lead.

'Doughnut! Why does bubba get the lead?' someone shouted out. 'Hardly able to squeeze himself out of a chopper at the best of times.'

'Go fuck yourself, Dogboy,' Mat fired back. 'At least when I do I know one end of me MP5 from another, which is more than can be said for a desk-bound fuck like you.'

'Calm it, lads,' the CSM interjected. 'Very funny. Anyone got anything serious to say? Anyone got any more questions?'

'You said you're still trying to work out when we hit the ship,' Jamie asked. 'Why's that, boss? Surely we should go in at the dead of night, to maximise surprise?'

'In an ideal world, yes,' the CSM grunted. 'But we're having a few problems with our political taskmasters over this one. Seems there's some saying we should hit it in daylight, so as not to frighten the poor crew members too much when the black death hits them.'

'You *what*, boss?' Tom Knight piped up. 'You can't be fuckin' serious.'

''Fraid I am – seems even terrorists have rights. Anything else?'

'Why is the first priority of attack the bridge?' Mat asked. 'Why not the ship's hold where the bomb is supposed to be?'

'You can have a bomb on board, lad, but it needs someone to detonate it. Take out the crew and your bomb's as good as safe. Make sense? Any more for any more?'

'How many crew on board and are they armed?' one of the SAS lads asked. 'And what sort of hardware have they got?'

'I'll leave all that sort of detailed stuff to the intel boys,' the CSM said, nodding in their direction. 'So if there's no more questions, that's that. I've still got to go negotiate what ruddy time we're allowed to hit this thing,' he added, shaking his head in disgust.

As the CSM disappeared into the ops room an intelligence officer stood up to start the next briefing. Mat noticed that he was all 'suited and booted', done up in a grey pinstripe suit and a pair of shiny shoes. City gent attire, Mat thought to himself, dismissively. Hardly appropriate dress for a military base. The Green Slime always seemed to look the same – grey men in grey suits with generally a lot of grey stuff to say. As the intel officer cleared his throat, Mucker leaned over to whisper in Mat's ear.

'About the only rights the fuckers on that ship should have is the right to choose how they want to die.'

'Too right,' Mat replied. 'Terrorist rights? It's a crock of shite, mate.'

'Gentlemen, the MV *Nisha* is a tramp steamer, a cargo ship some three hundred yards long with five main cargo holds,' the intelligence officer began, pulling up a slide of a cross-section plan of the ship. 'The rear super-structure is made up of four main decks, including a bridge – here – crew quarters – here – a mess – here – and engine rooms – here and here. Forward of the super-structure are the sealed bulkheads containing the cargo – some 26,000 tonnes of sugar. Any explosive device will be situated somewhere in the cargo area, we believe. The ship has recently been in the Red Sea, around Somalia, which first got our suspicions going and those of our US colleagues. We believe she may have picked up al-Qaeda terrorists in and around that area, before starting her present journey to London. We also have credible intel that she's got some kind of improvised chemical weapon on board.'

The intelligence officer stopped to catch his breath, and Mat and Jamie exchanged glances. This was going to be some operation. Sounded like they were up against a bunch of al-Qaeda fanatics in charge of a cargo ship that had basically been turned into a massive chemical bomb.

'We believe there's sixteen crew members and that they will be armed, although we have no details of what weapons they may be carrying,' the intel officer continued. 'There is a high possibility that they will violently resist attack – although whether they're carrying shorts, longs, grenades or whatever we don't exactly know. Some of the terrorists are likely to be Mauritanians, and they may be linked to Hezbollah, a group you'll all be familiar with, I'm sure. That's about it as far as intel is concerned. Any questions?'

'What sort of distances are we talking here?' Mat asked. 'Bow to stern and the like?'

'She's 450 feet end to end,' the MI6 officer said. 'And she's approximately eighty feet high at the stern, where the main superstructure is. Plus she's 17,000 tonnes unladen weight.'

'So, she's pretty bloody big then,' Mat remarked. 'Like, a lot of territory to cover looking for sixteen terrorists and a chemical bomb.'

'I suppose you could say that, yes,' the intel officer said. 'Anything else?'

'Yeah. Where was the ship bound for, mate?' Tom Knight piped up. 'Officially, like, before we was ordered to stop her?'

'London. To the Tate and Lyle sugar refinery. Which just happens to be on a dock on the Thames adjacent to the City of London. Hence our concern.'

'So, have you asked them – Tate and Lyle, like – what she's carrying?'

'No. For the simple reason that this is a highly sensitive mission and potentially an extremely dangerous target. It's been handled on a need-to-know basis only.'

'Fair 'nough, mate,' Tom acknowledged. 'I was just askin'.'

As the intel briefer stood down, the MOD lawyer stood up to commence the legal brief.

'From that intel alone you can see that you've got a clear legal right to go on board that ship and use whatever means are necessary to stop her,' he began. 'When you go into a room on that ship – they're armed, al-Qaeda terrorists or whatever, picked up illegally, there's some kind of chemical or biological warfare device on board – you're cleared for whatever means are necessary. If there were an inquiry, in a court of law the whole scenario would be put to a jury, and they would know that on the intel you have before you now it has been identified as a terrorist vessel. That intel comes from the highest level in Whitehall and it says that a ship crewed by terrorists is going to attack London with a chemical device. Clearly, you will be justified in using whatever measures you see fit.'

After the legal briefing, there was one by the doctor outlining where the emergency medical facilities would be established in case there were casualties. This was followed by a comms briefing, detailing call signs, frequencies to be used and any mission-specific reporting practices. Once the general briefing was over, the men broke down into their individual four-man teams to run through the whole brief several times over, until all the details were clear in their minds. Over in their corner of the giant hangar Mat's troop leader, Captain Pete Trotter, was running over their team-specific tasks one last time with Mat's team.

'As Team 1 – that's your lot, Mat – hit the bridge, you'll have Team 2 going into their primary target directly behind you, which is the radio room. After they secure that, two of their guys should move into their secondary, which is your primary, the bridge, so freeing you lot up to move on to your secondary target, the crew quarters. Team 2 will in turn be replaced on the bridge by an HQ element, which will run the show from there on in. So, you'll keep leapfrogging from one TAOR [tactical area of responsibility] to the next. Your TAOR is always the immediate target area your team is securing. Hell, you've all done this so many times, I don't need to remind you how it's done. Once the command-and-control element are established on the bridge, you'll be radioing in your sitreps to them. Are you all pretty clear on it now? Any questions?'

'Yeah, who's going to be first down the ropes then, boss?' Mucker asked. 'Cos it sure as fuck ain't going to be me.'

'Why ever not?' Captain Trotter replied, with a grin.

'Cos knowing my luck I'll get me balls shot off,' Mucker replied, 'and then I really will be in the shite, cos my old lady's very partial to them, she is.'

'That's honking sick, that is, mate,' Mat interjected, disgustedly. 'Filthy. What do we want to know about you and your missus's sex life for?'

'Cos it's a fuck sight more interesting than –' Mucker started to reply, but the captain cut him off.

'Well, if there's no volunteers to be first down the ropes . . . ?'

'I ain't bothered,' Mat spoke up. 'I don't mind doing it.'

'Well, I know I wouldn't want to be the first, Mat,' the captain replied. 'So let's pull straws to decide, eh?'

The captain grabbed hold of some plastic sticks used for stirring the tea. He took four and broke them into different lengths. As Mat's unit were to be first down the fast ropes, they all knew that they had been given the most dangerous part of the operation. They would be first into action hitting the bridge, the nerve centre of the whole ship, and it was bound to be manned at all times.

'Pick one then, Mucker,' Captain Trotter offered,

holding out the plastic sticks, their true lengths hidden in the palm of his hand. 'Longest one gets the honour of going first.'

'And gets his balls shot off,' Mucker retorted. 'No way am I choosing first.'

'Shouldn't it be the shortest one?' Tom interjected. 'It's drawing the short straw, innit?'

'Fine by me,' the captain replied. 'Whoever gets the shortest straw is first down the ropes.'

Mat drew the first straw, followed by the others. As it happened he picked the shortest. So, that decided it. Mat Morrisey would be first man down the fast ropes.

'Congratulations, Mat, looks like you got what you wanted,' the captain remarked. 'Right, if there's nothing else?'

'Just one more thing, boss,' Mat said. 'Whenever we've trained for this, we've been going in at the dead of night. So now it's for bloody real why're we being told we have to go in during the hours of daylight? Makes no bloody sense to me at all.'

'I couldn't agree with you more. We're still arguing for hitting it under the cover of darkness, but the powers that be don't want us to. We're being told it has to be a daylight op – which takes away the element of surprise, obviously. Maybe it's because a night-time assault is seen as being too aggressive – more aggressive than a daytime one is, anyway.'

'Too bloody aggressive?' Mat snorted. 'What, with a ship packed with a poor man's WMD, crewed by terrorists and bound for London? Nowt can be too aggressive with that little lot, if you ask me.'

'I agree entirely. But it's politics, isn't it?'

'Fuck all the politics of it, mate,' muttered Tom. 'Let's just get in there and get it on.'

'That's pretty much what we are doing,' the captain replied. 'We hope we're reaching a compromise that'll satisfy everyone. Officially, daylight time starts at 0530 hours. At 0530 hours this time of year it's still dark. So, that's when we're saying we are willing to hit the ship. Seeing as though it's midwinter it'll still be dark enough at that time to cover the assault, and then the follow-up can take place in daylight.'

'So, do we take it as read that we're going in at 0530 hours?' Mat asked. 'Cos if we are then there's time for a bit of kip, which'd be no bad thing.'

'If I hear otherwise I'll let you know,' Captain Trotter answered. 'In the meantime, you can get your heads down.'

It was 11 p.m. by the time Mat and his team finally settled down to get some sleep. The same thoughts were running through each of their minds regarding the assault: will it or won't it happen?

The nearest the SBS/SAS had ever come to a live ship assault was over thirty years ago. On 17 May 1972, the QE2 – the pride of the Cunard fleet of ocean-going liners – was in mid-Atlantic, en route from New York to London. That evening a call was received at Cunard's New York offices. An unidentified American male informed the company that he had two accomplices on board the QE2 with instructions to detonate six bombs and blow the ship out of the water. Both accomplices had terminal illnesses, he said, and neither cared if they lived or died. The only way to save the ship and the 1,438 passengers on board was to deliver $350,000 in cash into the caller's hands.

Almost immediately the search of the ship got underway. But William Law, the ship's veteran captain, informed Cunard that it was an almost impossible task to check the whole ship. She had thirteen decks, a thousand cabins and miles of corridors, not to mention the below-deck gantries, bulkheads and engine rooms. Scotland Yard and the FBI began scrutinising the passenger list to see if the bombers could somehow be identified that way, and all ship-to-shore communications were put under surveillance in case the shore-based blackmailer tried to contact his on-board accomplices. Meanwhile, the MOD put the SBS and SAS on standby, along with bomb disposal experts. Even if the *QE2*'s crew did discover any bombs, it would need experts to diffuse and disarm them.

Some eighteen hours after the blackmailer had made his initial bomb threat, two SBS operatives headed up to RAF Lyneham, in Wiltshire. They were joined by a colleague from the SAS and a bomb disposal specialist. After a short delay the four men boarded an RAF C-130 Hercules transport aircraft and headed out on the 1,500-mile flight across the Atlantic to the Cunard liner. En route Captain Williams, the bomb disposal expert, was receiving intensive coaching from the SBS operators on how to parachute into the sea. He had never done any military parachuting of any sort before, let alone jumping into the cold and uninviting waters of a choppy May Atlantic.

At 2.20 p.m. the captain of the *QE2* gave the order to 'Stop engines' and made his announcement to the passengers that a bomb threat had been received the previous evening. British soldiers were about to parachute into the sea and search the ship. Until this time, none of the ship's passengers had been any the wiser to the drama being played out all around them. By the time the C-130 reached the *QE2* the weather had taken a turn for the worse. Conditions were well beyond safety limits for parachute jumps into water, but the mission had to go ahead regardless. In a highly unorthodox manoeuvre, the C-130 had to make two drop runs, descending to below the three hundred feet cloud base to get the ship visual, then claw its way back into the overcast sky.

All four men made the jump – including a rather relieved looking Captain Williams – and were picked up by the QE2's lifeboat. The search of the liner turned up one suspicious container, which was blown up, but it turned out to be a false alarm and no bombs were found. The $350,000 in cash was delivered to a pickup point, which was covertly staked out by the FBI, but the blackmailer never called to collect his cash. And the QE2 sailed on to dock safely in Southampton.

Afterwards, the operation was analysed and dissected in detail by the SBS. The results of that analysis were used to help draw up an operational model for any future assaults on a ship at sea. But that was then and this was now. The 1972 QE2 assault had been a four-man jump to board a friendly ship that was stationary. Mat and the rest of the lads were well aware that they faced a very different threat: they were assaulting a hostile ship crewed by terrorists and sailing the high seas.

Just as he was dropping off to sleep Mat felt a tug on his sleeve. The SBS doctor was handing him a couple of white tablets and a plastic cup of water.

'What're these?' he asked, sleepily.

'NAPS tablets,' the doctor replied. 'Sort of an antidote, just in case there is any nasty stuff on board that ship.'

Mat glanced around at the other lads in his team to see if they were taking the tablets. He had heard all the horror stories about the NAPS (nerve agent pre-treatment set) tablets British soldiers had been given at the start of the first Gulf War. They were being blamed in part for Gulf War syndrome, the mysterious illness that some of the Gulf veterans had been suffering from ever since.

'Bottoms up,' said Mucker, with a grin, as he threw the tablets into the back of his throat and took a gulp of the water. That decided it for the rest of the team, and Mat, Jamie and Tom quickly followed suit.

'Which of you guys is the medic on your team?' the doctor asked.

'That's me,' Mat volunteered.

'OK, take these with you when you go in,' the doctor said, handing Mat a couple of British Army mark 1 antidote kits, which included two spring-driven injectors. 'Those are shots of atropine,' he added, pointing to the two phials of liquid. 'I take it you know how to use them?'

'No worries, doc,' Mat replied.

He knew very well what atropine was for. It was the only known antidote to nerve poisons. *Holy fuck! So that was what they feared was on board that ship – some sort of nerve agent.*

Pretty shortly, all of Mat's team started to feel sick – nauseous and feverish – and they could only put it down to whatever was in the NAPS tablets. As they tossed and turned trying to get some sleep, they cursed the doctor. Eventually, Mat, who was feeling the worst of all, gave up trying to sleep and started to double-check his assault gear. His body was having a bad reaction to the cocktail of drugs that the NAPS tablets contained. But on top of the nausea and fever, something else was bothering him.

As he sat there messing around with his gear, Mat

kept replaying in his mind the last time he'd been into action alongside the SAS. Several months earlier, they'd been on a joint marine counter-terrorism training exercise with the Hereford lads. But while the Hereford lads were very good on land and in the air, marine operations – like assaults against a vessel on the high seas – weren't their speciality. Three SAS lads had either forgotten to take their STASS (short-term air supply system) emergency breathing bottles with them, or deliberately chosen to leave them behind. Either way, it was a mistake that had almost cost Mat and his mates their lives.

The ship that they had then been practise-assaulting was called the *Maiden*, and she was steaming off the Bournemouth coast with a skeleton crew on board. Mat had been on the lead chopper, a Chinook CH47, and he'd had three blokes from the SAS alongside him plus ten fellow SBS. As they had come in alongside the *Maiden* the chopper had flared out to a hover. All the guys had been standing in line ready to fast-rope down on to the vessel and waiting for the aircraft's loadmaster to give them the Go! Go! Go! But suddenly Mat had heard what sounded like rounds from a paintball gun slamming into the side of the chopper – 'Pzzzt! Pzzzt! Pzzzt!'

Holy fuck! The fuckers are shooting at us, was the first thought that'd flashed through his head. *That wasn't in the bloody mission brief.*

But a split second later he'd realised with a shock that the noise was actually the rear rotor of the CH47 hitting the ship's superstructure – the Pzzzt! Pzzzt! Pzzzt! being the sound made by the rotors shearing off as they smashed into the steel mast and rigging. Immediately, the chopper started yawing over and going down towards the sea. The hold of the giant aircraft was filled with the ear-piercing whine of the massive turbines straining to keep the aircraft airborne, while one set of its giant rotor blades spun round and round, shattered and useless. Suddenly, the calm in the rear of the chopper had been replaced by frenzied chaos, as fourteen blokes started to frantically rip off their fast-rope gloves and struggled to remove their respirators (gas masks).

Pulling a knife from his belt, Mat began slicing through his webbing and his MP5 machine-gun strap, in an effort to get some of the weight off him before the stricken chopper plunged into the heavy seas below. But just at that moment, the three Hereford lads had made a break for the door. Luckily, the CH47's loadie (the loadmaster) was faster than they were and slammed the door lock into place. Mat and some of the other SBS lads dived on the SAS blokes and wrestled them to the floor of the stricken aircraft.

Mat was well aware that if the SAS lads jumped then they were as good as dead. The chopper was still some hundred feet or more above the water and the three SAS soldiers were carrying a lot of heavy kit. They would plummet into the sea like stones. Even if they did survive the drop, they were still at least half a mile out from the shoreline – which was one hell of a swim when weighed down with several dozen pounds of cumbersome, water-logged gear. And, presuming they did survive the fall, once they surfaced they could easily have the Chinook going down on top of them. The chopper's rotors – which would still keep on churning even under water – would chew them up into little pieces.

'Let me outta here! Fucking let me out!' one of the SAS lads was screaming.

'Fuck's sake, NO!' Mat roared, as he held him down on the floor. 'Fuckin' sit down and get ready, cos we're ditching.'

'But we've no fuckin' STASS bottles!' the SAS bloke cried out.

'Get back in your seats. Share air with our guys. Remember your ditching-at-sea drill.'

Just at that moment, the pilot of the stricken aircraft had come in over the intercom. 'As you can tell, we're in a spot of bother,' he announced. 'I'm going to try and put her down on the shoreline but brace yourself for the impact just in case we go down in the drink.'

Somehow, the pilot had managed to keep the chopper more or less level, steer it away from the ship and turn it back towards the beach. But not for long. By the time Mat and his mates had got everyone strapped into their seats the chopper was less than seventy feet above the ocean waves. They could feel the aircraft losing power and accelerating into a slide towards the sea. Suddenly, there was a sickening impact as the underside front of the chopper ploughed into the water, the force of it throwing the men forward in their seats. Within seconds, the massive machine was sinking fast. As it did so it began a slow-motion somersault, the top-heavy turbines and rotors flipping the aircraft upside down and dragging it, roofwards, towards the seabed.

Every special forces soldier dreads the moment when a chopper carrying him ditches in the open ocean. He may have trained for it over and over again – learning the strict evacuation procedure that must be followed – but that only makes it marginally less terrifying. The eleven SBS and three SAS soldiers remained strapped in their seats as the chopper plunged towards the seabed, waiting for it to hit rock bottom. Suspended upside down as they were in their seat straps, the water started gushing in all around them and was soon up to their necks. Now was the time to use the STASS bottles.

The STASS gas canister was strapped to the operator's chest webbing, for ease of access in an emergency. Now, each operator grabbed his beer-can-sized STASS bottle, clamped his lips around the rubber mouthpiece, squeezed the emergency operating ring and started to breathe. Only in this case, in marked departure from standard operating procedures (SOPs), the three SAS lads had no STASS bottles with them and were forced to share air with their buddies from Poole. A STASS bottle provides about twenty good, deep breaths of air – less, if you're hyperventilating with the shock of a crash landing at sea.

Finally, after what seemed like an age, there was a heavy Crunch! as the chopper hit rock bottom, followed by the groaning of collapsing metal as it settled on to the seabed. Quick as they could the men grabbed a breath from their STASS bottles and unbuckled their seat belts. Then they kicked out the emergency escape windows, took one last look in the murky gloom to get their bearings and headed for the open sea. It is still possible to use the STASS bottle as you swim, by holding it in one hand and taking short breaths. But in this case, Mat and two of his mates found themselves swimming buddy-buddy fashion with the three SAS lads, and sharing the last of their air with them as they made a break for the surface.

Luckily, the pilot of the CH47 had managed to nurse the stricken chopper close enough to the shoreline so that she had settled in relatively shallow water. All of the SBS and SAS soldiers and the aircrew made it out of the aircraft and to the surface alive, whereupon they had a short swim to the safety of the shore. But they'd been lucky. If the chopper had ditched a few seconds earlier and a few hundred metres further out to sea, it could have been a completely different story.

As Mat repacked his explosive charges and assault gear into his rucksack, he thought about those SAS boys and why they had failed to bring their STASS bottles with them. On the coming mission they would be crossing miles of open sea before they hit the target ship. If one of those choppers ditched in the drink it would be a long way down to the seabed. And no one would be offering to share their STASS bottles – for to do so would be akin to signing one's own death warrant. Putting his worries to one side Mat rolled over on his camp bed and decided to try to get some sleep.

As the seventy men of the assault force spent a restless night at Yeovilton, their target, the MV *Nisha*, was steaming doggedly up the English Channel towards London. But how had British intelligence – and hence the SBS and SAS – been alerted to the potentially lethal cargo this unremarkable ship was feared to be carrying? Following the terror attacks of 9/11, allied intelligence networks – chiefly American, British and Norwegian – had been tracing the whereabouts of twenty merchant ships dubbed the 'phantom fleet'. As passenger aircraft had been put to such horrific ends in the New York terror attacks, so it was now feared that cargo ships plying the world's seas could be the next weapons of mass destruction in al-Qaeda's arsenal. And by early November 2001, the ship that was at the focus of the most intensive scrutiny was the MV *Nisha*.

The MV *Nisha* was a battered old tramp steamer – a 'tramp' being a ship that moves from one port to another, depending on the business she obtains. In August and September 2001, she had been shuttling back and forth across the Red Sea between Africa and the Middle East. But on 4 November, the Mauritius Sugar Syndicate advertised a 26,000-tonne sugar cargo that needed to be taken from Port Louis, to the Tate & Lyle sugar refinery, in Silvertown, east London. On 8 November, the MV *Nisha* departed the Red Sea bound for Mauritius to collect the sugar cargo and ship it to London.

But for some time now there had been trouble brewing in the otherwise peaceful tropical paradise of Mauritius. The authorities there had recently been forced to declare that the Islamic group Hezbollah was operating a terrorist cell in their country, and planning to attack Christian churches and government buildings. The US Embassy, based in Port Louis, the Mauritian capital, had issued a terrorism alert to its citizens living in Mauritius and to any tourists planning to visit this popular holiday destination off the east coast of Africa. And the Mauritian government had begun rushing through new anti-terrorism legislation designed to enable it to outlaw groups like Hezbollah.

On the morning that the MV *Nisha* was steaming out of Port Louis bound for London, a Mauritian Security Services source reported to his CIA handler with some highly sensitive information. He proceeded to tell the CIA agent that a large quantity of Lannate, a pesticide, had been procured by two Hezbollah operatives in Mauritius. The Mauritian authorities had been placed on high alert, but the Lannate had already been spirited out of the country. It had been secreted on board a merchant ship, the MV *Nisha*, which had just set sail for London with a cargo of sugar.

After thanking his informant in the usual way, the CIA agent turned his attention to analysing the intelligence that had just fallen into his hands. What was its significance? he asked himself. How could Lannate be of use to Hezbollah? Could the pesticide somehow be

deployed as a weapon of mass terror? If so, the ultimate
target of such an attack would appear to be London, as
that was the final destination of the vessel. Of course,
there was always the possibility that the MV *Nisha* might
be hijacked by the terrorists en route and forced to change
course. But any self-respecting terrorist would know that
an abrupt change of course by the ship would attract
the attention of Europe's counter-terrorist authorities.
No. There was little doubt in the CIA agent's mind: the
target of an attack by the MV *Nisha* had to be London.

Within a matter of hours the CIA agent had started
to build up a picture of the potential terrorist threat.
Lannate, he discovered, is the trade name for a pesticide
whose chemical name is methomyl. Methomyl comes
from a class of chemicals called carbamates, some of
which are nerve poisons. They disrupt nerve signal trans-
missions by blocking the human enzyme acetyl-
cholinesterase. Such nerve poisons were first discovered
by German scientists in the 1930s. They were subsequently developed by the Nazis during the Second World
War to make the nerve agents sarin, soman and tabun.
After the war, several acetylcholinesterases, including
methomyl, were developed as pesticides for use in agri-
culture. Though less deadly than the nerve agents,
methomyl has 'acute mammalian toxicity'. In other
words, it is very poisonous to humans.

In fact, long before the CIA agent's suspicions were
aroused methomyl had been identified by allied intelligence as one of several chemicals that could be utilised
by terrorists to create a 'poor man's chemical weapon'.
Methomyl can be absorbed through the skin, is harmful
to inhale and can kill if swallowed. The effects of
methomyl poisoning are disturbingly similar to those of
a nerve agent attack: stomach cramps, involuntary urina-

tion and/or defecation, muscular tremors, staggering gait, pinpoint pupils, slow heartbeat, difficulty breathing, convulsions, possible coma and death.

But any terrorist wishing to deploy methomyl as a chemical agent to attack London would first have to 'weaponise' the highly toxic material. This would involve transforming the chemical into a form that could enter the bodies of targeted people in sufficient quantities to kill them. The only way of doing this over a large area would be to contaminate the air that people were breathing. In the case of a solid such as methomyl, this would mean dispersing the chemical as an airborne cloud so fine that it would be blown by the wind on to the target. If a terrorist could find a way of doing just that, then an attack utilising methomyl could cause widespread terror, injury and death. And it just so happened that the main cargo of the MV Nisha – sugar – burns fiercely once set alight. In fact, sugar is a well-known ingredient, when mixed with certain other commonly available chemicals, of the improvised explosive devices frequently used by terrorists. The question the CIA agent was forced to ask was this: was the ship now steaming its way towards London some sort of crude, but massive, chemical bomb?

Two days after the MV Nisha had set sail, the CIA agent decided it was time to pass his intelligence up the food chain to his bosses at the CIA's HQ, in Langley, Virginia. From there, the agent's report was passed to the CIA's sister organisation in the UK, MI6. Once MI6 officers started to examine the CIA's report, it immediately started ringing alarm bells with them. MI6 analysts now began to scrutinise the MV Nisha themselves, tracing the exact route the ship would take to reach its final destination, the Tate & Lyle sugar refinery in London.

The agents quickly realised that the MV Nisha would

have to travel along the Thames, passing by Canary Wharf, the home of London's tallest building and its City financial district. The potential terrorist scenario was becoming ever more terrifying: a cargo ship pulling into a Thames-side dock, carrying terrorists ready to detonate a poor man's nerve agent bomb in the heart of London. The consequences of such an attack were unthinkable. Such a device had the potential to kill and injure thousands, poisoning a huge area of London and forcing the evacuation of hundreds of thousands of terrified people from the largest city in Europe.

For a full seventy-two hours prior to the SBS being warned of the MV *Nisha* assault, an RAF Nimrod MR2 surveillance aircraft had been shadowing the vessel as it ploughed its way up the Atlantic, off the French coast. The Cabinet Office Briefing Room had been placed on full alert, so that it could provide strategic command and control for any measures that would need to be taken against the ship. Government ministers and top MOD officials were deliberating how best to deal with the perceived threat, as the ship steamed onwards towards London. The Prime Minister, Tony Blair, was being kept informed of every twist and turn as the terrorist drama unfolded. With the MV *Nisha* rapidly approaching the British coastline, there was only one way that she could be stopped: a lightning assault by the combined forces of the SBS and SAS.

2

OCEAN STRIKE

IT was the pitch black of a bleak winter's morning when the lead Chinook came swooping in low over the grey-flecked swell. Hungry wave crests seemed to reach up and snatch at the chopper's landing gear as the giant machine pounded onwards at 120 mph towards its target. Forward in the cockpit, the pilot was struggling to keep his aircraft low enough so as to avoid the radar sweep of the enemy ship up ahead, while at the same time preventing his chopper, and the thirty men he was carrying, from plunging into the freezing waters. If he ditched at sea, he and the SBS men could be dead from hypothermia within twenty minutes. Flying on night-vision goggles (NVGs) and instruments only, all that was visible below was the faint green glow of the sea spray whipped up by the wind before it slammed into the chopper's cockpit with the force of a raw, elemental nature.

Overnight, the weather had taken a decided turn for the worse: cloud cover was down to 150 feet, there was a thirty-knot wind and a fifteen-foot swell.

SBS / SAS Assault on MV Nisha

1. **4.55am:** Assault force of two squadrons of SBS/SAS in two Chinook CH47 helicopters lift off from Yeovilton Airbase for 15 min flight to assault ship. Two Lynx attack choppers and three Sea King helicopters are in support.

2. **5.30am:** 1st Chinook with one squadron of SBS/SAS on board approaches from rear and hovers over ship's bridge to allow five teams to rope down on to the ship.

SBS/SAS assault force rope down points onto ship.

Ship's bridge and radio room to rear.

Four main decks including the crew quarters, mess, Captain's cabin and engine room.

3. **5.30am:** Four RIB's approach bow of ship and attach hook and pole assault ladders. One troop of SBS/SAS forces assault ship from sea.

4. **5.30am:** Two Lynx helicopters hover over ship with SBS/SAS sniper teams on board.

Ships cargo holds containing 26,000 tonnes of raw sugar.

5. **5.30am - 6.00am:** SBS/SAS airborne teams clear and secure ships super structure. 16 prisoners taken out on deck.

6. **5.30am - 6.00am:** 12 of the RIB-borne SBS/SAS assault force move through the ship's cargo hold breaking open sealed bulkheads and searching for hidden bombs.

7. **5.30am - 6.00am:** 8 of the RIB-borne SBS/SAS assault force move through ship's cargo area above decks, securing vessel.

8. **6.05am:** SBS/SAS assault force hands over vessel to NBC specialists, Special Branch and H.M. Customs & Excise. All SBS/SAS taken off ship and return to base.

As none of the aircraft in this covert air armada were showing any lights, they raced past the dark waters like wraiths in the ink-black sky. Directly behind the two Chinooks, flying in staggered V-formations, were the two Lynx attack choppers carrying the sniping teams, and the three Sea King helicopters with the command, control and follow-up elements on board.

In the rear of the lead Chinook, even the scream of the chopper's giant turbines was unable to drown out the howling wind. As he sat there right behind the loadie, psyching himself up to be first down the ropes, Mat could already imagine the cold slap of the sea spray hitting the chopper as he stood at the open doorway preparing to jump.

Following his lead Jamie, Tom and Mucker would be ready to hit the fast ropes – which were coiled up like well-fed serpents on the floor – directly behind him. But it was a godforsaken night. *With weather like this, who needed terrorists?*

They were thirty-five minutes into the flight when the loadie signalled the ten minutes to target mark, by holding up two full hands of fingers. As he did so, the atmosphere inside the chopper became one of a muzzled, icy, killer calm. Mat and his three teammates stared out of the Chinook's portholes, straining their eyes in the leaden darkness to catch the first glimpse of the target vessel, some twenty miles to the south-east of them. They hit the six minutes to target mark and still there was no sign of the ship.

As the chopper closed in, each man on that aircraft was taking advantage of these last few moments to run through his team's specific tasks one last time – their primary and secondary targets, their place on the fast ropes, their call signs. Just as the loadie signalled the three minutes to target mark, Mat started jabbing his index finger excitedly at the rain-lashed window. He'd just caught sight of a set of ship's lights blinking in the darkness up ahead of them. The MV *Nisha*. The target.

As they hit the two minutes to target mark, the enormity of the task now facing the SBS and SAS soldiers hit them hard, like a blow to the stomach. They were four miles out from the ship now, and several of them felt physically sick as they imagined everything that could go wrong with this mission. Chinooks carry no armour plating at all, leaving them highly vulnerable to even small arms fire. Once over the ship they were basically sitting targets for anyone with a weapon below them. As they would have to hover some ninety feet above the vessel, and hold that hover for as long as it took the remaining troops to fast-rope down, the terrorists would have ample time to blast them out of the sky.

Up front, Mat could feel the blood thumping in his temples, the adrenalin pumping, his heart racing with the visceral thrill of imminent combat. Then, for a split second only, he was struck by a shiver of fear as an image flashed through his mind of a Chinook ploughing into the ship's mast – just as it had done on the exercise several months earlier – its rotors sheering and buckling with the impact. If their chopper went down now, this far out in the open ocean, they'd have a long way to go before she reached the seabed. And there was no way that any of them would be coming up again for air, of that Mat was certain.

But just as quickly as the image came, it went again, and Mat was on his feet, pulling his respirator down over his face, and signalling to the others to do likewise. He checked his MP5 machine gun one last time to make sure he had a round chambered and that the safety was off, then pulled on the thick leather gloves that would prevent him cutting his hands to shreds as he went down the fast ropes into action. Reaching behind his back Mat patted the bottom of his backpack just to reassure himself that the plastic explosives charges were still there. Then he glanced round to give the thumbs up to the other lads.

As he did so Mat realised just what an awesome sight it was in the rear of that chopper: all the guys were on their feet now; all were wearing their jet-black CT (counter-terrorism) gear (fire-retardant and rubberised cotton 'frizz' suits that were flexible enough to run and fight in, but also waterproof enough so that they could dive in them too); all had their respirators pulled down over their faces; all had their MP5 machine guns or pump-action shotguns slung from their chest harnesses, and flash-bang stun grenades and CS gas canisters hung from their webbing; and each operator had a knife and a Sig Sauer pistol strapped on where they favoured it for the quick, killer draw. When operating in constricted areas like a ship's hull a knife or pistol strapped to a leg might get caught as the soldier moved through a tight passageway or up a ship's ladder. So most of the men had opted to strap their knife, inverted, on their left chest plate and a pistol on the right hip.

For a split second, Mat put himself in the place of the terrorists down below him on that ship – asleep in the crew quarters, keeping watch from the bridge, or maintaining the vessel on a direct bearing, whatever they might be doing. Mat checked his watch: 5.15. Maybe, if they were good Muslims, they'd be getting ready to say their first prayers of the day, as it was about the right time for them to be doing so.

Holy fuck, Mat thought to himself, *how would he*

feel if he stepped out of his ship's cabin and caught sight of a load of blacked out men aboard this chopper descending from the heavens above – anonymous, mean as hell, armed to the teeth and with blazing blood-red eyes. As that thought struck and then left him, Mat was filled with a total, overwhelming confidence that they were going to take down that ship and win the day. *Somewhere on that ship was a deadly, evil weapon, designed and built by sick murderers. A ship crewed by men who sought to kill thousands of innocent women and children, and to kill them in the most horrible, horrific ways possible, using nerve poisons. And he and the rest of the lads were just about to put a stop to the bastards. How could they fail?*

He was but one of seventy members of the black death that were going to hit that ship like a whirlwind. *Let's fucking do this*, a voice had started screaming inside his head, impatient to get down the fast ropes and into action. *Let's fucking get in there, get it on and get at them. They were the best. They were the warriors. Who could stop them?*

Suddenly, there was a rip roaring blast of icy wind howling through the chopper's hold as the loadie threw back the side door, and the men felt the giant aircraft flaring out to hover. Peering out into the freezing ocean maw, wind whipping and tearing at his clothing, all Mat could see was the dark waters heaving and sucking below him. Then, on the crest of a massive swell, a set of ship's lights were carried above the seething blackness, as the giant superstructure of the MV *Nisha* emerged out of the sea some hundred feet below. The ship was six storeys high at least – including the hull – and she appeared like some surreal tower block looming out of the ocean waters.

The Chinook was barely sixty feet away from the ship now, and the pilot was edging his aircraft closer by the second. He would have to be directly over the vessel before Mat and his team would be able to hit the fast ropes. For a horrible second Mat was convinced that the pilot had brought the chopper in too close and that its rotors were about to collide with the ship's rigging. And then the loadie was kicking the fast ropes out the side door and they went tumbling away into the darkness below them. The thick ropes jinked and snaked with the roll of the aircraft – like two sea serpents reaching up to strike the chopper and drag her into the angry depths.

Slowly, the pilot edged the Chinook closer and closer towards the ship's bridge, fighting to hold her steady some fifty feet above the vessel. As he did so, Mat realised with a shock that conditions were so bad that he could barely make out the flat section of roofing that was their rope-down point. The ship was pitching about in the swell so violently that Mat wondered whether they could even make the jump. Ultimately, it was the pilot's call as to whether to abort the mission. Yet with the threat from the ship being so serious, they had little alternative but to go ahead. Either they hit the fast ropes and made it on to the ship, or there would be no stopping the MV *Nisha*.

Visibility was being made a damn sight worse by his respirator, Mat realised – the heat thrown off by his body among all the rain and sea spray was steaming up the mask's two glass eyepieces. As a spasm of frustrated anger surged through him, Mat ripped the gas mask off his face. He was just about to throw it back into the chopper when caution got the better of him, and he clipped it on to his chest webbing. Behind him, Jamie, Tom and Mucker followed suit. They were going in unprotected. So be it. Whatever nasty shite – *whichever nerve poisons* – they had on board that ship, they'd just have to make sure they hit it so hard that no one got a chance to use any of it against them.

To either side of Mat, the two sniper specialists – Bret and Chis – were ready at the open windows now. They had their G3 sniping rifles – shortened versions with retractable stocks – braced across their knees. Everyone was having the same visibility problems, and following Mat's lead both of them had ripped their respirators off. This would give them a better chance of being able to spot anyone through their laser sniping scopes who might be putting up armed resistance on the bridge, and kill them. As the pilot fought to bring the chopper in close enough to be able to drop the men, Mat found himself cursing the amount of time it was taking. They'd been closing on the ship for some sixty seconds now, and Mat couldn't believe that the terrorists hadn't detected them. At any moment he was expecting to see the flash of muzzles in the darkness below them and hear bullets slamming into the floor of the chopper.

Mat was practically hanging out of the aircraft, straining to jump, when suddenly the loadie gave him the Go! Go! Go! But as he grabbed the rope and went to step into the black void, the chopper banked violently, throwing him off his feet and out of the aircraft door. As he fell he made a desperate lunge for the rope, caught it, lost his grip, caught it again and then he was plummeting downwards at forty feet a second with the rope smoking through his fingers and the deck racing up to meet him. With all the strength he could muster Mat clamped his hands fast around the thick rope, the deceleration threatening to tear his arms from his shoulder sockets. A split second later his feet went slamming hard into the metal deck. As he rolled to his right to break the fall Mat realised that he'd slowed his descent just enough to save himself from serious injury. He'd been lucky.

Getting up into a crouching position, he was just about to remove his gloves when he felt his heart miss a beat. Time seemed to stand still as he watched the glow of an opening doorway some thirty feet below him. Then one of the terrorist suspects was standing silhouetted against the light from the ship's bridge, craning his neck to get a look at the Chinook high above him. Even as the enemy figure started up the metal stairway towards the roof, Mat knew that he didn't have time to rip off his fast-rope gloves and bring his MP5 to bear before the man would be on to him. And he also knew from countless training sessions that it was impossible to operate a weapon before first removing those thick gloves.

A split second later, reacting with pure instinct and raw aggression, Mat was on his feet. He took three steps forwards to the top of the stairway and before the shocked figure could react, Mat smashed his fist into his jaw. The single, massive right hook lifted him bodily off his feet. As the man's knees buckled beneath him he went down hard, falling backwards down the stairs. He hit the deck like a sack of shit and he didn't get up again.

As quickly as he could Mat ripped his gloves off, unhooked his MP5 from his chest harness and brought it to bear at his shoulder. Silently, he crept down the stairway towards the open doorway. As he moved forwards he stepped carefully around the unconscious figure. Mat knew without looking that Tom, Jamie and Mucker were right behind him on his shoulder.

This was the most dangerous part of the assault. The bridge was the nerve centre of the MV Nisha. While the rest of the enemy might still be asleep in the crew's quarters, the bridge was bound to be occupied at all times. If they could seize control of the bridge and hold it, then they could stop that ship.

Keeping his weapon forward and on the aim, Mat burst through from the dark night into the brightness of the bridge. For a moment he was blinded by the light. But his eyes adjusted quickly and he swept the area for the enemy.

'GET DOWN! GET DOWN!' he yelled.

He'd spotted three men at the rear of the bridge. He was waving his MP5 machine gun at them and pointing to the floor. But the men seemed frozen to the spot with shock. They'd been taken by complete surprise and none of them appeared capable of moving.

Mat took four quick strides across the bridge and grabbed the nearest, wrestling him to the floor. He shoved his boot into his back and forced him face downwards, while menacing the other two with his MP5. Then Mucker and Tom moved in. They shoved the other two face downwards on the deck. The prisoners were dressed in bulky waterproofs and overalls. They had dark, Asian features and they had been sat at a table, playing a game of what looked like dominoes. They appeared utterly terrified.

Mat swung his weapon around towards the front of the bridge now. As he did so he caught sight of a fourth figure crouched over the ship's wheel, some fifteen feet in front of him. By the looks of his tattered uniform he had to be the MV *Nisha*'s captain. But right at this moment he had his hands in the air, instead of on the ship's wheel – because Jamie was holding a pump-action shotgun to the man's head.

'Keep on this bearing if you want to live,' Jamie barked in his clearest, simplest English.

But the captain of the MV *Nisha* was scared out of his wits. He rolled his eyes in panic and made no move to hold the wheel.

'Grab the wheel and steer, man,' Jamie yelled.

He forced the captain's hands back down and placed them on the wheel.

'Now, stay on this course, dead ahead.' He used one of his hands to indicate a line out of the ship's window straight ahead of them. 'Dead ahead, got it?'

The captain finally seemed to get what Jamie was on about. He began nodding his head quickly. With both his hands on the ship's wheel he began to swing it from left to right, as he mimed steering the ship.

'You got it, but straight ahead, like,' Jamie said. He was trying to soften his voice so as to calm the captain down. 'And slow your ship to a stop.'

Mat glanced at his watch: they were sixty seconds into the assault, and already the ship's bridge was theirs. Suddenly, echoing up from below them there were the repeated Boom! Boom! Boom! reports of what sounded like pump-action shotgun fire. Somewhere in the crew's quarters, another of the fire teams was going into action and it was kicking off big time.

'Cuff 'em, Mucker, quick as you can,' Mat commanded, his voice laced with urgency as he indicated the three prisoners now prone on the deck before them.

There was no time to think now, only to act and react and keep moving through the ship. The quicker they could get all the enemy secured, the quicker they could move on to their secondary target and deal with whatever shit was going down below.

Mat turned to check outside. The enemy figure that he'd thumped was still lying in a heap exactly where he'd floored him. He dragged the unconscious crewman over towards a section of steel railing that ran up the stairs.

Boom! Boom! Boom! More gunfire rang out from below.

Quick as he could Mat whipped a length of plasticuff out of one of his chest pouches, bound the unconscious man's hands together, and then cuffed them viciously tight to the railing.

He'll have a shock when he comes to, Mat thought to himself, with grim satisfaction. *Not to mention the headache.*

Moving back inside, Mat glanced over at Mucker and Tom. They nodded back at him. All the prisoners had been secured. Mat pressed the switch on his radio first grip. He spoke into his mike, calling the command unit. The mike was held against his throat, where it could pick up even the most softly spoken of messages.

'Alpha One One, Romeo Control,' Mat intoned.

'Romeo Control. Go ahead Alpha One One.'

'Secured primary. Five times X-rays [enemy] detained. Negative Yankee [friendly] casualties. Maintaining heading and slowing ship to stop. Leaving two Yankees at primary and moving to secondary.'

'Roger that.'

That quick exchange on the radio meant that the SBS command element (and COBR in turn) now knew that control of the ship was in friendly hands. Whatever else happened Mat and his team had to hold the bridge. As long as they did so the MV *Nisha* would be getting no nearer the British coastline with any chemical weapon that she might have on board.

As soon as he'd finished making the radio call, Mat turned to the others on his team.

'Right, Mucker, Tom, you know the score. Stay here

and keep your eyes peeled. Once you're relieved, move to our secondary target. Then go on from there until you find us.'

'Roger that,' the two men replied.

Seconds later Mat and Jamie were back out in the icy blast of the sea wind, charging down the metal stairway to target deck three, below them. As they did so, they heard a series of massive explosions rippling through the lower decks of the ship. It sounded as if grenades were going off, although whether it was friendly forces letting them off or the enemy attacking, neither of them was sure. The shock wave from the blasts below blew open the ship's door up ahead of them, leaving it swinging crazily on its hinges.

Without a moment's hesitation, the two men charged through the open doorway and headed down a set of metal steps, which led into a corridor going through to the crew's mess. With their MP5s held at the shoulder they switched on the powerful torchlights attached to their weapons and entered the darkened mess room. As the torch beams groped ahead in the echoing darkness they swept the cavernous space for targets. But the room appeared to be completely deserted.

Just after Mat's team had hit the ship's bridge, Team 2, coming in directly behind them, had hit the radio room to their rear. Teams 3 and 4 had hit the ship's cabins on the third floor, while Teams 5 and 6 had hit the second floor, where the crew's quarters were located. As soon as the first CH47 had pulled away from the MV *Nisha*, its men successfully on board ship, the second had taken its place. And to either side of the vessel the two Lynx attack helicopters had moved in close, their sniper teams combing the decks below them for any terrorist targets.

The MV Nisha was assaulted by air and by sea; the SBS fast roping from Chinooks and using the rigid inflatable boats (RIBs) to establish a foothold on board. Black-clad figures swarmed onto the vessel as she crashed through the waves with the RIBs being thrown about like toys alongside. It would have been a horrendous way to assault a ship in training, let alone for real and in mountainous seas.

Once safely over the sides, the four seaborne teams had been tasked with securing the ship's cargo holds – the most likely location of any chemical weapon. Two teams were now passing through the bowels of the ship, one on either side, working from the bow to the stern and breaking their way through the sealed bulkheads. This was tense, difficult and physically challenging work. The cargo holds were pitch black and airless. The men moved along slippery walkways, metal gantries and ladders. Their torch beams pierced the gloom, searching for enemy figures or for any signs of a bomb. One mistake could be fatal, as they would fall into the bowels of the ship.

Meanwhile, the other two RIB teams were working their way through the ship in the same direction, but above decks, in the open cargo area. While they might not discover any bombs up there, they had every intention of capturing or killing any terrorists hiding out in this part of the ship.

Barely two minutes into the assault and the attacking force of SBS and SAS soldiers had swamped the MV Nisha with fire teams going in from every conceivable entry point.

Back up in the ship's mess Mat and Jamie were making their way towards the exit now. As they did so, Jamie's torch beam caught on something swirling, amorphous, glowing white as it snaked its way up the metal stair-well below and into the mess room. *What the fuck is that?* Jamie wondered. But before he could act, he was engulfed in the wraith-like substance and had sucked a first, burning gasp into his heaving lungs. As the gas – for gas it was – seared its way down inside him, Jamie felt like his windpipe was collapsing, choking the very breath and the life force out of him. He clutched at his throat and turned to Mat to cry out a warning.

'Get your fuckin' ressy on! It's fuckin' gas!' he tried to shout, but the words just seemed to be strangled in his throat and came out in a rasping, suffocated whisper.

In the next second, Jamie lunged for Mat, grabbed him and tried desperately to drive him back out of the mess area towards the open deck. But already it was too late, as Mat had just taken the first gulp of the gas into his hungry lungs. For a split second Mat stood there, uncomprehending, wondering why he couldn't breathe any more and why Jamie was trying to rugby-tackle him and force him back out of the mess room. And then he caught sight of the thick, white, oily fumes dancing in the light of his torch beam. And suddenly the realisation hit him like a sledgehammer.

Holy fuck, it's gas.

Quick as they could the two men stumbled back outside, choking and coughing their guts up, dragging at their respirators and trying to unhook them from their webbing. As they did so, Mat found himself wondering – in a dislocated, unearthly sort of way – exactly which type of nerve gas they'd just been hit by. *Was it sarin? Tabun? Or soman? Or maybe the deadliest of the lot – VX? And how long had they left to live?* They'd known what they'd been doing when they'd come in unprotected like this, without their respirators on. And oddly enough, there was no real fear now, just a desperate urge to get it over with, one way or the other. As Mat dragged his gas mask over his head and down on to his face, the first waves of nausea swept over him and suddenly, a jet stream of vomit went spattering into the front of the mask.

Cursing himself and wondering how it could all have gone so suddenly to rat shit like this, Mat fumbled in his chest pouch for his medical kit. Kneeling on the deck, his fingers numbed by the cold, he scrabbled inside his medical bag for the syringes of atropine antidote that the SBS doctor had given him the night before. As he did so, he glanced over at Jamie, dreading what he would discover. He half expected to see his best mate lying on the deck, twitching and writhing in his death throes, shitting and pissing himself as the nerve poisons coursed through his blood, cauterising his veins and blowing his nerve endings all to fuck.

But while the big man *was* bent double choking his lungs up, he appeared to be pissing himself laughing at the same time.

What the fuck? Mat found himself thinking, in shock and confusion. *What the fuck?* He'd finally got his hands on the atropine syringes, but at the same time Jamie seemed to be going totally fucking insane. *Jamie? JAMIE? WHAT THE FUCK IS GOING ON?*

'It's nothin' . . .' Jamie rasped in a hoarse whisper, as he tried to explain to Mat what was happening. 'It's . . .' his words tailed off into a fit of mixed coughing and laughter, before he turned and vomited all over the deck.

Just then, an icy blast of sea wind cut around Mat's face, blowing both the reek of the vomit and the fog of confusion away. With a blinding flash of realisation Mat suddenly understood what it was that Jamie was finding so bizarrely, shockingly funny. Relief and ecstatic release flooded through him, as Mat *recognised the smell of the gas*. It was a type of gas that they'd used countless times before during SBS training.

This ain't no fucking nerve agent, Mat found himself screaming inside his head, joyfully. *It's CS. It's CS. It's only fucking CS.* As Mat and Jamie stumbled about on the deck, choking their guts up, the two men turned tearful faces to each other, pissing themselves laughing as they did so.

CS gas – more commonly known as 'tear gas' – is a highly debilitating crowd control agent, but it is largely harmless at the end of the day. Some of the lads must've been letting off the CS rounds down below, and that was the gas that Mat and Jamie had stumbled right into. The two men felt an overwhelming wave of relief flood through them now that they knew they were going to live. They cleared out their respirators of vomit and got them well and truly strapped on. There was still a major task ahead of them – the taking down of any terrorists below decks on that ship.

As they prepared to head back into the mess room, they were joined by Tom and Mucker. Their two fellow SBS soldiers had just been relieved on the bridge by one of the follow-up fire teams. Pretty shortly now the command and control element would be taking over on the ship's bridge, and the SBS/SAS assault force would be one step closer to their overall objective of stopping the ship.

Mat, Jamie, Tom and Mucker headed back through the mess room and down into the crew's quarters. As they advanced along the ship's corridor they ran into the lads from Team 4, who were preparing to shoot the locks off a cabin door. Boom! Boom! Boom! Three rounds from a pump-action shotgun went slamming into the wood and metal door frame, immediately followed by a boot smashing the door open. A split second later a CS gas rip round had been fired inside, and thick white smoke started pouring out of the room.

Bang on cue, three Team 4 lads sprang inside the cabin, their weapons at the ready. Just seconds later, two enemy figures were thrown out into the corridor, coughing and choking as the CS gas took a hold of them. They were dressed only in their underwear and pyjamas, and must have been taken completely by surprise.

'GET DOWN!' a Team 4 operator screamed, as one of the prisoners tried to get to his feet and flee. While the words were distorted and muffled by the gas mask, his meaning was crystal clear, the menacing pump-action shotgun showing that the SBS operator meant business.

Now that Mat's fire team had made visual contact with the Team 4 lads they could safely move on to their secondary target without fear of a friendly-fire incident (getting mistaken for the enemy and shot by their own side). Giving the thumbs up to one of the Team 4 lads, Mat indicated by hand signals that they were coming through – advancing through Team 4's TAOR and then moving on towards their next target.

'Alpha One One, coming through,' Mat announced, switching from his team-specific radio frequency to that which enabled him to communicate with the other fire teams and with headquarters.

'Alpha One Four, roger that,' came back the reply from the Team 4 leader.

As Mat and Jamie moved past the Team 4 lads, the prisoners were lying on the floor gasping for breath and puking their guts up with the CS gas swirling all around them. They were also shivering uncontrollably, but whether from the cold or the shock of it all Mat wasn't certain.

Poor bastards, Mat thought to himself, as he watched the prisoners being plasticuffed by the Team 4 lads. He knew himself what it was like to be CS-gassed now, and it wasn't a pleasant experience. *It would take one hell of a hardened terrorist to resist that sort of wake-up call*, Mat reckoned. *And that was the intention. Hit them with such overwhelming force so as to make any sort of resistance impossible. And – no mistake about it – right now it seemed to be working.*

Mat still found himself feeling a twinge of pity for the prisoners. Not all of them would be terrorists, he reasoned. Some were probably just regular seamen: they would have no idea why the Black Death had suddenly descended upon their ship. The terrorists would probably be few in number and holed up in the cargo area, where any bomb was likely to be situated. Mat made a mental note that when his team had completed their tasks and secured their targets, he would come back and fetch the prisoners out on to the open deck, where they could get some fresh air into their lungs.

Carefully, Mat led the way down the corridor ahead, which would take his team directly into the rear of the ship's quarters. As he did so Mat knew that they were about to move into a part of the vessel that had not yet been secured. As their torch beams probed ahead in the darkness a white figure suddenly came crashing through one of the doorways to Mat's left. It turned and then came charging in his direction. Just as Mat was about to open fire, the figure must have spotted him, as it stumbled to a halt. For a split second there was a tense and potentially deadly stand-off, as Mat and the figure stared at each other. And then Mat realised with a shock that

the figure was one of their own, black-clad operators –
but somehow he seemed to have got himself covered
from head to toe in a thick white scum. And for some
reason his gas mask was missing.

There was the faint crackle of radio static in Mat's
earpiece. 'Alpha One Five, you frobbers,' came a breathless voice on his radio. It was the man in white up ahead
of Mat identifying himself. 'Let me the fuck past, will
you?'

As his team stood aside, Mat realised that he recognised the figure in white goo. He had an unmistakable
Geordie accent that Mat knew well. It was 'Stretch', one
of the SAS lads that he knew from previous operations.
Recently, they'd been on a week-long quad-bike training
course together. What the hell had that crazy bastard
been up to this time? Mat wondered. He was clearly
trying to get away from all the CS and find his way to
the fresh air outside the ship.

Once they'd pointed Stretch towards the open deck,
Mat led his team onwards, taking care as they probed
deeper into hostile territory to the rear of the ship. Finally,
they came to a heavy metal bulkhead. It was locked and
it looked like it might be barring the way to somewhere
important. Opposite the bulkhead was a storeroom of
some sorts, but a quick search revealed it to be deserted.
Still, as it did contain several crates of booze Mat made
another mental note: to return once the action was over
and help themselves to a few bottles. The team had been
shown plans of the MV *Nisha* during the mission briefings. But they hadn't gone into enough detail to map out
every room, so they had little idea what was behind the
heavy bulkhead.

Mat signalled that he wanted the bulkhead blown
open. Kneeling down before it, Jamie set the charges and

all four of them stepped back to take cover. Immediately,
there was a massive BOOM! A cloud of smoke and debris
went thundering down the corridor, and then the metal
doorway toppled outwards into the walkway with a loud
crash. The second they were inside the room, MP5s and
pump-action shotguns at the ready, Mat's team realised
what they had found.

By the light of their torch beams they could see that
they were in some sort of ship's workshop, festooned
with wires, cables, sheets of metal and every sort of tool
imaginable. On the workbench bang in front of them
was an old oil drum that had a series of wires attached
to it. The drum had a hatch cut in one side by a welding
torch, and inside it was packed with what appeared to
be bales of cotton wool. With a surge of excitement Mat
and his men realised that if there was a bomb-making
facility on board this ship, then they had just discovered
it. They couldn't be certain, of course, until the bomb
disposal experts arrived. And it wasn't their job to poke
around – just to secure the ship. But it certainly had the
looks of a bomb-making facility.

Once they'd checked that the room was clear, Mat
told Tom and Mucker to remain on guard until the bomb
disposal people relieved them. In the meantime they were
to touch nothing and leave the room exactly as they'd
found it. Then he and Jamie moved off to clear the rest
of their target area. Some five minutes later the team
was able to declare deck three clear of the enemy.

As they headed back down the corridor towards the
open deck, every cabin that they passed seemed to have
had its doors blown off their hinges. Splintered and
buckled metal sheets, spent shotgun cartridges and gas
canisters littered the floor, and CS gas blanketed the
corridor like a thick mist. The prisoners were lying every-

where, face down in the corridor. They were handcuffed to the ship's rails and any other solid objects. They were all in a state of undress and clearly suffering badly. It crossed Mat's mind that the MV *Nisha* below decks had all the makings of a scene from a major action movie. But unlike a movie this was for real and the captured crew members would not be able to survive much more of this exposure – of that Mat was certain.

'We've got to get these blokes outside, or they're dead,' Mat said to Jamie. 'Give me a hand will you, mate?'

The two men helped one of the prisoners to his feet and started to frogmarch him outside. But they had barely taken a couple of steps before the prisoner's legs buckled. He went down hard on the deck. The CS gas had taken a horrible toll, and the prisoner was dizzy, sick, fighting for breath and freezing cold. Eventually, Mat and Jamie had to half carry him by his shoulders out of the crew's quarters.

'Look, there's a load more of these poor sods down there,' Mat announced to the Team 4 leader, as they laid the prisoner down on the open deck. 'You'd better get 'em outside, double quick, mate. They're dying a bloody death in there from all the CS.'

Within minutes the SBS/SAS assault force had the prisoners lined up face down in the open. Mat counted fifteen in all. Together with the ship's captain, who was still up on the bridge steering the vessel under guard, that made sixteen prisoners – which accounted for all of the men that Green Slime had told them would be on board the ship. It looked as if they had captured everyone.

As the first rays of a chill winter's sun began washing over the ship, Mat could see that the prisoners were in a bad way. In addition to the effects of the CS gas, and the shock, the prisoners were now in real danger of going

down with hypothermia – a life-threatening body collapse
due to exposure to intense cold. They were dressed in a
motley assortment of underwear, pyjamas and workmen's
clothes, and with the serious wind-chill factor out there
the conditions were murderously cold. Mat knew about
the effects of hypothermia from his medical experience.
In the extreme stages, a victim would become totally
disorientated. They would become convinced that they
were burning up and rip all their clothes off. Victims of
hypothermia were often found curled up naked, with
their clothes scattered nearby. If Mat and the lads didn't
do something, the prisoners wouldn't survive for long.

'Look, it's bloody Baltic out here and most of these
fookers are dressed in their skinnies, and nowt else,' Mat
commented. 'Take a look in their cabins, Jamie mate.
Grab some coats, blankets, whatever you can lay your
hands on.'

'Okey-dokey,' Jamie replied. 'Mucker, Tom, lend me
a hand, will you? Never know what you might find.'

'Any porn, mate?' Mucker asked.

'What, like a bunch of good Muslims are gonna 'ave
a load of porn on board?' Tom cut in. 'Get real, mate.
Most you're likely to find is a dog-eared copy of the
Koran tucked under the mattress.'

'What about all that booze in the storeroom, then?'
Mucker fired back at him. 'Eh? Eh? Reckon we'd find
a few rashers of streaky bacon in the galley if we looked
hard enough, mate.'

'Bloody get on with it then, lads,' Mat butted in. 'Do
something, will you – before these fookers freeze to death.
Don't call us blokes the Special Boat Circus for nothing,
do they?'

Five minutes later Jamie, Tom and Mucker returned
laden down with an assortment of coats, jackets and

blankets. Together with Mat they started handing them out to the freezing prisoners. But as Mat went to hand one of them a yellow oilskin, the prisoner raised an objection.

'No, no – not my coats, sir,' he ventured, nervously.

'*You what?*' Mat asked, incredulously.

'Yes, sir, this one is most seriously not my coats, sir. Sir, my jackets is that one, sir, the most excellent, most divine leather ones, sir.'

'Listen, mate, you'll take what you're bloody given,' Mat replied, throwing him the yellow oilskin. 'That bloke's got the neck of a giraffe,' Mat remarked to the others. 'The bloody cheek of it. Just had the Black Death descend on him and now he's tryin' to rob someone else's jacket.'

'How d'you know it isn't his, mate?' Jamie asked.

'"Seriously not my coats, sir,"' Mat answered, mimicking the prisoner's Pakistani-sounding accent. '"My jackets is the most excellent leather ones, sir." Would you believe that shit?'

'Still, got to admire his nerve, haven't you, mate?' Jamie said, with a grin.

By now the SBS/SAS assault force were some fifteen minutes into the assault, and sitreps had gone out from all of the fire teams reporting that their target areas had been cleared. As the ship was now secure, the Sea King helicopters started coming in and dropping off the bomb disposal teams and the anti-terrorism experts from Special Branch. A grey-painted HM Customs & Excise vessel pulled alongside the MV *Nisha* and began shadowing her off the port bow. Shortly, a Royal Navy skeleton crew would be taking over crewing the vessel. The time was fast approaching when the assault force would formally hand over control of the ship to the civilian authorities. But just before they did there was one last remaining task for Mat and his mates inside the ship. Having a celebratory drink on-board.

Mat, Jamie, Tom, Mucker and several of the other lads made a beeline for the ship's storeroom. Upon arrival they stuffed as many bottles as they could of ship's brandy and rum inside their Frizz suits. Next, they headed for the captain's cabin, which they knew was at the rear of the ship, on deck two. Grabbing a Polaroid camera off the captain's desk, the lads ripped off their gas masks and lined up for a couple of souvenir photographs, posing with one of the MV *Nisha*'s lifebuoys. But as they did so, first one and then the rest of the lads started pointing at Mucker's face and pissing themselves laughing. He seemed to be the only one who wasn't finding it funny.

'What? *What the fuck?*' Mucker asked, angrily. 'What the fuck is it, you wankers?'

In answer all Mucker got was a further burst of hilarity and a chorus of piss-taking.

'Blacked up for the mission then, did you, mate?'

'What's that instant tanning lotion you're using, mate? I gotta get me some.'

'He'll fit in better in Bradford now, mind.'

'Someone fetch the Hobbit a mirror.'

Before the assault force had gone in one of the lads had played a practical joke on Mucker. He'd rubbed boot polish all over the inside of his gas mask. Once Mucker had removed it for the group photo, he had the black polish smeared all over his face. This time, the joke really was on him.

Barely thirty minutes after hitting the MV *Nisha*, the SBS/SAS assault team was winched off deck by the two Chinooks and rotated back through the reception point on Thorny Island. During the whole of the ship assault not a single hostile shot had been fired at them. The ship's crew had been taken by such surprise that if they did have weapons to hand, they'd not had time to use them.

The only casualties on the assault team's side were two minor, self-inflicted ones. One of the SAS operators had hurled a ship's fire extinguisher into a door, in an effort to smash it open. But the door had resisted and the fire extinguisher had rebounded into him, setting itself off and covering the operator in foam. That accounted for Stretch – the mysterious, ghostly figure who'd come rushing past Mat's team covered in white scum. And one of the SBS operatives had fired a CS round into a door only to discover that it was made of reinforced steel. As the round had bounced back, it had caught him on the thigh, spewing CS gas all over him. Both men had suffered little more than bad bruising. And while there were several injuries among the prisoners, none of them were life-threatening. The assault had been a textbook operation.

From Thorny Island the assault force made its way back to Yeovilton by Chinook. As they did so Mat, Jamie, Tom and Mucker felt rightfully proud of themselves. Whatever the outcome of the forensic investigations on board that ship, they had pulled off a tough and risky assault in appalling conditions. As far as they were concerned, the mission had been a resounding success: it was the first ever operationally tested DAA against a hostile vessel. And Mat's worries about the performance of the SAS lads on a maritime assault such as this had proven totally unfounded. They had gone into action alongside their SBS teammates with just the right combination of aggression and professionalism that the mission had required.

On arrival back at their Poole base later that morning, there was no major debrief, no 'yin yang goo hoo' as the lads liked to call it. This was largely because the CO of the SBS was away in Afghanistan and everyone else was winding down for Christmas. While the men were deservicing their kit, CSM Gav Tinker just did an informal walk-around of all the fire teams, congratulating them on a job well done. The CSM was one of the old and the bold and had seen it all before. But he was still unable to hide the pride he felt in the way that the lads had performed. They had done exactly what he'd asked of them and made it look so easy.

The CSM found Mat checking his weapons back into the armoury.

'Mat! Come 'ere, lad,' he said, throwing an arm around his shoulders. 'I'm bloody proud of you. You were awesome out there. First down the ropes n'all. Don't think I didn't notice, cos I did.'

'Cheers, boss,' Mat remarked. The CSM rarely gave out any praise, so to hear it now meant one hell of a lot to him. 'No dramas. There was a couple of times when it was touch and go. But we pulled it off, like.'

'Too bloody right you did,' Gav Tinker enthused. 'Listen, lad, you go enjoy that Christmas break. You've more than earned it.'

'Don't mind if I do, mate.'

'And one more thing,' the CSM added, as he turned to leave. 'Don't you go eating too many of them doughnuts. I need you to stay in shape for the next time those bastards try and hit us. Cos mark my words, they will.'

Predictably, news of the seizure of the MV *Nisha* leaked out to the press. The day after the assault the story was splashed all over the front pages of the British newspapers. 'UK HALTS SHIP AFTER TERROR ALERT', 'SECURITY

ALERT AS CHANNEL SHIP IS SEIZED', 'ANTI-TERROR SQUAD SEIZES SHIP', and 'AL-QAEDA'S PLAN TO NUKE LONDON' ran the headlines. The authorities seemed keen to stress that the ship had been boarded in international waters in accordance with international law, and that the speed and success of the assault proved the readiness of the UK's counter-terrorism forces.

'Even where the risk is only a potential risk, we will not hesitate to take any action we think necessary to investigate a potential threat,' Prime Minister Tony Blair told the press. While playing down the threat that the ship had posed, he was keen to stress that the MV *Nisha* assault demonstrated the 'top-level vigilance of our security services'.

Pretty quickly, the media moved on to other, more pressing, issues. Within days, the MV *Nisha* story seemed to have vanished without trace. After the initial investigations carried out on board the ship, the MV *Nisha* was taken into a mainland port and kept in isolation. Not surprisingly, the main cargo found in the vessel's hold was raw sugar. But in the ensuing days, scores of scientists came and went on board the ship, and containerloads of materials were taken away for further testing.

Back at Poole, there were initially rumours that the ship had been a red herring – and that nothing sinister had been discovered. Then word filtered back to the men that quantities of a deadly nerve agent had been found. But none of the SBS lads knew – or cared that much – which version of events was true. As far as they were concerned, at the end of the day it was mission accomplished.

It was time to wind down and enjoy the Christmas break. The lads felt they'd earned it, too. After the tension and intense activity of the MV *Nisha* assault they were shattered. And prior to that they had just spent three months in Afghanistan, hunting down AQT terrorists. They'd faced freezing temperatures, towering mountain ranges and an all-but-impossible mission. Mat's team had ended up fighting an epic battle that none would ever forget, against a fanatical enemy who wanted nothing more than to kill American and British soldiers – or die in the process.

Ahmed was a massive bear of a man, with tiny eyes set deep in an imposing, black-bearded face. His skin was cracked and worn by years of fighting in one of the world's harshest theatres of war. Over several centuries, the armies of the world's main superpowers had come to grief here, fighting the mujahidin of Afghanistan, and had given up trying to tame the warriors of Afghanistan. And now the Taliban were following in the footsteps of the mighty Afghan mujahidin, or so Ahmed liked to believe.

By contrast, Ali looked puny besides the giant Taliban fighter. But he'd more than earned Ahmed's respect several months earlier, when he'd turned up as one in a group of new Taliban recruits. At a training camp somewhere on the Afghanistan border Ahmed had been introduced as their trainer. That first week, he'd started by instructing them in some basic, close-quarter combat, teaching them the quickest ways to kill using only their bare hands. Ahmed demonstrated several lethal moves. One involved driving the palm of the hand into the opponent's nose with maximum force, so ramming the nose bone up into the brain. It wasn't necessarily a killer blow, but the damage done would be enough to disable any opponent, whereupon he could be finished off. Ahmed's real favourite was a savage blow from behind the opponent, using both hands to deliver a karate chop to the base of the neck. The crushing shock wave travelled down the spine, shattering the opponent's vertebrae and severing the spinal cord. Death was more or less instantaneous.

A week into the training Ahmed had asked for a volunteer to fight him. Understandably, no one was that keen to do so. So, Ahmed had picked on Ali. Ali was the only Westerner in the whole of his unit, and this, he knew, made him something of an oddity. There were hardly any Afghan recruits here – as this camp was for the international jihad brigade, the foreign fighters. But there were scores of other nationalities – Yemenis, Saudis, Egyptians, Sudanese, Chechens, several Europeans of Pakistani origin and a couple of Muslims from the Balkans. But what really set Ali apart was that he was from Britain and he was black – his great-grandparents had come from Africa – and there were no other black Britons in the training camp.

Britain was the foremost ally of the Great Satan, America, the arch-enemy of all the fighters drawn to the Afghan jihad. So Ali really felt that he had to prove himself. But he could deal with that. Ever since childhood he'd always felt that he had to prove himself – because he was a black man living in a white man's country. As a kid he'd lived in a London suburb that was predominantly white. At school he'd learned to fight first and ask questions later if ever he suspected that someone might be 'dissing' him. By the age of twelve he was carrying a knife and 'doing' drugs. He'd flunked school and drifted into a life of crime, women and alcohol. It was only when a distant uncle had taken him to a mosque in his late teens that his life had taken a drastic new turn.

Five years later and Ali was a twenty-three-year-old

devout Muslim, with a successful career in IT. But he'd still felt that his life in Britain was empty. Since first finding Islam, he'd become increasingly religious and had memorised vast tracts of the Koran. He'd also learned a deep hatred for the non-Muslim West – a society that Ali believed was in terminal decline. It was a society that Ali felt had rejected him, a society that he believed was rotten to the core with immorality and decadence. And, worst of all in Ali's eyes, it was a society that had turned its back on the word of God. Ali had no wife or children to tie him down, and he had ample savings. Eventually, he had decided to head for Afghanistan, where the Taliban were fighting to build a pure Islamic state.

Three months later and Ali found himself in this training camp, being challenged by a veteran mujahidin to trial by unarmed combat. Realising that he had no choice but to accept Ahmed's invitation to fight and make good account of himself, Ali calmly stepped forward. As he and Ahmed squared up to each other, the rest of the brothers formed a ring around them to watch. There was no betting who the other recruits believed was going to win. But Ali just kept reminding himself that back home in London he had accounted for himself well in the training sessions at his local mosque. Before leaving for Afghanistan he'd earned himself a black belt in karate. And he'd beaten guys this big, and bigger, before. *Insh'Allah* – God willing – he would prevail.

'So,' shouted a grinning Ahmed, as he prepared to jump Ali, 'ready yourself for *shihada* – martyrdom – brother, and for the fruits of Paradise that will then await you!'

Ahmed was speaking English, the lingua franca of the foreign Taliban in Afghanistan. As many of the brothers were non-Arabic speakers – from Europe, the Balkans,

South-East Asia and Africa – he spoke Arabic words only where they were commonly used in Islam. And whenever he used an Arabic expression, he was careful to give the English translation, to help the new recruits learn their Islamic phraseology in Arabic, the original language of the Koran.

The two men began circling each other now, slowly, watchfully, each waiting to see who would be the one to make the first move.

Suddenly Ahmed sprang forward and made a grab for Ali, throwing his whole weight behind the charge. As he did so Ali performed a dancing sidestep, and the big Taliban commander lunged past, completely missing his target. In a lightning move Ali grabbed Ahmed's shoulder, spun him off balance and using all of the big man's momentum and body weight he hurled him on to the ground. A huge bear of a man, Ahmed fell hard. The ground shook and threw up a big cloud of dust, and Ahmed lay flat out where he'd fallen. There was a moment of deathly silence before Ali swooped down over Ahmed's prostrate form and made a dummy jab to his nostrils, in a blow that would have driven the nose bone up into the eyes and brain. He did so just to demonstrate his point – just to show that he could have used one of Ahmed's favourite moves to kill him.

'*Allahu Akhbar!*' Ali yelled as he did so. '*Allahu Akhbar!* God is Great! And if you were an infidel you'd be dead by now, which is more than such a godless dog deserves.'

Calming himself a little, Ali reached down to make sure that Ahmed was all right. Luckily, he'd had his black turban wound tightly around his head, and that is what saved his skull from cracking when it hit the rocky earth. After checking him over, Ali helped the big man to his feet. But he was groggy and unsure of himself for a good few minutes afterwards.

'I knew you were going to fall hard, brother,' Ali remarked. 'So I'm glad you're still with us and not in the land of Paradise yourself. Big guys like you are strong, but you move slowly, and that's your weak point. It's the small, quick ones that are more difficult to fight.'

'Al-hamdu Lillah – praise be to God,' Ahmed replied, leaning on Ali for some support. 'This brother fights like the fierce lion, like a true mujahid. From now on I am going to call you "Ali the Lion Cub". And if Allah the All Merciful One so wills it, my brother Lion Cub here shall be one of the chosen ones and he will be first to be shaheed – to be a martyr.'

After the fight, word went through the training camp like wildfire. Ali al-Britani – Ali the Briton – had beaten Ahmed! Soon, a large crowd of the brothers gathered around him. There was a frenetic religious fervour within Ali's unit, which was a melting pot of different nationalities. The Taliban's war in Afghanistan had become a rallying cry, and Muslims from all over the globe were converging to fight the jihad. The brothers trained together, prayed together and would fight and die together. It was a type of brotherhood that Ali had never experienced before. For the first time in his life he had found a family, a new home, where he felt he absolutely belonged.

Just as the brothers were congratulating Ali on his fighting prowess, Omer, the commander of their unit, came tearing out of a nearby communications bunker, his arms flailing wildly and his eyes bursting out of his sockets with excitement.

'ALLAHU AKHBAR! ALLAHU AKHBAR! ALLAHU AKHBAR!' he roared, punching the air with both his arms as he did so. 'By the grace of Allah, brothers! VICTORY! Victory to the NINETEEN LIONS! Come, brothers. Come,' Omer announced, waving around a sheet of paper and hardly able to contain his excitement. 'Come hear about our glorious victory over the *kafir* – the infidels.'

The brothers gathered around as Omer began to read from the paper.

'This is a communiqué from our brothers,' he began. 'It reads: "By The One who allows the seas to scream, the waves to crash, the winds to howl: we will never rest while our homes are flooded by the blood of our slaughtered children. On a historic sunny 11 September morning, 2001, a few men, armed with little more than their faith have brought the greatest modern military might to its knees. Today, nineteen of the most heroic brothers have struck a mighty blow against our enemies. Today, the Nineteen Lions have crashed four passenger airliners, two of them into the mightiest symbols of America – the World Trade Center Twin Towers."'

'*ALLAHU AKHBAR!*' A huge roar went up from the brothers, as they crowded around to hear their commander speak. Over the previous few days they had heard rumours of a coming victory, but none of them had even dreamed that it could be anything as spectacular as this.

'There is more, brothers,' Omer announced, holding his hands up to silence them. '"So, imagine the scene. 'Fasten your seat belts,' the sign flashes. The plane is ushered on to the runway, the sound of the engine rises to a crescendo in tandem with the adrenalin surging through your blood. Your pulse is racing, you feel your heart thudding against your chest; you admonish yourself to increase your remembrance of Allah. You pick up an in-flight magazine, act as if you are flicking through it, while once more you go over the details of the operation: soon, there will be no room for error. The minutes move too slowly and you are eager for Paradise. Finally the time arrives. Without a glance you rise from your seat and dart to the cockpit. Securing control of the plane you set your sights on your target. As the building approaches, you look about you at your brothers and all you see is the blazing light shining from their faces. Attempting to conceal your delight you direct the plane towards the north tower. With a prayer you shout, '*Allahu Akhbar! Allahu Akhbar!*' as you graciously glide into the tower, obliterating an Idol of the Modern Age."'

More ecstatic shouts of '*Allahu Akhbar*' rang out from the brothers.

'"For now there can be no doubt that men with impenetrable beliefs and impeccable character have arrived,"' Omer continued reading with obvious relish. '"The hearts of the infidels tremble in fear that there are more on the way. Remember the words of the Holy Koran. 'Oh Prophet Muhammad – peace and blessings be upon him – urge the believers to fight. If there are twenty steadfast persons among you they will overcome two hundred, and if there be one hundred steadfast persons they will overcome one thousand of those who disbelieve.' The World stands aghast, frozen in panic. Where has the American dream gone? Where is the great USA now? Where is the tyrant of the last century? Where is the superpower 'modern' Muslims quiver at the thought of?"'

'By the grace of Allah, the Great Satan has been struck a mortal blow!' Ali cried out, excitedly.

'"Have not the Nineteen Lions attested to the strength of a few armed with Imam – belief – against the many armed with disbelief?"' Omer continued. '"Did not this handful of a handful annihilate the CIA, the NSA, the FBI, the US Army, the US Navy, US Marine Corps, US Air Force, Navy SEALS and Delta Force? Did not the Nineteen Lions, financed comparatively by only nickels and dimes, overcome the hundreds of billions of dollars spent by the US Government on defence? Did not these Nineteen Mujahidin manage to enter the Lion's Den itself?"'

'Yes, brother, YES!' Ahmed roared, triumphantly. 'Brother Omer, he speaks the truth!'

'"The hearts of the US and her allies are trembling,"' Omer read on from the communiqué. '"Dark clouds lie overhead. When, and not if, the Call to Prayer bellows through the cities of New York, London and Sydney, and all the people worship none other but Allah, the Muslims will remember the Nineteen Lions, the Nineteen Martyrs. When the chronicles of Islam are written, when the World is ruled by the Book of Allah, then will we remember that these Nineteen Martyrs changed the course of history. Let it be known in the Heavens and on Earth that on Tuesday 11 September 2001, the Nineteen Lions of Islam roared. *Allahu Akhbar!*"' Omer shouted, as he finished reading out the communiqué.

Again the brothers took up his cry, punching the sky as they did so and embracing each other.

'The fresh blood is still dripping from the hands of the Crusaders!' Omer cried. 'The Nineteen Lions were men who could no longer sit back and watch the rape and humiliation of our sisters. These men realised that to liberate Muslim lands from the claws of the enemies of Allah required the blood and the sacrifice of the Martyrs. And that is you, brothers! Jihad, brothers! Jihad!'

'Death to the infidels!' the brothers roared in reply.

Two days after the brothers had received the news of the 9/11 terror attacks, the men of Ali's unit were given their marching orders. All of them knew that a great battle with the USA and her allies would be coming soon now. It was just a matter of time. They were ordered to deploy to the front line around the sacred town of Mazar-e-Sharif, in northern Afghanistan. The name Mazar-e-Sharif means 'the Tomb of the Saint'. In the twelfth century the burial place of the son-in-law of the Prophet Muhammad was discovered there. Thus Mazar-e-Sharif was a sacred place within Islam and one that the brothers felt they would be honoured to defend with their very blood.

As they were preparing to depart, Ali looked around at the thirty fellow fighters in his unit. He had become very close with three of them. One was Mohamed al-Jihadi, an Algerian doctor who'd taken the name al-Jihadi – the jihad – because he didn't want to identify himself with Algeria, a country ruled by a secular regime. As far as he was concerned, he belonged to no country – his allegiance was only to the Umma, the world Islamic community united under Islam. Over the last few weeks, Mohamed had given away little of his personal background. But Ali was drawn to him because Mohamed was so zealous in his views. He even resented the fact that the foreign fighters spoke in English, because, he argued, it was the language of *kofr*, of disbelief.

Then there was Sadiq al-Saudia – a lawyer from Saudi Arabia. Sadiq was married and had a family back home in Jeddah. Ever since the brothers had arrived in the training camp, the local Afghan kids had kept begging for money, and Sadiq had never been able to refuse them, partly because the children reminded him so much of his own. Ali had asked Sadiq what it was like to leave a family behind and join the jihad. 'The bond between the wife and husband, it is even stronger than that of a mother and son . . .' Sadiq had responded. From the sadness in his voice, Ali had realised how tough it must have been to leave his wife and two young sons behind. Sadiq had also talked about how hard he'd had to work to provide for his family while he was away from them.

It was Ali's giant friend Ahmed who was the odd one out. Ahmed was uneducated and came from a dirt poor farming community in the Yemen. He had only managed to make it to the Afghan jihad with the help of money donated by his local mosque. Four years earlier the Taliban Army had seized control of Afghanistan, and Ahmed had decided to join them. He had been swept up in the movement and had proved himself a fearless warrior. He had no wife or children to return to in the Yemen, and felt that Afghanistan was now his personal and spiritual home. He had no intentions of ever leaving, unless he did so on the path to eternal Paradise.

Despite their differing backgrounds, all of the brothers shared one thing in common. They had all come to Afghanistan with one sole intention – to wage jihad and kill the infidels, their enemy. As they set off for the front line Ali prayed that it would not be long before the killing could begin.

3

FIRST INTO ACTION

ON the morning of 11 September 2001, Mat, Jamie, Tom and Mucker had been up at Hereford (the location of SAS headquarters). Earlier in the week they had been on combined SAS/SBS exercises. They'd finished the training ahead of schedule and gone to the ranges for some shooting practice. But around mid-afternoon, the stillness of the countryside had been shattered by a bleeper going off. As the lads pulled out their various mobile communication devices, Mat took a look at the message on the screen of his Blackberry handheld.

'Holy fuck!' he exclaimed in horror. 'They've just hit the Twin Towers in the States!'

Five days later, on 16 September, the men of the SBS gathered to listen to the first formal post 9/11 briefing. Mat had never known such a sombre atmosphere at their Poole headquarters, with a raw undercurrent of anger running just below the surface. As far as the men of the SBS were concerned, they served on the front line of the battle against terrorism in all its forms. And the 9/11 attacks had been a declaration of war by Islamic extrem-

ists against the Western world. While the terror attacks
had hit America, the lads still felt as if they were an
assault on their own beliefs, on their own way of life.
And now they wanted nothing more than to go into
battle against those responsible for the atrocities – which
had to mean hitting Afghanistan. That was the only way
to boost their battered morale – to go into action fast
and hard.

As Colonel James Saunders, the CO of the SBS, stood
up to speak, a deathly silence settled over the room.

'Gentlemen, you all know why we are here,' the colonel
began. 'Our foremost ally, America, has been attacked.
In a cowardly and unprovoked action, terrorists from
al-Qaeda have flown passenger aircraft into the Twin
Towers in New York and the Pentagon in Washington.
Thousands of innocent people have been killed. Some of
the intended terror strikes were foiled. If it were not for
the brave acts of the passengers on board those hijacked
aircraft, the casualty figures might be even higher. That
much you are all aware of. Now, as we speak, America
is preparing her response: Operation Enduring Freedom.
And make no mistake, that response will be rigorous
and deadly and aimed at taking out those responsible
for planning, financing and executing these heinous acts.
As our own Prime Minister has made abundantly clear,
Britain – and her armed forces – will stand shoulder to
shoulder with America in this struggle against world
terrorism.'

The CO paused and took a look around the assembled men. 'I know that you are all itching to be in on
the action, to play your part in bringing to justice or
otherwise dealing with those responsible,' he continued.
'You will be aware that the main alleged culprit is Osama
bin Laden, presently being sheltered by Afghanistan's

Location of UKSF operations in Afghanistan

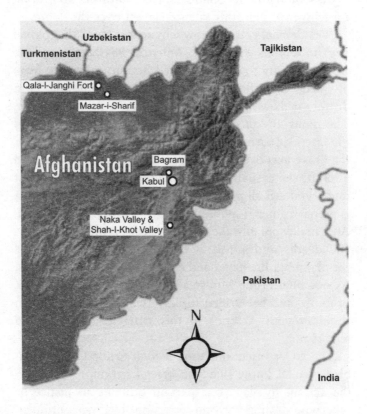

Taliban regime. Unless he is handed over to US authorities, which is looking increasingly unlikely, then Afghanistan will be the first target of any US, and British, response. That much is abundantly clear. However, should the war kick off in Afghanistan, as I am certain it will do, I have to inform you that the SAS have been given Afghanistan as their theatre of operations. We have been given the rest of the world.'

As soon as the CO had spoken those words, a groan went up from the lads assembled in the room.

'Now, I know that every man among you would want to be in Afghanistan, where you believe the war will be fought at its fiercest,' the CO continued. 'But your role is equally, if not even more, vital. On 11 September the world changed. A group of extremist Islamist terrorists – al-Qaeda, bin Laden, call them what you will – declared war on Western interests. That war will now be fought anywhere and everywhere that they feel they can strike at us. We are fully expecting there to be further attempts at terrorist attacks. Which means that the global counter-terrorism role you are being given is a vitally important one. The visible war will be fought in Afghanistan. But the covert, shadow war will be fought wherever these people try to hit us. And that, gentlemen, will be your responsibility: to stop those terror strikes before they can do us any harm.'

As the men of the SBS filed out of the briefing and wandered off in groups, there was no disguising the disappointment that they all were feeling. Despite the CO's words of encouragement, they felt that, once again, the SAS had been given the real mission, and that they were being left with the scraps from the big boys' table. For several years now the SBS soldiers had been complaining that their higher profile, sister special forces unit took the lion's share of any juicy operations. And years of experience had proven to them that counter-terrorism duties rarely resulted in any active combat missions. The key to CT work was to prevent any attacks from happening, rather than taking the terrorists on in full battle.

'Fuckin' bunch of shite, that's what that is, mate,' Tom remarked to Mat, as they strolled away from the briefing. 'We're on CT – fuckin' "Cushy Time" – again, while the SAS gets the whole of the Stan. Fuckin' nightmare, that's what it is, a fuckin' nightmare.'

'Too bloody right, mate,' Mat grunted, morosely. 'It'll be kicking off in the Stan left, right and centre, and we'll not get a sniff of anything. Bloody typical.'

A massive US and British war machine was gearing up for action in Afghanistan. Each morning since the 9/11 terror attacks, officials from the MOD and Defence Intelligence met with Geoff Hoon, the Defence Secretary, and General Sir Michael Boyce, Chief of the Defence Staff. Secure lines of communication had been set up with General Tommy Franks, head of US military Central Command (CENTCOM), based in Tampa, Florida. As the US and British military planners examined the potential for a conventional ground offensive, just about every aspect appeared negative. Afghanistan was a landlocked nation the size of Texas, a logistical nightmare for getting allied troops in to the country. Large-scale troop movements would need helicopter support, and many of the Afghan mountain passes were too high for heli-borne operations. In addition to which, enemy forces numbered some 50,000 Taliban soldiers, including hundreds of foreign fighters – battle-hardened religious fanatics from across the Islamic world.

A conventional ground offensive had all the makings

of a disaster, and was clearly a non-starter. A plan was therefore drawn up to use small units of US and British special forces to fight alongside the Afghan resistance, the Northern Alliance (NA). At the same time a massive allied air campaign would target terrorist training camps and air defences, followed by communications and command and control facilities. Then the so-called 'targets of opportunity' would be hit: enemy tanks, fuel tankers and other military vehicles. Finally, the Taliban and al-Qaeda forces would be targeted, using munitions designed to kill large troop numbers. At the same time the NA forces would be strengthened by weapons supplied from Russia. And all of this activity was to be coordinated on the ground by US and British special forces.

In late October the SAS were inserted into Afghanistan, using the HALO (high-altitude low-opening) parachuting technique. But their operations on the ground were frustrated by terrible weather conditions and confusion over appropriate mission tasking. In early November, after spending just two weeks on the ground, the main body of the SAS were withdrawn from Afghanistan. Upon hearing that the SAS were being pulled back, Rear Admiral Boyce, a powerful Navy man in Whitehall, contacted the Director of Special Forces to discuss SBS tasking. The Rear Admiral had been fighting the SBS's corner for some time now and he made an impassioned argument for the deployment of the SBS to Afghanistan. The Director of Special Forces agreed that the SBS should be sent in to secure Bagram airbase, the gateway to central Afghanistan.

And so, on a day in early November, the best part of C Squadron found themselves leaving the UK at short notice, en route to Afghanistan. As the men left their

Poole base, they threw pitying looks at their mates in M
and Z Squadrons. Barely six weeks earlier, they had been
told that they wouldn't be deploying to Afghanistan.
Every man in the SBS had been bitterly disappointed.
Now the C Squadron lads were getting to go, and they
departed Poole giving the finger to the others, knowing
that every man jack of them was dying to be on this
mission.

'Looks like you poor sods've been left behind, again,'
Mat shouted over at the lads from M and Z.

'Have fun. Enjoy your Cushy Time,' Jamie added.

'Yeah – an' keep Britain fuckin' safe for us, won't
you, lads?' Tom chipped in.

'Anything in particular you'd like us to bring you back
from the Stan, lads?' Mucker piped up, grinning from
ear to ear.

All they received in return was a barrage of abuse.

C Squadron departed the UK from RAF Brize Norton
in three C-130 Hercules transport aircraft. It was a
sixteen-hour flight with a couple of fuelling stops. They
came into Bagram airbase in Afghanistan under cover of
darkness and showing no lights. When the lead C-130
pilot went to put his giant aircraft down, he found himself
having to dodge shell craters and the wreckage of ancient
Soviet aircraft in order to make a safe landing. As the
roar of the C-130's turboprops reverberated through the
still, night-dark landscape, the men of C Squadron discovered that they had arrived in a deserted wasteland.

Some forty-eight hours earlier, Bagram airbase had
been in the hands of the AQT forces. It had only been
due to the pounding by US air strikes, plus the repeated
attacks by the Northern Alliance troops massed to the
west of them, that the enemy had been forced to abandon
the airport. As the lead C-130 came to a halt on the

battle-scarred central runway, its rear ramp was already opening. Mat, Jamie, Tom and Mucker drove off the still-moving aircraft in their Land-Rover with orders to immediately take possession of this no man's land. As soon as they hit the ground they were battle-ready, and they headed out to secure the airbase perimeter.

The crumbling and ramshackle Bagram airport sits within a massive series of mountain peaks – the Paghman range – that overlook it on three sides. Although these mountains were now lost in the towering darkness, the SBS knew that the high ground was held by the heavily armed forces of the enemy. It was only the threat of further US air strikes that was preventing the Taliban armour and heavy guns from pounding Bagram further into oblivion. Yet the men of C Squadron now securing the airbase had just flown into an even greater danger than that posed by the enemy – a danger emanating from one of the most unexpected of quarters.

Bagram was built in the early 1980s by the Soviets, strategically located some forty kilometres north of the Afghan capital, Kabul. Control of Bagram was crucial to holding central Afghanistan. The Soviets had known this, as did the Taliban and al-Qaeda. And it was a fact not lost on the Northern Alliance now fighting alongside the US and British. But the US high command had decided that it wanted to take control of Bagram airbase, as it provided the perfect bridgehead via which to pour US ground troops into Afghanistan. And so the men of the SBS had been quietly inserted into Bagram without the Northern Alliance's knowledge or prior approval. As the Afghan commanders woke up to the fact that British troops had flown in to secretly occupy 'their airbase' they began threatening war.

Mat, Jamie, Tom and Mucker took up positions on

the eastern perimeter of Bagram, finding cover in the fuselage of an ancient Soviet MiG fighter jet. The base was a veritable graveyard of aircraft, with the gutted carcasses of MiGs, Antonov cargo planes and Mi-24 helicopter gunships lying around where the Soviets had abandoned them. The Mi-24s were painted sky grey underneath with green-brown camouflage above, and each had the five-pointed red star of the old USSR displayed on its fuselage. It was a poignant reminder to the SBS troops of how former superpowers had come to grief here on the Afghan plains.

It was a bitterly cold night, with icy winds sweeping down off the surrounding hills. Mat's team rolled out their down sleeping bags inside the hold of the MiG, which provided a modicum of shelter. They ate some rations and organised sentry duty. As Mat took the first, freezing cold watch of the night, little did he realise that some 20,000 NA troops were massing to the west of them, poised to wipe out the British forces now in Bagram and take back 'their' airport. The men of the SBS were outnumbered some 200-1 – which were odds that even C Squadron wouldn't have relished, if they had known about it.

By now, angry radio and satphone exchanges were flying backwards and forwards between the enraged NA commanders and the US and British high command. The NA were demanding that the SBS withdraw immediately. They gave the British until dawn to comply with their demands: otherwise they would launch a massive offensive to retake the airport. The Afghan commanders were angry on two counts. First, their so-called allies had 'stolen' Bagram airbase from under their noses. Second, it was *British* – not American – troops that were now in possession of the airbase. And as far as the Afghans were concerned, British forces were far from welcome in their country. The British had a long history of waging war in Afghanistan, as opposed to the Americans, who had only ever come to their country as allies.

The Americans had first aided the Afghans in their battle against the occupying Soviet forces – which had all been part of the Cold War struggle between the communist East and the democratic West. The chief contribution that the US had made was to provide the Afghan fighters with US Stinger missiles, which were used to shoot down Soviet Red Army choppers as they ferried in supplies over the high mountain passes. A staggering 315 Soviet helicopters had been lost in that conflict. Finally, the Soviets had been forced to recognise that the war was bankrupting their country. The US policy of providing surface-to-air missiles had been a major factor in helping to drive the Soviets out of Afghanistan and bring victory to the Afghan mujahidin forces.

As an angry dawn smote the sky towards the east of Bagram blood red, Mat tried to breathe some life into his stiff, frozen fingers. All night long the bitterly cold Afghan wind had howled through the wrecked MiG fuselage, penetrating their thick down bags and duvet jackets and chilling the men to the bone. Mat was tempted to light a fire to warm himself, using some old, discarded packing crates that lay nearby. But he knew the smoke from the fire would be visible for many miles around and could betray their position. Instead, Mat broke out his tiny hexy stove (a collapsible, metal grill that burns smokeless solid fuel blocks) and started to get a brew on. If they could get some hot, sweet tea inside them, that would help the thawing-out process no end.

As he was heating the water, Mat spotted the first of several Hercules C-130 aircraft in-bound towards the airbase. This time they were US aircraft and they were flying in an attachment of Delta Force troops – the nearest US equivalent to the SAS. The arrival of Delta Force signalled that the stand-off with the Northern Alliance forces was coming to an end. Overnight, senior US military figures had presented the Afghan commanders with a counter-ultimatum: unless they allowed British forces free access to their country, including Bagram, the US military would call off all air strikes against enemy forces. 'The Brits are our allies and they're part of the equation,' the US commander had told the Northern Alliance. 'They're here to stay.'

As Mat and his team stretched their ice-cold limbs in the feeble light of dawn, with little idea how close they'd come to a showdown with their Afghan 'allies', the newly arrived Delta Force operators began deploying around the airbase to shore up the SBS positions. The US soldiers were surprised to find their British counterparts camped out in the wrecked Soviet aircraft with the most basic of kit, as far as they saw things. Four Delta boys came over to join Mat and his team. They found the elite British troop brewing up some tea on a tiny little stove, and cracking jokes as if there was nothing in the world to worry about.

'Want a brew, mate?' Mat asked, as he welcomed one of the Delta operators. 'Take it you didn't fancy a night at the airport, then?'

'We, like, only just got here, buddy,' the operator replied. 'Guess we kinda didn't fancy our chances bedding down in one of those Russian crates alongside you guys.'

'Don't blame you, mate,' Mucker called over from the inside of the MiG fuselage, where he was still cocooned in his sleeping bag. 'Cold enough to freeze the balls off of a brass monkey, it was.'

'Fancy a brew, mate?' Mat asked again. 'I just got this on the go so you're welcome to some.'

'Coffee'd be good, buddy,' the operator replied, as he crouched down next to Mat at the stove. 'Say, you guys are the S-B-S, aren't you? Cos, like, that's what the briefer told us on the ride out here in the Herc.'

'That's us, mate,' Mat said. 'SBS – Special Boat Service. And proud of it. Why? You expecting someone else?'

'Well, I kinda thought the S-A-S were the first of you guys sent out here,' the operator said. 'I mean, I sort of expected –'

'They was, mate,' Mat interrupted. 'But they found the weather a bit too cold for their liking. So, they all just been sent home again.'

'Bring any Hershey bars with you, mate?' Mucker shouted over from the MiG. 'Swap some for the coffee. I could murder some decent chocolate.'

'I guess you guys don't, you know, realise how close you just come to the shit going down, do ya?' the operator asked, with a grin.

'The Afghans? They've been no trouble, like,' Mat said. 'Quiet as the grave it was all night long. Apart from Mucker there snoring, of course. The whole fookin' fuselage was shaking, he was so loud. I should know, n'all. I didn't sleep a bloody wink, I was that cold.'

At the centre of the airbase was a massive hangar painted a dirty green colour, which was large enough to hide a jumbo jet in. It was pockmarked with bullet and shrapnel holes, but was more or less serviceable. To one side of the hangar was a three-storey accommodation block, and this is where the SBS now made their quarters. As soon as the men had slung their beds, they began work on the infrastructure required for an operational airbase. Further flights were expected in the coming days bringing in the SAS, the Paras, the Royal Marines and several hundred assorted US troops. Inside the hangar itself they set up the SBS ops tent, the nerve centre of their operations. Next to that was the quartermaster's tent, containing the stores and the armoury, plus a mess tent and a field hospital. And on the opposite side of the hangar they made room for the heads and the shitters.

Some eighteen hours after their arrival at Bagram, the SBS gathered in the giant hangar for their first operational briefing. As they did so the men were wondering just what might now lie ahead of them. But the briefing was to be short and sweet. No missions had yet been allocated, the officer commanding (OC) of C Squadron told them. After the near disaster of the threatened attack by the Northern Alliance, it was abundantly clear that UK forces had no status in Afghanistan. Or rather, what status they did have was an altogether negative one. The men were ordered to keep a low profile and integrate with the US Delta teams as far as possible. Having only been allowed into the country by the skin of their teeth, the SBS would now have to show willing to their Afghan allies – which meant taking the fight to the enemy as soon as they possibly could.

The OC finished the briefing by stressing one other aspect of their deployment: Afghanistan in general and Bagram airbase in particular was seen as being a nest of vipers. Enemy spies were everywhere. Standard operating procedures (SOPs) concerning operational security (opsec) – and in particular communications back to the UK – were to be adhered to at all times. No mobile phone calls were allowed and no email facility was to be made available for troops to contact their families. Any letters home would need to be sanitised in the normal way, with no references made to their location, mission details, troop numbers or operational plans. All mail would be read and checked by the SBS officers.

Over the next twenty-four hours more men and supplies started arriving by air, including the troops of the US 10th Mountain Division and operators from the CIA. But with enemy forces putting up stiff resistance all across the country, allied commanders remained unsure where best to deploy their forces, the SBS included. The main focus of the US-led air campaign was north of Bagram, around the city of Mazar-e-Sharif. Here, the US 5th Special Operations Forces group had deployed on the ground in support of General Rashid Dostum and his Northern Alliance troops. But sustained US aerial bombardment of enemy positions had yet to produce any significant breakthroughs. As predicted, the Taliban forces were proving a tough nut to crack.

Some months prior to the Afghan deployment, Mat had been sent on an all-terrain-vehicle (ATV) training course in the UK. The focus of the course was to learn how to operate quad bikes. The main reason that he'd been sent was to satisfy health and safety regulations, which had now even started getting into special forces. Unless someone had a piece of paper to show that he was a 'qualified' ATV instructor, then the SBS weren't supposed to teach ATV use at Poole. On the morning of their third day in Bagram, Mat decided to hold a quad-bike training session for those who'd missed out on it back in the UK. There was little else to do and somehow his instinct was telling him that the quad bikes would prove invaluable in the harsh Afghan terrain.

Bagram airbase was arranged in an elongated H shape – the two long arms of the H being the two main runways. At one end there was a short section of runway that was pockmarked with bomb craters and totally unserviceable

– which made it a perfect quad-bike training ground. Mat, Mucker, Tom and Jamie marked off a course in a figure of eight, and called together a bunch of the lads. The quad bikes were big, hefty machines with chunky wheels: to the fore and aft they were fitted with racks for carrying bergens, weapons, ammo, jerrycans of water and fuel.

Prior to the lads trying their hands at the machines, Mat stood out front and began to give some verbal instruction. But just as he did so there was a noisy interruption from Gobbler, one of the comparative newcomers to C Squadron.

'What the fuck're we listening to all this shite for?' Gobbler began, in his thick West Country accent. 'You cain't fuckin' teach me nothing about quad bikes. I was brought up on a fuckin' farm, weren't I? Been riding 'em since I was born. I'm fuckin' ace on a quad bike, mate, just you watch.'

With that Gobbler jumped on one of the quads, gunned the throttle and shot off round the first bend. Just seconds later there was an almighty crash, and Gobbler and his bike had disappeared from view. As one, the lads rushed over to see what had happened, only to discover Gobbler lying in a heap in one of the bomb craters with his quad bike wrapped around a rock. It would have been exceedingly funny had Gobbler not been so badly hurt. Being a medic, Mat jumped down into the crater to take stock of Gobbler's injuries. As far as he could tell, Gobbler had broken both his arms and a leg, so he must have been going at one hell of a crack when his bike had hit that rock. As fast as they could they got Gobbler on to a stretcher and wrapped in some warm blankets, with a casualty evacuation chopper on the way. Whatever the prognosis when they got Gobbler to hospital, it looked as if this was going to be the end of his war. And as for the quad bike, it was a write-off.

'"Fuckin' ace quad-bike driver, me." Fuckin' idiot, more like it,' Tom remarked under his breath, as they waited for the casevac chopper. 'Tragic, wasn't it, mate?'

'The bloke's a numpty, mate,' Mat said, nodding at Gobbler's prostrate form. 'Reminds me of that time in Norway. You was there, weren't you, mate? The CSM trashed his OSV [over-snow vehicle]. Remember? Now that was a bloody classic.'

'Nah, I didn't make it, mate,' Tom replied, shaking his head. 'Stayed behind in Poole – can't remember why now.'

'Well, it was on Arctic exercises, a couple of years back,' said Mat. 'The CSM was that really hard fooker, Bob Wort, tiny and wiry and bloody hard as nails. We were all in white camo and had the skidoos with a trailer on the back loaded up with ammo. We was following old Worty in line astern, and every time he stopped, the OSVs'd go crashing into each other.'

'Yeah, we were following the tracks of the man up ahead,' Jamie interjected.

'The throttle wasn't up to much on the OSV – it was really all or nowt,' Mat continued. 'You'd be hammering along when suddenly the bloke in front would put on the brakes and you'd slam on the anchors. Then there'd be a smashing of plastic and crunching of metal all along the line, and there'd be half a dozen smashed brake lights and crumpled snow guards. Anyhow, Worty finally blew his top.'

'Steam was coming out of his ears, mate,' said Jamie.

'Yeah, he was honkin' angry,' Mat agreed. '"Now listen up, you twats," Worty yelled, his face red with anger. "Treat these fookin' machines with some fookin' respect, like you would your wives or your girlfriends or sommat. They're ten grand a piece and I don't want you fookin' smashing them up any more. You hear me? Treat them with some fookin' respect. Next bloke who smashes one up will be returned to unit. Got it?" With that, Worty spun around on his OSV, gunned it full throttle and shot off. We looked at each other, shrugged and headed off after him. Then his OSV just disappeared from view. One moment it was there, the next gone. We all slammed on the anchors. "Where the fuck's the CSM gone?" we're all asking. We started searching around when suddenly there was a yell and someone had found him. Worty'd managed to find the one part of the snow-field where there was a crevasse. Admittedly, the light was bad, but even so . . . Worty's OSV'd gone plunging down some fifteen metres. He'd had a trailer on the back towing a GPMG, and it'd gone smashing down on top of the OSV, totally wrecking it.'

'Bit like Gobbler's quad bike, then?' Tom asked. 'Smashed to fuck, was it?'

'Yeah. For a second, we'd all stood there on the edge of the crevasse. Then someone spotted Worty's legs, wiggling wildly . . . He'd been catapulted off the OSV and landed head first in a snowdrift. He must've been suffocating in there. Couple of us roped down and pulled him out fast as we could. But the rest of the lads just couldn't help themselves, they were standing up there on the rim of that crevasse pissing themselves laughing.'

'So, which was the biggest fuck-up then, mate?' Tom asked. 'Worty's on the OSV, or Gobbler's on the quad bike?'

'Dunno,' Mat replied, taking a few seconds to think it over. 'Probably Worty's, cos he was the CSM and all. "Treat these machines with a little fookin' respect."

Bloody classic. He didn't need casevaccing to hospital, mind.'

'"Fuckin' ace quad-bike driver, me,"' Jamie said, indicating Gobbler's figure prone on the stretcher in front of them. 'Talking of which, where the hell's that casevac chopper?'

After the disastrous quad-bike training, Mat went and found a quiet corner in the SBS quarters. He wanted to write a letter to Suzie, his girl back at home. He'd met her just a few months back, but he knew already that she was the one. She was an educated woman with a degree, and sometimes he felt a bit unequal to her because of that. But she told Mat that she loved him and he believed her. He'd even started thinking about what it'd be like to have some kids. But whether he could stick with the SBS if he had a wife and family was another matter.

Honey, I can't tell you nowt about where I am or what I'm doing or how long I'm going to be here, Mat began his letter. *Sorry, love, that's just how it is and you know that. What I can tell you is that I've got the ring you gave me and it's now tied round my neck with the morphine and dog tags. That's about as romantic as it gets, especially as I know the ruperts will be reading this letter . . .*

A couple of hours after Gobbler had been air-evacuated Mat heard back from the military hospital that his condition was stable. But, as predicted, it was the end of Gobbler's war in Afghanistan. It was also the end of any quad-bike training at Bagram, as the lads had lost all enthusiasm for it. That evening, Mat and his team were to receive news of another of the C Squadron operatives being taken out of action. And this was to prove far more serious for them.

Mat, Tom and Jamie were sat around in their makeshift quarters, moaning on about the fact that they didn't have any of the normal luxuries of deployment. There wasn't even a TV on which to show DVDs of their favourite war films (*Apocalypse Now*, *Platoon*, *Full Metal Jacket*) and the odd porn movie. Not surprisingly, Mucker had one of the best porn collections of anyone in the SBS, and he'd brought a load of DVDs with him. But now they had nothing to play them on. Officially, there was no beer allowed on the base yet, as operational security meant that the men were on high alert at all times. But some of the lads had managed to smuggle a few beers in, although only in limited quantities. Just as Mat, Tom and Jamie were bemoaning this shocking lack of beer, war movies and porn, Geoff, one of their C Squadron mates, came barging in.

'You blokes not heard?' Geoff announced, as soon as he laid eyes on them. 'The Hobbit's deep in the shit.'

'What?' said Mat. 'What's that silly fooker Mucker been up to now?'

'Reckon he's on his way out of here, mate,' Geoff replied. 'He's fucked up fucking big time.'

'What the bollocks d'you mean?' Mat asked.

'Well, it's to do with all this opsec. Security's so tight just about all you can write home to your missus is something like you're missing her and the kids, and how's the dog? And that's hardly going to put her mind at rest, is it? Well, rumour has it the Hobbit wasn't satisfied writing a letter home, specially as he knew that the head sheds would read it. Apparently, he had some real personal stuff to deal with. So the silly fucker made a call home on his mobile phone, didn't he? To his missus. Anyhow, the phone call was traced and Mucker's deep in the shite.'

'What the fuck did he do that for?' Mat said, incredulously. 'First any of us have heard he had trouble back home, and we're his bloody mates.'

'Well, you know that old joke, don't you, mate?' Geoff replied, with an evil grin. 'You know – the one about the Canadian chicken farmer?'

'Never heard of it – and what the fuck's it got to do with Mucker, anyways?'

'Well, there's this chicken farm in Canada. One day the chickens start producing these huge, one-pound eggs. Now they're the biggest fucking eggs in the world a chicken's ever produced and the Canadian egg marketing board won't sell them, cos they don't meet with their strict rules. You know, size, how many they pack to a box, that sort of thing. So the guy who runs the chicken farm is going spare. Anyhow, he calls in this expert on chickens to try to sort it out. This expert can speak chicken language, so he goes in and starts speaking to the hens. "Cluck, cluck, cluck, cluck," he goes. Sure enough the chickens reply, and so the chicken expert tells the farmer: "Well, the chickens aren't much help – they say it's a secret. I'm gonna have to go talk to the rooster."'

'Yeah, all right, bloody ha ha,' Mat interrupted. 'Just tell us what the bloody score is with Mucker.'

'I haven't finished yet,' Geoff retorted. He was relishing the fact that he was dragging out the joke and keeping Mat and the rest of them on tenterhooks as he did so. 'So – "Cluck, cluck, cluck, cluck, squawk," goes the chicken expert as he talks to the rooster. And sure enough the rooster replies to him. The chicken expert shakes his head, smiles then turns to the chicken farmer. "Think I may have found your problem," he says. "The rooster just told me: 'I dunno why the hens are producing one-pound eggs,' he said, 'but can you help me find that fuckin' ostrich that's been shagging my hens?'"'

'Yeah, cracking joke, mate,' Mat snorted. 'Nowt funnier. Mucker's gettin' sent back home cos he told a joke about chickens to his missus on his bloody mobile, is that it?'

'Don't you get it?' Geoff shot back at him. 'Mucker's missus has started fucking with some local ostrich back home so he wants to go and pan the guy's head in, doesn't he? So he calls up his missus on his mobile threatening to go and do the guy in. Doesn't see that it's his missus who's got hooked on shagging the local playboy that's the problem, and that he ought to dump her.'

'Holy fuck, Mucker's got problems with her indoors?' Mat said. 'I never knew nowt about it. How the hell did you get all the sordid details, anyway?'

'Well, Mucker was just hauled before the OC, wasn't he? Straight away he knows that he's been rumbled, so he tells the OC everything, I guess to try to stop himself being RTU'd. Just blurts it all out. A couple of the lads overheard it. But you know the score – it doesn't matter a fuck to the OC what's going on back at home. Ever known an officer make allowances for that sort of thing?'

'Domestics? They don't give a shit,' Mat said. 'So what's the bottom line, mate – what's happenin' to Mucker?'

'Well, they're paranoid about opsec and I reckon he's on his way out of here. Which'll leave you guys one man short. Fucks your team right up. Bit of a bummer, what with a shitload of juicy ops just about to be allocated.'

'Thanks for all the sympathy, mate,' Mat retorted. 'Bloody arseholes. Mucker! What a dumb time to pull a stunt like that.'

Sure enough that evening Mucker was put on a C-130 flight back to the UK. He'd escaped being RTU'd (returned to unit – in effect being kicked out of the SBS and returned to his parent unit, the Royal Marines) only by the skin of his teeth, on compassionate grounds. But with Mucker gone that left Mat's fire team down to three men – at the very moment when they were hoping to get deployed on active missions. Not only that, but Mucker was one of their team's forward air control (FAC) specialists, and Mat had a strong suspicion that calling in air strikes was going to make up the lion's share of how they would fight this war. Mat went to sleep that night cursing Mucker's stupidity. He feared that it might just end up costing the rest of them a happy war.

The following morning C Squadron were called together for their second briefing. This time, the atmosphere in the giant hangar was completely different and very businesslike. One corner of the cavernous building had been turned into the SBS's briefing area. It was covered in maps of Afghanistan with coloured pins stuck in them and noticeboards full of high-resolution satellite photos showing specific target areas. As Mat filed into the hangar he could see the US special forces teams setting up their multigyms and plasma TV screens over on their side. If only the British forces had the same sort of resources as the Yanks, he thought to himself, ruefully.

As Mat waited for the briefing to begin, he knew that he ought to be feeling some degree of sympathy for Mucker, as it must have been a bloody awful situation to find himself in, stuck out in the Stan with his wife getting it on with some local boy back at home. But even so, it was the dumbest of ways to have reacted – to have called home on his bloody mobile phone. It was just the sort of thing that he should have expected from the Hobbit. As the OC of C Squadron, Major Peter Griffin, stood up to address the men, Mat feared that his fire team was going to be the one left out of the action.

Thanks to Mucker and his stupidity they were down to three men, which meant that they were no longer an operational unit in the eyes of the SBS commanders.

'R-r-right, we've finally got some m-mission taskings, and some j-juicy ones they are too,' Major Griffin began. The major was known as 'Grizzly' to his men, because he talked with an unfortunate 'grrrrr'-like stutter. 'So l-l-listen up, l-l-lads. First half a dozen of you will be deploying north to Mazar-e-Sharif, transiting via Uzbekistan. As you all know Mazar is in this region.' The OC indicated an area on one of the maps close to the north-western border of Afghanistan. 'This is where US air power is giving the enemy a right good pounding, so you'll be in the h-heart of the action. Fire Team 4, you'll be h-heading up that way shortly. Now, Mat, because you're down to three men, we're splitting up your team: Tom and Jamie, you will accompany Fire Team 4 to Mazar. The six of you will d-deploy via the US special forces base in Uzbekistan – low p-profile, in civvies, not showing any w-weapons. On arrival at Mazar you're to co-locate with US special forces and get stuck in. As you all know, our arrival here didn't exactly go down a bundle w-with the Afghans. So, w-we now need to show them that we have teeth.'

The OC paused for a second to let his words sink in. 'R-right, mission two: a s-similar sized unit will be d-deploying south of Shah-i-Khot, here, to the Naka Valley. You'll be co-locating with US special forces as part of their Task Force 11 – otherwise known as "Task Force Dagger". You've all heard what Task Force Dagger are up to, and it's s-some pretty s-serious s-stuff. They're joint units of Delta Force and the CIA, and they're going after some of al-Qaeda's top people. The CSM will give you a m-mission specific briefing, but suffice to say intel has identified what must be the biggest terrorist training facility ever in the Naka Valley. US air intends to obliterate the place. Mat, you'll be heading up there, along with our SEAL guest, Sam Brown, and the guys from Fire Team 6. You're to go in and get eyes on the target and guide in the air strikes. This is one of the biggest hits of the war so far, so I don't need to impress upon you the importance of your m-mission. You're going into the lion's den, and I have every confidence you'll be up to the job.'

Major Griffin then went on to outline the other operations allocated to the remaining men of C Squadron. But as far as Mat was concerned none of them sounded anything like as dramatic or dangerous as theirs – the Naka Valley mission.

'Now, if there are no questions,' the OC said, as he rounded of the briefing, 'you'll break down into your units and the task-specific briefings w-will begin. Of one thing I want you to be absolutely certain: you are going in there as the vanguard of UK armed forces, and I want you to draw blood quickly.'

'Just one question, boss,' Mat piped up. 'Who's the team leader on our op – the Naka Valley?'

'You are, Mat. You are to head up your six-man team, and then w-work very closely with your US counterparts.'

'Sure thing, boss.'

'Any more questions?'

'Yeah, I've got one, boss,' Tom said, barely able to disguise his frustration. 'What exactly are we tasked with up around Mazar? Sounds like we're going to be a talking shop and not much else.'

'You're chiefly on an advisory role,' the major replied. 'The main w-warlord up there is one General Dostum,

a key ally in our war effort. Your r-role is to get close
to him and act as his eyes and ears on the ground. The
General's land f-forces are well-equipped and capable
f-fighters – but tactically, they're lacking in knowledge
and experience of how to engage the AQT f-forces dug
in around Mazar. Your r-role is to help them work all
of that through – and coordinate all of that with allied
air strikes.'

'So, basically it's a non-combat mission, like?'

'Yes. But make no mistake, it's no less important
because of that.'

'So just how exactly are we supposed to "draw blood
quickly", if we're on a non-combat mission?'

'You're s-supposed to enable the Northern Alliance
f-forces better to draw blood, that's how. Now, if there's
no more q-questions, we'll break down into individual
unit briefings. And, gentlemen, good luck. I want to wish
you every s-success with your missions.'

'F-f-fucking d-d-deploying in c-c-civvies on a n-n-non-
c-c-combat m-m-mission,' Tom said, once the briefing
was over. 'Ain't exactly w-w-what I c-c-came out t-t-to
the f-f-fuckin' S-S-Stan f-f-for.'

'Me neither,' Jamie responded, morosely. 'Sounds like
we'll be up there miles back from the front line holding
the General's hand. "Draw blood quickly" – what a load
of bollocks that is.'

As Jamie, Tom and the Team 4 lads tasked with the
Mazar deployment bitched among themselves, the rest
of the SBS troops broke down into their operational
units. Mat, Sam Brown and the others slated for the
Naka Valley mission went into their own little huddle
in one corner of the hangar.

'Holy fuck, mate, look what we've just landed,' Mat
said to Sam, as they settled down to listen to the CSM.

'Looks like we're going into the heart of the action. Christmas has come early this year, eh, mate?'

'Just awesome, bro, awesome,' Sam replied, in his laconic East Coast drawl. Sam was a US SEAL – the nearest US equivalent to the SBS. He was on a two-year secondment to the SBS. 'Like the man there said, bro, looks like we'll be headin' right into the lion's den.'

On the one hand, Mat was disappointed to be splitting from Jamie and Tom. But on the other, he was chuffed to be teaming up with Sam, an operator for whom he had masses of respect. In his early thirties, Sam had sandy hair and thin, chiselled features. He had been based with the SBS for the best part of eighteen months. He was a combat veteran, having proven himself in the Balkans conflict when deployed there with US forces. Mat had heard the rumours that had done the rounds of the SBS – that Sam Brown came from a seriously rich landowning family. But the American was a man of few words and he certainly never bragged about being megawealthy. When he'd moved over from the States to Poole, all Sam had brought with him were his two favourite things in life: his wife, and his Harley-Davidson.

During his time with the SBS Sam had earned a reputation of being a genuinely decent guy who would do anything for his buddies. He held strong Christian beliefs, but he didn't talk about them that much. He was far from being the archetypal American soldier, and had quickly cottoned on to the unique sense of humour common to Britain's special forces. Quiet he might've been, but Sam had rapidly acquired a proficiency in sarcasm and piss-taking, which meant that he could hold his own with even the sharpest-tongued guys in the SBS. In short, he was considered by the men of C Squadron – Mat included – to be very much one of the boys.

Mat and Sam had hit it off immediately when they'd met back in Poole. They'd been on several training exercises together, and Mat had been impressed by Sam's combat abilities. The two men shared a maverick outlook on soldiering: they'd try anything once if it might just offer them an advantage over the enemy. Sam called all his fellow special forces soldiers 'bro'. But for those that he really warmed to he reserved the ultimate term of affection – which was 'bitch'. On several occasions Sam had introduced Mat to some of the other American soldiers based in the UK with: 'So, this here Brit's called Mat . . . He's ma bitch.'

Sam was especially keen to get blooded in Afghanistan. He felt the 9/11 attacks had been an assault on America, on his own way of life and beliefs. Sam knew from experience that the SBS were the elite of the elite – as good as any special forces that they had in the US. He loved their way of doing things – their can-do attitude that was second to none. Too often US special forces seemed wedded to technology and their logistical support. The emphasis in the SBS was on operating independently wherever and whenever required, on using physical strength, stamina and ingenuity to get the job done. Sam felt honoured to be in Afghanistan with the SBS. With them he felt sure that he'd be at the heart of the action.

CSM Gav Tinker came over to brief Mat, Sam and the Team 6 lads on the Naka Valley mission. 'OK, as you know you're co-locating with Task Force Dagger. What that means is you'll be teaming up with their people and using US vehicles, air and intelligence assets, and working very closely with their commanders. Sam, you're going cos you're an American and you understand the way the US military thinks. Mat, you're lucky to be on this op and you can largely thank Sam for that. Seems he asked that you go with him, and the Americans are happy to have you cos of your photography skills. You're going to have a CIA bloke joining you – probably at a safe house somewhere en route. We're still working on the detail. He'll be gathering intel and reporting back what you find. Your photos, Mat, are going to play a big part in those intel briefs. As for the rest of you, this is your lucky day. You've been chosen cos you're good operators, and you're basically a protection force for that CIA dude. Make sure you bring him back alive.

'You'll be deploying at first light tomorrow morning by Chinook,' the CSM continued. 'As much as possible we want you to deploy in civvies. No green army kit where you can avoid it. You'll be operating at altitudes of 12,000 feet plus. At that height it'll be twenty degrees below, maybe more. If there's a wind blowing it'll be more like sixty below – cold enough to freeze your bollocks off. Plus it's winter right now, so the weather's unusually dry and cold. You'll need to take your full allotment of alpine equipment from stores. Take enough food and water for a week-long deployment. And remember you're going to need to carry all this kit, plus weapons and ammo, on your backs. Don't ask me how you're going to manage it, cos buggered if I know. Work it out for yourselves. Don't underestimate your enemy: there's some five hundred hard-core al-Qaeda and Taliban in that valley, according to our intel. They're carrying out early-morning combat and PT-type exercises in the afternoon. The USAF is preparing for the largest bombardment of the war, and the Naka Valley is going to be obliterated. Is everyone clear?'

'Sure thing, boss,' Sam replied.

'Yeah – clear as mud, mate,' Mat added, sarcastically. 'Don't s'pose you've got a few packhorses you could lend us? No chance you'll be volunteering to come with us, then?'

'I would if I could, lad,' the CSM said. 'These old bones could still out-climb and out-fight you, any day of the week. Trouble is, I'm needed back 'ere to help steer the ship. So, you'll just have to manage without me. It's a tough one, this Naka Valley op, but it's a beauty of a mission if ever there was one.'

'Any idea who's in there, then?' Mat asked. 'Any of our Most Wanted, like?'

'There's a good possibility any one of 'em could be. There's been no specific names mentioned, but even Mullah Omer or bin Laden's possible. Back when I was your age, lad, I'd have given me eyeteeth to be on this mission. So don't go letting us down, will you, lads?'

After the CSM's briefing, there followed one from the Green Slime presenting all the intelligence they had on the Naka Valley. Then, an Aussie NCO came over to give a final briefing. He'd recently joined the SBS and was an expert in escape and evasion (E&E) procedures. He proceeded to rip Mat, Sam and the Team 6 lads to shreds on their E&E procedures, repeatedly going over the emergency rendezvous (ERV) measures to be used if the mission got compromised. Mat was scribbling madly in his notebook as the Aussie NCO spoke, but with the full knowledge that he'd have to destroy all the notes he was making before he left the briefing.

SBS standard operating procedures meant that no one was allowed to take anything away from a briefing that might compromise them if it fell into enemy hands. All written details of a mission, even pencil marks on maps, were strictly forbidden on an active combat mission. They weren't even supposed to fold their maps in a way that might emphasise any specific areas. So all details of the mission, intelligence, communications and E&E briefings had to be committed to memory. That was why the men would run through the briefings over and over and over again, until they had everything fixed in their minds.

'As usual, we'll work out our special codes – in case we're under duress or captured,' the Aussie NCO said. 'If you slip that code into your oral comms we'll know you're in trouble, right? If you quote the emergency code at any stage, air cover will know that you blokes're fucked. That's your last resort if it's all going to rat shit and you need to let us know. Remember: the codes. Only use them if you're captured or on your own and heading for the ERV.'

'Got it,' Mat, Sam and the Team 6 lads replied.

'OK, so I'm going to run through it one more time, just to make sure you guys know what you're up to. But this time, you're going to tell me how we do it, right? So, let's start at the beginning. You lot are on patrol and you're taking point. Now, let's say you spot a big, easily recognisable rock and you choose that as your first muster point if your patrol gets compromised. How d'you indicate to the rest of the blokes in your patrol that that's your first ERV?'

By lunchtime the mission briefings and rehearsals were finally over. As Mat, Sam and the other lads came out of the hangar they spotted a further flight of C-130s putting down on the runway. These turned out to be carrying a large force of SAS – the majority of two squadrons. It was barely three days since the SBS had seized Bagram and it seemed that everyone wanted a slice of the action. But with the airbase secured there would be little for the SAS lads to do but sit around killing time and awaiting their mission orders – just as the SBS had been forced to do before them. As for Mat and Sam, they'd be departing for the Naka Valley mission that night.

Winter on the Afghan front line was harsh for Ali, Ahmed and the other brothers. They had deployed to trenches positioned around a battle-scarred and run-down ex-Soviet base. All drinking water came from a nearby stream, which was also where they washed, and the freezing waters came straight off the mountainside. Every morning in the pre-dawn light Ali had to shake himself awake from his bedroll and break the ice on the stream, so that he could make his first ablutions of the day. As a Muslim, he had to undertake *wudu* – the ritual washing of his hands, face and feet – before making each of his five daily prayers to Allah.

Now that the Nineteen Lions had unleashed the wrath of Allah on the Great Satan the brothers knew that war was upon them. The American air attacks had started already, hitting strategic targets all across the country. Soon, there would be a ground offensive and the brothers knew that they had to be ready. They had started training with some of the heavier weapons that the Taliban had in their arsenal. That morning, after breakfast, Ahmed had the brothers gather around an ancient, Soviet-era DShK 'Dushka' machine gun. The massive, 12.7mm heavy machine gun (HMG) was suspended on a tripod that had clearly seen better days.

'Do I have a volunteer, brothers?' a grinning Ahmed asked, looking around at the assembled group. 'There is not much to it really. It is just like an AK47, but bigger. You aim it in the same way – you line up the sights, hold the big gun very steady and squeeze the trigger. And the target we will make that old Soviet Gaz jeep over there. And, *insh'Allah*, the godless American infidels driving the jeep, they will be no more. So, who's my first volunteer?'

There was a second or so's silence and as no one else seemed that keen, Ali stepped forward.

'I'll give it a go, brother,' he remarked, quietly.

'So, Brother Ali the Lion Cub is the one to volunteer again,' Ahmed announced. 'The rest of you are not so keen to be *shouhada'a* – martyrs – so quickly? Fine, Brother Ali, then it is all yours.'

As Ali prepared to fire the weapon, Ahmed and the rest of the brothers backed off a good distance. Ali slammed the first of the rounds into the Dushka's heavy breech and glanced over at the others. Though it was still early morning, the sun was already beating down from a hot Afghan sky and Ali could feel the sweat pouring off his forehead. As he squinted through the sights of the weapon and tried to line up the target, it kept dripping into his eyes. Taking his hand off the machine gun for a second, he wiped away the moisture and dirt, but still he couldn't stop it from obstructing his vision. None of the brothers were exactly rushing forward to help him, either.

'There is one more thing, brother,' Ahmed called over from where he was standing. 'When you fire the gun, remember to keep shouting "*Allahu Akhbar! Allahu Akhbar!*" as loud as you can. If you do not do this, the concussion from that gun when it is firing can blow your eardrums.'

Ali lined up the metal sights on the wreck of the Gaz jeep as best he could. It was a rusting hulk of a thing, some five hundred metres away across the flat, hard-packed desert. It clearly hadn't been driven by anyone, anywhere for a very long time. But in his mind's eye, Ali could now see a group of American soldiers together with their Afghan guide crouched over the wheel of the jeep, powering across the desert, oblivious to the destructive power that he was about to unleash on them. What would they be doing in there? he wondered, excitedly. Eating some dehydrated rations? Chewing gum? Drinking from their flasks and chatting about their girls back home? It didn't matter, really, did it? All that mattered was that they were infidels who had invaded a Muslim country and slaughtered Muslims. *This is what jihad is all about*, Ali told himself, as he tightened his grip around the trigger. *This is what jihad is all about. This is what I came here for.*

Ali gradually increased the pressure, waiting for the trigger point. As he did so he started yelling, '*Allahu Akhbar! Allah Akh –!*' But he never got to finish the last word. The firing pin slammed home and as it did so his world just exploded around him. Flames and smoke shot out in front of him, as the massive weapon rocked back on its tripod, the force of the recoil of each of the heavy-calibre rounds tearing into his shoulder muscles. Suddenly Ali's world had become one of the deafening roar of the gun, of the pain in his upper torso, and of the smoke and concussion of the weapon firing.

As a series of rounds tore into the Gaz jeep, punching massive rents in the rusted bodywork, it just seemed to crumple before him. Again, in his mind's eye, he could see the US soldiers, now being cut to pieces by the massive destructive power of the gun. *This is what I have come here for*, he told himself again, with grim satisfaction. *To kill the kafir, the infidels, the unbelievers. To kill them all.* Then Ali watched, transfixed, as a massive blast convulsed the dry desert air and the jeep just seems to vaporise. Whatever petrol had been left in the Gaz's fuel tank had just ignited, throwing a huge mushroom cloud of black, oily smoke high into the air. As debris from the exploding jeep clattered to earth, Ali ceased firing.

After the deafening roar of the giant machine gun, the desert seemed strangely silent. Ali sat there behind the smoking gun, unsure of what to do next. He heard footsteps approaching from behind him, and then Ahmed was clapping him on the shoulders and congratulating him on a job well done. Ali felt as if his legs were about to buckle under him, after the strain of operating the huge weapon. He was grateful when he felt Ahmed lifting him out of the gun carriage and placing a conspiratorial arm around him.

'This is very good shooting, Brother Ali,' Ahmed said, as he helped Ali to stand. 'If there had been any of our American friends inside that vehicle – *that Humvee* – they would all have gone to their infidel hell by now, that is if they even have one.'

'*Insh'Allah*,' Ali replied. 'May the grace of Allah keep us safe from this American bombing so that I may get the chance to use this weapon for real, brother.'

'*Insh'Allah*, brother,' Ahmed replied, '*insh'Allah*. But I think it's not just the Americans that you will need to be protected from. You'll need all the protection of all the Holy Prophets, peace be upon them, if you truly want to be a Dushka gunner. Nine times out of ten, brother, the Dushka destroys the target and kills the *kafir*. But there is always the chance that a round explodes in the barrel, and then it will take your arm off in the process.'

Ali looked up at Ahmed sharply.

'Oh yes,' he continued, 'it will take your arm right off. Or, if you are really lucky and the tripod is as old and worn as is this one, it just collapses with the force of the recoil, so crushing you. One minute you would be there, brother, bravely firing the weapon. The next you would be gone, crushed under the weight of the weapon. A martyr. And would that not be great and glorious? For then you would have gone to join the other *shouhada'a* and your seventy-two virgins in Paradise.'

Ali looked down at the still-smoking Dushka. He noticed that the breech was held together by nothing more than a length of twisted wire, and that the tripod was worn and badly buckled and missing several bolts from the mounting. Which meant that the giant machine gun was about as well maintained and functional as most of the other weapons that they were using.

'Did you not wonder why the rest of the brothers stood so far back from that thing when you were firing it?' Ahmed continued, nodding at the Dushka. 'The answer, Brother Ali, is that although they all may want to be *shouhada'a*, they let you volunteer, because they wanted you to have the chance to be the lucky one, the *shaheed*. That is the truly great thing about the jihad, brother – how blessed we all are by Allah: either you kill the *kafir*, the unbelievers, which is the very essence of jihad, or you are killed, and then you are swiftly off to join the Prophet in Paradise.'

Beneath his jovial air, Ali knew that Ahmed was deadly serious. Most of the foreign fighters that he'd met so far seemed to desire nothing more that to meet a rapid and violent end in battle. They were actively seeking to be martyrs, at the first available opportunity. They were rushing headlong towards death, embracing the promise of eternal Paradise. It was this unyielding death wish that Ali found so difficult to understand. Why were they so desperate to find death, he wondered, when there were so many of the cursed enemy out there to kill?

As far as Ali was concerned every mujahid was a

volunteer and an individual and free to speak his own mind. In the training camp he'd had several discussions with the other brothers concerning this death wish. Ali had argued that the true mujahid should not seek the quickest route to death and the reward of Paradise. He should fight purely for the cause, for the jihad, and seek no reward for himself at all. He should wage the jihad with ultimate selfless dedication. As Ali had explained all this to his brothers, he had found himself earning a new respect in their eyes. Many had concluded that they should be more like him, because he was on the purest path of jihad seeking no reward.

Ali cherished the respect that he was earning from the other brothers. He walked tall in the knowledge that he was a true mujahid. And he longed for the day when he could prove himself so in battle.

4

IN HARM'S WAY

ON the night of 12 November, Mat, Sam and the Team 6 lads set off on stage one of the Naka Valley mission. They deployed by Chinook to a forward mounting base (FMB), an old fort some twenty kilometres short of their destination. From here Mat and his team would travel on into the Naka Valley, scale one of its highest peaks and set up a covert observation position. They would then feed back intelligence on the terrorist activities they observed. This would be used to plan the US air strikes, which were scheduled to take place in nine days' time. They would guide in those air strikes using laser target designators (LTDs) – a portable device used for 'painting' the target with a laser beam, so that a guided munition could home in on it.

The FMB turned out to be a mud-walled Afghan fort, with a few single-storey buildings clustered along one wall. The fort was small by Afghan standards, some two hundred yards from end to end, and there were sixty US military personnel of Task Force Dagger based there. For these Delta Force and CIA operators accommodation was pretty basic: camp beds slung in the open or under a sheet of canvas. The fort's main gates were just tall enough to allow US Army trucks to enter. The walls were thirty feet high and topped off by battlements, from where defenders in ancient times would have shot at an attacking enemy. Little seemed to have changed, as the fort kept on being attacked by probing AQT patrols. No one knew the exact number of enemy in the region surrounding the fort. But the attacks were taking place on a more or less daily basis and the fort was on a permanent high state of alert.

After a few hours' snatched sleep Mat and his team began planning the mission ahead of them. At first they considered deploying directly from the fort into the Naka Valley by chopper. Mat was dead keen on the idea, especially as it meant that they wouldn't have to hump in all their own gear on their backs. But the more he and his men looked into it, the less feasible that option became. They had been warned during the briefings that the enemy were dug in on the ridgelines at around 10,000 feet. They were just waiting for a heavily loaded allied chopper to fly over within range of their hand-held surface-to-air missiles (US Stingers and Soviet SAMs). The mujahidin had learned this method of attack when fighting the Red Army, and the British and American assault planners felt certain that they would now repeat such tactics wherever possible.

And there were other drawbacks with getting choppered into the Naka Valley. First, any flight into the area – even at night – risked alerting the enemy to the arrival of British and US forces. That would mean that Mat's team would have been compromised before the mission even began. Second, the peaks around the Naka Valley were over 12,000 feet high, which was approaching the limit of the Chinook's operating ceiling. The choppers would be laden down with more than a dozen SBS operators and flight crew, extra fuel, food supplies, water and weapons. So it would be touch and go as to whether the aircraft would actually be able to make it. And no one fancied making a crash landing in the middle of hostile territory. Eventually, Mat, Sam and the Team 6 lads were forced to conclude that flying into the Naka Valley was a non-starter.

Once he knew that the air route wasn't feasible, Mat went to have a chat with the US base commander about their possible onward deployment overland. The man in charge at the fort was a charismatic Delta Force officer known as 'Commander Jim'. It was late afternoon when Mat found him sitting outside his tent in an easy chair, sporting a Stetson and enjoying a cold beer. Mat got stuck in straight away and began a detailed explanation of the nature of his mission: that he and his team needed to get dropped on the outskirts of the 'Knackered Valley', as they'd started calling it; that they'd then have to yomp over the mountain ranges with all their kit, set up a covert OP and stay there for several days getting eyes on the enemy targets; that this was all in preparation for the mother of all air bombardments, to be carried out by US warplanes.

'You're what?' Commander Jim said, once Mat had finished outlining the mission. He tipped his Stetson back on his head a little to get a proper look at Mat. 'Buddy, you're tellin' me you're gonna walk in there with enough kit for a week's mission? Up them mountain peaks, n'all? You know how fuckin' high they are? What are you Brits, goddam mules or somethin'?'

'I reckon,' Mat replied, with a grin. 'Talking of bleedin' mules, you don't happen to have a couple knocking around the fort, do you, mate? We could do with some to carry all of our kit in.'

'I mean, we'll get you in there all right, I ain't worried none about that,' the Delta commander continued, ignoring Mat's joke. 'We'll get you some 10th Mountain boys and an escort of Humvees, some Predator drones up top as eyes in the sky, and we'll snuck y'all in there under cover of darkness. Piece of cake, buddy. I ain't worried none about that. It's the next part of your mission I ain't too sure of. You're gonna walk in there for a week's duration? Carryin' all your kit n'all? I mean, all your goddam water? Man, that shit is *heavy*. Then you gonna just hide away in them rocks – which're crawlin' with al-Qaeda and Taliban – and then just walk right on out of there again after it's all over and done with. After our flyboys have flattened the whole place. Is that it? *Is that your plan?* I mean, I'm just kinda checking to see if I heard you right.'

'More or less, mate,' Mat replied. 'It's sort of pretty standard stuff for us. It's just the next leg to get us into the Knackered Valley – that's where we need your help.'

'Well, all I can say, buddy, is that they must make you guys pretty goddam tough over there in England.' The Delta commander disappeared into his tent and came back with a map and a couple more beers. 'Right, buddy, crack open a beer cos by God you deserve it, and let's take a look-see at the map here. Now, this is the shithole where y'all are now, see? And that there's your intended destination, 'bout fifteen miles away, I guess. Now, the roads between there an' here were first made in hell and haven't been worked on much since. But we've driven 'em and we know 'em – so we can get y'all in there all right. Question is, where exactly d'you wanna get to before, you know – *Jesus* – we just drop you off with your packs and you begin your 12,000-foot climb?'

'Round about here,' Mat replied, pointing out a mountain peak straddling the Afghanistan-Pakistan border.

'Right, you folks are part of Task Force Dagger, aren't ya?' Commander Jim asked, levelling his steely-grey eyes at Mat.

'Far as I know, mate, we are, yeah,' Mat answered.

'Well, OK, then it's fine by me. We got permission from the Paks that our Task Force Dagger boys can chase these Talibuttfuck motherfuckers right into their country if we have to. Only problem is, nearest we can take you boys to is around here – 'bout, let me see, eight miles or so short of where you wanna get to. After that, even the roads made in hell run out. Far as we know it's all just mountains, bush and Injun country from there on in. Maybe there's some old tracks and paths in there someplace, but if there is we ain't looked for 'em or used 'em.'

'Reckon we'll be yomping in from around about there then, eh?' Mat said, indicating the proposed drop-off point on the map.

'Whatever you say, buddy. So, when d'you wanna start? Just give me a day to get the Predators sorted, then it'll be overnight we'll take you in there. Hell, the drive in there takes, you know, about eight hours or so. Sounds long, but we'll be crawlin' in there in convoy and them roads is real bad, lethal, and we'll be checkin' ahead for the bad guys all the time. We'll leave here around 2000 hours, kinda gives us time to get you in and us out again under cover of darkness. Means we'll be dropping you sometime around 0400. Hell, but I just thought of somethin'.' The Delta commander tipped his hat back and scratched his forehead. 'We maybe got us a problem . . . You folks ain't gonna wanna do most of your climb in daylight, are ya?'

'Not if we can help it, mate.'

'All right. Then this is what we'll do. We'll aim to drop you guys around 2400 hours – gives you six or seven hours before sun up to get some miles under your belt. An' that means us doin' the first leg of the drive from here in the daylight, which should be all right, long as we can keep the fuckin' Talibuttholes' heads down. How does that sound, buddy?'

'Bleedin' near perfect, mate,' Mat replied. 'A good six or seven hours' darkness to get lost in the hills should do it.'

'Yeah. Should be plenty of time. Guess you wouldn't say no to another beer, buddy? Cos you sure as hell won't be takin' any with you on that climb, that's for certain.' As Commander Jim jumped to his feet to fetch some beers the stiff rim of his Stetson jabbed Mat right in the eye.

'Hey, mind where you put that hat of yours,' Mat remarked, tapping the brim of the Stetson with the neck of his beer bottle. 'That went right in me bleedin' eye, mate.'

'No one ever, EVER, touches ma hat,' Commander Jim growled, anger flashing across his face. 'Make no mistake about that, buddy.'

With that he turned and stalked back into his tent. *Bollocks*, Mat thought to himself, as the commander disappeared from view. It looked as if he'd just managed to piss off the one person they needed to get their mission underway and into the Naka Valley. As Mat rubbed his eye – which was stinging like mad and had started streaming tears – Commander Jim came back out with another couple of beers.

'How's that eye of yours, buddy?' he said, flipping the top off a beer and pushing it in Mat's direction.

'Guess you folks don't have 'em much in England, do ya?'

'Don't have what, mate?' Mat asked.

'Stetsons. Best hat ever made in the whole goddam world,' Commander Jim responded, with a mischievous gleam in his eye. 'Now, I'm thinkin' it's because you don't have 'em in England much that you committed the major sin of touchin' the brim of ma hat with your beer bottle? Am I right?'

'You're right, mate,' Mat said. He reckoned he needed to mollify Commander Jim a little. The best way he could think of doing so was to use a few 'quaint' English stereotypes. 'You know how it is in England, mate. Afternoon tea. The Queen Mum. Cricket. Warm beer. Us blokes don't go in much for Stetsons over there.'

'Yeah, I figured. And that's why I'm not gonna have to kill you. Any other guy touches ma hat, I'd have to whup his ass.'

For a split second Mat almost lost control of himself, and he gave Commander Jim a blank stare. He didn't appreciate being threatened and had never backed down from a fight in his life. But then he told himself to cool it, as they badly needed Commander Jim's help with this mission.

'Sorry for any offence, mate,' Mat said, with a forced grin. 'I'm just a dumb Brit who's only ever seen a Stetson on JR's head in *Dallas*, or in them old John Wayne movies.'

'No offence taken, buddy. Let's take a drink to your mission,' the Delta commander replied, as he raised his beer bottle at Mat. 'I been to England a couple times. My folks are from there way back. Say, buddy, that eye looks to be in a pretty bad way. You need to see the medic or somethin'?'

An SBS/SAS operator in CT gear prepares to assault ship - note gas mask, knife inverted on right chest, MP5 submachine gun and Sig Sauer pistol on hip.

SBS/SAS operators fast rope 90 feet from a Chinook MH47 helicopter onto the target in the English Channel, poised to hit the ship like a whirlwind.

SBS/SAS operators fast rope from a Sea King helicopter onto the target ship and rush into their battle positions. Any terrorists on board will be killed or captured.

Smiles all round as SBS/SAS operators pose with beers and an MV Nisha life ring after they have successfully taken down the ship and stopped her reaching London.

SBS operators on exercises in Norway. Artic warfare is an integral part of the SBS's intensive training, which rivals that of the SAS.

Having just warned his men to 'treat the vehicles with a little respect', SBS CSM Bob Wort drives his OSV over a crevasse, completely wrecking it.

Afghanistan's national sport, Bushkasi, involves riders fighting to drag a goat around a racetrack on horseback. As with many things in Afghanistan, anything goes.

BoySoldier-NA: Northern Alliance forces fighting the Taliban and Al Qaeda included boy soldiers like this one, proudly sporting his pistol and ammo belt.

The hangar at Bagram airbase where SBS, SAS and Delta Force made their headquarters. Wrecked Soviet fighter aircraft lie to the front, a reminder of how past superpowers came to grief in Afghanistan.

Upon arrival in 'the Stan', the SBS lads put down thousands of rounds on the ranges, zeroing in their weapons for the fight that was to come.

The Squad Assault Weapon (SAW) Minimi 5.56 mm drum-fed machine gun gets put through its paces on the ranges.

A 40mm grenade scores a direct hit out on the ranges – a devastating weapon of choice for the SBS lads waging war in Afghanistan.

At Bagram airbase SBS lads practise assaulting from a vehicle and ambush,
as they prepared to do battle with the terrorists.

SBS on a vehicle patrol. They carry Diemaco 5.56 mm assault rifles with under-slung
Hechler & Koch 40 mm grenade launchers. A satellite comms antennae can just be
seen on the roof of the vehicle.

British, US, Aussie and New Zealand special forces deployed by Chinook on low level flights. One hit from an enemy stinger and this chopper would be blasted out of the sky.

Flying in line astern, MH47 Chinooks deployed special forces teams deep into hostile Afghan terrain.

Later that night, at around 0100 hours, a massive fire-fight broke out on the outskirts of the fort. One moment Mat and his team were asleep, the next they were wide awake as rounds slammed into the mud walls. An enemy patrol had hit the sleeping base with a barrage of rocket-propelled grenades (RPGs) and machine-gun fire. The enemy fighters had somehow worked out how to fire their RPGs at a forty-five-degree angle, so that the grenades acted something like mortar rounds. It increased the operational range of the RPG by three hundred yards or more, and meant that the enemy had a chance of lobbing their grenades over the fort walls. But the RPG was seriously inaccurate when fired in this way. Rounds were firing off all over the place, scorching fiery trails across the dark sky above the fort.

As soon as the attack started, Mat, Sam and the Team 6 lads headed up on to the fort roof to join the US forces returning fire. The enemy had taken cover some three hundred yards away in a heap of jumbled rocks, which meant that they were still within effective range of the SBS soldiers' Diemaco assault rifles. Mat and his team took cover as best they could and began returning fire, aiming at the muzzle flashes out there in the darkness. It felt good to be finally taking the fight to the enemy. As the skirmish intensified, the two sides exchanged heavy machine-gun fire across the valley floor, the tracer arcing back and forth in the night sky. On their arrival at the base, Commander Jim had warned Mat and his team to expect such night-time attacks. This was the enemy's way of reminding the US forces that they were out there some-where, just beyond the walls of the fort. These probing, strafing attacks were designed to test the fort's defences and provoke Commander Jim into doing something silly.

As the battle escalated, the US forces responded with

50-cal heavy machine-gun fire and mortar rounds. But Commander Jim had decided that this night, he wanted to hit the enemy forces really hard – largely because he knew that he had to get Mat's patrol out of the fort during daylight hours in the next day or so. And he couldn't do that if the enemy kept him pinned down in his own base. Some twenty minutes into the firefight, the Delta commander called Mat on his radio and told him to get over to his command post smartish, as there was 'somethin' pretty special goin' down'. Mat scuttled across the fort roof, keeping to the shadows of the battlements so as not to make an easy target for the enemy, wondering as he did so what the US commander had in mind.

'How's that eye of yours, buddy?' Commander Jim asked, as soon as he caught sight of Mat.

'Bearing up,' Mat replied, with a grin. 'How's that Stetson of yours, mate?'

'Still allergic to goddam beer bottles,' Commander Jim growled.

The two men laughed.

'How many of the fookers d'you reckon there's out there then, mate?' Mat asked, nodding in the general direction of the enemy.

'Aw, not many, say fifteen or so. But they're sure as hell makin' a racket and forcin' us to lose some sleep these last few days.'

'So, what's the crack now then?' Mat asked.

'You what? The *crack*? You Brits sure got a strange turn of phrase. I guess you mean "what's goin' down", right? Well, I reckon it's time to show them Talibuttholes we ain't puttin' up with this no more – disturbin' our sleep n'all. Gonna hit 'em with some JDAMs.'

It turned out that Commander Jim had called in an

air strike from some fast air that he had on standby. As the Delta commander began talking the F-18 pilot down on to target, Mat was surprised to hear a female voice coming back to him from the lead aircraft. Commander Jim gave the woman pilot a set of coordinates that pinpointed the enemy muzzle flashes out there in the darkness. Almost before the aircraft was audible there was the unearthly scream of precision-guided munitions rocketing overhead, followed by a series of massive explosions. Two JDAMs (joint direct attack munitions – GPS-guided 2,000-pound bombs) slammed into the enemy positions, followed in quick succession by two more. The giant explosions lit up the night-time scene, momentarily throwing everything – rocks, scrub, squat mud buildings – into stark relief. By the time that darkness had descended again, the enemy guns had fallen silent.

'Nice shootin', Thunder Thighs,' Commander Jim drawled into his radio. 'I reckon them Talibuttfucks are toast.'

'You stay safe down there,' came back the F-18 pilot – whose call sign was actually Thunder Ranger One. 'I'm goin' away wet, boys.'

'Jesus, that's one horny bitch,' Commander Jim remarked, as he came off the radio. '*I'm goin' away wet.* Jesus! Horny little bitch. I wanna kiss your ass, Thunder Ranger, I wanna kiss your beautiful ass.'

'What'd she mean, "going away wet"?' Mat asked, feigning ignorance. 'That some sort of code for mission accomplished or something?'

'Jesus, it ain't just Stetsons you don't have a lot of over there in England, is it, buddy? You *got* any women over there? Like, *real* ones? She means that she's creamed herself, buddy. An' she's doin' that just to wind us up cos she knows we been down here for days on end and there ain't no women for a thousand fuckin' miles around. Not real ones like her, anyways.'

After the air strikes the enemy didn't trouble the base any further that night. Early the following morning the CIA agent that would be joining Mat's team arrived by chopper. He introduced himself to the lads as Bob Frankell. He was a short, wiry guy with a big, bushy beard. He was looking flustered. Apparently, he had a huge task ahead of him collating all the intelligence for the forthcoming mission. He quickly made his excuses and disappeared into the CIA's end of the base. As far as Mat was concerned, CIA Bob looked like he'd spent too much time alone in his log cabin out in the Oregon back woods. Either that, or too long staring at a CIA computer screen. Mat hoped to hell that CIA Bob was going to be up to the challenging mission ahead of them.

Departure time for their insertion into the Naka Valley was set for 1600 hours the following afternoon, which left Mat and his team a good twenty-four hours in which to sort and pack all their gear. The lads broke out their maps, compasses, charts and some less than perfect satellite photos, and began planning the route they'd take to reach their objective. The Naka Valley itself was some eight miles west of Shah-i-Khot – the Valley of the Kings – a renowned stronghold of enemy forces in southern Afghanistan. Recent allied air strikes on the Shah-i-Khot had reportedly forced large numbers of enemy fighters to retreat into the shelter of the Naka Valley, hence the need for the present mission. Mat's team aimed to set up a covert observation post (OP) in the heart of the Naka Valley, on a ridgeline running between two of the highest peaks. This would give them a good line of sight into positions to the north of them, where US intelligence sited the mother of all terrorist training camps.

Their route in with Commander Jim's convoy would take them barely to the foothills of the Naka Valley. There, the maps showed, all roads came to an abrupt halt. The climb from the drop-off point to the intended OP was around eight miles as the crow flies, through pretty much uncharted territory, and it would take Mat and his team from an altitude of 2,500 feet to over 12,000 feet, with several major climbs and descents in between. All in all, Mat calculated that they'd be making some 15,000 feet of ascent to reach their final destination. At best, they would have seven hours' darkness in which to make the climb, which was nowhere near enough time.

As Mat and his team studied the maps, a local Afghan guide was brought over to help with the planning. Because Mat's team was attached to Task Force Dagger, they were – like all US forces under Dagger – cleared for crossing the border into Pakistan. But only if they absolutely had to. The role being played by Pakistan in this war was sensitive enough as it was. The Pakistanis were allowing US forces to use their bases and to operate on their soil in the hunt for terrorists. But with Pakistan being a fiercely Muslim country this risked inflaming Muslim sentiment, both within Pakistan and across the wider Muslim world. All troops under Task Force Dagger had been ordered to cross on to the Pakistani side of the border only if they absolutely had to.

Unfortunately, Mat's map put the border with Pakistan in a different place to where their Afghan guide said it ought to be. The guide maintained that the border had been changed, which would mean that the maps that the SBS lads were using were wrong. If this was true, it put their intended OP some ten miles *inside* Pakistani territory. Mat suspected that the Afghan guide was right, and that their maps were wrong. But the location that he had chosen for the OP was on the highest peak, and anywhere else just wouldn't give them the vantage point that they required. So Mat decided to ignore the Afghan guide and argue that if their maps put the OP bang on the Afghan–Pakistan border, then that was what they would go by.

Having planned their route in and pinpointed their intended OP, Mat, Sam and the Team 6 lads began packing their bergens. They were scheduled to be on this operation for six days, but had been told to prepare for anything up to eleven. And Mat just had a sneaky feeling that this might turn out to be a long mission. As they laid out the food rations, weapons, ammunition, photographic kit, communications gear, cold-weather survival equipment and water that each man would need to carry, they realised the enormity of the task before them. Hauling all this kit to over 12,000 feet was going to take a superhuman effort.

Luckily, prior to deployment, the SBS had put up a 'war fund' from which the lads had been free to purchase any personal gear they required. First priority had been boots, and all the lads were now sporting tough Berghaus, Karrimor or Scarpa Gore-Tex walking boots. None was wearing British Army issue footwear – if they had been Mat would have been truly worried. A lot of the standard-issue British Army gear had a bad reputation with the soldiers, and deservedly so. In addition to the boots, everyone on Mat's team had purchased a couple of sets of thermal underwear, a windproof Gore-Tex jacket and a down-filled duvet jacket, all in civvy colours.

Into their bergens went a camo poncho liner and a poncho – to be used as a makeshift ground sheet to sleep on at night and as a sunshade to rest under during the day. Weather conditions in the area were expected to be freezing cold at night and burning hot by day, with very little chance of rain. Each man packed two spare sets of socks, one spare set of thin cotton trousers, a thermal balaclava and gloves, a woolly hat, a Gore-Tex bivvy bag, an inflatable Thermarest and a down-filled four-season sleeping bag. Taking pity on his under-equipped fellow warriors, Commander Jim had given each of the SBS soldiers a giant US Army issue fur-lined winter Parka. But, regretfully, the men decided these were too heavy and bulky and would have to be left behind.

All the lighter clothing and survival gear went in the bottom of the pack. Heavier kit would then be packed into the upper reaches of the bergen, as weight balances better the higher up on a man's back it can be carried. Food went it next, a selection of the best from the British Army twenty-four-hour ration packs and the US military MREs (meals ready to eat). As everything was to be eaten cold, they discarded such things as the hot-drink packs and the self-heating meals. Mat's team were going in on 'hard routine'. This meant no hot food or drinks, as even the aroma of a cup of soup in the clear mountain air could give the game away. And they took plastic freezer bags for crapping in, as the smell of fresh human faeces would be even more of a dead giveaway.

Each man broke his food down into one-meal-a-day packs. Other than that, the men would survive on snacks like chocolate bars. Back in Poole Mat had purchased several bags of Brazil nuts. These were a near-perfect food for this kind of mission, being a rich source of energy and protein and unbeatable weight-for-weight. Another vital piece of kit was the baby oil. Baby oil had achieved an almost mythical status in the SBS (and SAS). Long periods spent at the mercy of the elements in hostile environments had proven its worth. Baby oil kept exposed skin soft and moist, preventing lips and hands from cracking. Intense cold and heat could cause cracks to deepen and get infected. This could quickly render a soldier useless, as it was all but impossible to operate a weapon with cracked, painful hands.

Mat, Sam and the Team 6 lads each stuffed six water bottles into their packs – allowing 1.5 litres for each day spent in the OP, if it did turn out to be a six-day mission. At 12,000 feet and with daytime temperatures such as they were, it would be far too little fluid, but any more than this would be prohibitively heavy. Mat was banking on their finding a mountain spring or stream from which they would be able to replenish their supplies. Two Katadyn pump-action water filters were added to their loads, so that they could render any water they found drinkable. Each man also carried his own set of basic field dressings and a personal medical kit, in case of injury.

Next, the men began packing their weapons and ammo. Four of the team would be taking the Diemaco 5.56mm assault rifle (a modified version of the standard US M16), while the other two opted for the Minimi SAW (squad assault weapon) 5.56mm drum-fed machine gun. The four men with the Diemacos also had Heckler & Koch 40mm grenade launchers attached to the barrel of their assault rifle. This devastating weapon was accurate up to three hundred metres. While at close range a 40mm round could pass straight through a man's body, a direct detonation would blow a man's torso in two. It was a fearsome weapon, and one favoured by the special forces troops.

During the climb up the mountain, each man would carry his weapon in his hands, in case of contact with the enemy. But a Diemaco with attached grenade launcher was a hefty piece of kit – weighing 11.79 pounds in all. The 40mm grenade launchers also made the assault rifle very front-end-heavy. So on the mountain ascent the team chose to detach the 40mm grenade launchers from their weapons and sling them on to their webbing. One of their webbing pouches would be stuffed full of 40mm rounds. Each operator also carried a 9mm Sig Sauer pistol as his emergency weapon, plus two smoke and two white phosphorous grenades. And then there were the five kiwi-fruit-sized high-explosives grenades that Commander Jim had given each of them, just for 'good luck'.

With their personal gear, food, water and weapons packed, the men moved on to their ammo. Each man carried sixteen full magazines for the Diemaco, with three tracer rounds at the start of each mag. That way, if there was a contact and one of them needed to show the others where the enemy was, all he had to do was yell out, 'Watch my tracer.' One magazine was loaded purely with tracer – and marked as such with a length of gaffer tape – in case of a night-time contact. Plus a couple of the magazines were loaded with armour-piercing rounds, just in case they came up against any heavy weaponry. In addition to the magazines, each man took an extra dozen boxes of ammunition, which meant that he had some five hundred rounds in all for his main weapon.

Everyone also carried a BE499 TACBE (tactical beacon). The TACBE is used for line-of-sight communication if a patrol gets compromised, and acts as an emergency beacon that can be located by allied aircraft. Each TACBE was assigned to the SBS operator's own call sign, so that an allied aircraft would automatically know exactly which operator was using it. Notebooks, pencils, compasses, binoculars and other small kit were stuffed into the bergen's side pockets.

Each man carried a PRM (personal radio mike), which allowed him to communicate with the rest of the men on his team, and this was slung on to his webbing. And the most delicate equipment was packed into the top of the bergens. Each operator carried a set of night-vision goggles for operating during the hours of darkness and a hand-held, infrared sight and laser device. This could be attached to their weapons and used as a night sight, or switched on to steady beam laser mode to 'paint' a target, thus marking it out as an enemy position to be hit by allied aircraft deploying laser-guided bombs. And then there were the spare batteries required for each piece of electronic kit, which added yet more weight to the load.

Finally, there were several pieces of 'communal' kit: telescopes, cameras, secure comms, radios and satphones, all provided with a mountain of batteries and extra weight!

Once Mat's team had finished packing, each bergen weighed in excess of a hundred pounds. They were stuffed to bursting with gear and packed so tightly that nothing would rattle or clank about as they climbed. Last but not least, a 'grab bag' full of emergency kit was strapped to the top of the bergen, containing ammo, basic medical supplies, a personal radio and a two-day ration pack. If the men got compromised on the climb up the mountain and had to ditch their bergens, they would still be able to detach the grab bag and take it with them. During the six days spent in the OP the men would live out of their bergens, and never go into their grab bags unless forced to. This ensured the grab bag was always kept intact. As a rule all kit would be kept permanently packed, in case they needed to make a rapid getaway.

By mid-afternoon the lads were putting the finishing touches to their gear. As Mat was double-checking some of the communal equipment, he realised that one of their most vital bits of kit was malfunctioning. The ECM117 radio – the one piece of kit that they would use for secure communications back to headquarters – had gone down. There was no way that they could leave without the radio being in working order, so Mat put a call through to Bagram to ask for a replacement set to be sent out. As they were scheduled to leave the base the next day with Commander Jim's convoy, headquarters agreed to send out a replacement radio as soon as possible. All being well a Chinook would be with them that evening with the new equipment.

Mat spent the rest of the afternoon running over comms procedures and escape and evasion plans if the mission got compromised by the enemy. Normally, as they were an SBS patrol, they would report directly to their HQ, in Poole. But on this mission they had been ordered to report directly to US command at JSOC (Joint Special Operations Command) – the nerve centre of Task Force Dagger. The patrol was supposed to make contact with JSOC at regular twelve-hour intervals, to report in that all was well. If one call was missed, it would raise the alarm at JSOC (and at SBS headquarters), and intensive efforts would be made to contact the patrol by radio and satcom. If two calls were missed, allied air assets would be alerted to listen out and watch out for the patrol. If three calls were missed, the patrol would be presumed compromised, the men either captured or heading for the ERV for pickup by an extraction chopper.

If the patrol was split up and unable to reach the ERV individual patrol members could contact allied aircraft via their TACBEs. Using tiny infrared strobe lights they could mark their position for pickup by an extraction chopper. If the casualty required a medevac, the patrol was to give the grid reference of the casualty, the type of injury suffered, the type of assistance needed (such as helicopter extraction with stretcher) and the grid reference of the nearest usable landing zone. If any of the patrol members were captured, they would give the 'Big Four' and nothing more: name, rank, serial number and date of birth.

At the allotted time Mat and Sam headed out to the landing zone (LZ) to await the arrival of the chopper with the replacement radio. But when an aircraft finally did come lumbering over the horizon, it wasn't a CH47 Chinook. It was a giant, four-engined C-130 Hercules. As Mat and Sam had been expecting a chopper, they hadn't bothered to mark out a usable landing strip. Yet the C-130 definitely looked like it was preparing to land. Mat and Sam began rushing about popping light sticks in order to mark out a rough LZ. But they soon realised that they had to abort the landing, as the strip was full of rocks and unusable. If they couldn't take delivery of the new radio it was bad news indeed.

As Mat dropped a red smoke grenade to signal the C-130 pilot to abort the landing, he was cursing their bad luck. First, the ECM117 had gone down. And now they had a C-130 trying to put down on a non-existent airstrip, as opposed to the chopper that they'd been told was coming. They waited for the plane to fly over and abort, and sure enough the C-130 did do an overflight. But then it circled back as if it were preparing to land, just on a different angle of approach. Mat and Sam raced across the LZ waving frantically, but the pilot proceeded to ignore them completely. As the giant aircraft hit the dirt it was engulfed in a cloud of dust, and Mat and Sam just stood there with their hearts in their mouths, fearing the worst. But just as suddenly as it had disappeared, the C-130 came powering out of the dust storm, bumping and bucking its way across the rough, uneven terrain.

'Holy fuck,' Mat exclaimed, turning to face Sam. 'The bloke flying that thing's a bloody nutter.'

'US pilot, gotta be,' said Sam, as he tried to make out the marking on the plane. 'Those guys just don't give a damn, bro. If you've got the balls to fly a C-130, you know, there ain't a lot that's gonna faze you.'

As the plane drew to a halt, the pilot popped his head out the window and greeted Mat and Sam with a wave. Sure enough, the C-130 was decked out in USAF markings.

'Gee, guys, thanks for the smoke – guess that was to help with the wind direction?' he yelled down at them, with a beaming grin. 'That sure was one of the better strips we've had the pleasure of putting this bird down on. Gee, what a goddam dump this country is.'

'Pretty smart piece of flying, buddy,' Sam yelled back, choosing to ignore the fact that they'd just been trying to get him to abort the landing. 'Say, you got us a radio on board?'

'That's why we're here,' the pilot shouted, giving the thumbs up. 'Ain't for the sheer fun of it, that much's for sure. Take a look-see at the back there – should be there's one of the crew ready to hand it to ya.'

Mat and Sam walked round to the back of the plane, giving a wide berth to the C-130's propellers, as the pilot had kept the engines running. Upon arrival they could see the rear ramp descending and one of the aircrew standing there.

'Guess you'll be needing this,' he remarked, as he handed the replacement radio set to Sam. 'Oh yeah, message from the pilot – that was the best LZ ever. See you around, guys.'

Now that they had the new radio set the mission could proceed as planned: Mat and his team would be departing with Commander Jim's convoy the following afternoon. Because it was their last night in the base, and because he couldn't carry it with him on the mission, Mat decided to break out a bottle of Jack Daniel's that he'd brought with him from the UK. It was a treat that he'd been saving for a special occasion, and he couldn't think of a better one than their first combat mission in Afghanistan. Together with Sam and the Team 6 lads, Mat sat under the dark Afghan sky and sloshed a good shot of whiskey into each of their plastic mugs.

Sam raised his and proposed a toast: 'To the Naka Valley mission.'

'The mission,' the others echoed, as they clunked mugs.

'To absent wankers – like Mucker,' Mat announced.

'Absent wankers,' the others replied.

'To Commander Jim,' Sam added.

'Commander Jim,' the men repeated, heartily.

Just as Mat was pouring out a second round of shots, CIA Bob came over to join them. He had with him a tiny little backpack, hardly larger than an average daysack. Mat wondered if that was where he had stashed all his gear for the mission. If it was, either CIA Bob didn't need to eat and drink and didn't feel the cold, or he was going to starve and freeze to death on top of that mountain, while dying of thirst at the same time. It was on the tip of Mat's tongue to raise the issue with CIA Bob. But he decided instead to strike up an amiable conversation with the CIA spook, in an effort to try to get to know him a little before the mission proper began. Maybe in the process of doing so he could work the diminutive nature of CIA Bob's backpack into the exchange.

'Cheers. So, here we are again then, eh, mate?' Mat said, after he'd poured CIA Bob a generous shot of Jack Daniel's.

'Yeah, cheers,' said CIA Bob. 'But what d'you mean, buddy, "here we are again"?'

'Well, you know – like the last time we was down here to do some serious damage was on the Crusades, weren't it? Did a bit of Muslim bashing back then too, just to keep 'em in hand.'

'Whoa, hold on there a minute,' CIA Bob replied. 'Dunno where you learned your history, buddy, but there ain't never been no Crusaders this far east. Never, ever. But you Brits sure do have a history of trying to whup the Afghans' asses. Mostly you failed, n'all. Fancy a quick history lesson, buddy? You may as well know something about the people you've come here to kill.'

'Sure, mate, that'd be grand.' Mat wasn't proud, and CIA Bob certainly seemed to know his stuff. 'Fire away.'

'Well, OK, buddy. So you guys waged three wars down this ways – the Anglo-Afghan wars, they called 'em. In fact, first time the Afghans were ever bombed was by you guys. In 1919 it was, and you guys used Bristol BF2 bombers against Jalalabad. Most of the city was left burned out, and it was sort of in revenge for what the Afghans had done earlier.' CIA Bob paused to take a swig of his whiskey. 'You want me to continue, buddy?'

'I'm gripped, mate,' said Mat.

'Well, back in January 1842, you Brits were retreatin' from Kabul – 16,500 troops set out into the hills around Bagram. As they hit the mountains the snow begun to fall. Then the Afghan tribesmen attacked from above. That retreat turned into a goddam death march. Only one Brit soldier ever made it out alive. So the following year your guys went in and trashed the Afghan capital. The Afghans have long memories, buddy. Famously long. They ain't forgotten what happened back then. And I reckon they ain't forgiven, neither.'

'Fair 'nough, mate,' Mat remarked. 'And the Crusades, they're nowt to do with Afghanistan then? Cos that's what the ragheads keep crapping on about, ain't it? I mean, way they see it, this war now's "a Crusade", ain't it –'

'The Crusades never got further than Syria,' CIA Bob cut in. 'Which is about a thousand miles from here as the crow flies. And for their part the Muslims got as far as Spain before you guys decided to finally get your acts together and whup their asses. Kinda took your time, didn't you, buddy?'

'The Muslims got as far as Spain? I thought it was all about Richard the Lionheart heading on down to their part of the world with his band of merry knights.'

'It takes two to tango, buddy, and what Richard the Lionheart did in Syria, Saladin – that's the biggest, meanest dude of a Muslim commander that there ever was; Jesus, the guy makes Osama bin Laden look like a goddam pussy cat – Saladin then went and did in Spain. In fact, the Muslims got as far as central France before you guys piled in and rescued 'em – the French that is. Not the first time we Anglo-Saxons have had to wade in and rescue the goddam French, n'all. Not that they ever show any gratitude for it.'

'Too right, mate,' announced Mat. 'Still, way it was taught me, mate, was that we went down there on the Crusades pretty much just cos we fancied a rumble.'

'You reckon it was all one-sided, buddy? As if war's ever been like that, ever since war was invented. You lopped off a few heads here, raped a few hot Muslim chicks there, and then they came and did the same with a few French heads here and a few pretty English girls there. Clash of religions and civilisations then, just like it's gearing up to be now. In the one battle where Saladin whupped your asses more 'n any other, his forces captured several hundred Knights Templars. Now, the Knights Templars, they're like the medieval equivalent of Delta Force or your SAS –'

'Sorry? SAS? You mean *SBS*, don't you, mate?'

'What? Oh yeah . . . my mistake. Medieval equivalent of you guys, the *SBS*. Anyways, Saladin says to the Knights Templars: "Look, guys, you got two choices. Either you convert to Islam, right here 'n' now, and you'll be spared. Or, you know, we're gonna have to execute y'all." Well, the Knights Templars were mean sons of bitches, and to a man they refused to convert. So Saladin had them all beheaded. Now, you tell me if that's the way it's taught by those pansy-assed, tea-drinking English schoolmarms of yours. The Muslims gave as good as they got – and each side gave no quarter. It was no different then than it is now. Just look what them motherfuckers are capable of with the Twin Towers. Civilians. Women. Children. Made no difference to them on 9/11, did it?'

There were a few seconds silence as everyone stared into their plastic mugs of JD. Then CIA Bob continued.

'Listen, buddy. I ain't gettin' at you none. Must be the drink talkin'. I always get like this when drinkin' JD. Talkin' of which, you got a drop left in that bottle of yours? Don't wanna let it go to waste.'

'Pass us your mug, mate,' Mat said, quietly. 'There's a smidgin left in the bottle and you're welcome to it.'

'Cheers.' CIA Bob raised his mug, then carried on.

'It's just, you know . . . War's a fuckin' nasty business
– whoever's fighting it and whatever religion they profess
to follow. Period. We're Christian. They're Muslims. Bad's
been done on both sides. And it looks like bad's gonna
be done some more before we finally learn to live with
each other in peace. Which is the only way all this shit's
ever gonna end. You know where I'm coming from on
this one, buddy?'

'That I do, mate,' Mat replied. 'Tell you the truth,
what you've been saying makes a lot of bloody sense.'

'Thanks, buddy.' CIA Bob got to his feet to leave.
'Appreciate it. And thanks for the JD.'

With CIA Bob having gone the conversation quickly
died down, and one by one the men wandered off to bed.

'Holy fuck, that CIA lad is one smart cookie,' Mat
remarked to Sam, once it was just the two of them left
with the dregs in the bottle. 'I could sit and listen to him
all bloody night.'

'Yeah, well, you just kinda did, bro,' Sam replied. 'I
guess just occasionally you do meet an American who
kinda knows what he's talking about.'

By mid-afternoon the following day the convoy of
vehicles bound for the Naka Valley began assembling at
the fort entrance. There were six Humvees carrying the
10th Mountain troops, and a half-dozen 'civilian' Toyota
pickups driven by the Delta Force operators. Mat and
his men were riding in the centre of the convoy, in the
rear of one of the Humvees, together with CIA Bob.
Commander Jim had made his reluctant apologies – his
responsibilities as base commander meant that he couldn't
accompany them on the fifteen-mile drive into the Naka
Valley. At 1600 hours exactly the convoy began crawling
out of the fort gates.

'Good luck, boys,' Commander Jim shouted across at

them, as he saluted their departure. 'Stay safe out there. Aim true an' die laughing.'

The first two hours' driving were uneventful enough, as the convoy passed along some decent desert roads. But as dusk settled over the surrounding landscape, the vehicles entered a narrow mountain valley, the walls crowding in on both sides. It was ideal ambush territory. As night blanketed the scene, the soldiers donned NVGs and the darkened convoy crept forward driving on infrared lights only. All that could be heard was the creaking of strained metal, the crunch of tyres on rock, the grinding of gears and the straining of powerful diesel engines as the vehicles negotiated the terrible terrain. A herd of metallic beasts from some prehistoric era were moving through a night-dark valley, and all around there was only hostile territory.

It was now that the Predator pilotless aircraft really came into their own. The RQ1 Predator UAV (unmanned aerial vehicle) is a remote-operated drone armed with AGM-114 Hellfire short-range, laser-guided, air-to-surface missiles. Two Predators were now flying above and before the convoy to scout the route ahead. Mat could hear the constant updates from the Predator control centre coming in on the radio net. An operator based in the US was watching real-time video footage beamed back live from the Predators, as they identified potential enemy positions up ahead of the convoy.

'Right, about a mile and a half up ahead of you we can see a lot of activity,' the US operator's voice came through on the radio. 'Looks like some forty-odd potential hostiles to the east of you, grouped on the valley wall, bearing 9694. Wait out, wait out. We're going in to take a closer look with the infrared and thermal imaging. Await further instructions.'

In this fashion the convoy inched forward, repeatedly stop-starting as the Predators identified, and then cleared, potential danger spots. But despite all their technological wizardry, there were some things that the Predators were not best suited for – like the mission that Mat and his men were now undertaking. It was impossible for UAVs – or any surveillance aircraft for that matter – to replace good men on the ground. Mat and the team were well aware of this. They would be able to see things that the Predator would miss: hostile vehicles hidden beneath trees, camouflaged enemy positions, or enemy fighters based in caves. Besides, no surveillance aircraft could ever remain in position for seven days and seven nights, as Mat and his men were planning to do.

For several hours the convoy's halting progress continued up the valley floor, the vehicles winding their way along rutted river beds and dry wadis. As they edged closer to the drop-off point, the atmosphere in the back of Mat's Humvee was edgy. The men were impatient for the tense waiting to be over and for the mission proper to begin. In the cab the driver and co-driver had a couple of Kurtz machine guns (a shortened version of the Heckler & Koch MP5 sub-machine gun) slung across their knees. At any sign of trouble, they could grab these snub-nosed weapons and put down a barrage of fire from the open windows.

Finally, the lead vehicle ground to a halt in the cloying darkness of a narrow mountain defile, the rest of the convoy following suit. This was where the road from hell ran out, and where Mat and his team would begin their epic climb.

For several days now, the brothers had been expecting a resupply of ammunition from the Taliban headquarters. Just after dawn Ali spotted a plume of dust to the east of them, backlit by the early-morning sun. Soon, he could hear the noise of approaching vehicles. It turned out to be a convoy of three battered Toyota pickups, one of which was painted a fluorescent green. The brothers who were driving it had obviously made no effort whatsoever to camouflage it, despite the ever-present danger of attack from US aircraft that were patrolling the Afghan skies.

Just as the three pickups were rolling into camp, out of nowhere there was a Whoosh! above them, followed by the roar of a US jet tearing past overhead.

'Fighters!' one of the brothers yelled, his words lost in a massive explosion.

As the dust cleared from the bomb blast Ali could see that the pilot had overshot his target, but only just. The US warplane started screaming around for another attack run on the pickups, and the brothers began unloading in a mad frenzy. Weapons – RPG rounds, cases of AK47 ammunition, grenades – rucksacks and food were thrown into a heap on the ground. Just as the last bundle had been offloaded the fluorescent green pickup roared off, and the jet came in for its second attack run. Ali hit the deck just as there was an ear-splitting detonation, the bomb impacting right where the green pickup had been a second earlier. Ali could feel the shrapnel flying past him as he buried his head in the sand. When he finally glanced up he could see the pickup still miraculously intact and weaving crazily as it roared off into the desert. And behind him a group of brothers were standing around laughing, seemingly completely unperturbed by the US bombing.

'Welcome to the front line,' one of them called over at Ali. He was a big, bearded brother whom Ali hadn't met before. He helped Ali to his feet and to dust himself down. 'Come, brother, come and join us for breakfast,' the bearded one continued. 'Don't worry about the bombs. Who taught these infidels how to fight, anyway? Their mothers? This is nothing to worry about. And if they get lucky, well, then you'll be *shaheed*! Seventy-two virgins, brother. Come, brother. Pitta. Some roast goat. You helped us unloading. Now, come and eat with us like a true brother.'

As the men led Ali over to their position, it was immediately clear to him that morale was very high among their unit. They were positioned on the crest of a hill overlooking a shallow valley. To their left and right along the ridge there were further Taliban positions. But higher above them, on the next mountaintop, the US-backed Northern Alliance had their forces. Ali figured that it must have been these Northern Alliance troops who had spotted the fluorescent green pickup from their vantage point, and called in the US air strike.

Ali was amazed, and somewhat concerned, when the brothers proceeded to serve breakfast out in the open, despite there being a secure underground bunker nearby. And in no time, the Northern Alliance forces spotted them. They started to target the breakfast party with a long-range howitzer, calling in the shots from their vantage point high above. The incoming fire wasn't that accurate, but the barrage was gradually creeping closer, and Ali could tell that the gunners were zeroing in on their position. But the brothers just sat there eating and made no mention of the bombardment, and it was as if they were playing a game of chicken with each other.

Ali took his plate of food and sat down with his back to a large rock, which gave him a small sense of security. Another brother joined him and they struck up a conversation. He could feel the man's shoulder against his, the reverberations of his voice box rumbling on and on as he talked about the glory of jihad. It turned out that this brother had been on the front line for many months now, and refused to be relieved. He loved it here, he told Ali, because it was the one place where he really felt alive. He started to tell Ali all about his family back home in Algeria. Then he began asking Ali all about life in the West – which seemed to hold a strange fascination for so many of the brothers.

It was a special moment for Ali and he suddenly felt very close to his Algerian brother. But just as he started telling him all about his life back in the UK, there was the scream of another incoming shell. For a second Ali flinched as the round slammed into the desert some fifty feet away from them, jagged chunks of shrapnel whirring off in all directions. The explosion was deafening and it threw up chunks of rock high into the air. For a few seconds Ali and his brother sat there in silence, watching the smoke and dust from the shell drifting into the air.

'That was a close one, brother,' Ali remarked, before returning to their conversation.

Ali told the brother about his life in the UK and how glad he was to be away from it all, from the self-indulgence and depravity of the decadent West. He described his deep abhorrence of a British society where worshipping God had been replaced by worshipping football, money and sex; a society that encouraged homosexuality; where morals had been abandoned in preference for drugs, alcohol and debauchery; where family values were collapsing and where so many children were born to illegitimate, women-only families. As he talked Ali was swept away by a wave of revulsion. As far as he was concerned there was only one thing that could save the West from destroying itself. It required a total conversion – by force, if necessary – of all its people to Islam, and strict adherence to the codes of Islamic sharia law. The UK needed to be remade along the lines of Afghanistan.

But as he spoke, Ali started to notice that his brother wasn't responding. His brother wasn't saying a word in reply, and he couldn't feel him nodding or reacting. Come to think of it, Ali couldn't feel him breathing, either. And there was also something odd about the way this brother was sitting. Slowly, Ali turned to check if he was all right. As he did so, he twisted around, removing the support of his shoulder, and the brother slumped away, falling sideways on to the ground. He lay there, unmoving, his eyes open and glazed. Then Ali caught sight of a jagged rent torn in the side of the brother's head, a rivulet of fresh blood running down his temple and into the sand. The man was dead, killed by a fragment of shrapnel thrown up by the exploding shell.

How do I feel? Ali asked himself, as he stared down at the corpse of this brother – his newest and so short-lived friend. *Sad that he's dead? Elated because he's shaheed? Or enraged, and in need of revenge?* Ali knew that he had been that close to being killed himself. That razor-sharp chunk of shrapnel had torn into his brother's head right next to his own. *Am I glad that it's him that's been killed and not me?* Ali wondered. But most of all he was frustrated and angry that the brother's life had been thrown away so needlessly – before he'd had a chance to fight and to kill any of the *kafir*. It was such a pointless waste and could have been so easily avoided.

That evening, Ali brought this up in conversation with Ahmed, Sadiq and the rest of the brothers in his unit. Why did the brothers here on the front line never take cover? Didn't they want to fight the *kafir* and kill them, and to defend the Umma – the greater body of Islam – from the Jews and the Crusaders invading the Muslim lands? Or did they all just want to be snuffed out at the first available opportunity? But the brothers replied that if it was Allah's will, then they would be taken out by a shell or a bomb or a bullet and be *shaheed*. Or if it was Allah's will that they should survive and fight, then they would survive and fight. It was all in the will of the Almighty Allah.

Ali said that he had a different view on things. His mission in being there was clear: it was to wage jihad against the infidel invaders of a Muslim country. The best way to do that and better serve Allah was to keep himself alive and fighting fit, not to sit under the first shell that came along. Ali quoted the Prophet's words at the brothers: 'Do for your living life as if you will never die; do for your late life as if you will die tomorrow.' The meaning was clear, Ali explained: it meant that this life was precious and the brothers should not squander it needlessly. He was here with one mission: to kill the infidel Americans and their lapdogs, the British.

5

DEATH VALLEY

MAT glanced at his watch. It was twelve midnight. They had seven hours to go before dawn, during which they had to cover eight miles and some 15,000 feet of ascent. After the comparative warmth of the Humvee the Afghan night was chilling. But Mat and his men knew that once they started the climb the exertion would keep them warm. Every inch of terrain ahead of them now was hostile territory. If they didn't make the mountain peak and the comparative safety of their observation position by daybreak, then they were in trouble. According to their intelligence, the Naka Valley was crawling with the terrorist enemy. If Mat and his small team ran into them in broad daylight, he had few illusions about who was more likely to win any firefight. They may have been Britain's (and America's) finest special forces, but they were not superhuman.

As each man helped his mate on with his massive backpack, they were reminded just how horribly heavy their bergens were. As soon as they were ready, Mat led the team some hundred yards away from the mountain track that the vehicle convoy had been following. Once the seven of them were in a position of cover, they dropped to the ground. Mat then gave the pre-arranged signal using his infrared torch to let the US vehicle convoy know that they were free to return to base.

Down below them, the Humvees and Toyota pickups began executing awkward three-point turns, their engines snarling and revving in the darkness. Finally, when all the vehicles were pointing back the way they had come, they began to crawl down the valley floor and away from the watching special forces soldiers. As the convoy rounded the far corner of the valley, the noise of the engines faded into the night. Silence descended upon Mat and his six fellow patrol members. Immediately after being dropped at the start of a mission was one of the most dangerous times for a covert patrol. Any enemy in the region could easily have detected their arrival and be poised to attack.

As the men squatted in the darkness, each with their bergens propped against a boulder, they strained their ears to catch any sound that might indicate that they had been compromised: the soft crunch of a sandalled foot on gravel; the clink of an AK47 magazine against a webbing belt; a faint cough, strangled in the dense mountain blackness. But all they could hear was their own, laboured breathing pounding in their ears. It seemed that they were alone out there in that dark valley. As his eyes adjusted to the faint moonlight filtering down to the valley floor, Mat searched the hillside for the best route up on to the ridgeline high above them.

After some fifteen minutes waiting, watching and listening – soaking up the night-dark atmosphere and acclimatising to their new environment – Mat got to his feet and signalled for the others to follow him. During

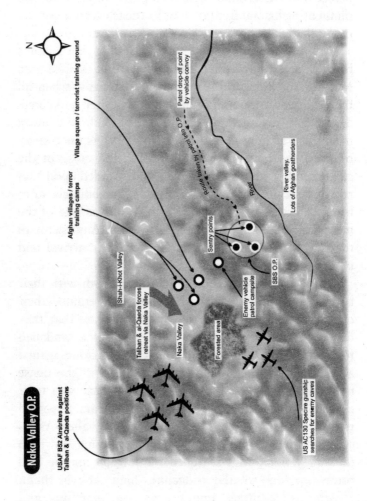

Naka Valley O.P.

N

USAF B52 Airstrikes against Taliban & al-Qaeda positions

Shah-I-Khot Valley

Taliban & al-Qaeda forces retreat via Naka Valley

Naka Valley

Forested area

Afghan villages / terrorist training camps

Village square / terrorist training ground

Patrol drop-off point by vehicle convoy

Route taken by patrol into O.P.

Sentry points

Enemy vehicle patrol campsite

SBS O.P.

River

River valley. Lots of Afghan goatherders

US AC130 Spectre gunship searches for enemy caves

that short wait, the cold had already started to seep into his limbs and he knew that he had to get his legs moving before they seized up. The men swung their packs around on their backs one last time, just to check for any rattles or clinks that might betray their passing – and then they set out into the unknown. Sam took point, heading off on a bearing due west, and Mat brought up the rear. Mat put CIA Bob in the middle of the column, surrounded by the Team 6 lads, where he would be best protected. The patrol was operating on 'silent routine' now, which meant that all communications would be by hand signals only, unless absolutely necessary.

SBS standard operating procedures for this sort of patrol make it the man in front's responsibility not to lose sight of the man directly to his rear. But Mat's team were now employing an old trick to help keep the patrol together. Each man had attached a compass to the rear of his bergen. The faint luminosity of the dial would show up just enough for the man behind to keep track of the guy in front of him. As the seven men started to climb out of the valley, each footstep shifted the balance of their packs slightly, making the bergens creak alarmingly. In the deathly still night air sounds like this would be audible for hundreds of yards. But there was nothing the men could do about it. The heavy loads they were carrying were about as silenced as they could possibly make them.

From his position at the rear of the column, Mat began to wonder just what they had let themselves in for with this mission. Barely thirty minutes into the climb and already his shoulders were on fire as he hauled his pack up the steep incline. Prior to departure, there had been an animated debate among the men as to whether they should make the climb using NVGs, to help find their way. Mat had been adamant that they should not: using goggles over a seven-hour period would put an unbearable strain on the eyes, as well as eating up their supply of batteries. And so they had opted against NVGs.

As he climbed, Mat's eyes adjusted to the darkness remarkably well and he found that he could make out most of the detail of the surrounding terrain. During the Afghan spring, the valley would become a raging torrent swollen by melt waters from the snowfields above. But now it was the dry, cold season and just a thin sliver of water snaked its way along the valley floor. The men trudged ever upwards, scrub and thorn trees tearing at their clothing. As they continued to climb, the terrain underfoot became a moonscape of broken rock interspersed with larger boulders, with here and there a stunted pine tree looming out of the darkness. Many of the trees were no taller than the patrol members: it was hardly surprising, as the dry, cold earth offered little in terms of shelter or nutrients.

The first hour of the climb passed without incident and finally the patrol reached the ridge, which marked the limit of the river valley. Beyond lay a series of higher ridges, stretching away to their final destination, the mountain peak now towering some 8,000 feet above them. From here on in, Mat reminded himself, the going would only get tougher. But his greatest worry was fast becoming the lack of water. After leaving the river bed, they had yet to come across another water source: neither mountain spring nor stagnant pool relieved the unrelenting dryness of the terrain. No doubt about it, Mat reflected, this was a harsh, unforgiving landscape; it was hardly surprising that it had spawned a harsh, unforgiving people; and maybe it took a harsh, unforgiving mission like this one to get the better of them.

The patrol crested the ridge and descended into a plunging valley. On the far side, they began climbing again, and the ascent now was even steeper, the slope rising up before them at a sixty-degree angle. In places Mat found himself bent double as he tried to stop himself from overbalancing and being dragged backwards down the mountainside. At the same time he was prevented from grabbing hold of any boulders or undergrowth to help haul himself upwards because he had his weapon gripped in his hands. He wondered how the rest of his team were faring.

Eventually, the inevitable happened. One of the Team 6 lads up ahead of Mat must have put a foot wrong, and suddenly he went tumbling and crashing down the mountainside. Rocks and debris dislodged by the fall went clattering past Mat, the sound deafening in the deathly still mountain air. After he'd fallen some fifty yards, the SBS soldier had his momentum broken by a tree.

As the rest of the patrol waited for him to rejoin them they were glad of the few minutes' break. Mat rested the weight of his bergen against a rock and pondered their predicament. Any enemy in the immediate area would certainly have heard the racket made by that fall. The only way that he could think of to make the going any easier was to ditch some of the weight in their bergens, which wasn't really an option, or to free up their hands to help with the climb. But it was a cardinal rule among the SBS that an operator should never let go of his weapon. He should eat with it, sleep with it, walk with it and always have it to hand. They would have to press on as best they could.

Unfortunately, the going kept getting worse. As they climbed ever higher, the rock strata began changing. The boulders and gravel gave way to hard-packed fields of black, flint-like rock. All too often, it was smooth underfoot and difficult to get a grip with their boots, and in places the incline worsened to some seventy degrees. Straightening up momentarily on one of the worst stretches, Mat realised that he'd overdone it and that his bergen was pulling him backwards. Reacting on instinct, he dropped his Diemaco and made a desperate grab for the nearest tree. As his assault rifle went clattering to the ground, his hand found a branch, and for a split second it checked his fall. But then there was a sharp crack as the branch broke, and Mat felt himself going over, the weight of his bergen dragging him off his feet and down the precipitous slope below him.

For several seconds Mat went plummeting down the hillside, his body a flurry of arms and legs and backpack and webbing. Finally, he came to rest where a massive boulder blocked his fall. Luckily, his bergen took the brunt of the impact. But Mat still felt a juddering pain stabbing up through the base of his neck, and for a moment he blacked out. As he came to, his first instinct was to look for his weapon. But as he glanced back up the slope he caught sight of a mini avalanche of rocks tumbling down towards him. As the hard, black, igneous rocks went smashing into each other, they sent showers of white sparks shooting into the darkness. It was one of the weirdest sights Mat had ever seen. He buried his head in the dirt to shield himself from the falling rocks. As he did so, he reflected on the fact that here they were in the middle of hostile territory on a covert mission, yet he'd just set off a massive mountainside firework display.

Once it seemed like the avalanche was over, Mat risked a glance upwards again. Sure enough, the rockfall appeared to have stopped. He could see a faint line of luminous green lights glowing in the darkness up ahead – the compasses of the rest of his team sat atop their bergens. The lads had stopped and were waiting for him. Using the boulder as leverage he hauled himself to his feet, checked for any signs of damage and then went in search of his weapon. If he remembered correctly, he'd hurled it away from his body into a little natural depression to the right of him. As Mat retraced his steps, one of his biggest worries was if all the camera gear in his pack had survived the fall.

When Mat reached the little hollow in the hillside, the Diemaco was lying exactly where he'd remembered throwing it. But just as he stooped to retrieve his weapon, he froze: something had caught his attention. As he swivelled his head slowly to take a better look, Mat caught sight of an object faintly glowing on the ground, just a few yards ahead of him. It was too white and too regular to be any product of nature. Reaching down, Mat slipped his hands around the cold steel of the Diemaco, and flipped the safety to off. He was relieved to see that his weapon had suffered nothing more than a few small dents and scratches.

Crouching low and stepping as gently as he could on the rocky ground, Mat crept towards the mystery white object. As he got closer, another appeared out of the darkness, and then another and another, stretching away in line across the hillside. He was almost on top of them before he realised what they were: someone had placed a series of squarish boulders running across the hillside, and they were all painted a bright white. Out here on this darkened, deserted mountainside, they were about the last thing that Mat had expected to find.

From where he was now standing, one line of white boulders stretched away across the mountainside following the contours, and as he looked uphill Mat could see another running directly up the slope ahead of him. Someone had deliberately marked off a corner here – and Mat was standing at the apex of the right angle. But a corner of what? It could hardly be a field or a garden on this barren hillside, and the terrain was far too uneven for it to be a landing strip or a path. Mat was completely mystified. He made a mental note to consult the other lads when he rejoined them. Seven heads were better than one – maybe together they could figure it out. Whatever it was, it was man-made and had to have been put there by the local Afghans – which more than likely meant the enemy.

Mat turned and made his way back towards the waiting line of compasses, bobbing and faintly glowing in the darkness.

'Sure did appreciate the firework display, buddy,' Sam drawled as Mat hove into view. 'Say, but next time can we have some rockets an' maybe a couple of air bursts, too?'

'Piss off, mate,' Mat replied, as he dropped his bergen to the ground. 'Take five, lads,' he added, as he began rubbing the base of his neck, which was badly bruised from the fall. The rest of the team gathered around, dropping their packs on to the hard earth.

'Ace quad-bike driver, me, mate,' Mat remarked to no one in particular, making a reference to how stupid he felt for having taken a tumble down the mountainside.

'Say, you sure you're OK, buddy?' CIA Bob asked. 'You taken a bad knock on the head or somethin'? Cos you weren't drivin' no quad bike, buddy. 'Less I'm mistaken, you was walkin'.'

'It's just an expression, mate,' Mat replied. 'One of

our blokes wrapped his quad bike around a rock on training back at Bagram. Now I can't even manage to walk me way up a bloody mountain without taking a tumble. Bugger it, you Yanks wouldn't understand anyways.'

'Whatever,' CIA Bob said. 'Still, you know, by the looks of all them pyrotechnics down there, I guess you took a bad fall, huh?'

'Yeah, could have done without it. Anyhow, listen up, lads. Way I see it is we're in a honkin' filthy place right now. What are we, two hours into the climb? And this is bad and only getting worse. Way we're going, any AQT in the region will be able to hear us and see us coming bloody miles off. And we've taken two falls already. I had to drop me weapon, obviously, and I'm lucky it's still OK. So, I know it goes against SOPs and all, but each of you's got to feel free to do this climb as it's easiest for you. So, if you want to sling your weapon, sling your weapon. You've all got some Paracord, right?'

'Right,' the rest of the guys confirmed.

'OK, then use that to strap your weapon to your bergen, or, alternatively, sling it from your front,' Mat continued. 'Best way to protect your weapon is to strap it tight as buggery to your bergen. But if we're compromised, you'll have a bloody nightmare trying to get to your weapon. It's your call. And we've got to try to avoid the worst of these rock slopes. Only way I can see us doing that is using NVGs. I know we decided against it back at base and for all the right reasons. But unless anyone's got a couple of broomsticks and a pointy black hat so we can fly up there, it's the best I can think of.'

'Maybe we should've, you know, brought the quad bikes in with us, bro,' Sam remarked. 'Got the 10th

Mountain boys to tow them in behind the Humvees. Might have been kinda neat for gettin' in closer to the OP.'

'Yeah, well, we could've loaded the bloody bergens on them, that's for sure,' Mat replied. 'I did think about it, back at the fort. And we might've done so had Gobbler not buggered up our little training session back at Bagram. Anyhow, the noise might've alerted the enemy, although the quads're pretty bloody quiet. Well, bugger it, mate, the only way forward now's on foot. Talking of which, did anyone else stumble across them painted white rocks? Long lines of 'em slung out across the hillside. Bollocksed if I can work out what they're for, mind.'

'Buddy, you sure you didn't take a crack on the head when you took that fall?' said CIA Bob, with a wicked gleam in his eye. 'Cos if I didn't know you better I'd say you been seeing things.'

'Bob, are you taking the piss, mate?' Mat was getting the measure of the little CIA spook by now, and had realised that he was a real joker. 'Cos if you are all I can say is it's very bloody un-American of you. As all us Brits know, you Yanks don't do sarcasm, specially not Southern boys like you. Anyhow, you open your eyes a bit, mate, and you'll see 'em soon enough. White rocks. Painted white rocks. Long lines of 'em. Off to the right of us. OK?'

'Whatever you say, buddy,' CIA Bob replied, shaking his head in mock amazement.

'You know, whatever drugs he's on, I wanna get me some,' Sam added, nodding in Mat's direction.

'Like I said – ace quad-bike driver, me,' Mat retorted, with a grin.

There were a few seconds' silence finally broken by Sam. 'Say, I dunno about the rest of you guys, but I'm kinda whacked. I guess, you know, you guys kinda do more of this sort of mule work than we do.'

'You never yomped up a hill with a pack on your back before, mate?' Mat asked.

'Seriously, bro, it ain't somethin' we do much of in the SEALs,' Sam replied. 'Like, I ain't never done nothin' like it before. Reckon I don't ever want to again, either.'

'Nowt like learning on the job then, is there, mate?' Mat said, unsympathetically. 'Anyhow, thought you SEALs were tough. We'll make a real man of you yet, mate, don't you worry.'

'You'll make a goddam mule of me is about all, bro.'

'All right then, lads, come on, let's get going,' Mat announced, grabbing his pack and lifting it on to his shoulders. 'We got a lot of climbing to do before sun-up.'

As he got to his feet Mat flipped his NVGs down over his eyes. With the aid of their night vision, the patrol members soon spotted the lines of rocks that Mat had mentioned. And not just the white ones, either. Within the next half an hour or so, they'd passed long lines of blue and red ones too. But none of them were any the wiser as to what they might be for. And the NVGs proved to be only a marginal help in finding a better route. While the goggles were good at picking up movement or colour, static black rock was static black rock. The eerie green glow of the NVGs didn't pick up a lot more detail than that. Within the next two hours fatigue really began to take a toll, and two more of the team took a fall down the mountainside. One of them had his NVGs ripped from his head as he went plunging down the slope. When he found them again they were completely ruined.

With all the falls they were taking Mat found himself wondering whether Commander Jim hadn't been right after all. Maybe they were attempting the impossible.

It was five hours into the climb when they hit a particularly nasty section of slope. Suddenly, Mat heard Sam and CIA Bob cursing and yelling, and almost simultaneously they both took a fall. As CIA Bob went crashing past Mat – a flurry of rocks sparking down the hillside after him – Mat couldn't help himself any longer and just cracked up laughing. Here they were, an elite special forces team supposedly on a covert night infil deep into enemy territory, and they couldn't be making any more of a balls-up of it had they tried. You had to see the funny side of it. As the Team 6 lads gathered around to wait for CIA Bob and Sam, the merriment quickly spread. It was, after all, a ridiculous situation to find themselves in.

'Tell you what,' Mat said to the lads, 'if them AQT wankers haven't spotted us by now I reckon we've got nowt to worry about on this op. If they're all they're cracked up to be, we should've had Osama himself and all his merry men after us by now. Couldn't have made more of a song and dance of it if we'd flown in here in a couple of Chinooks, all guns blazing.'

What made it even funnier as far as Mat was concerned was that CIA Bob had finally taken a tumble. Mat was rapidly warming to the funny little American spook and his evil sense of humour, and now it was his chance to give CIA Bob some grief in return.

'Take a couple of Yanks on the mission and it all goes to rat shit,' Mat called out, in the general direction of Sam and CIA Bob. 'You guys still alive down there?'

'Ace quad-bike drivers, us!' a voice floated up from down below them.

'Reckon bloody Spooky there's two sandwiches short of a picnic,' Mat remarked to the others, as they waited for the two Americans to rejoin them. 'Seen the size of that pack he's carrying? More like a girly handbag than a rucksack. You blokes took a bit of a tumble, did you?' he said, as he spotted Sam and CIA Bob emerging from the darkness.

'Well, you know, we were feelin' kinda all left out,' Sam retorted.

'Don't want you Brits havin' all the goddam fun, do we?' CIA Bob added.

Once the two Americans had checked themselves over, Mat was keen to press ahead. But as he got to his feet and reached for his pack Sam drew him to one side to have a quiet word.

'Listen, bro, I'm real whacked,' Sam said.

'Yeah, well, we're all bloody hooped, mate, what of it?' Mat replied.

'No, really, I mean it, bro, I'm kinda finished. I mean, with all that goddam weight I'm carryin', I ain't sure how much longer I can do this for.'

'You serious, mate?' Mat asked, finally realising that Sam was in trouble. He knew this tough American soldier well enough to know that he never normally complained.

'Yeah, I'm real serious, bro. My shoulders are ripped to shreds from that goddam pack. My back's on fire. And my legs feel like Jell-O. I wouldn't be sayin' nothin' unless it was bad.'

'All right, well, this is what we'll do, mate. First off, lose that pack,' said Mat. For some reason Sam had chosen to carry a standard-issue British Army bergen, not a civilian pack. And Mat rated the British Army backpacks about as highly as he rated the boots. 'Try my bergen. It's a civvy version. If it suits, we'll swap and I'll also take some of your extra weight. And then we'll just have to crack on.'

'Shit, buddy, I feel goddam awful about this.'

'No problem, mate. Just don't forget to buy me a couple of pints when we're back in Poole. And take your grab bag, mate. Fat lot of good that'll be if it all goes noisy and we've got the wrong bags to hand.'

Back at the fort Sam had volunteered to carry the team radio, a big, chunky piece of kit. Mat wondered if maybe that was part of his problem. After they had redistributed some of the weight, Mat and Sam and the rest of the patrol recommenced the exhausting climb. By now, they had been on the move for six hours, and the first glimmer of dawn was just starting to lighten the mountain peaks to the east. As the soldiers trudged upwards, they broke out from a wooded area on to a barren hillside. By the light of the coming sunrise they could see that the top of the ridge they were climbing now lay some five hundred yards directly ahead of them. And between them and the ridgeline lay a snowfield, glowing a fantastic fiery orange in the rarefied dawn light.

The men stopped for a second to catch their breath. Beyond the ridge, towering above and behind it, lay the peak for which they were heading – the snowfields on the near side of the mountain picking up the dawn light and throwing it back at Mat and his team in a thousand different shades of red. Despite where they were and the nature of the mission, it was an uplifting, awe-inspiring sight. At last they could finally see their destination. Mat felt the tension and exhaustion of the climb dropping away from his shoulders. He consulted his Trek GPS, which showed that they were at 9,000 feet now. The summit lay 3,000 feet above them. Which meant it was three hours' walk away, but well within their reach.

Once they got off the ridgeline – where they could easily have been spotted, silhouetted against the sunrise – Mat called a short break. It was light now, and no amount of hurrying was going to change that. The team slumped to the ground, broke out some chocolate bars and began munching quietly, psyching themselves up for the final ascent. As they did so, Mat was running a new scenario through his mind. They had barely passed any river or stream or other source of water in the six hours that they'd been climbing. But now they had reached the snowline, and Mat was wondering if they could melt the snow and use it to replenish their water supplies. Trouble was they were on hard routine, and using a fire or a stove to melt the snow could betray their position to the enemy. It was a risk Mat wasn't willing to take, not at this stage of the mission, anyway.

They recommenced the climb with Mat taking point and Sam bringing up the rear, sticking to just below the ridgeline. When they reached the point where the ridge met the base of the mountain, Mat noticed a little damp-ness in the earth at his feet. Stooping down, he realised that there was a tiny spring just at the base of the moun-tain wall. It was emitting a feeble flow, barely enough to wet his boots. But it was more than enough to work the Katadyn intake pipe into so they could filter the water. Pulling his GPS unit out of his smock pocket, Mat waymarked the coordinates of the stream. This could be their lifesaver: the nearest water source to their moun-taintop OP. It certainly meant they had other options than to risk melting the snow.

Mat led his team on the summit climb and, at that altitude and with all the weight they were carrying, they quickly found themselves all but crawling up the barren, shattered scree of the mountainside. Progress was painfully slow, and they were all gasping for breath in the thin air. Each man had to force himself to place one foot in front of the other and keep moving forwards.

They reached the summit just before lunchtime and collapsed, gasping for breath, into the weird, cactus-like undergrowth that was all that seemed to cling to the peak. Before them stretched an undulating vista of ridges and plunging valleys. But a harsh, midday sun beat down from the sky now, painting everything – rocks, snow-fields, vegetation – an unrelenting drab grey brown. The Naka Valley was an inhospitable, unforgiving landscape if ever there was one.

By the time his patrol had reached the mountain summit, Mat knew that they were all suffering from the onset of acute mountain sickness (AMS), a life-threatening condition of high altitude. At 12,000 feet the oxygen present in the atmosphere is only half that found at sea level. Which meant that every time the lads breathed in, they were taking in half as much oxygen as normal. Oxygen is vital to physical well-being and survival. The early symptoms of AMS are like a bad hangover: a thumping headache, nausea and a general feeling of lousiness. An AMS headache is generally believed to be the worst a man can get: a blinding, pounding pain that thuds like a jackhammer inside the skull.

As AMS worsens, the nausea turns to vomiting, the headache becomes even more unbearable and the sufferer finds himself gasping for breath. Then balance and co-ordination begin to fail, a symptom known as ataxia. Mental confusion, slurred speech and drowsiness follows. The sufferer may have a horrible gurgling in the lungs, and be coughing up bloody phlegm. At this point death is just hours away, and the only cure is to rapidly descend the mountain and use oxygen. The one way to avoid getting AMS is to climb slowly. SBS SOPs for high-altitude missions suggest making no more than three to five hundred yards of ascent for each day's climb.

Yet Mat's team had just made a 12,000-foot climb in less than twelve hours.

It was no wonder that they were feeling so awful, Mat reflected, as he staggered off into the bush to vomit. He had a splitting headache, a churning stomach and was struggling to drag enough air into his aching lungs. He had vomited three times on the last stage of the climb, and the rest of the lads were suffering just as badly. Mat knew the symptoms of AMS well, having carried out several Alpine and Arctic training missions. He also knew that they would just have to grit their teeth and bear it, as descent was not an option. Over the next forty-eight hours either the AMS would become life threatening, or they would acclimatise. The men were parched from the climb, and drinking plenty of water is one of the main ways to avoid AMS. Mat knew that his men should be drinking five litres of water per day, but they could only allow themselves less than a third of that on this mission.

It was crucial that Mat got his men into the cover and shade of a secure observation position as quickly as possible. Scanning the ridgeline ahead of him with his binoculars, Mat spotted a giant heap of boulders about a mile ahead. It should provide some protection, and offer a clear view down into the Naka Valley to the north. After a short break Mat urged his men on with the promise of a proper feed and a rest. Some twenty minutes later they arrived at the mound of boulders, and it did indeed appear to be a classic site for an OP. It provided good cover, great arcs of fire across the surrounding terrain, several escape routes and views both to the north and south of the ridgeline.

While the rest of the men settled down to rest, Mat goaded Sam into one last effort. He wanted Sam to help him do a quick recce of the OP. They needed to

check if there were any signs of human presence in the
region: hidden pathways, a makeshift shelter, a goat
track even. If there were, they would have to search
for another, more secure location. Sam had also offered
to be the comms man on the team, and Mat wanted
him to do a quick comms check of their position. There
was no point in choosing this location for the OP unless
it had good reception for the radio and satcoms. Mat
and Sam spent five minutes doing a quick walkabout.
As far as they could see, there was no sign of human
presence at the OP and their signal strength appeared
to be excellent.

Mat also wanted a chance to be alone with Sam so
he could check on his welfare. While the other lads were
suffering, none of them – CIA Bob included – had
complained about the gruelling climb. If anything, they'd
chosen to make light of it. Only Sam had vocalised his
discomfort – and from what Mat knew of him this was
completely out of character. Mat suspected that the British
Army bergen Sam'd been carrying had really cut into his
shoulders. If so, it was Mat's duty as the team medic to
make sure his injuries were treated properly. Sam had
refused to complain about the bergen until it was too
late and he was just as likely to refuse to ask for medical
help now.

'You all right, mate?' Mat ventured. Despite their
exhaustion, it was a joy just to be relieved of the massive
weight of their packs. 'Seems like you were suffering
honkin' bad back there.'

'Sure, bro, I'm fine,' Sam replied, as he turned to face
his fellow soldier. Sam was almost a full head taller than
Mat, but he didn't let that fool him into thinking that
he was any the tougher because of it. Mat was squat
and solid as a rock, and he'd more than proven his

endurance on the climb. Sam didn't doubt that Mat's pack, which was laden down with all the photographic gear, would prove to be the heaviest of the lot of them if they ever checked. He rolled his shoulders. 'It's just that goddam backpack, you know. It beat the crap out of my shoulders big time, bro.'

'Yeah, I thought as much. Listen, you got to let me take a look at that, OK? You leave it untreated, those cuts could fester bad and infect your blood. Six days from now you could have septicaemia and you'll be buggered. There's little chance of getting you medevacced at this altitude, is there, mate?'

'You got it, big man,' Sam replied, with a smile. 'Appreciate the concern, bro. Say, what is it with you Brits anyways and all this "yomping" shit? Couldn't hear none of you guys complaining. It's, like, weird – I mean, you guys enjoy this shit, or somethin'?'

'Look, mate, you're as fit as any of us, make no bloody mistake about it. It's just that we do a lot of this shit, specially in the Boot Necks – the Royal Marines, that is. The Paras too. Gets to be sort of automatic after a while, mate.'

'Bitch, I ain't never done nothin' like this before in my life,' Sam said, shaking his head in bemusement. 'And I ain't got no desire to start learnin' now. SEALs just don't do this sort of shit, period.'

'Well, it ain't over yet, mate, cos you're going to have to get back down the bloody mountain again. Look, it's mainly just psychological. With us lot it's cos we done it before that we know we can do it again. Plus none of us had the bergen from hell, did we, mate? Anyhow, truth be told all of us found that tough. At this altitude, with all that weight? Bloody honkin' filthy it was. We just cracked on with it cos we had to.'

'Really? You guys made it look like a goddam walk in the park.'

'Bloody take a look at us, mate. Bloody hanging out of our hoops we are. Just we ain't saying it.'

'Bro, what in God's name is "hanging out of our hoops"?'

'Means we're shagged, mate. Knackered. Wanked out. Bollocksed. Cream-crackered. Buggered. Hanging out of our hoops. You name it, mate, we're feeling it.'

The patrol's OP consisted of a flat patch of bare, rocky earth just large enough for seven men to sleep on, surrounded by a series of massive boulders. Over and above this was a tangled thicket of pine trees that helped keep their position hidden from prying eyes. The northern end of the OP dropped away abruptly into an all but sheer escarpment, plunging some several thousand feet down into the Naka Valley. This gave a perfect vantage point from which to observe goings-on in the target area. During the day this viewpoint would be manned by two members of Mat's team – so that they could keep two sets of eyes on target. The only entrance to the OP was located at the southern end where a man could just squeeze himself between two boulders. Three claymore mines were bedded into the ground guarding that entrance point – just in case they had any unwanted visitors.

There was a view southwards into a gorge on the other side of the ridge, which ran parallel to the Naka Valley. It had a river snaking along the valley floor. Although the gorge was too steep and inhospitable to be permanently inhabited, Mat knew that any river would be a magnet for goatherds who would bring their animals there to drink. That much had been explained to him in the mission briefings. Every goatherd had to be treated as a potential enemy. So a second sentry point was set up looking down into the southern end of the gorge. A third sentry point was established at the western end of the OP, in a crevice between two massive boulders. At any one time four of the six SBS soldiers would be on sentry duty. This left the other two free to eat, sleep or file reports, while CIA Bob got on with the job of spying on enemy forces in the region.

Mat and Sam took first turn watching over the Naka Valley. As they gazed down, Mat got out his map and started identifying some of the key features that had been mentioned in the mission briefing. Directly below them lay two villages of mud-walled houses, which were reportedly the source of much of the terrorist activity in the region. In front of the two villages lay a wide, open area that had been identified as a parade ground. It was here that US intelligence had observed the terrorist training sessions and afternoon combat exercises taking place. As it was now 2 p.m. and the hottest part of the day, there was little activity that Mat and Sam could observe. It seemed that even terrorists needed to rest through the heat of the afternoon.

Mat and Sam took it in turns to do alternate watching duties of thirty minutes each. Any longer than that and eye strain started to be a real problem, as did the ability to concentrate. Back in the cover and security of the centre of the OP, CIA Bob was busy setting up his spying equipment. Keeping one eye on the Naka Valley, Mat and Sam watched as CIA Bob strung a dull metal Christmas-tree-like device from the branches of one of the trees. With a set of headphones clamped over his ears, he then proceeded to twist and turn the device, minutely adjusting the orientation. Finally, a broad smile broke out on his bearded face. By the looks of it this was some sort of listening device, and CIA Bob had just picked up a good signal.

Next, he set up a spindly metal tripod with a set of eight metal fingers extending like a splayed hand from the top of it. Between the ends of the fingers there was a delicate silver wire. Above this, CIA Bob pulled out an extension and unfolded four flat blades set in a cross shape. Both Mat and Sam had come across a similar device before: this was an aerial for a satcom device. CIA Bob set the device to search for communications satellites in the sky above, and then pulled out an Iridium satphone from his tiny backpack. Once the satcom had found three satellites, he was able to put through a test call to JSOC headquarters back in the USA.

Using his tiny Psion laptop computer, CIA Bob would be able to upload written information, photos and even video footage back to base via the satcom. This was the way in which he, Mat and the rest of the patrol would be reporting their intelligence back to headquarters. The Psion also had two state-of-the-art chips embedded within it, which could descramble any encoded signals that enemy forces in the region might be using. And the tiny computer not only allowed him to upload information back to headquarters, it also enabled him to download information from Global Hawk and Joint-STARS – US spy planes now patrolling the skies above Afghanistan.

The Joint-STARS (Joint Surveillance and Target Attack Radar System) jets – a Boeing 707 equipped with radar and electronic communications systems – have the technology to look deep into hostile regions. They can search some 150 miles of territory and distinguish between a tank and a wheeled vehicle. The Joint-STARS aircraft were a boost to special forces, because they enabled them to do real-time data links, helping coordinate ground actions with air assaults. The Global Hawk unmanned spy planes were making their combat debut in Afghanistan. These drones have the ability to carry out surveillance operations from 60,000 feet, for more than thirty hours at a time. Both aircraft provided just the sort of back-up that Mat's team would need while calling in air strikes on the Naka Valley.

Mat and Sam were fascinated to watch CIA Bob at work. He looked more like a mad scientist than an officer with the Central Intelligence Agency. All afternoon he sat around with his headphones on, most of the time acting as if he wasn't really listening to what he was hearing. Then, just as Mat and Sam were convinced that he was dropping off to sleep, he'd start scribbling crazily in his notebook, before lapsing back into inactivity. He must have been monitoring the headphones traffic and listening for pro words – phrases that would signal to him something important was being said. CIA Bob spoke Arabic, Pashtun, Farsi and several other local Afghan languages, and Mat and Sam found themselves itching to know what sigint – signals intelligence – he'd picked up.

'You know, I heard some of the guys talkin' about spooky there back at the fort,' Sam whispered, nodding in CIA Bob's direction. 'Word is the guy's worth a fortune back in the States.'

'You what?' Mat replied, incredulously. 'You telling me he's minted? Then what the hell's he doing freezing his bollocks off with us lot on a 12,000-foot peak in Afghanistan?'

'Guess he must be madder than he looks, which sure is sayin' somethin',' Sam responded.

'Whatever tickles your fancy, I suppose. Still, just goes to show it's not all about money, don't it?'

'Guess it ain't so different from us, though. He's here to do a specific job, just like we are, bro. Listen to all the frequencies, monitor the sigint and get a handle on the enemy comms.'

'Yeah, but just look at him, mate. Bit of a spotter's job, ain't it? I mean, hanging up all those wires and coat hangers in that tree. Doing that would send me nuts. No wonder he looks like a Vietnam vet who's been locked up by the Vietcong for too long in a bamboo cage full of rats. I'd rather have me gun, any time, mate.'

By the time Mat and Sam had been relieved of their sentry duty, the sun was fast sinking towards the distant horizon. Night came quickly in the Afghan wildlands, and with it the temperature dropped to well below freezing. Both men spread out a poncho to shield them from the damp of the ground, and rolled out their down-filled sleeping bags and Gore-Tex bivvy bags. Each was so exhausted from the climb that they knew sleep would come easily that night, no matter how inhospitable the surroundings. As he crawled inside his down bag fully clothed, Mat glanced across at CIA Bob. Somehow, he wasn't surprised to see the state of the CIA agent's sleeping bag: it looked as if it had been made for a summer camping trip in Yosemite National Park.

'You sure you're going to be warm enough in that bag, mate?' Mat asked.

'Damn right I am, buddy,' CIA Bob responded, with a grin. 'They breed us Yankees hard as nails, not like you pansy-assed Brits. That's how we managed to whup your butts when you tried to lord it over us a few hundred years back. Whupped 'em good 'n' proper, too.'

'Fair 'nough, mate,' Mat replied. 'Only I was going to offer you me thermals. But if that's how you're going to be I ain't offering twice.'

'Gee, *your thermals*? Really appreciate the offer, buddy.'

'Well, I ain't offering again, mate,' said Mat, trying his best to ignore CIA Bob's sarcasm. 'How was the sigint, anyways?'

'Kinda awesome, buddy. We've got comms going back and forth between some guys down there and it's all about Mullah Omer and some others of our "Most Wanted". No mention of old Osama Binliner yet, but I'd say this place is crawling with bad guys.'

'Awesome, mate. That is, as long as they ain't realised we're here,' Mat said. 'No mention of us lot, was there, mate? I mean, no mention of our patrol?'

'Us lot? Gee, now I gotta think about that for a second,' said CIA Bob, in mock puzzlement. 'Yeah, come to think of it there was some mention of five Brits and two Yankees bedding down for the night on top of the mountain. Said we were the SAS, too, which kinda got my back up cause we're the SBS, ain't we? And I didn't appreciate them Talibuttfucks sayin' otherwise.'

'Piss off, mate.' For once Mat was lost for a sharp reply to CIA Bob's piss-taking.

'What's eatin' you, buddy? You still pissed I didn't kinda fancy wearin' your thermals?'

'Night-night, mate,' said Mat, ignoring CIA's Bob's comment. 'Sleep well. But keep one eye open – you don't want any of them bad guys creeping up on you in the middle of the night, do you?'

Within seconds, Mat had drifted off into an exhausted sleep. He had no worries about any enemy stumbling across their OP that night, as they had sentries out on all three positions. As for Sam, tired though he was, he found time to say a short prayer before sleep. He was a strongly Godly person, although he chose to keep this pretty quiet as he saw his religion as a private thing.

Some time after they'd fallen asleep, Mat found himself being shaken out of a deep, deep slumber. As he tried to clear the grogginess from his head, he heard Sam's urgent whisper.

'Listen, bro, one of the sentries has spotted a shitload of activity going down in the valley there. There's several vehicles on the move and we reckon it's AQT.'

Somewhat begrudgingly, Mat extricated himself from his sleeping bag and crawled over to the sentry point. Surely the enemy couldn't be on to them already? Down in the valley he could see the lights of half a dozen vehicles converging on a central point. Grabbing a pair of NVGs he took a closer look. The vehicles were Toyota four-wheel drives. As he watched, they pulled up and formed a circle, with their lights facing inwards towards a central point. Several figures in white turbans and loose robes got out and set about building a fire in the centre. Once it was burning well the car lights were switched off. Some two dozen figures gathered around, warming themselves in the blaze. Every now and then Mat caught sight of the twin lights of other pickups heading towards or away from the firelight. There was clearly a considerable active presence in the valley.

Mat glanced at his watch: it was 9.30 p.m., and he'd been asleep for two hours.

'Bollocks. They can't know we're here already,' Mat whispered to Sam, voicing the concern that was on everyone's mind. 'I mean, you reckon they're out searching for our patrol or something?'

'Shit, bro, if they know we're here, I think they'd be on top of us by now.'

'Reckon you're right,' Mat replied, with obvious relief. 'Reckon it's the bloody altitude getting to me, mate. Air's so bloody thin can't seem to get me bloody head together. But if they ain't looking for us, what are they up to?'

'No idea, bro,' Sam replied. 'Maybe it's a bunch of AQT getting together for a heads-up around the camp-fire. Maybe it's just a bunch of villagers. But my guess is if the AQT knew we was here, they'd be keeping a real low profile. They'd be coming for us in as quiet a way as possible. And that ain't what's happening down there around that fire.'

'In which case, what the fuck did you wake me up for, mate?' Mat said, with a grin. 'Stone me, it's cold. Freeze the balls off of a brass monkey, it would. I'm heading back to me sack. Best tell the boys to keep a close eye on 'em, though – just in case anything develops.'

'You reckon you're cold, buddy?' Sam remarked under his breath. 'Take a look-see how ol' Spooky over there's doin'. And listen to that, bro. You hear it? Sounds like a goddam machine gun. That's Spooky's teeth chattering.'

'You're joking, aren't you, mate?' Mat glanced over in CIA Bob's direction. 'Poor guy must be freezing his cock off.'

'You betcha,' said Sam. 'Say, bro, why don't you offer him your thermals again?'

The following morning, Mat awoke with the dawn. As soon as he opened his eyes he realised that his skull was pounding with an altitude headache. He felt like he had the worst hangover in his life. His throat was dry as sandpaper, as if he'd spent the whole night gasping for air through his mouth. He had a bitter, iron-like taste on his lips, and he wondered for a moment if he'd been coughing up blood. It tasted as if he had been, which would mean that the AMS was getting serious. As he spat phlegm on to the back of his hand, Mat had images of the seven of them having to abort the mission and struggle back down the mountain, fighting AMS all the way. He checked his spittle for flecks of blood, but it appeared clear. On previous high-altitude missions Mat had always found the symptoms of AMS at their worst in the morning. If possible, it was better to climb high and sleep low: a few hours' kip on 50 per cent oxygen wasn't very healthy for anyone.

Mat lay there relishing the warmth and dryness of his sleeping bag, and waiting for the worst of the AMS to pass. As he did so, he gazed up into the pine trees above him. They appeared to be dripping with moisture – which meant that even at this altitude there had to be a considerable early-morning dewfall. He wondered why the outside of his bivvy bag wasn't soaking wet from the dew. And then he realised that what had at first looked like water droplets were in fact tiny icicles. It was so cold that the very air around him appeared to be frozen. The ice would burn off pretty quickly in the Afghan sun, which accounted for the lack of it upon their arrival in the OP the previous day.

Fortunately, Mat had put his water bottles inside his sleeping bag for the night, where his body heat would prevent them from freezing solid. All of the SBS lads – Sam included – had done Arctic survival courses in Norway, and Mat knew that he didn't have to remind them about such tricks. As for CIA Bob, he was so full of himself that Mat half hoped all his water had frozen solid. In which case, it'd be a great excuse to rip the piss out of him. Mat made a mental note to gather up all the batteries and the electrical gear and distribute them among the team – so that each man could keep it warm inside his sleeping bag at night. Such extreme cold would exhaust batteries in a matter of hours, and quickly render all their electronic gear unserviceable.

Eventually, Mat got up and shuffled over to join the hunched figures on sentry duty. His limbs ached like never before – doubtless the result of the previous day's climb and a night spent comatose on the hard, unforgiving ground. Maybe he was getting too old for this lark, he thought, ruefully. Thirty was still a good age to be in Brit special forces, and it was possible to still be in the SBS at forty. But few made it much further, unless they were from the senior ranks. Around thirty was really decision time, Mat reflected. Either you stayed in and made a life career out of it, or got out and went into private military work. Sometimes – like when he was freezing his bollocks off at 12,000 feet – a cushy private security job on big bucks did seem appealing.

Mat sat down next to the two, frozen Team 6 sentries in their position overlooking the Naka Valley. They acknowledged each other with a silent nod. Then Mat gazed down below him and the sight that met his eyes all but took his breath away. The floor of the valley was completely obscured by a vast bank of rolling cloud and mist, which was tinged a fierce, fiery pink by the rays of the sun now groping their way over the ridgeline. After a few minutes' silent contemplation Mat moved over to take a look at the opposite valley.

On that side of the ridgeline the whole of the valley bottom was visible in the dawn light. The river that snaked its way along the valley floor looked as if it were on fire, thick banks of steam rising wraith-like from its waters. Mat had seen something similar to this once, back home at Poole. In winter the River Frome remained warmer than the surrounding land and air, and so the water would throw off clouds of steam in the first light of day. The sight below him now was stunning, and strangely reminiscent of home. Feeling uplifted Mat turned and headed back to the OP.

'Say, bro, I've been kinda noodling over those painted rocks seems like all night long,' Sam said, as soon as he caught sight of Mat returning to the OP. 'And I guess I got it figured: they're minefields, bro. Back there at the fort one of the Delta boys mentioned it – that's how the Afghans mark off their minefields.'

'Holy fuck. You're right, mate. It's all coming back to me now. Painted rocks as markers . . . Which means we've spent the best part of the journey in here yomping through an effing minefield. Nice of the effing Green Slime to warn us about that in the briefings, wasn't it, mate?'

'Go figure. Well, at least we'll know for the exfil, anyways.'

Neither Mat nor Sam were feeling very hungry, what with the nausea of AMS. They forced a few nuts and some chocolate down them, then went to take over the next sentry duty. Gradually, the mist cleared from the valley and they got sight of the forces camped out below them. The men had spent the night huddled around their campfire and were now readying what looked like a series of armed vehicle patrols. Mat and Sam watched carefully as the force split up. Half of the men – some fifteen fighters armed with AK47s and RPGs – headed off in the direction of a patch of thick forest towards the north-west. The other half set off into the north-eastern hills.

'Stay here, mate,' Mat whispered to Sam, as he belly-crawled away from their viewpoint. 'I'm going to check on the other sentry position – see if we can work out what they're up to down there.'

Keeping as low as he could, Mat scuttled over to the

western edge of the OP. The sentry point was set in a defile between two massive rocks, and the sun never seemed to make it into the shadows down there. Consequently, as Mat squeezed himself into the deep crevice it was freezing cold. After a quarter of an hour or so, there was still no sign of the vehicle patrols, and so Mat extricated himself from the icy embrace of the rocks and headed back to the OP. As he did so, he felt the early-morning rumblings in his intestines that signalled a need to defecate, and quickly. As an added evil, AMS had the tendency to create massive amounts of wind in the sufferer.

Squatting down behind a large rock, Mat pulled out a plastic freezer bag from his pocket and proceeded to try to perform the difficult task of crapping into it. It wasn't an altogether successful attempt, especially as the farting made it a somewhat explosive effort. It was made all the worse by the knowledge that they had no water to spare for washing. When Mat got back to the OP he proceeded to rub his hands vigorously together in the rough, gritty soil. Somewhere he'd learned that in the absence of soap and water, dry grit would act as an abrasive and a cleaner. As he was trying to 'wash' his hands in the sand, Mat caught sight of CIA Bob watching him. The little CIA spook was staring at him as if he had gone completely nuts.

'What? What is it?' Mat asked, irritably. 'Look, I've just been having a dump, all right? I'm trying to clean me hands. And unless you got any better ideas, this is the best I can come up with.'

'Buddy, by "dump" I presume you mean you were tryin' to use the bathroom, right?'

'Right.'

'Well, question is, buddy, how d'you manage to do it

on your hands? You got no toilet paper or something? I mean, I know you Brit soldiers ain't always the best equipped. But if Her Majesty ain't up to providing y'all with some loo roll, sure Uncle Sam can loan you some.'

'Dumb Yank,' Mat murmured. 'Well, if you don't know, mate, it's standard procedure on a covert op like this one to dump into bags, OK? That goes for spooks like you too, mate. Don't they teach you nowt in CIA training?'

'They teach us a lot of things, buddy. But they sure as hell don't teach us 'bout crapping into plastic bags. Guess the Agency don't see it as bein' too high a priority, you know. So what's all the bags of crap for, buddy? Don't tell me – it's some kinda Brit secret weapon. You know, like Her Majesty can't afford any hand grenades, so you chuck bags of crap at the enemy instead. Is that it?'

'I'll be chucking a bag of shite at you soon, mate,' Mat muttered. 'If you want to know, you carry all the bags of crap out with you. Otherwise, in no time this place'll be stinking to high heaven, which'll be a dead giveaway, won't it?'

'Listen, I ain't no soldier, right? But I figure there ain't no need up here. You been over to that sentry point between the two rocks, right? You seen how cold it is in there. If we dig a latrine where the sun don't shine, our crap'll stay frozen all day and all night long too. Ain't no one gonna smell nothing from a heap of frozen shi-ite, is there, buddy?'

'Smart-arse,' Mat said, with a grin.

'If any of you guys've got a spade, I'll go dig the latrine myself. I got a feeling like I gotta go bathroom myself right now.'

CIA Bob disappeared into the rocky terrain with one

of the Team 6 lad's folding spades. But barely a minute had passed before he came rushing back again, looking decidedly agitated.

'What's up, mate?' Mat asked, as soon as he caught sight of him.

'Just seen an enemy patrol,' CIA Bob hissed. 'Workin' their way down the ridgeline right this way, three hundred yards from us at present. Lucky I was havin' a crap at the time, so they didn't see me.'

'Take it you shat yourself, then?' Mat said.

'What kinda dumb-assed question is that?' CIA Bob hissed again.

'Right, get the lads together, mate,' Mat said, nodding at Sam. 'Looks like we're about to be pinged.'

'You got it, bro,' Sam whispered back at him.

'How many enemy?' Mat asked, turning back to CIA Bob.

'I only saw the one, an' I wasn't waitin' for the rest, buddy.'

'Weapons?'

'AK47 looked like.'

'Uniform or Arab civvies?'

'Kinda mixture of the two.'

'Right, lads, looks like shit's about to hit the fan,' Mat announced, as the SBS soldiers gathered around. 'We've no idea how many of the fookers there are. But you know the form – get in position covering your arcs of fire and be ready to rumble. If it does kick off, fire on my signal and let's mallet the fookers. As soon as there's a chance to break out of here, I'll pop some smoke and we're gone. On my lead be ready to move. Grab bags only, and load 'em up with as much ammo as you can carry. You all know the E&E procedure: it's a fighting withdrawal to the ERV. Got it?'

'Got it,' the rest of the lads replied.

Mat settled down behind his Diemaco and laid out half a dozen 40mm grenades on the ground in front of him. He slotted a 40mm round into his grenade launcher, and it slid home with a reassuring clunk. If the enemy were about to hit the OP, he was determined to give them a warm welcome. His mind was racing now, trying to work out how the enemy might have discovered them. All he could think was that the enemy vehicle patrols had picked up their trail and tracked them to the OP. It was a pretty dire situation: fifteen miles of enemy terrain lay between them and the nearest friendly forces, they were surrounded by hostiles and at this altitude they had no hope of calling in an extraction chopper. Welcome to Afghanistan, Mat thought to himself, grimly.

Suddenly, he detected a voice yabbering away up on the ridgeline. From the few words that he understood he knew the language had to be Arabic. If they were about to be ambushed, the enemy sure were making one hell of a lot of noise about it. The soldier came into view, moving slowly down the ridgeline towards them, all the time speaking into an enormous radio handset that he had glued to his ear. The radio was of an ancient Soviet vintage and it all but obscured the soldier's head. Mat signalled to the rest of his team that they should hold their fire. Nothing about the way the enemy soldier was behaving suggested that he had detected their presence. The radio handset was so large it reminded Mat of a scene from a cartoon. He had visions of a string looping across the rocks to link up with another, equally vast, handset on the other side of the valley.

'Pssst . . . Buddy! I ain't never used one of these things before,' CIA Bob whispered across to Mat, as he tried to bring his own Diemaco to bear on the enemy figure. 'What do I do if he points his gun at me?'

'Nice time to tell me, Spooky,' Mat hissed back. 'You pull the trigger and try to bloody shoot him, mate, that's what.'

'Tee-hee . . . Well . . . OK, then,' CIA Bob chortled. 'Come an' get it, Talibutthole.'

'Bloody CIA Bob,' Mat muttered under his breath, as he kept the enemy soldier in his sights. 'Bloody little midget with a big bushy beard. 'Bout as much use as an ashtray on a bleedin' motorbike, that's what you are, mate. If it all goes noisy, don't you go getting us all killed now, Spooky. And whatever else you do, don't go pointing that gun anywhere in my direction.'

For fifteen minutes or so, the enemy soldier remained where he was carrying out a long and animated conversation on the radio. Mat figured that he had to be oblivious to the fact that a unit of heavily armed British special forces were ready to blow him to pieces. He was itching to ask CIA Bob what the enemy soldier was talking about. But before he got the chance to do so, the enemy figure moved off down the ridgeline, passing by some fifteen yards from their position. Mat felt sure that he was going to spot them, but his concentration still seemed focused on the giant radio handset. In normal circumstances, Mat would have captured or killed the enemy soldier, just in case. But it was impossible to do so with the guy permanently talking on the radio.

Mat followed the lone operator in his gun sight as he proceeded down the ridgeline and linked up with the rest of his unit, about half a mile further on. Together, they disappeared into the trees to the west of them. Some twenty minutes after the enemy had disappeared Mat stood his men down from their ambush positions. They gathered around for a hurried 'Chinese parliament' – a group discussion to take stock of what had just happened.

'I reckon he saw us and was bluffing and they'll be back later with a larger force,' Mat announced. He said this partly in order to see what the others were thinking.

'Bullshit – the guy never even realised we were here, bro,' Sam replied. 'He was kinda glued to the radio set, and that was where his world ended. He coulda stepped right over you, bro, and still not noticed.'

'Say, that was the largest radio piece I ever seen in all my born days,' CIA Bob added. 'You reckon it was steam-powered or somethin'? Has to be some reason to build 'em that goddam big.'

'You must've had a handle on what he was saying,' Mat said to CIA Bob. 'Any clues there, mate?'

'Heap of crap from what I could make out. First, he was trying to locate his buddies cos he'd lost them on the hillside and was tryin' to rejoin them. You probably guessed that much, anyways. Then there was a lot of stuff about Ramadan comin' up – that's the big Muslim festival a bit like Christmas but lasts one hundred times as long or seems to –'

'I know what bloody Ramadan is, mate,' Mat interjected.

'Hey, take it easy, I was just explainin' . . . Then he was going off on some story about a lost goat which they wanted to catch and kill for the Ramadan feast – by which time, buddy, I lost interest, tell you the truth. They're just the little guys, far as the AQT set-up round here goes. And they sure as hell weren't out lookin' for us, I got no doubts about that.'

'Well, that's a bloody relief,' said Mat. 'Means we can stay put, instead of hauling all this kit over to another OP.'

After the surprise visit by the enemy patrol, the men went back to their sentry positions. By mid-morning things started to liven up down in the Naka Valley. On the flat stretch of ground several hundred young men and boys had gathered together. They were dressed in white djellabas – long, flowing robes – and the ubiquitous white turbans. Under instruction from half a dozen older men they began carrying out running, jumping, press-ups, sit-ups and other exercises. There was nothing overtly sinister in these PT-type exercises, and no weapons were involved. But Mat figured that this had to be what the US intelligence boys had picked up on – in which case it had to be some sort of unarmed combat training school for terrorist recruits. Mat shot off several dozen rolls of film using his massive telephoto lens, and took notes of the numbers and ages of the trainees.

As the heat built into the afternoon the training came to a halt and the valley became deserted again. Mat wondered whether the terrorist recruits were all in the classrooms now, learning how to make chemical bombs so as to nuke London or something. It was a frightening prospect. He used the down time to transfer his digital stills on to CIA Bob's Psion, so that they could compile and file their first intel report. In the briefings back at Bagram they had been told that the massive bombardment of the Naka Valley was scheduled for five days from now, which gave them time to research and prepare the targets to be hit. By the time they settled down for their second night in the OP there had been no further significant enemy activity in the valley.

But sometime in the early hours Mat felt himself being shaken awake.

'Hey, buddy, break out your NVGs,' Sam whispered. 'I got a treat in store for you.'

Somewhere above them in the brilliant starlit sky there was the indistinct drone of an aircraft. As Mat donned his goggles, Sam pointed over towards the far side of the valley. As he searched in that direction, Mat picked up a giant tunnel of infrared light beaming down from the sky. It was only visible with the aid of the NVGs. In the eerie green glow of the goggles Mat could follow the infrared searchlight as it illuminated whole swathes of the mountainside. The aircraft operating the searchlight was flying a grid pattern. Mat watched the invisible beam probing among the crags for what he presumed were cave entrances where the enemy might be hiding.

'Holy fuck,' he said, under his breath. 'That's some Maglite they're using up there.'

'That, bro, is a Spectre gunship searching for the enemy,' Sam replied, proudly. The Spectre is a US Airforce C-130 Hercules aircraft transformed into an armoured aerial gun platform, with an unparalleled search and destroy capability. 'You see it, bro, you know, lighting up the whole hillside with infrared? It's checkin' for any signs of the enemy. Awesome, ain't it, bro?'

'Yeah . . . awesome . . .' Mat replied. 'I just hope they don't clock our position and decide to hose us down by mistake.'

Mat had heard too many stories of friendly-fire incidents involving US aircraft during past conflicts in the Gulf and elsewhere. After half an hour or so the Spectre flew off in the direction of the Shah-i-Khot valley, to the east of them. It hadn't engaged any targets, which suggested that its search of the Naka Valley had been a fruitless one.

After an otherwise uneventful night Mat shook himself awake at the start of their third day in the OP. As he did so, he spotted CIA Bob rooting around in his tiny rucksack and pulling out some rations.

'Where the bloody hell's he keep getting it from, mate?' Mat whispered to Sam, in amazement. 'I mean, we're all rationing ourselves. I dunno how he does it, but, what are we, three days into the OP, and that tiny little rucksack of his is still full of chocolates, biscuits and the like.'

'Jesus . . . I've no idea, bro,' Sam replied, stifling a yawn. 'Reckon Spooky there must've been up half the night stealing yours.'

'Reckon you've got a point there, mate,' Mat said with mock suspicion, turning to inspect his bergen. 'Wouldn't put it past him. He's got the neck of a giraffe, Spooky has. My sack keeps bloody well shrinking, yet he just keeps on pulling stuff out of his. It's like the bloody Tardis, that little bag of his.'

It had already become a standing joke among the SBS soldiers that CIA Bob would eat almost anything. He even seemed to like the British Army ration biscuits. These were dry, tasteless lumps of cardboard, which were pretty universally despised. But CIA Bob always seemed to be munching away contentedly from an open packet. As they were impossible to eat without water, the SBS lads were more than happy to unload all their biscuits on to him. The men were trying to stick to their daily 1.5-litre water ration, but the heat and the altitude was making it impossible to do so. Mat knew that soon he would somehow have to replenish their water supplies. He kept thinking about that tiny spring that he'd discovered some 3,000 feet lower down the mountain. At some stage they'd have to use it, regardless of the risk.

By lunchtime that day they had observed another of the early-morning PT sessions. Mat and CIA Bob were now ready to send in their first sitrep to JSOC headquarters. That first sitrep contained several transcripts from CIA Bob's intercepts, reports of the enemy movements in the region, a detailed description of the PT sessions and photos to illustrate. The report concluded that so far, at least, the Naka Valley looked to be bang on target for the planned air strikes. And in sending that report, Mat, Sam and CIA Bob had pretty much given the go-ahead to bomb the Naka Valley back into the Stone Age.

As first light touched the mountain peaks above Balkh a golden yellow, Ali shook himself awake. It was time. He joined his brothers for pre-dawn ablutions and prayers. It was still dark all around them. Despite the hardship, it was exhilarating being on the front line – especially on a morning like this, when a counter-attack was about to get underway. The previous day, Commander Omer, Ahmed, Ali and the rest of their unit had 'surrendered' to the Northern Alliance forces. Only, it had been a mock surrender, a ruse. And just as the brothers had expected, the NA had taken the brothers at their word, as honourable Muslims, and accepted their so-called surrender at face value. In keeping with Afghan tradition, they had even allowed the brothers to keep their weapons.

The fools, Ali was thinking, as the brothers prepared for their treacherous attack. *We will take no prisoners. The fools – we will show them no mercy and we will annihilate them.*

During the night, Commander Omer had related the story of the seven hundred Jews of the Bani Quraiza tribe who were beheaded in the time of the Prophet Muhammad. According to Omer here was proof that it was justified in Islam to kill prisoners. 'Remember what it says in the Koran,' Omer had told them. '"It is not for the Prophet that he should take prisoners of war until he has made a great slaughter in the land."' As far as Ali was concerned, the Northern Alliance had sided with the infidels, and so they deserved no mercy anyway. He would happily slaughter them all and needed no encouragement from Omer to do so.

Last night, Omer had put the final touches to their plan of attack. It would be a lightning raid across the valley, the brothers deliberately launching their assault through a minefield. This would be practically suicidal, which is why the enemy would never expect it of them. It would give the brothers the vital element of surprise. Ali was disappointed that he had not been placed in the vanguard of the assault, but he knew that in some ways his role was even more dangerous. He was to create the diversion, so that the brothers would have a clear run of things as they launched their surprise attack.

As they finished their prayers, brothers from other units started to file silently into their positions. Omer had sent word out that they would be starting the counter-attack at first light. Soon, there were some hundred fighters gathered together with Ali's unit. Shortly before the start of the attack, Ali moved off with Sadiq, his Saudi brother, to the far end of the group of mud-walled buildings where they were being held 'prisoner'. They settled down behind a large rock and Ali prepared the RPG launcher for action – the weapon that he would use to create the diversion. Sadiq squatted down next to him with a rucksack stuffed full of RPG rounds.

Ali was glued to his watch as the second hand swept round towards 0600 hours, the pre-arranged time for the attack to start. By then he figured it would be just about light enough for him to aim and fire the RPG. He checked for one last time that the launcher was properly loaded and that the fuses were set on the first round. He flipped up the sight and made sure that it was clear of grit and mud. Then, in a hushed whisper, Ali ran through the battle plan one more time with Sadiq.

'You remember Omer's instructions, brother? We fire the first rocket from here at six o'clock dead. Then we get back down the rock. Then we make for a position higher up the hill, behind those buildings. After thirty yards or so, we stop, reload and fire again. Then we move again, and fire again, drawing the enemy fire as we do so. For as long as we have rockets left we keep firing – so that we give the brothers as much diversionary cover as possible. You got it?'

'*Al-hamdu Lillah*,' Sadiq replied. He had given up so much to come and join the jihad. But the fact that Sadiq had a family back home in Saudi Arabia hadn't seemed to hamper his performance as a holy warrior. Sadiq had more than proven himself steadfast under fire. He took risks and fought as hard as any of the brothers, Ali included. And he made an excellent RPG loader, of that much Ali was certain.

A few seconds before 0600 hours, Ali hauled himself up from cover, bracing one foot on the rock in front of him. He already had the launcher on his shoulder. It always felt so strangely front-end-heavy with the grenade attached. He began searching for the target that he and Sadiq had identified. There was an army truck some three hundred yards away across the valley – well beyond the accurate range of the RPG. It would be a miracle if Ali managed to hit it. Taking his time, he lined up the metal sights on the truck, which was just visible through the dawn stillness. He braced himself for the recoil and squeezed the trigger gently. Even if he could just get a couple of shots close enough it would create the desired diversion. On the dot of 0600 hours the RPG let out a great whoosh and gout of flame and the rocket streaked out in front of Ali towards the target.

Without even stopping to check if the rocket had struck home, Ali jumped down and suddenly he and Sadiq were running hell for leather up towards the higher ground. Now he could hear the loud crackle of a Degtyarev (a 7.62mm light machine gun fed by a circular magazine) just to their backs, where another of the brothers was providing covering fire for their RPG attacks – one more element of the planned diversion. Then Ali heard the answering clatter of a Degtyarev starting up from across the other side of the valley, and bullets spattered into the sand and rocks where he and Sadiq had just been standing. The enemy had woken up to the attack.

They raced up to the cover of a low building and then stopped. As they reloaded, Ali could see that Sadiq was excited, the adrenalin coursing through his veins. His hands were shaking, fumbling as he tried to slot the second rocket on to the launcher. *Come on Sadiq, come on*, Ali urged, as he imagined the other brothers charging down into the valley below them. It wouldn't take the enemy long to work out that far from surrendering, the brothers were launching a massive counter-attack and battling for their very lives.

Finally, the rocket clunked home. As Ali leapt up to fire, the first mortar round slammed into the buildings some thirty yards away, and machine-gun bullets started kicking up the dirt all around him. '*Allahu Akhbar! Allahu Akhbar!*' Ali began yelling as he lined up the sights, fired and dropped down again, all in the space of a few seconds. This time, Ali heard the crump of the rocket exploding across the valley. As they broke cover and ran further up through the village, the mortar barrage seemed to chase their very shadows. They reloaded, aimed and fired again in a frenzy of activity, and then they heard a heavy diesel engine starting up from across the valley. Sound travelled well in the early-morning still-ness, and Ali and Sadiq knew that the enemy must have started up the truck to move it out of the range of the RPG. Their diversion was working.

Ali heard the clatter of a third Degtyarev machine gun opening up now, this time out in the no man's land lying between their positions and those of the enemy. In his mind's eye he could see Ahmed, his huge Yemeni bear of a brother, spraying the Degtyarev in front of him as he led his unit in a crazed charge across the minefield. Back in the training camp the brothers had been taught how to use the Degtyarev to pour machine-gun fire into the ground as they ran forward. The Degtyarev could put out four hundred rounds a minute. At that rate, rounds shot into the ground some thirty feet ahead of a runner would detonate any mines without harming him. At least that was the theory. It was a method of surprise attack that the mujahidin had perfected over the years spent fighting the Red Army. But it was a pretty basic technique and it often went wrong.

Ali knew he had to keep firing the RPG, drawing the enemy's attention away from the main thrust of the attack. It was about four hundred yards across the no man's land before Ahmed and the sixty brothers with him would hit the enemy positions. Ali figured it would take the brothers a good minute to cross that terrain. Another rocket was ready. Ali leapt up, aimed and fired, and as he did so one of the enemy tanks opened up, a heavy shell slamming into the earth just behind him.

Diving back behind cover Ali couldn't believe that he

and Sadiq were still alive. They had mortars and heavy machine-gun fire pouring down on them, and now a tank had opened up with both its main cannon and heavy machine gun. The supporting fire of the Degtyarev to their backs had been silenced: perhaps the gun had jammed, or maybe the brother had achieved glorious *shihada*. All Ali knew for certain was that they'd drawn a murderous barrage of fire down upon themselves. For a split second, he felt pinned down, unable to move, trapped in the ebb and flow of the explosions. But he forced himself to his feet, grabbed Sadiq and they ran, bent double, along a drystone wall towards a nearby bunker, red-hot lead and shrapnel thrumming the air as they passed. Ali wanted to get in one last shot before the brothers reached the enemy positions and attacked.

As they reached the bunker a tank shell slammed into the wall where they'd just been crouching. They loaded the RPG again. Then they heard a new noise, a series of dull flat crumps from across the valley. Ali and Sadiq didn't know it yet, but this was the sound of mines exploding. One of the brothers had just had his legs blown off as he charged across the minefield. It was Mohamed al-Jihadi, Ali's Algerian doctor friend, the brother whose name signified that his only allegiance was to the Umma, the world Islamic community united under Islam. Ironically, he had just died while charging down positions occupied by the Northern Alliance troops – who themselves were fellow Muslims.

Ali was just about to jump up and fire again, when he heard the frenzied cries of, '*Allahu Akhbar! Allahu Akhbar!*' drifting across the valley. The brothers must have reached the enemy lines already. There were the sharp reports of AK47s being fired and the crump of grenades going off. Then Ali was up again, above the parapet, and firing the RPG. He was sorely tempted to take a look to see how the attack was going, but he knew that it would be suicide to do so.

As the incoming fire rained down on their new position, Ali and Sadiq dived into the bunker to take cover. They knew now that their diversion had worked. Ahmed and the other brothers had taken the enemy by surprise and were across the valley, getting in among them.

6

VILLAGE PEOPLE

BY the evening of day three in the Naka Valley, Mat and his team were becoming increasingly aware of just how inhospitable it was up on that mountain summit. They had more or less acclimatised to the altitude now. The remnant symptoms of AMS were little more than a mild headache and persistent nausea. But they were becoming badly dehydrated, and the cold was sapping their strength and alertness. Bundled up in all their Arctic survival gear they were still feeling the chill, and their ability to operate effectively was being compromised.

Nothing else was living up there on that barren peak. The goatherds stayed down in the valleys. Even the wildlife kept away. The only other living thing seemed to be the eagles that occasionally soared overhead. Apart from the one enemy patrol, the SBS team seemed to have the mountain all to themselves. As they prepared for their third long night on the summit, each of the patrol members checked their weapons, just to make sure that no water had got into them during the day. This had become a regular ritual before bedding down for the night. If any moisture had got into the gun barrel it would freeze overnight, which could cause the gun to explode upon firing.

On the morning of day four, Mat decided that they had to risk breaking cover and head down to the spring at the bottom of the mountain. They were desperately low on water, and they needed to stay in the OP for three more days at least, until the scheduled air strikes went in. As he was bored stiff of staying in one place, Mat volunteered himself to go, with Sam as his support man. They set off at 8 a.m., glad to be on the move again. At first they retraced their steps uphill, keeping off the ridgeline. They skirted the mountain summit and began the descent, keeping some ten yards apart so as not to make an easy target if they ran into any enemy. Suddenly, as they were descending the bare escarpment, a lone figure appeared from nowhere. Mat, who had taken point, spotted him first, and dropped to a crouching position. As soon as he did so Sam followed suit.

There was no real cover to be had, so Mat signalled to Sam that they should stay down and wait out. They remained in a squatting position, their eyes glued on the lone figure as he made his way towards them. As the man approached Mat could see that he was shooing a herd of scraggy goats ahead of him. The Afghan looked to be as ancient as the hills and he was armed with nothing more than a stout stick. There were no standard operating procedures governing what to do in a situation like this: it was down to the individual operator's choice on the day. Mat remembered the written brief they'd been given on the locals back at Bagram: 'Avoid – treat as hostile.' But there was no way that he was going to shoot this old boy. If he spotted them, then they would take him prisoner. If he failed to spot them, they'd let him go on his way.

As the old man herded his goats up the slope, he was humming gently to himself, seemingly lost in a world of his own. Eventually, he ambled past some thirty yards away, seeming oblivious to Mat and Sam's presence.

'Dozy old bugger,' Mat said, once the old goatherd was well out of earshot.

'You reckon he didn't see us, bud?' Sam asked.

'Nope. Reckon he can't see sod all,' Mat answered. 'The poor bloke looked deaf as well as blind.'

'You sure?'

'Anyhow, even if he did see us he'd have thought he was bloody hallucinating,' Mat replied. 'You seen yourself recently? You look more like a mountain goat than you do an ace US Navy SEAL.'

'You ain't lookin' too hot yourself, bro,' Sam retorted. 'If I'm a goddam mountain goat then you're the yeti himself.'

On the day of their departure for Afghanistan, the lads had stopped shaving, and Mat and Sam had two weeks' facial growth by now. In addition to which, both of them were wearing a dirty shamag – a traditional Arab scarf – wrapped around the lower half of their faces, with a black woolly hat perched on top. Dressed in civvy-style combat trousers and jackets, they were far from easily identifiable as being from any conventional military force.

'You think we should just let the old guy go?' Sam added, as they watched him meander his way up the mountainside.

'Yep. Even if he did spot us, from thirty-odd yards away he'd have trouble telling us from a bunch of Talibs. Sure, they don't carry Diemacos. But they have got some pretty weird ex-Soviet kit – like that fuck-off radio set. I reckon the old boy'd be none the wiser.'

Mat and Sam continued down the mountain and some twenty minutes later the two men reached the spring. As Mat provided cover, Sam began to pump the filter, the clean mountain water spurting out the exit pipe into their bottles. The Katadyn filter was newly purchased out of the SBS's war fund, and it made short work of the little pool of spring water. Mat thanked his lucky stars that he'd remembered to bring it with them. It was going to prove a lifesaver on this mission.

The climb back up the mountain was uneventful. Once they were safely back at the OP Mat decided that they could allow themselves no more water resupply runs. Although he felt pretty certain that the old man hadn't spotted them, any foray down the mountain greatly increased their chances of being compromised. They would have to survive on the twenty-one litres of extra water that Mat and Sam had between them managed to carry back to their position. That was an extra three litres per person. On present rates of consumption it was not enough to last them through to the day of the air assault. But somehow they'd have to make do.

Once Mat and Sam had dumped the water in the OP, CIA Bob called them over to the sentry point overlooking the Naka Valley.

'Take a look at this, guys,' he said, quietly.

Down below them a large crowd of people was milling about in the mid-morning dust. The whole population of both villages seemed to have gathered together on the parade ground. Mat reckoned there had to be a couple of thousand or so in total. At the far end, a large black banner with white Arabic writing was displayed between two poles. Beneath the banner a wooden table had been set up, and a couple of elders in white robes and turbans were seated at it, addressing the crowd. Every now and then a lot of wild chanting and wailing would go up from the crowd. Pretty clearly, something important was taking place in the Naka Valley that day.

'What's the banner say, mate?' Mat asked CIA Bob.

'It's a verse from the Koran about the path from death to the afterlife, followed by an exhortation, "*Allahu Akhbar*" – "God is Great".'

'Reckon it's a recruitment drive for AQT?' Sam asked. 'You know, like advertising the glory of being martyred fighting the enemy?'

'Could be,' CIA Bob answered, non-committally. 'That'd fit with the intel we've been given on this area and the threat.'

'Looks like a big mobilisation drive to me,' Mat remarked. 'Means this must be one massive terrorist recruitment ground.'

'Possibly,' said CIA Bob. 'But somehow it just don't feel like that to me, buddy.'

'What else could it be then, mate?' Mat asked. 'I mean, it's no village fête, is it? You see any cake stalls? You see any apple-bobbing going on down there? Coconut shies? Are the Women's Institute down there, mate, selling raffle tickets for goldfish in bags or giant teddy bears?'

'*Apple-bobbing? Coconut shies?* What the hell you on about, buddy?' CIA Bob retorted.

'I'm just saying it's no village fête, is it?' Mat countered. 'And what the bollocks is going on down there – if it ain't a terrorist rally.'

'Well, let's look at this another way,' said CIA Bob. 'For starters, you see any guns down there, buddy? You see a single AK? A Degtyarev? An RPG? A pistol? A grenade, even? No. An' I don't either. We got more hardware among the seven of us than those couple thousand Afghans down there. Now, don't that strike you as being just the slightest bit strange, buddy? Especially now you've listened to my history lessons, and you know what a warlike race the Afghans are?'

'What're you suggesting, then?' Mat asked. 'You saying it's a rally for global peace or something?'

'Nothin'. I ain't suggestin' nothin'. I don't know what it is. I got no idea, buddy. No goddam idea. We just gotta sit here and do nothin' and watch and wait. An' we just gotta keep on doin' that until we figure out what the hell they're up to down there. It'll come to us, buddy, just takes a bit of time is all.'

'Fair enough, mate. Whatever you say.'

'Tell you what, though. It'd be real useful if you could grab a bunch more shots with that camera of yours. I wanna upload some to headquarters, so our boys back there can take a look see.'

Mat was glad to have something to do, so he went off to fetch his Nikon and the giant telephoto lens. By mid-afternoon the gathering was reaching some kind of climax, and Mat shot off several dozen photos. As Mat and Sam did a rough headcount, CIA Bob uploaded some of the shots back to JSOC headquarters. There were around 2,500 people down in the valley now, and every minute the behaviour of the crowd was becoming wilder and wilder. As the rally built to a crescendo, the women began an ululating, chanting cry that was repeated over and over and over again. Even at such a great distance it felt strangely hypnotic to the watching soldiers.

While the women wailed the men formed up into a long line, stretching up into the foothills. Then the team spotted a long, squarish object being hoisted up on outstretched arms and transported overhead. It moved along the line of men as if it were on a gigantic human conveyor belt. As the object passed, the women rushed forward to touch it, as if it were somehow magical or sacred.

'Goddammit!' CIA Bob suddenly cried out, as he smacked his fist against his forehead in frustration. 'Goddammit! I got it! That ain't no goddam al-Qaeda recruitment rally. You guys know what that is? It's fuckin' simple. It's a traditional Muslim funeral, that's all. It's just a fuckin' funeral.'

'Holy fuck. You sure, mate?' said Mat.

'Take a closer look at what they're carrying, buddy. You see it? It's a fuckin' coffin is all. A coffin. It's just a normal everyday goddam funeral takin' place in the Naka Valley, that's all it is.'

'You mean we've been uploading digital images of a bloody funeral back to headquarters at JSOC?' Mat asked, incredulously.

'You're goddam right we have, buddy,' CIA Bob responded. 'Jesus, I should've spotted it hours back. It just goes to show what preconceived ideas can do, don't it? I was seeing it like it was an AQT recruitment rally cos that's what we'd been told to expect. Do your head-count again, guys. But this time, only count how many women and children there are down there. See, it all depends on how you look at a situation, what perspective you take on it. It could be a terrorist training camp. And they could be Taliban. They could be al-Qaeda. Or then again they could be just a bunch of Afghan villagers. And it could just be a simple village funeral.'

'So what's the big idea with the coffin going overhead like that?' Mat asked.

'Simple, buddy. The men line up and move the coffin hand over hand – representing the journey from death to Paradise. The women, hell, they wanna piece of the action, too. So when the coffin goes past they rush forward to touch it, to pay their last respects to the dearly departed. See, the line of men goes uphill towards the base of the mountain – that's where they'll have their cemetery. In the Muslim faith the body has to be buried before sundown on the day of death, so they're carrying the coffin away to the burial ground. Simple, ain't it, when you don't view it all through a filter that says it's gotta be a fuckin' terrorist recruitment rally?'

'All right, but if you reckon it's only a village funeral where does that leave us with unleashing the mother of all air strikes?' Mat asked. The ramifications of what CIA Bob had been saying were just starting to hit home. 'I mean, those early-morning "unarmed combat training sessions" we were told about in the mission briefings – they could just as easily be schoolkids doing their physical training lessons. PT at the local village school. Couldn't they, mate?'

'Exactly what I just been thinkin', buddy,' CIA Bob said, quietly.

'I mean, you ignore the pre-mission intel briefing that the Naka Valley was the mother of all terrorist training camps,' Mat continued, 'and then you take what we've seen over the past few days at face value. And what does it all add up to? Bugger all. One enemy patrol with the world's biggest radio looking for a lost goat. And a few Talibs driving around in circles in their pickups. As for those two villages down there, all we've seen is one pretty wild funeral and what may as well be some early-morning gym lessons. It's a fookin' joke to mallet the place for that, ain't it?'

'Too right, buddy,' CIA Bob responded. 'But it'll cause a lot of upset back at headquarters if that's what we go an' tell 'em now, three days before the mother of all air assaults an' all. There's a lot of people if they were put in our shoes would stay firm on the original analysis, so as not to cause any dramas. Take the easy path and bomb the valley anyways, just in case.'

'What, it'll look stupid us changing the story now so let's go ahead and bomb the cunts anyway – is that what you're saying?' asked Mat, angrily. 'You're telling us it ain't nowt but a village funeral. And a village school. But let's bomb the fookers, anyway, just to be on the safe side? Is that what you're saying?'

'Hey, take it easy, buddy. That ain't what I said and I don't appreciate you puttin' the words in my mouth that I did. I'm just tellin' you there's a lot of high-up intel boys who've staked their reputations on this one. So, if we're gonna turn round now and tell 'em they're full of shit, we'd better be ready for the blow back. We'll have a fight on our hands, that's all I'm saying. We'll have a fight on our hands and we need to be prepared for it.'

'He's right, bro,' said Sam. 'He's just tryin' to warn you what's gonna happen if we report back that there's a school and a funeral and fuck all else to hit in the valley. Lot of big egos involved. Lot of unhappy boys back at home. But Mat's right, too,' Sam continued, turning to face CIA Bob. 'No ways can we bomb the shit out of this place if there's just a bunch of innocent villagers down there. That'd be a war crime, and it sure ain't somethin' that I wanna be part of.'

'Me neither, buddy,' said CIA Bob. 'Listen, I'm with you boys all the way. You think I'd have told you it was a fuckin' funeral if I wasn't? No way can we obliterate the place on the present evidence. So, unless a bunch of AQT boys turn up in the valley with Osama Binliner himself carryin' an atomic bomb in a suitcase or some-thin', I vote the air strikes are off. We came here with a job to do – to gather accurate intel on the target. We done our job. Right now, the intel we have says the targets're a couple of innocent villages. Intel says there ain't gonna be no bombing.'

'Too right, mate,' said Mat. 'Looks like the intel boys gave us a load of intel that was a crock of shite. So what's new? Takes men on the ground to work out just how shite it really was, though, don't it?'

'Ain't it always thus,' Sam remarked.

'You're right though, Spooky mate,' Mat said. 'There'll be nowt so difficult as convincing the fuckers they got it all wrong. Green Slime're a bunch of arrogant wankers. And they think us lot're a load of numpties with nowt between our ears. They'll have a right fit when we tell them they're full of it.'

The three men turned back to observe the valley. It was late afternoon by now and the funeral ceremony was coming to an end, villagers drifting off in various directions. It was time for CIA Bob and Mat to put together a report outlining their reassessment of the situation. The way they figured it, the more notice they could give that the target was a no-go, the easier it would be to get the air assets reassigned to other missions, which would make it easier to justify calling off the air strike. Their report was short and to the point, and once it was ready CIA Bob dialled up the satellites and prepared to send it to JSOC headquarters. But, as he fiddled with the lead connecting the Psion's serial port to the satphone, he couldn't get a connection. Eventually, he realised that the lead must've been damaged during the climb up the mountain and had finally stopped working.

'Goddammit!' CIA Bob cursed, throwing the lead to the ground. 'Fuckin' lead's shot. That's all we need.'

'What's the problem, mate?' Mat asked. 'The satphone

still works, don't it? There's nowt wrong with that. Just dial 'em up and tell 'em the air strikes are off for the reasons following.'

'Look, trust me, I know these guys,' CIA Bob responded. 'Without concrete evidence – photos and a written report they can place in front of the guys who call these things – there's no way they're gonna call this thing off. Careers are at stake. Heads can roll. No one wants to make the call. This thing could go as high as the President. And without a report and some images they can throw on the big man's desk, we stand about zero chance of gettin' them air strikes cancelled.'

'Listen, mate, take it easy,' said Mat. The frustration that CIA Bob was feeling was written all over his face. 'I'm a wizard with me hands, as all the girls in Poole know to their delight. I'll take a look at your lead – but in the morning, when it's light. In the meantime, Sam, you shoot some video of that funeral. Just in case they do try to flatten the bloody place we want as much evidence as possible to stop 'em. And Bob, why don't you make the satphone call anyway? Warn them that it ain't a justifiable target, and that we'll be getting the hard evidence to them in the morning.'

'You reckon you can fix it, buddy?' CIA Bob asked, hopefully.

'I reckon,' Mat replied, with a grin. 'Let's sleep on it. Tomorrow's a new day. And I'll be fresh as a bleedin' daisy in the morning.'

As Mat bedded down in his sleeping bag and tried to get some kip, his mind kept replaying the events of that afternoon. It was weird how things could have changed so quickly. One minute it was a massive terrorist training camp, the next a couple of innocent villages. Once CIA Bob had realised that it was just a funeral he and Sam had done another headcount, which was the deciding factor. Three-quarters of the people in the valley were women and children. Mat's mind drifted to Suzie, his girl back home. Mat knew he was good with children: nieces, nephews and those of their friends. He made them laugh. They liked him. He'd make a good dad, of that he was certain. And he'd only make a good soldier if he got the air strikes called off. He was dead certain of that, too. Just the very thought of bombing the Naka Valley now sent shivers up his spine.

After their fourth freezing night on the mountain summit, Mat awoke to an overcast, grey morning, with freezing fog blanketing the OP. It was bitterly cold, but he forced himself to get at least halfway out of his down bag, so that he could work on the Psion lead. After unscrewing the back of the serial connector with his Leatherman, he could see that three of the wires had come loose from their connecting pins. They would need resoldering if the lead was to work again. He broke out his tiny hexy stove and set light to a couple of the paraffin fuel blocks. As the flames started burning blue, Mat began heating up the tip of his Leatherman blade. Once he had it red hot, he used it to melt the remains of the solder on the connecting pins. After several unsuccessful attempts, he finally succeeded in reattaching all three wires.

'Was wondering why I brought that stove with me,' he said to CIA Bob, as he screwed the serial connector back together again. 'Seemed a bit pointless as we're on hard routine. But I'm bloody glad I did. Here you are, mate. Fingers crossed. Fire up the Psion and give it a whirl.'

The men gathered around CIA Bob as he got his computer up and running and set up the satphone. Then he connected one end of the lead to the phone and the other to the Psion, and started to dial up headquarters. Within seconds, the look on CIA Bob's face told Mat and the others that the lead was working. They slapped each other on the back, as CIA Bob gave a grinning thumbs up. Shortly after making a successful connection, the urgent intel report calling for the cancellation of all air strikes on the Naka Valley had been uploaded to JSOC in the USA.

'Message sent,' CIA Bob said, as he glanced up from his computer screen. 'Now we just gotta sit back and wait for the reply.'

'How long d'you reckon, mate?' Mat asked.

'No telling with these guys,' CIA Bob answered. 'But it's forty-eight hours or so 'til the air strikes're scheduled to go in – which is more than enough time, I'd say. Or should be.'

They spent the rest of that day checking on any further activity in the valley, just to make certain that they'd not made a wrong call. But all they could see now was a couple of villages and a school. No one was armed in the villages. The majority of the inhabitants were women and children, and the men who were there seemed to be living with their families. Of course, the Taliban was a religious movement and a sense of identity, so in theory any one of them could have been 'Taliban'. But the same could be said for any village across the country. There was certainly nothing that justified the intel assessment that the Naka Valley was the biggest terrorist training facility in the whole of Afghanistan.

'You still glad we called off the strike?' Mat asked Sam, as they were resting in the afternoon heat.

'We ain't called if off yet, bro,' Sam replied. 'But am I glad we trying to? You're damn right I am. Afghan

terrorists attacked my people on 9/11. They hit
Washington and they hit New York. But that don't mean
the whole Afghan nation are my enemies. I can't see
those young kids down there pulverised by my own coun-
trymen. Fact is, it'd be a war crime, and we'd have failed.'

'Reckon you hit the nail on the head, mate,' Mat said
'Hey, Bob, there any reply yet from JSOC on the report
we filed?'

'Yeah . . . there's a reply of sorts.' CIA Bob turned
around from his computer. 'It says our intel conflicts
with their previous intel assessment of the target. So,
they're sending a patrol up overnight to link up with us,
go through all our intel and get eyes on the target. Patrol
should be with us first thing tomorrow morning.'

'Who's it coming, mate?'

'Some Delta boys. Maybe a couple of CIA guys, too.
It's some of Commander Jim's lot who're out in the area
anyway. Probably been deployed to help lase the targets
when the air strikes go in. The air strikes that ain't now
happening, that is.'

'So JSOC don't trust what we're telling them?' Mat
asked.

'Somethin' like that, yeah, buddy,' CIA Bob replied.
'Still, let 'em come. Be kinda fun to see if they can manage
to go against our analysis, won't it?'

By late that afternoon, Mat knew that their water
situation was becoming desperate. His men had been
without water for nearly twenty-four hours now. Despite
having exceeded their original water rations and getting
the resupply from the spring, all of them were starting
to feel badly dehydrated. The classic early symptoms of
dehydration are extreme swings between hot and cold,
slurred speech, an inability to think straight or even to
make the simplest of decisions. In the mid-stages fingers

and feet become numb, body muscles cramp up and the tongue starts to swell. Finally, hearing and sight are affected and serious hallucinations occur: a shadow becomes an enemy soldier or a dangerous wild animal. Eventually, brain seizures can occur.

At 12,000 feet of altitude and suffering extremes of heat and cold, the patrol's resistance to dehydration was greatly impaired. Mat knew that he was suffering badly, and that some of the other lads were worse. His speech was becoming slurred, his movements sluggish, his thought processes laboured and muddy. But there was clearly no way that they could pull out of the OP. If they did, the bombing of the Naka Valley would go ahead, of that he was certain. From being tasked to guide in the mother of all air strikes, Mat and his team had suddenly become the protectors of the valley. It was an odd feeling for men who were basically trained to wage war. But if they were to stay on the mountain Mat knew that they had to find water. The one half of his brain that was still functioning properly was screaming at him that he had to get some fluid into his body, and fast. Desperate situations called for desperate measures, as far as Mat was concerned. Rousing himself, he ordered his men to break out all the trauma packs from their medical kits. Each pack contained three saline drip bags, or the equivalent of two litres of water. Forcing himself to keep going, Mat attached the first two bags to the branches of an overhanging fir tree. Then he got CIA Bob and Sam, two of the worst affected, and inserted a drip into their arm.

Over the next hour he fed both of them the contents of three saline drip bags. Then he repeated the process with the other patrol members, giving each man as much as he felt his condition warranted. Finally, an exhausted

Mat settled down to administer the last couple of drip bags to himself. As he did so the sun was sinking over the mountains to the west. The influx of fluid from the saline drip felt wonderful, like a complete lifesaver. But at the same time Mat wondered if the saline bags had provided enough fluid to keep his team going until the end of their mission.

Shortly after sundown, Mat began drifting into an exhausted sleep. Severe dehydration causes the body to go into shock. Even the saline drips hadn't prevented the body's natural defences from kicking in, and the craving for sleep was irresistible. With his men in such a bad way and no major enemy presence in the region, Mat took the tough decision to call off sentry duty for the night. They all needed a good night's sleep, as the following day was crunch time. If they didn't get confirmation that the air strikes were off, then it was likely that the valley was going to get blasted. Military inertia and the fog of war would have ridden roughshod over their objections, and the Naka Valley would have become just one more example of the 'collateral damage' of war.

Just after sunrise the following morning, the Delta patrol they had been told to expect made radio contact, and announced their imminent arrival at the OP. A couple of minutes later and they were there.

'Mat Morrisey, patrol leader,' Mat said, extending his hand to the lead Delta operator.

'Hi, Jim Beyrer, good to hook up with you guys at last,' the Delta patrol leader said, taking Mat's hand. 'Jesus, buddy, but you guys look like the walkin' dead.'

'Yeah. You got any water, mate? We're dying for some. I'd offer you a brew, but we've been on hard routine so hot drinks are off the menu. Plus, we've run out of water.'

'Sure, you guys take all the water you need. We just got

to make it down the mountain again today, then we got some vehicles waitin' for us with supplies. You can take it all, buddy. Or at least most of it. You need some rations too? We got some MREs. Take some MREs an' all, buddy.'

'Nice of you to offer,' Mat said, as he grabbed the Delta patrol leader's water bottle. 'Take a seat,' he added, offering him a boulder to sit on.

'You got any news on those planned air strikes?' Mat gasped, after draining a whole water canteen. 'Cos there's no AQT training camps down in that there valley, that's for bloody certain.'

'Yeah, so we figure from your reports,' the Delta patrol leader replied. 'You been causin' some real fireworks back at JSOC. Commander Jim sends his regards, by the way. Says he'd expect nothin' less from you guys than to cause a fuckin' riot, which seems like you have done. But this here's the CIA dude on our team, an' he can tell you more about that side of things.'

'Hi. Name's Shorty. I'm the Agency guy. I know Bob – how you doin', buddy?'

'Good, buddy, good. Just a little thirsty is all.'

'I bet,' CIA Shorty said. 'I guess the rest of you must be the SAS boys.'

'It's S-*B*-S,' Mat replied, through gritted teeth. 'SBS. That's us.'

'Sure, S-*B*-S. Well, whatever, you boys have been causin' some serious ructions back home,' the grinning CIA officer continued. 'You'll be pleased to know your report went right to the very top. To the desk of the President of the USA, cos no one else felt like callin' this one either way. Word is it went to your own top dog, too, Prime Minister Blair.'

'Pleased to hear it, mate,' Mat said. 'So what's the result?'

'Result is air strikes have been called off, that's as long as we concur with what you guys're sayin'. Seems like they had a bit of a problem with your intel at first, cos you're a bunch of Brits and the initial intel assessment was done by our boys. Went down like a lead balloon. So we been sent up to check you out – make sure you're sane and you ain't seein' things or somethin'.'

'What's the verdict then, mate?' Mat asked, breaking into a grin.

'Well, I reckon you guys gotta be a bunch of certifiable lunatics to stop out on this godforsaken mountaintop for, what is it now, five days?'

'Six,' CIA Bob interjected. 'Get it right, buddy, it's six.'

'Six is it? Like I said, you guys gotta be mad,' CIA Shorty continued. 'But one thing I am sure of, you're a damn sight smarter than those desk-bound fucks who did the initial intel assessment in the first place. Fuckin' "mother of all terrorist training camps" my ass. I seen your photos. Like you all said, a goddam funeral's a goddam funeral, and no amount of hoping can turn it into an AQT recruitment rally. And a school's a goddam school, whichever way you look at it.'

'Does make you wonder, don't it?' Mat interjected. 'I mean, we was briefed that this was the biggest al-Qaeda training camp in the whole of Afghanistan. The Naka Valley? It's no more a bloody al-Qaeda training camp than Butlin's or Disneyland.'

'Yeah, them desk-bound fucks sure must have some active imaginations,' said CIA Shorty. 'Still, that's why you always gotta get eyes on the ground . . . Tell you what though, any more of those images you took of the funeral or the school, they'd be real useful on calling this one.'

'Sure, mate. You can take a couple of the gigabyte memory cards from the camera,' Mat replied. 'I've uploaded all the pics on to me computer anyways, so you're welcome to 'em.'

'You're a real gentleman,' CIA Shorty said. 'An' I'd expect nothin' less from a Brit and a member of the SAS, ain't that right, Bob?'

'S-B-S, buddy,' CIA Bob replied. 'Get it right – SBS. May seem like a small thing, but these guys don't take kindly to a "B" being mistaken for an "A". Kinda touchy about it. But you're darn right, you do have to watch your manners around these Brits. And as for the toilet etiquette, that sure takes a while gettin' used to.'

'So, if we're all agreed we'll upload some more of your photos to JSOC,' said CIA Shorty, ignoring CIA Bob's last comment. 'We'll send a recommendation that you boys are still pretty much sane, and then we'll get confirmation up to you guys just as soon as we can that the air strikes're off, at which time I guess your mission will be over.'

'Be sad to leave this place.' Mat gazed around at the heap of boulders and the pine trees. 'It was starting to feel just like home.'

Pretty quickly, the Delta patrol members offloaded their food and remaining water supplies and set off back down the mountainside. By mid-afternoon, CIA Bob had received confirmation from CIA Shorty that the bombing of the Naka Valley had been postponed indefinitely. As Mat, Sam and CIA Bob gazed down into the valley the first flakes of a snowstorm began to swirl around them. They could just make out a bunch of kids playing in the village far below. As they watched, they realised that it was their work that had prevented the valley – and the kids – from being pulverised. These men were soldiers first and foremost. But to have saved so many lives that otherwise would have been so senselessly annihilated was a mighty good feeling.

The path was rocky and it was a pitch-black night. The brothers were moving carefully so as to try to keep their footing. Everyone was exhausted, having been on the move for eight hours continuously without a break. To make matters worse it was bitterly cold. So cold that the water in the bottles in the brothers' packs had frozen solid. Six hours' walking and no chance of a drink. A biting wind was ripping through the brothers' clothing, chilling them to the bone.

As they snaked their way down the mountainside they knew that, somehow, they had to hurry, or at least find a way to delay their pursuers. After the glorious assault where Ahmed had led the attack across the minefield and they had slaughtered the enemy, Omer's unit had lost battle after battle as the US warplanes had pounded their positions. And now they were on the run again. The Northern Alliance dogs, aided by the infidels and hypocrites, were hot on their trail.

Every time the brothers reached a trench that had recently been occupied by their fellow Talib fighters they would split into two groups. One, led by Commander Omer, would advance down one side of the trench, shining a flashlight to see if anyone was still alive in there or if there were any walking wounded. The other group would take the opposite side of the trench. But each time they did so, the dark earth was littered only with corpses, the blasted trench empty of life. It seemed as if there was no one left alive from their Taliban brothers on that bleak mountainside – that they were the last group of brothers in their position to have started the retreat.

It always seemed to be like this, Ali reflected, with a flash of stubborn pride. During the weeks of conflict, the foreign fighters were always the last to fall back from the enemy, always the keenest to fight to the last man. He glanced back up the mountainside. Their pursuers were gaining on them – he could see their torches high up on the ridgeline. Maybe Allah might choose him this night, Ali reflected, with grim satisfaction, offering him the glorious chance to be *shaheed*. If so, he would join the other martyred brothers in Paradise. But somehow he felt as if he was not yet finished with this war and this world and he would prefer to survive and to fight.

Commander Omer took advantage of a slight pause in their headlong descent, while his men crossed a perilous mountain stream, to order some mines to be placed on the path behind them. There was a fumbling of cold, stiff fingers in the darkness as fuses were primed and safety switches thrown to the armed position, then the mines were shoved into rough holes dug with a bayonet in the rocky earth.

They knew they had to get to the road somewhere below them and then across the river, to reach any modicum of safety. On the far bank, their Talib brothers had established a new front line, or at least that's what the last radio message had told them. How long that new front line would hold was another matter entirely, particularly when the US warplanes discovered their new positions, sometime the following morning. Then the relentless pounding would begin again.

The brothers set off, hurrying down the path as best they could. After some twenty minutes they heard a faint Boom! echoing out across the darkened valley behind them, followed by an unearthly screaming. One of their mines must have found its mark. Checking behind them, the brothers could clearly see the torch beams of their pursuers converging on one spot, which must have been their casualty. Ali prayed to himself that it was one of the *kafir* American dogs who had been hit by the mine. Whoever it was, it might just slow the enemy down a little.

A few minutes later, there was the soft pffuuuttt of a flare being fired high up on the mountainside. Half a dozen more followed, the streak of the rocket followed by a blinding white light hanging in the dark sky, like some bizarre front-line firework display. Soon, the whole mountainside was lit up in an unearthly, phosphorous glare. All the brothers could do was to take cover, crouching down behind rocks and flattening themselves on to the earth, so that their pursuers couldn't pick them off from above. For many a fighter, this would have been a terrifying experience – feeling so totally pinned down and exposed. But not for the brothers. If death found them, then so be it. It was what they had come here for. They would fight until Allah willed it otherwise, and then they would welcome death's embrace. For Paradise beckoned.

As the flares drifted lazily to earth, the brothers heard excited shouting from up on the hillside, directly behind them. The Northern Alliance soldiers had spotted them. They were less than half a mile away now, and so the brothers were within range of their Kalashnikovs. Within seconds, the first rounds started cracking into the rocks all around them. At that range the crack of the enemy weapons remained muffled, the incoming fire still pretty inaccurate. But it wouldn't remain so for long. The brothers knew that they were outnumbered and outgunned. If they stayed where they were, their pursuers would close in on them and they would be finished.

Suddenly, Omer was on his feet and urging his men to break cover and follow him. There was no doubt about it, he was a fearless and talented commander. The brothers raced ahead now, all attempts at concealment abandoned as they went sliding down the mountainside.

Then, somewhere behind them, the brothers heard a firefight breaking out. There were bursts of AK47 fire going in either direction. Their pursuers must have stumbled upon another group of retreating Taliban – giving the brothers a few precious minutes in which to try to make good their escape. They surged ahead, reached the foot of the mountain and hit level ground. In the mad scramble down the mountainside weapons had kept banging against rocks and several were damaged. The brothers raced on across a darkened field and finally reached a road with a few shadowy houses grouped around it. Here, Commander Omer paused for a second so they could catch their breath.

'Shall we ambush them here, brothers?' he panted, gesturing to the mud houses. 'We have cover. We can turn and fight. We have the ammunition to take them on. And we have God on our side and so, *insh'Allah*, we cannot fail.'

Looking around them, the brothers could see that the village offered great cover for an ambush. And Commander Omer was right – they were well armed. Between them they had six RPGs (and scores of RPG rounds), two Degtyarevs, dozens of hand grenades and several AK47s.

'*Al-hamdu Lillah* – let us do it,' Ahmed urged excitedly, his teeth showing white in the darkness. 'Either we kill them all, or die here fighting if Allah – peace be upon Him – so wills it. And if that happens we will be most glorious *shouhada'a*.'

'Yeah, we might well be *shouhada'a*, but is that the best way to kill as many of the *kafir* as possible?' Ali countered. As the weeks had gone by Ali had become more and more assertive, showing a greater willingness to voice his opinion. His innate intelligence made him a natural leader, one prone to taking the initiative. 'That's what I came here for,' he continued. 'I'm not so keen to find death before I kill the *kafir*, the invaders of the Islamic lands, the killers of our Muslim children. These cowards refuse to face us like men in battle, but rain death down on us from the skies, with their warplanes. I came here to kill them. To kill them all. If Allah – peace be upon Him – so wills that I die in the process, then so be it. And if Allah – peace be upon Him – so wills that we live to fight another day, then He may grant us all the glorious chance to do what the heroic Nineteen Lions did: to get close to the *kafir*, the Great Satan, the Americans, and kill them. If we die here then in that we will have failed.'

There followed a quick discussion among the brothers, but Ali's viewpoint eventually held sway. So they headed on across the plain towards the river, avoiding the road bridge and the road itself for fear it might be watched. As they crossed the open fields in single file, there were dead bodies sprawled in the dust. As Ali hurried on, he accidentally stepped on a corpse, and it made a sharp, whooshing noise like a massive belch, as the air trapped inside the body escaped under his weight.

Ali noticed there were five or six other corpses near him. Black beards. Black turbans. Faces glowing faintly in the moonlight. All of them brothers. All of them drilled through by American bombs and bullets dropped from the air. Brothers who'd died fighting for what they believed in, their religion, their cause. It struck Ali then

A C130 Hercules delivers vital supplies to the SBS lads, as they prepare for their mission to assault 'the mother of all terror training camps'.

US Delta Force operators head into the Naka Valley with their British SBS brothers-in-arms. A rocky river bed provides the only route in.

The SBS team on the climb into the Naka Valley, location of the 'mother of all terror training camps'. CIA Bob is second from left, clutching a packet of 'inedible' British army ration biscuits!

SBS troopers on climb into Naka OP, carrying 100-pound bergens and with Diemaco assault rifle and Minimi SAW machine gun held at the ready.

SBS soldiers on climb into the Naka Valley hit the snow line. As well as all their cold weather gear, they're each carrying 500 rounds of ammo, grenades, comms kit, food rations for a week and nine litres of water.

The Naka Valley observation post (OP), at 12,000 feet, overlooking 'the mother of all terror training camps'. The SBS team spent a week here in freezing conditions, surrounded by the enemy and running out of water.

An SBS operator keeps watch over a 'terrorist training camp' in the Naka Valley. A Nikon D1 digital camera is used for close observation work.

Using a Katadyn filter dehydrated SBS soldiers extract life-saving water from a seepage at the foot of the mountain.

Naka Valley elders peer into the vehicles carrying the special forces soldiers – as they befriend the villagers, instead of blasting them into oblivion.

Having been sent in to flatten the 'terror training camps' of the Naka Valley, the SBS soldiers realise the valley is full of women and children.

SBS, CIA and Delta Force operators meet the locals. Forty-eight hours earlier they had been poised to bomb their village back into the stone age.

SBS soldiers in cave entrance. They fought their way into caverns in Afghanistan, and found huge caches of Al Qaeda and Taliban weaponry.

Subterranean tunnels were terrorist bases holding huge caches of Al Qaeda and Taliban weapons, which were destroyed by UK special forces.

Hiding their faces with their turbans, the foreign Taliban prisoners arrive at
Qala-I-Janghi fortress by the truck-load.

One of the entraceways to Qala-I-Janghi. Its massive mud walls made the ancient
fortress all but invulnerable to Allied airpower.

that this was the field of the Martyrs. Yet none of them had been given even a chance to get close to the *kafir* and fight them, as they had all been killed from the air. It was all so one-sided, so frustrating and so wrong.

Commander Omer led the way, avoiding the soft, sandy areas and sticking to the hard-packed soil where other people had already trodden – their passage marking a safe route through the minefields that were bound to have been planted here at one time or another. Closer to the river, they passed a burned-out car. Something resembling a black statue of a human form was hunched over the steering wheel, silhouetted against the dark night sky. One of the brothers had burned to death here, as a US warplane had hit the vehicle and turned it into a raging funeral pyre.

As they reached the river, the men noticed with relief that there were soldiers massed on the other side. *Our Talib brothers*, they thought to themselves, as they prepared to swim across and join them. But just as they were about to enter the waters, one of the soldiers shouted a challenge across to them from the far river bank. He repeated the challenge and the brothers realised he was speaking in Persian – the language of the Northern Alliance, of the enemy. And then the brothers knew. Somehow, the enemy had already got ahead of them. Where the new Taliban front-line positions were supposed to be there were now only enemy soldiers.

As none of the brothers could speak Persian they were momentarily at a loss as to what to do. Suddenly, the soldiers on the far bank opened fire on them, bullets slamming into the river bank and RPG rounds ricocheting off the river. Within seconds two of the brothers went down, screaming, and then Commander Omer himself took a bullet in the right shoulder.

'ALLAHU AKHBAR!' Omer roared, rousing himself from the shock of the attack and opening fire with his AK. He was followed a split second later by the rest of the brothers, who put down a wall of return fire on the enemy across the river.

The brothers fought ferociously, blind to the danger before them. Within minutes the enemy guns had fallen silent. None of the brothers were under any illusions that the enemy had been routed though. Far from it – they had been fighting the Northern Alliance for far too long to fall into that trap. The enemy soldiers would have retreated into cover, waiting for the brothers to try the river crossing. And if they did so, the enemy would open up on them and cut them down when they were in the waters, at their most defenceless.

The brothers clambered back up the river bank, carrying their wounded with them. Ali was deeply saddened when he realised that one of them was Sadiq al-Saudia, his RPG loader from the battle at Balkh. He had a horrible wound to the chest and was begging the brothers to finish him off, so that he could leave this world of pain and hurt and be *shaheed*. Ali knew that Sadiq was close to Paradise now, but he still hated to see him suffer. Despite this, Ali knew that he couldn't help Sadiq. In Islam it was absolutely forbidden for a Muslim to kill a fellow Muslim in cold blood, even as a mercy killing. If Ali did so, then the both of them would go to hell.

As best they could the brothers squeezed in among some rocks, which provided at least a little cover from the enemy. The wounded were going into shock now, drifting off into a fitful half-consciousness and shivering uncontrollably. Every now and then, sporadic shots rang out from behind them, away towards the mountain, as

the enemy must have been finishing off the odd strag-
glers.

'That's it, brothers,' Commander Omer announced,
breaking the eerie post-battle silence that had enveloped
them. He had blood seeping from the bullet wound to
his shoulder, and was clearly in a bad way. 'By the grace
of Allah – peace be upon Him – we are surrounded.
They are behind us on the mountain and to our flanks,
and they are before us on the river. *Insh'Allah*, this is
where we will die.'

Ali thought about this for a moment. He was not one
to go wilfully against his commander, but he was
convinced that he and some of the other brothers still
had the fight left in them. There had to be a way out of
there and Ali wanted nothing more than to be able to
live to fight another day. He searched desperately in his
mind for a plan, a way to escape. And then he hit on
something.

'Listen, Brother Omer. *Insh'Allah*, some of us could
make a break for it,' Ali said in a hushed whisper,
addressing his injured commander. 'We could use the
river, swim out and let it carry us away downstream. We
could live to fight another day, brother. What do you
say?'

'But what about the wounded brothers?' Omer replied,
weakly. 'Are you willing to abandon them? You have
lived and prayed and fought alongside them on the front
for many months now. Surely you should stay here and
help defend them and, if Allah wills it, be martyred alongside them?'

'Brother Omer, I can't depart this world for Paradise
with peace in my heart knowing I have not killed at least
one infidel, preferably a cursed American.' As far as Ali
was concerned, his studies of the Koran had made it

clear that it was his Muslim duty to wage jihad against
the unbelievers, until injury or death prevented him from
doing so. As of now, he was neither injured nor dead,
so his priority had to be to carry on. 'Brother Omer, it
says of the infidels, in the Holy Koran: "Do you fear
them? Surely, Allah is more worthy of your fear. If you
are true believers, make war on them." I am not yet
ready to abandon the path of holy jihad.'

'You must do what you feel is right, Brother Ali,'
Commander Omer replied, after several seconds' silence.
'And what you feel the Prophet – peace be upon Him –
would want of you. As for me, I am finished. And you
will be leaving Sadiq and the other wounded brothers
here. That much is clear – they can go no further. For
us there is no escape,' Omer concluded, pulling a grenade
from one of his chest pouches.

'You are most gracious, brother,' Ali said, quietly, his
voice choked with emotion. 'You know we do not do
this – desert our brother warriors in their hour of need
– lightly. We do this so that – *insh'Allah* – we get a
chance to fight again and kill the *kafir*. Glorious Paradise
awaits you, Brother Omer, have no doubt. And when
you get there and when you have the honour of meeting
the Nineteen Lions, embrace them for me, brother. Listen
to their story of that glorious day. So that when we join
you there in Paradise, then you can tell us all about their
glory.'

'*Al-hamdu Lillah*,' Commander Omer replied. 'Brother
Ali al-Africani, the Lion Cub, get on your way. Take
whichever of the brothers will follow you. Take command
of them, Ali. Lead them well. I know that Ahmed will
choose to go with you. Keep him always by your side,
and heed his counsel. He is not a born leader, brother,
but he is a tireless and loyal deputy. I pray that Allah

blesses you with a safe journey . . . This is my journey to another place,' Omer added, raising up the hand grenade. 'And Brother Ali, if you do get the chance to get close to the *kafir*, kill one for me, will you? Slice off his cursed head. And write my name in blood across his infidel's forehead.'

Quickly as he could, Ali gathered together the brothers who wished to join him and outlined the plan to them. Then, slipping his AK47 across his back, he led the way down towards the river. As the cold water lapped around his feet, he turned to take one last look at the brothers they were leaving behind – among them Commander Omer and Brother Sadiq, two of his closest friends. Then he let the freezing waters carry him off downstream. As he did so he heard a series of chants ringing out from behind him – '*Allahu Ahkbar! Allahu Ahkbar!*' – followed by a massive explosion.

Finally, his brothers had found what they had come here for. Their path to Paradise.

7

MOUNTAIN INFERNO

SOME twenty-four hours after the cancellation of the Naka Valley bombing Mat, Sam and CIA Bob found themselves driving into the valley to meet the locals. In one of those crazy, flip decisions that define the madness of war, it was decided by the powers that be that they'd put a team in to do a 'feel for it on the ground'-type mission, as they weren't going to bomb the place. So, along with some of Commander Jim's 10th Mountain troops and the Delta patrol, Mat, Sam and CIA Bob found themselves heading into the valley to meet the people they had at first been sent in to bomb back into the Stone Age. Overhead, there were a couple of Predator UAVs providing top cover, and just to make a show of strength they had some F-18s roaring across the sky with their afterburners.

As soon as their convoy pulled up at the 'parade ground' – which turned out to be the village square – it was mobbed by a bunch of raggedy kids who came rushing out of the mud-walled buildings. Mat got down from one of the Humvees and spotted a bright-eyed

Afghan boy of about nine years old holding out his hand towards him. As he had a couple of boiled sweets still in his pocket from the OP, he placed them in the kid's hand. Pretty quickly, all of the soldiers were handing our toffees and Hershey bars and there was something of a carnival atmosphere in the village.

With the help of Ahmed, one of Commander Jim's translators, Mat tried to engage the Afghan boy in conversation. As he did so, CIA Bob decided to play a trick on them. With his laser-gun sight he put a red dot on to the kid's chest and began moving it around in a figure of eight. Realising what CIA Bob was up to, Mat had to think of an explanation fast. He told the Afghan kid that it was one of the F-18 jets overhead that had put the mark on him. Mat was quick to reassure the youngster that he was in no danger. He explained that he could talk to the aircraft without the kid even being aware of it and tell it exactly what to do. The Afghan kid went wide-eyed with amazement.

Just then, Ahmed told Mat that they had been invited into the village proper to meet the headman. Together with Sam, CIA Bob and CIA Shorty, Mat was led over to one side of the square where a rough shelter of branches provided shade. Four battered plastic chairs had been placed in a semicircle, and a group of ancient Afghan men were seated opposite on a carpet on the ground. Mat reckoned that one of the Afghan elders was the old goatherd that he and Sam had run into up on the mountain. He nudged Sam in the ribs, and indicated with his eyes the suspected goatherd, and from Sam's reaction he knew that he was right. After some formal introductions, the old man pointed at Mat and Sam and began speaking.

'He says he has seen you two before, up on the mountain,' Ahmed translated. 'Three days ago, he was with his goats. Strange men with guns up in the mountains are often dangerous, he says, so he tried his best to avoid you.'

'Yes, we saw him, too,' Mat said. 'Tell him he did a good job of pretending not to notice us.'

'The old man asks what you were doing up there?' Ahmed continued. 'He says you looked like you had been living up on the mountain and no one in their right mind does that.'

'Tell him we're not complete nutters,' Mat replied, grinning. 'We were doing a recce of this area from a distance, in preparation for paying the village a visit. But ask him who he thought we were and what he did about it?'

'The old man says he didn't know who you were, but he felt uneasy,' Ahmed said. 'So, he came down and told the other village elders what he'd seen. They decided not to say anything to anyone, because they don't like to get involved in the war.'

'Tell him that sounds very sensible,' Mat replied.

After they had been served with hot, sweet tea in tiny glasses, the village headman began speaking. He appeared very earnest and had a spirited glint in his old eyes.

'I have a question for you,' Ahmed translated. 'You come here with your vehicles and your guns. You have your aircraft flying overhead. They have their bombs. Is all of this directed against us? What have we done to you? I have never even met you before. I have never met any American before. I have never hurt your country or your people.'

'We're not all Americans, actually. I'm British,' Mat said. 'But tell him there were reports that al-Qaeda and Taliban soldiers had been gathering in this area to attack us. So we came to check if it was true.'

'So, you are British,' Ahmed continued, translating the village headman's reply. 'You British come back again? You have waged war on us many times before, and yet you come back to attack us again? You don't remember what happened the last time? You lost. Every time we defeated you. You had better guns, aircraft, vehicles – but still we beat you. You didn't learn the lesson then?'

'Tell him Afghan memories are long and it's a fair point, but we haven't come back to fight him,' Mat replied, with a grin. He had a soft spot for the belligerent old devil already. 'Tell him we have no desire to get beaten for a second time. But we would like to ask him about any AQT movements in the region.'

'The village headman wants to correct you. He says if you British lose again, it would be for a *fourth* time.' Even Ahmed was enjoying translating the conversation now. 'And even if you are British you look just like the Americans, he says, only you are more scruffy and untidy.'

Mat couldn't stop himself from letting out a chuckle. The headman was running rings around him.

'Tell the headman that we've just spent a week living on top of his mountain,' he said, once he'd recovered his composure. 'That sort of accounts for our appearance. We were up there trying to get an idea of what goes on in his valley.'

'The headman says he doesn't understand why you wanted to spend a week on top of the mountain, where it is freezing cold and there is no water. It would have been much easier just to have come here and asked him. Nothing goes on in this valley without his knowledge. If you had done that, you could have at least come here looking clean and respectable. He says that in the old days when the British came, at least they took pride in their appearance.'

Mat turned to the others in exasperation. But all he saw was a line of smirking faces as Sam, CIA Bob and CIA Shorty joined in the peculiarly light-hearted moment – one of Britain's finest special forces soldiers getting upbraided by an unarmed Afghan elder. With a mischievous glint in his eye the village headman carried on.

'He says he has seen many Afghan fighters – Taliban – going through his valley over the past few weeks. They are running from attacks by your warplanes in the Shah-i-Khot. They travel through here to Pakistan, where they know you cannot reach them. They do not stay long. Three or four days ago, several dozen men passed through in vehicles. They camped the night, and then moved on to the border with Pakistan. And one patrol passed through the hills on foot.'

'Yeah, we saw them,' Mat remarked.

'When the headman first saw your warplanes flying over, he thought you had come to bomb the Naka Valley. He says this would be a very bad thing to do, for all you would achieve is to make more enemies among the Afghan people. And he says that you are right, Afghan memories are very long.'

'Exactly,' Mat said. 'Which is why we've come here to talk to him, face to face, as friends.'

'He says in our tradition you do not come to someone's village, to the door of his house, bearing weapons – and expect a warm welcome.'

'Yep, I can appreciate that,' said Mat. 'But tell him we are in a strange country and we need to protect ourselves.'

Once Ahmed had finished translating Mat's last words, the village headman nodded, rose to his feet and swept his cloak around his shoulders. Then he strode away across the square, several of the other elders following him. As he did so, he muttered something over his shoulder.

'What did the mad old bastard say, Ahmed?' Mat asked.

'He told you to follow him. He will show you where the terrorists hid their weapons before they crossed the border into Pakistan.'

'What? After all he just said he's going to help us?' Mat grinned. 'Bloody hell, I'm warming to this old bugger. Doesn't beat about the bush much, but I can handle that.'

Over the next half an hour, Mat and the rest of the team did a complete 360-degree tour of the village. In deserted mud buildings they were shown massive caches of weapons, including RPGs, AK47s, Degtyarev and RPK light machine guns, grenades, and cases and cases of ammunition. There was enough weaponry hidden in the village to equip a good-sized army. At the end of the tour, the headman spoke again.

'He says, as he told you, there are no Taliban here,' Ahmed translated. 'You should know that they are regrouping in Pakistan and that they will keep fighting from there. He says that the Taliban killed his eldest son, because they caught him playing a tape of Western music. He says he would fight the Taliban tomorrow, if he had the means to do so, but up until now they have been too strong. He says there is one last thing he would like to show you.'

Mat and the others followed the village elder a good distance out of the village, into the foothills of the mountains. The path led past a massive boulder, behind which lay the opening to a cave. As Mat's eyes adjusted to the darkness, he realised that he was standing at the entrance to a huge, cavernous space which was stuffed full of arms. This was obviously where the AQT forces had hidden their prized weaponry: the Dushka heavy machine guns, heavy calibre mortars and boxes of mortar rounds, plus several Metva bazookas and what looked like crates of rockets from Soviet-era multiple rocket launchers. It was a veritable Aladdin's cave of weaponry.

After discussing with the village elders what to do about the arms caches, Mat and his men rigged the cave and the other weapons stores with plastic explosives. Once they had cleared all the villagers from the danger area, they proceeded to blow the arms dumps, a series of massive explosions ringing out across the Naka Valley. It wasn't quite how they'd imagined the climax to their mission playing out, when they'd first been briefed about it back at Bagram. But it was a more than satisfying – if unexpected – outcome to the mission. Before Mat, Sam, CIA Bob and the others made their departure, the village headman spoke to them one last time.

'He says that if you leave Afghanistan, the Taliban will return,' Ahmed said. 'It is like a cancer – you have to treat it all, kill it all. He says that if the Taliban come back and discover what you have done here today, you do not want to know what they will do to the people of his village. He wishes you a safe journey and he hopes that you may soon return. Next time, he says, come directly to his house and stay with him and his family. Don't spend a week on the mountaintop first, watching them and deciding whether it would be a good idea to drop bombs on his valley.'

'Can you believe it?' Mat said, as they drove away from the village. 'The headman knew what we'd been up to all along. He knew we'd been up there about to call in the JDAMs.'

'Ain't you glad you called off them air strikes now, buddy?' Sam asked.

'Too right, mate,' Mat replied. 'Weird, ain't it? One moment we were just about to mallet the place and the next we're sitting down having a chinwag with them. One minute you're thinking you're going to drop the whole world on them and then you're having tea together. Bloody bizarre.'

'Say, that old boy sure ran the shit out of you though, didn't he, buddy?' CIA Bob said. 'Next time you go a-visiting, you'd better be wearin' your Sunday best, or he'll whup your ass again.'

'You guys reckon that old boy was genuine?' one of the US soldiers driving the Humvee interjected. 'You know, like he wasn't AQT? Or was he just shit-scared of the air attacks?'

'They got far more reason to hate the Taliban than we have, buddy,' CIA Bob replied. 'With 9/11, we just been attacked by them once is all. These guys have had to live with them every fuckin' day of their lives.'

'He was genuine all right,' Mat added. 'You don't need to worry none about that, mate. It's our side you need to worry about – whether our politicians are genuine about keeping the Taliban wankers out of this country long term. Cos if they aren't, his village is fookin' toast.'

That evening, back at the fort, Mat, Sam and the rest of his team said their goodbyes to CIA Bob, CIA Shorty and Delta Commander Jim. A Chinook was arriving shortly to take them back to Bagram, where they were to be retasked to other missions. Mat, Sam and the Team 6 lads had all bonded with CIA Bob. They'd warmed to his enthusiasm for the job and his strength of character. In a way they'd enjoyed looking after him, too, as he'd always been wide-eyed and fascinated by what Mat and his men were up to. CIA Bob was also full of riveting stories about Afghanistan and its people, which had made for a far more interesting mission. And they would miss his biting sense of humour.

Mat felt that he'd learned something important from working with the little CIA spook. As the two men walked out to the LZ, it was as if CIA Bob had been reading Mat's mind.

'Funny, ain't it, buddy,' CIA Bob remarked. 'But when we first met I reckoned I needed to teach you somethin' about the people you came here to kill. Cos you sure knew jackshit back then. Well, you ended up killin' no one. Instead, you ended up savin' a lot of innocent lives. And the fact is, it's just as tough savin' people as it is killin' 'em. Wagin' the war in this country's the easy part: winning the peace is gonna be the challenge. It's been a real privilege serving with you guys. If the S-B-S ever need a good spook on any of their ops, just you guys go givin' me a call, y'hear?'

'Too right we will, mate,' Mat replied. 'It's been one big eye-opener working with you, Spooky mate. We're trained to fight, and all we want is action. The challenge of taking on the enemy. But tell you the truth, calling off them air strikes was one of the toughest things I ever done.'

'Sure thing, buddy,' said CIA Bob. 'We was takin' on the whole of the US military, the intel boys, the air force, the lot of 'em. Shit, buddy, it went right up to the goddam President. We was tellin' ol' George W himself to wind in his warplanes. And we was tellin' 'em all that they didn't know jackshit. Kinda awesome, eh, buddy?'

'Awesome,' Mat agreed. 'And tell you another thing, mate, I never knew a dumb Yank could have such a wicked sense of humour. Nearest I got to death on that trip was fookin' dying laughing at you. Just you keep telling it like it is, buddy. And you make bloody sure you tell all your spooky mates: if they're ever in any real trouble – real trouble, that is – it's the SBS they should call for.'

Mat, Sam and the Team 6 lads climbed aboard the Chinook and were given a royal send-off by their American brothers in arms. On arrival back at their Bagram HQ they were welcomed by Major Peter Griffin, the C Squadron OC. As they clambered off the chopper he handed each of the men a cold can of beer. Having just spent some dozen days on operations, Mat and his men were hoping for some well-earned R&R before the next mission. But once the OC had congratulated everyone on the Naka Valley op, he dismissed all the lads – except for Mat and Sam.

'Mat, Sam, you've got to get your kit together, I'm afraid,' the OC announced. 'You're deploying to Mazar to join some of the other lads from C Squadron – to make up a QRF around Mazar. All US forces are heading down to the siege of Kunduz, to the east of Mazar, where there's several thousand enemy holding out. Not a lot is expected to happen up at Mazar, but we want some people on the ground to lend a hand with the Northern Alliance generals. You'll be leaving by CH47 this evening. I'll leave the CSM to brief you on the specifics of the Mazar op. Good luck.'

'Holy fuck,' Mat said to Gav Tinker, once the OC was out of earshot. 'We've just come in off a major op in the middle of honkin' nowhere, and we're getting turned around again. There'd be nowt as good as a bit of R&R, boss. You know, time to pull the plonker, have a good hot shower and a chance to write home to the missus. Ain't there no one else who can go?'

'Sorry, lad, everyone's out on ops,' the CSM replied. 'Anyway, like the OC said, it's quiet as the grave up at

Mazar. Nothing much is likely to kick off, so you'll have all the time in the world for playin' with yourself and writing your love letters home. You'll be deploying as low profile as possible. Again it's no uniform, only civvies. Don't go in showing any weapons either. You need to break down your longs and pack them inside your bergens. Likewise with any ammo, pistols and the like. No big stuff either – you're to leave behind all your LAWs, even your grenade launchers.'

'Fat fookin' chance of any action, then,' said Mat, morosely. 'Looks like we're on a punishment op for having put the kibosh on those Naka Valley air strikes.'

'Yeah, well, you did put a few of our American friends' noses out of joint,' said the CSM. 'But we're proud of you lads – you did the right thing up there and I don't reckon it was easy. To tell you the truth, you're getting the Mazar op in part cos we think you need the down time, and there's fuck all happening up there. The Northern Alliance have got the whole area pretty much under control. Mazar airport is in allied hands and we'll soon be getting flights in there. The enemy forces are badly demoralised from all the bombing and they've been surrendering by the bucketload. Pretty much safe as houses right now.'

'Sounds wonderful,' Mat remarked, unenthusiastically. 'What's the weather like? Any chance of getting a good tan?'

'Well, anyway, 'ave a good one, lads,' the CSM replied, ignoring Mat's sarcasm. 'And behave yourselves up there.'

'Bloody hell, what are we, mate?' Mat said to Sam, as they made their way over to the SBS quarters. 'I mean, what are we? A bunch of bloody UN peacekeepers? Didn't get a sniff of action in the Naka Valley, did we? Lovely scenery and all that. Great food. Wonderful company.

Nice to have saved the place from total devastation, too. But we didn't exactly get our honkin' hands dirty, did we? Looks like there'll be even less chance over at fookin' Mazar, don't it, mate?'

'You never know, bro,' Sam replied, trying to sound positive. 'We were supposed to flatten the Naka Valley, an' ended up kinda savin' the place. So who knows what might kick off in Mazar.'

Mat wandered off grumpily to have a dump. In the ten days that they'd been away, Bagram had been transformed. It was now very much a functioning airport, with lots of the luxuries of home having been flown in by the US military. As he was enjoying his first crap for many a day in reasonably civilised conditions, Mat glanced up at the metal door of the toilet cubicle. There was a piece of graffiti scrawled in black marker pen right in front of his eyes. The spelling left a bit to be desired, but the words struck him as being particularly ironic after the Naka Valley mission.

Yee, though I walk thru the Valley of the Shadow of Death I shall fear no evil, for I am the meenest mother-fucker in the Valley.

Well, that wasn't quite how things had transpired in the Naka Valley, Mat reflected. As far as he was concerned, the 'meanest motherfucker' in the Naka Valley had turned out to be the Afghan village chief. After running rings around Mat the old boy had then disclosed the location of the enemy ammo dumps, so they could blow them. Which was a pretty major result for the mission, in military terms. And in a way it had proved harder not to mallet the place, to choose to call off the air strikes, than it would have been to go ahead as planned and flatten the valley. In an odd sense perhaps the meanest motherfucker in the valley had turned out to be those with balls enough to tell it like it was – and to get the air strikes cancelled. And that had been CIA Bob, Mat and his men.

'OK, brothers, listen up,' Ali announced, as he strode across to the trench with Ahmed at his side. 'We've been given our marching orders by Mullah Fadhal. And you're not going to like it. The enemy have agreed to give all Afghan Taliban safe passage out of here if the foreign Taliban – that's you and me, brothers – are handed over to General Dostum. Brothers, we've been ordered to lay down our arms to those who have massacred our Muslim women and children on the plains and in the mountains of this pure Islamic land. We are being ordered to surrender to the *kafir* Americans, the cowards who have not beaten us in fair battle, brothers, who have not even been brave enough to meet us man to man on the battle-field, brothers, but have chosen instead to bomb us from the air because they fear us so much. Brothers, we have been told to surrender to them.'

'No way, brothers!' Ahmed yelled, from his position beside Ali. 'No surrender, brothers! We fight to the death.'

'*Al-hamdu Lillah*,' Ali said 'Brother Ahmed speaks true, brothers. I'm sure the rest of you are with him on this. No surrender to the American dogs or their Northern Alliance whores.'

Some several days earlier, Ali and the surviving brothers had succeeded in escaping from the Northern Alliance forces by swimming down the river. Commander Omer, Sadiq and a dozen more had died on the river bank, and they had lost three more brothers in the freezing river as they had made their escape. So now they were down to less than a dozen of their original number. After the escape, they had travelled through the mountains at night, bypassing Mazar – which had just fallen to the enemy – and heading for Kunduz, the eastern stronghold of the Taliban. With Commander Omer gone, Ali had now taken iron control over the men in his unit.

Upon their arrival in Kunduz, they had been placed in the front-line positions around the city, along with several hundred fellow foreign Taliban. That had been three days ago, and ever since then they had been subjected to fierce US bombing from the air. The besieging US and Afghan forces were now threatening to bomb Kunduz back to the Dark Ages, unless the defending forces agreed to lay down their weapons. As there were several thousand women and children still trapped in the city, the Taliban leaders had reached a surrender deal with General Dostum's forces. Under that deal, while the Afghan Taliban were being allowed to go free, the foreign Taliban – including Ali's unit – were being handed over to General Dostum's Northern Alliance troops.

'But if we refuse to surrender, we'll be going against the mullah's orders. We cannot go against our brother Taliban and fight them – even thought their wish for glory and death in the battle against the *kafir* is less than our own. So, brothers,' Ali continued, lowering his voice as he did so, 'you remember the glorious battle we fought at Balkh gorge? Where we "surrendered" and the Northern Alliance whores let us keep our weapons, and then we slaughtered them like dogs at dawn? You remember the glory and bravery of the giant Ahmed as he charged through the minefield, the grace of Almighty Allah rendering him invulnerable to the mines?'

Ali paused for a second as he looked around at the assembled men. 'None of us can ever forget the glorious battle of Balkh, brothers. We all remember the sweet taste of victory. Then let us prepare to do the same again, brothers. We will "surrender" to the *kafir* dogs, as the mullah has ordered, so we can save the Muslim sisters and the Muslim children. But keep your weapons close, brothers, and hide your grenades, your pistols and your knives in your clothing. And remain alert, brothers. We will await our chance. And when we are close enough to the *kafir* to attack, we will slaughter them like the infidel dogs they are.'

8

NO SURRENDER

It was the night of 23 November when Mat and Sam deployed by Chinook to Mazar-e-Sharif, via a short refuelling stopover at a secret US airbase in Uzbekistan. The two men slept the whole of the flight, as the physical and emotional strain of the Naka Valley mission caught up with them. The highlight of the journey was their arrival at Mazar airport, whereupon they were met by an SBS reception party including Mat's old teammates, Jamie and Tom. The last time they had seen each other was back at Bagram, when Mat had landed the Naka Valley mission and Tom and Jamie had got Mazar. They loaded all their kit into a couple of Land-Rovers and set off on the drive into the city.

'What's with the paint job, mate?' Mat asked Jamie, indicating the Land-Rover's bright white bodywork. 'They shipped you out an Arctic vehicle by mistake, or something?'

'I wish, mate,' Jamie replied. 'It's worse than that. Cos we're here on an "advisory" role to the Northern Alliance, we've been told to make like aid workers. We're supposed to look like we're the UN or something.'

'What, like we're the UN – despite the fact there's a great big fuck-off GPMG mounted on the back of the truck?'

'Yeah, well, it makes no sense to me, either,' said Jamie. 'Something about the place crawling with press and them not wanting it known there's Brit special forces in with the Northern Alliance.'

'Northern Alliance – sounds like a bloody building society,' Mat grunted. 'So what was all that shit in the OC's briefing about "drawing blood quickly", if we're to make like UN aid workers? The UN're hardly known for kicking arse, are they?'

'No idea, mate,' Jamie replied. 'This op's been a crock of shite since day one. It's you guys who've been having all the fun, calling in the mother of all air strikes down south so I heard.'

'Calling *in* air strikes?' Mat snorted. 'Calling *off* air strikes more like it. Ace quad-bike drivers, us, mate.'

'How d'you mean, mate?'

'Tell you all about it sometime,' Mat said, pulling his woolly hat down over his eyes. 'I got to get some kip, mate. What's on the menu tomorrow? Bugger all, I take it?'

'Watching a bunch of AQT surrender, or some such shite,' said Jamie. 'You might just want to spend the whole day snoozing, mate.'

On arrival in Mazar city, the two Land-Rovers made for the SBS's base at the Old Turkish Schoolhouse (once a working school, until the Taliban shut it down). The three-storey building was the US military's combined services headquarters for the Mazar region. The top floor housed the Delta Force operators and the CIA, the first floor housed the US 5th Special Operation Forces group

(5th SOF) and the Rangers, while the ground floor was for the 10th Mountain troops. The British special forces had an ill-defined place in that hierarchy. Strictly speaking, the SBS lads were co-located with the 5th SOF, as they jointly made up the Quick Reaction Force (QRF) with responsibility for the Mazar region. But they spent most of their time on the top floor of the Old Schoolhouse, where the CIA and Delta boys loved to get a brew on for their British counterparts, swapping stories about what they'd been up to in various obscure corners of the world.

The US special forces community is far larger than that in the UK, and more disparate. There are some 45,000 US active and reserve Special Operation Forces (SOFs) across all the services – comprising some 1.3 per cent of the US military. By contrast, there are less than 2,000 active and reserve SAS, SBS and related units in the UK. In the US military, SOFs are known as Tier 2 Special Forces. The level of training and specialist military skills achieved by the Tier 2 troops puts them on a par with the British Parachute Regiment's Pathfinder Platoons or the Royal Marine's Recce Troops. The only US units that rival the SBS and SAS are Delta Force and the SEALs, their Tier 1 Special Forces, who number no more than a few thousand.

By the time that Mat and Sam had reached Mazar, the whole of the US Delta Force contingent was away at the siege of Kunduz. So for that first night they were billeted on the top floor of the Schoolhouse in the deserted Delta Force quarters. It made no difference to Mat and Sam where they spent the night, as they were dog-tired from the Naka Valley op and could sleep just about anywhere. At 10 a.m. the following morning the eight SBS soldiers making up the Mazar mission gathered for a briefing by Captain Lancer, their OC.

'Welcome, lads, to marvellous Mazar,' Captain Lancer began, nodding in Mat and Sam's direction. 'I hope you got a good night's sleep, as I guess you must be knackered from your last op – you lucky bastards. I trust you'll brief us all on the Naka Valley mission later. Now, I'm not going to beat around the bush – this is a dead-end op if ever there was one. You've seen the Land-Rovers painted for Arctic conditions? Well, that just about says it all. That being said, we've got a job of sorts to do, so we may as well do it to the best of our ability. At its simplest, we're here to hold General Dostum's hand, not that he needs it. He's a tough cookie if ever there was one, with a track record it's best not to delve into too deeply. Suffice to say he commands the loyalty of all his men, some 30,000 troops and irregulars under arms.

'Mazar fell to the Northern Alliance forces and US air power a few days back – in fact, just before we got here. So, we've spent most of our time getting to know our Afghan hosts and our US military counterparts and doing a bit of hearts-and-minds work. The action's moved east of here, to Kunduz, which is the second city in Northern Afghanistan. There's some 6–7,000 enemy forces holed up in Kunduz, and the whole of the US military machine has refocused there – as have the majority of the Northern Alliance. And that's largely why you're here. With all of the Delta boys and most of the 5th SOF away at Kunduz, it's left a vacuum. We're here to fill it.'

'Silly question, boss,' Mat said, 'but why aren't we off mixing it with the Delta boys down at Kunduz?'

'Well, we'd like to be,' the Captain replied, ruefully. 'Unfortunately, we were ordered not to go – on the personal intervention of the Prime Minister, so I'm told. Seems he fears Kunduz is going to be a bloodbath. US jets are on standby to flatten the place and wipe out the AQT forces. Trouble is, there's a whole bunch of women and children holed up in the city. That's probably the wrong word – it's more like they're trapped in the city. Afghanistan is crawling with press – newspapers, TV crews, the lot. And Blair's paranoid that British forces are going to end up involved in some terrible human rights abuse and that it'll be all over the papers.'

'Makes you wonder what the fuck we are,' Tom interjected. 'Special forces, or some fuckin' public relations wing of Her Majesty's Government.'

'Oh what a wonderful war,' Jamie added, quietly.

'Anyhow, here at Mazar we make up the Quick Reaction Force (QRF),' Captain Lancer said. 'We're on standby in case any shit goes down, which is unlikely. Then there's a skeleton crew of 5th SOF, most of whom are admin staff tasked with manning Boxer Base.'

'Seems pretty much like the party's goin' down elsewhere, boss,' Sam remarked. 'I take it "Boxer Base" is the code name for this place?'

'Yes, Boxer Base is the code name for the Schoolhouse, our HQ,' said the captain. 'Other than that, I can't think of much else to brief you on. We, like you, came in low profile – so we have Diemacos and that's about it – not that I expect we'll be needing any heavy stuff. That's the one saving grace about the Land-Rovers. Although they're supposed to look like aid vehicles, we do at least have a couple of GPMGs bolted on the back of them, just in case we run into any trouble.'

'So, what d'you want to do with us, boss?' Mat asked.

'We've made up two QRF teams, one commanded by myself and the other by Sergeant Major Trent. Now you're here, we'll put one of you on each of the teams. If nothing else it'll give you the chance to tell us your war stories from the Naka Valley op. So, Mat, you'll join my team, along with Jamie and Ruff. And Sam, you'll join Sergeant Major Trent's team, along with Tom Knight and Jake the Snake, OK? Your team leaders can brief you up on your individual call signs, comms and other procedures in your own time. Any questions?'

'What have we got on the menu today, then, boss?' Mat asked. 'I hear there might be a gripping mass surrender.'

'Yes, some six hundred AQT have agreed to surrender to General Dostum's forces, somewhere to the east of Mazar. We've been asked along simply to "observe" today's surrender. So once again, we've got no role, really. I reckon it's just our US buddies taking pity on us and inviting us along for the ride.'

By mid-morning, the two SBS teams were in their Land-Rovers following a US 5th SOF Humvee out of Mazar. The SBS soldiers trundled along the baking tarmac in their gleaming white vehicles, with their faces wrapped in shamags and wearing battered jeans and T-shirts – so that no casual observer would be quite certain who the British soldiers really were. They headed out into the desert towards the east of the city, on the main Mazar–Kunduz road. They made for a fortified mound that housed a vehicle checkpoint manned by NA soldiers. From the top of the mound, they would have a clear view of the surrender taking place about a mile or so to the east of them.

They had been ordered that on no account should they allow themselves to be seen by the surrendering enemy. General Dostum feared that the sight of British and American forces might inflame the situation and jeopardise the surrender deal. To the east there was a sea of tiny, indistinct figures shimmering in the distant heat haze. Mat broke out his binoculars to take a closer look. Under high magnification he could just make out what was going on. It looked like a scene from some period action movie, with a crowd of berobed and beturbaned AQT on one side of the desert, and a bunch of Northern Alliance soldiers in a motley collection of uniforms on the other. They appeared to be in the middle of some kind of stand-off, with the six hundred heavily armed AQT refusing to give up their weapons. Like anyone else of any import, General Dostum was away at Kunduz, and perhaps that accounted in part for the enemy's reluctance to surrender. Perhaps they wanted the General on hand to personally vouch for the terms under which they would be laying down their arms.

The tense negotiations dragged on for hours. Finally, Mat observed the first weapons being handed over. But the Northern Alliance soldiers were making little or no attempt to search the AQT fighters. According to Captain Lancer, that was the nature of the deal struck between the enemy and General Dostum – that there would be no degrading body searches of the AQT fighters. In the Afghan tradition of warfare, you were supposed to surrender with dignity, and with a respect that was reciprocated by the victors. As an honourable Muslim it was taken as given that you would have handed over all your weapons, which meant that no search was required. It all struck Mat as being more than a little suspect, but who was he to criticise such ancient traditions?

From the fortified mound on which they were standing a road ran some three miles south to Mazar airport. At first, the six hundred AQT were scheduled to go to the airport after their surrender, as hundreds of prisoners were incarcerated there already. But US warplanes had now started operating from out of the airport. Not surprisingly, the US military didn't want any more enemy prisoners to be held in such close proximity to their air operations. As a result, the prisoners were loaded on to trucks and diverted to the only other large structure capable of holding so many captives – the ancient, mud-walled fortress at Qala-i-Janghi, about eight miles to the west of Mazar city.

The first truck to rumble past the checkpoint where Mat and the other lads were standing was piled high with surrendered weapons: AK47s, rocket launchers and heavy machine guns. Shortly after that, the first truck-load of prisoners drove past the checkpoint en route to Qala-i-Janghi. As it did so, Mat, Sam, Jamie, Tom and the other SBS lads hid their faces from the enemy captives' gaze.

After several hours of suffocating travel in the baking heat of an ancient Soviet truck, Ali and his brothers finally arrived at a location they immediately recognised, Qala-i-Janghi – the 'Fort of War'. Until a few days earlier, this ancient, mud-walled fortress had been one of the Taliban's key bases, which was how the brothers knew the place so well. But now, General Dostum's forces had seized control. During the journey there had been much animated discussion among the sixty brothers crammed on to the back of the truck – and it was clear to Ali that his was not the only group of foreign Taliban who had no intention of surrendering.

Ali knew that Qala-i-Janghi was used as a major arms store, and was kept permanently stuffed full of weaponry. It seemed inconceivable to him that General Dostum's men could have already removed all the arms that were stored there. In which case, being incarcerated there might just serve Ali and his brothers very well. If they could only get their hands on those weapons and the ammo dumps, then the much hoped for counter-attack would have every chance of succeeding beyond their wildest dreams. *Insh'Allah*, they could equip a whole army for jihad with the hardware stored in that fort.

As the brothers were unloaded from the truck, Ali noted how lightly they were being guarded. The Northern Alliance fools seemed to have learned little from the events at Balkh and elsewhere – where the brothers' so-called 'surrender' had turned into a bloodbath for the enemy. Well, the whores would be made to pay for it with their lives. At their surrender earlier in the day, the brothers had been made to give up their main weapons – their RPGs, AK47s and their heavy and light machine guns. But scores of them had secreted smaller weapons under their traditional Afghan robes. All they had to do now was fight their way into one of the weapons stores. Then the glorious uprising would be underway, and, if Allah so willed it, unstoppable.

Ali glanced around him, checking out the fort's defences and the number of guards. As he did so he caught sight of a group of foreigners chatting with some of the Northern Alliance soldiers. They were dressed in jeans, T-shirts and baseball caps, and Ali knew that they had to be either Europeans or Americans. *At last he had sight of the people that he had come here to kill.* He felt his blood thrill at the very thought of it. Before now, the hated *kafir* had always appeared as the pilots of distant aircraft screaming through the skies, cowards dropping steel and high explosives from the safety of 10,000 feet. *Until now they had always been out of reach and untouchable.*

Ali watched as three of the men separated themselves from the group and wandered over to where he and the brothers were waiting in line to be processed into the fort. They were carrying a large video camera, microphones and a tripod, so they had to be news journalists. They were members of the despised *kafir* media, Ali reflected, the propaganda machine of the Great Satan. All of the *kafir* media were biased and evil, because they ignored the murder of innocent Afghan women and children by US warplanes, focusing instead on their so-called victories. Just as they ignored the suffering in Palestine, because the *kafir* media was controlled by the stinking Jews. Ali hated the *kafir* journalists almost as much as he hated the *kafir* soldiers.

'Hi. Mind if we have a word with you guys?' the sandy-haired man at the front of the group asked one of the brothers. 'Just roll the camera, Brad, and let's see what we get,' he added, speaking over his shoulder. His accent was clearly American, and Ali just stared over at him without saying a word, hatred burning in his eyes.

'You mind if we have a word? OK? No? Yes? Well, I guess that's a "no"?' the journalist continued. 'Hey, maybe he doesn't have any English,' he said, turning to his cameraman, who just shrugged his shoulders. 'Hey, you know, you speak any English? I just wanna know why you're here and why you surrendered? I guess he's got no English. Hey, Brad, I guess we may need to get the translator over here, eh?'

'I speak English,' Ali spat out. 'And we have NOT surrendered. We have not surrendered to the *kafir* dogs and we will never be surrendering.'

'Hey, well, y'know, it looks to me pretty much like a surrender,' the journalist countered. 'And I guess that's what the Northern Alliance guys think too, or you wouldn't be here, now would you? Anyways, where're you from?'

'When the time comes, *insh'Allah*, you will be the first American pig to die,' Ali snarled, deliberately speaking in Arabic so the journalist wouldn't understand him. 'Remember this *kafir* dog's face, brothers, and remember it well.'

'Hey, you're defeated, disarmed and being held prisoner, buddy: looks pretty much like surrender to me,' the journalist said, walking away. While he couldn't understand Ali's words, the sentiment was crystal clear. 'But, whatever. Go figure.'

'Brothers, we have waited so long to get the chance to fight the *kafir*,' Ali continued, turning his back on the journalist. 'Sooner or later, we knew that chance would come. Now, by the grace of Allah, we are being granted that chance. Brothers, by the grace of The One who makes the sun shine, the wind blow and the oceans roar, may we now be worthy to the call of the jihad.'

Within the hour, Ali and his fellow brothers were processed into the fort, along with hundreds of other prisoners. Before being taken down into the fort's basement – where the majority of the prisoners were being held – Ali and his brothers suffered the indignity of having their hands bound. But none of them objected. They were waiting for the right moment to take the initiative and attack those holding them captive. They would only do so when the time was right – when some of the *kafir* American or British dogs were close enough at hand for the killing.

ULTIMATE BETRAYAL

THE morning after the surrender of the six hundred enemy fighters, Mat, Jamie, Captain Lancer and the fourth member of their team, Stevie 'Ruff' Pouncer, headed out of Mazar on what was basically a body-guarding mission. Mat knew Ruff as a tough, uncompromising soldier. His alternative nickname was 'the Animal' and he had a reputation for being a killing machine when the shit went down. While Ruff wasn't exactly the world's greatest conversationalist or philosopher, Mat always appreciated his presence in a potential combat situation.

Not that he felt they were going to get much action on today's mission. A US Navy admiral was scheduled to visit a local Afghan hospital around lunchtime. The hospital building had been damaged during the fighting, and as part of the ongoing hearts-and-minds activity in the Mazar region the US had offered to rebuild the facility. The Admiral's visit was the first step in that process – to assess what help the US could best provide. Captain Lancer's four-man QRF team were tasked with checking out the security in the area prior to the Admiral's visit.

They left Mazar city and drove out into the open desert, passing by an ancient mud-walled fortress. Its sloping ramparts rose some sixty feet above the desert, and were topped off by a massive, crenellated wall some ten feet high. Squat towers dominated each of the six corners of the fort, which were laid out in a rough hexagonal shape, and it had to be at least five hundred yards from end to end. It resembled a giant sandcastle, straight out of the *Arabian Nights*. But while it looked like something from the history books it was obviously still very much in use: a couple of Toyota pickups were parked up at the gates, and a dozen or so Afghan troops were wandering along the walls.

'Holy fuck,' Mat exclaimed. 'What the bollocks is that?'

'That, mate, is Qala-i-Janghi,' Jamie replied. 'Means "Fort of War". Like something out of *Lawrence of Arabia*, ain't it? That's where Dostum has his HQ now.'

'Awesome place,' Mat exclaimed, shaking his head in amazement. 'Awesome place. Ain't that where the prisoners from yesterday are being held?'

'You got it, mate, that's the place,' Jamie confirmed. 'Never been in there – but inside it's supposed to be a maze of compounds and bunkers and underground passageways.'

'Sounds like something out of *Lara Croft*,' Mat said. 'Best place to put the fookers, anyways. Looks like they won't be breaking out of there in a hurry.'

'I reckon,' Jamie replied. 'So, spill the beans, mate. What d'you get up to in the Naka Valley, then?'

'Not much. Like I said, ace quad-bike drivers, us,' Mat grunted. 'I got the verbal shit kicked out of me by an Afghan elder cos I wasn't dressed smart enough to be paying a visit to his village; we were compromised by a wrinkled old goatherd, but we never realised it; and the US top brass refused to believe our intel reports cos they thought we were a bunch of nutters.'

'That good, was it, mate?'

'Yep. That and the fact that the US intel's "mother of all terrorist training camps" turned out to be a school; their "unarmed combat training sessions" turned out to be school PE lessons; and their "terrorist recruitment rally" turned out to be the village funeral. So we called off the air strikes, gave the kiddies some sweets, had tea with the village elders, blew a few ammo dumps and came home.'

'Doesn't sound like we missed much then, mate.'

'You know what, mate, in a way it was a cracking op,' Mat replied, all serious for a moment. 'Us lot stopped a load of innocent Afghan women and children from getting malleted by the US Air Force. Wasn't what we went there intending to do, but what plan ever survives contact with the enemy?'

There were a few seconds silence while Jamie reflected on what Mat had just been saying.

'Tell you what, mate, I'd rather've been on that op than this one, any day. At least it sounds like you *did something*. Over here, what are we? I mean, what are we? Special forces or a bunch of glorified bodyguards? Shakyboats, or tour guides for the US and Afghan top brass?'

'That bad, is it, mate?'

'It's worse,' Jamie snorted in reply.

Once they had arrived at the destination village, they set up fire positions wherever they could find a bit of shade, and waited for the top brass to show. Captain

Lancer then accompanied the US Admiral on his walk-about of the village and the ruined hospital, while Mat, Jamie and Ruff tried not to look too bored. By lunchtime the visit was over, and the SBS lads were going out of their minds with the tedium of it all. When they'd left Poole for deployment to Afghanistan, some three weeks earlier, the last thing they'd expected to end up doing was acting as armed escorts to the US officer class. That sort of work did not require the unique skills of special forces soldiering.

They were glad to get in the vehicle and get on the move again. At least there would be a bit of a breeze on the drive back to Mazar. But they hadn't been on the road for more than ten minutes when their Land-Rover slowed to a stop. Looking over the cabin roof Mat could see that there was a roadblock made of burning tyres up ahead, with a couple of very agitated-looking Afghan policemen waving all vehicles to a halt. The Land-Rover pulled off the tarmac and drove up to the front of the queue of stationary pickups and battered cars.

'What the fuck's that?' Mat asked, as they came to a stop at the roadblock. He'd caught the distant noise of what sounded like gunfire. 'That's shooting, ain't it, mate?'

'You're not wrong,' Jamie said. Both of them were on their feet now, listening intently to the noise up ahead of them. 'Sounds like a bevy of AKs – going at it hammer and tongs.'

As Captain Lancer went forward to speak with the two Afghan policemen, Mat and Jamie kept a close eye on him. There was an air of panic and confusion about the roadblock, and Mat doubted whether the Afghan policemen knew much more than they did about what was going on up ahead of them. Every now and then, among the distant crackle of small-arms fire, they could hear the heavier crump of larger weaponry, which sounded like RPGs and mortar rounds going off.

'Sounds like a bit of a bloody rumble,' Mat remarked, hopefully.

'Yeah, about two miles distant, I'd say,' Jamie replied. 'Back up on the road to Mazar – the route we're supposed to be taking.'

'That's all good then, mate,' said Mat, with satisfaction. 'Let's get back on the bloody road, cos there's no way we're missing out on this one.'

'Lads, something pretty major's kicked off up at Qala-i-Janghi fort,' Captain Lancer announced, as he strode back to the Land-Rover. 'The police are going to let us through, but keep an eye out as it's very confused out there. Before we go, I'm just going to see if I can raise Boxer Base.'

The Captain put a call through to headquarters on the Land-Rover's radio, but it turned out that the 5th SOF officer on duty at Boxer Base seemed to know little more about the firefight than they did. He had confused reports coming in of US personnel missing in action (MIA) at the fort. Some sort of rescue mission was being mooted, but the officer couldn't say exactly who the MIAs were, or who had captured them. The one thing the officer was sure of was that he wanted Captain Lancer and his QRF force back at Boxer Base as soon as possible.

Some twenty minutes after making that radio call, the SBS Land-Rover pulled into Boxer Base compound. Captain Lancer and his men now knew that there was one hell of a shit fight going down at Qala-i-Janghi. On the drive past the ancient fortress they'd seen scores of Northern Alliance troops on the outside firing in, with a barrage of fire coming back at them from the fort's occupiers. There was little doubt in the minds of the SBS soldiers what had taken place: the enemy prisoners had launched an uprising. As Mat had pointed out, none of the AQT prisoners had been properly searched, so they could easily have used hidden weapons to start an armed revolt. Captain Lancer headed off into Boxer Base to have a word with his opposite number from the US 5th SOF.

'Any of you lot know what the fuck's going on?' Tom asked, as he and Sam came ambling over to the Land-Rovers.

'Dunno exactly, mate, but it's kicking off big time over at the old fort,' Mat replied. 'Reckon the shit's hit the fan with the prisoners.'

'That's what it looked like to us, anyways,' Jamie added. 'What's the score from your end?'

'Don't know a fuckin' lot,' Tom said. 'Just what we've been told by the 5th SOF boys – which is to get our shit together cos there may be some US boys in the fort that need rescuin'.'

'Reckon we'd better go get tooled up, then,' said Mat, excitedly. 'You never know, lads, but we may be getting a piece of the action, after all.'

The SBS soldiers made their way over to their own small storeroom and armoury and started breaking out boxes of ammunition and other kit. But just as they had started doing so, two of the 5th SOF soldiers came charging through the doorway into their room.

'Grab all your fuckin' kit, now, cos we're movin' out!' one of them yelled.

'What's up, mate?' Jamie asked, glancing up from an ammo crate, the contents of which he was stuffing into his backpack.

'There's been a breakout in the fuckin' prison, an' you

guys are needed over there, pronto,' the soldier replied, at volume.

'Yeah, we know that, mate,' said Jamie, calmly. 'We're just getting our shit together.'

'A'right, cos we're movin' out,' the US soldier yelled back at him, and then they were gone.

'What the fuck?' Jamie tried to stifle a chuckle. The US soldiers were charging around the base like headless chickens.

The SBS lads ignored them and carried on arming their weapons. Whatever shit might be going down at the fort, there was little point rushing in there unprepared. No one knew how long they'd be in there for, but one thing was certain: once they'd fought their way into that fort there would be little chance of a resupply. Which meant that they needed to take all of the kit that they might need with them now, plus maximum ammo.

Because they had been ordered to deploy to Mazar low profile and showing no weapons, the men only had their Diemaco assault rifles and 9mm Sig Sauer pistols with them. This meant that they had no light or heavy machine guns, grenades or anti-armour weapons. Having seen the ferocity of the firefight now underway at Qala-i-Janghi, Mat would have chosen to take the heaviest weaponry possible, if only it had been available. As it was, they'd just have to make do.

Each man loaded up three mags of 9mm ammo for the Sig Sauer pistols, and some fifteen mags of ammo for the Diemacos (each of which contained thirty rounds) – making up some five hundred rounds per man. That sounds like a lot of ammo, but in an intense firefight such as was now going down at the fort, five hundred rounds could be used up in no time. Each man slung nine mags on to his chest webbing, and the rest of them were stuffed into a grab bag, along with the pistol mags, some emergency field dressings, extra water, a twenty-four-hour food ration pack, NVGs, a torch and a knife.

Special forces legend generally has SBS/SAS soldiers deploying with giant, commando-style knives – seven inches long and with cruel, serrated edges – for close-quarter combat. But Mat and the rest of the lads preferred to pack a Leatherman each – a multi-use tool comprising of several short-bladed knives, pliers, a file and a screw-driver set. If it ever got to the stage of close-quarter combat, they would prefer to use their Sig Sauer pistols and shoot the enemy in the head. Last but not least, the men packed a couple of laser target designators (LTDs) and the related comms kit, as they had little doubt that they'd be calling in air strikes once they got to the fort.

It took the SBS soldiers the best part of thirty-five minutes to get fully tooled up, by which time they were ready to hit Qala-i-Janghi and get into action. But first, the lads gathered to listen to the intel briefing on the top floor of the Schoolhouse, along with the ten soldiers from the US 5th SOF who would be going in alongside them. In theory, Major Michael E. Martin, the 5th SOF commander, was in overall command of any joint SBS–5th SOF operation, as he was the most senior officer on the ground. But in practice the SBS lads would be under the orders of their OC, Captain Lancer. As Qala-i-Janghi fort had been under the control of the Northern Alliance and the CIA, the intel briefing was being given by a CIA officer.

'Listen up, guys, this is as much as we know,' the CIA agent began, hurriedly. ''Fraid it ain't much, but first off, there's some six hundred AQT prisoners held at that fort and they've broken out in some sort of uprising. Seems the fort was also General Dostum's ammo store, and we reckon they've got into those stores. Y'all heard about this Afghan and Islamic honour shit? Well, the prisoners were kinda supposed to behave themselves in there. Instead, they captured or killed – we ain't too sure yet, reports are still real confusin' on this one – two of our CIA buddies. They broke out the weapons and they've now started fuckin' World War Three in there. So, we gotta get in there, lift the siege and rescue our boys. That's about as much as I know.'

'Where were your two CIA blokes when they were captured?' Mat asked. 'And who've we got up there that we're in contact with?'

'Good point, buddy. They were interrogatin' the AQT prisoners in the southern end of the fort. That's where the uprising took place. The fort's kinda split into two halves with a dividin' wall in between – you'll see it when you get up there. And that's where our boys were, in the southern half. They had some Afghan guards with 'em, but only a handful, and it seems a couple of 'em were killed and the others escaped. Now we ain't really got comms with anyone directly, cos the Northern Alliance guys don't have fuckin' radios. There's been a satphone call from one of our CIA boys, but that comms link has now gone down so seems like we lost him. The NA are keepin' the prisoners holed up in the fort for now, but they can't do that for much longer.'

'Any idea how many Alliance soldiers are up there?' Jamie asked.

'Between fifty and a hundred, but again we ain't too sure.'

'You reckon your CIA blokes are still alive, mate?' Mat asked. In the back of his mind he had an image of CIA Bob being captured – and tortured – by a murderous enemy. When they'd left CIA Bob at Commander Jim's fort, he'd been scheduled to remain there for a long and detailed debrief on the Naka Valley operation. So the chances of him having ended up in Qala-i-Janghi three days later were next to zero. But for Mat it nevertheless made the uprising all the more real.

'Far as we know they are,' the CIA agent replied.

'So this is a mission to rescue them, first and foremost? I mean, the twenty-odd of us aren't going to retake that fort, however good we are.'

'In terms of the mission brief, we're gonna have to keep it fluid,' the US 5th SOF Major cut in. 'First off, we're gonna head for the fort entranceway – cos we do know that's still in friendly hands. We got some CIA and Northern Alliance boys in there holding firm – at least for now. From there, we're gonna have to take a view. Like I said, we're gonna have to keep it real fluid.'

'To clarify, the mission priority has to be to rescue the two CIA agents,' Captain Lancer said. 'After that, it's to contain the enemy in the fort and stop them breaking out any further.'

'Any chance of some reinforcements?' Jamie asked. 'I mean, I don't want to sound like a homo or anything, but we could do with a few more men.'

'Right now, we're on our own,' Captain Lancer replied. 'All of our lot are committed elsewhere across country, and Delta and the other US forces are down at Kunduz. Plus the Northern Alliance are down there too. Word is we've got to contain this, at least until they get some reinforcements up to us.'

'Well then, let's fookin' do it,' Mat announced. 'Got the names of the two captured CIA blokes, mate?'

'Yup. One's Johnny Michael Spann,' the CIA agent replied. 'An' the other's Dave Tyson. I'll be up there with you all, so if there's anything else you need you can ask me on the job.'

With that, the men got to their feet and filed down to the waiting vehicles. Mat was relieved to know for sure that neither of the captured men was CIA Bob. But it turned out that Jamie and Tom both knew Dave Tyson. During the previous two weeks stationed at Mazar they'd become pretty friendly with him. Several evenings they'd sat around with Dave Tyson on the top floor of Boxer Base, cracking jokes and telling war stories.

Before coming to Afghanistan 'CIA Dave' had been based in neighbouring Uzbekistan. For years he'd been the Agency's field officer there. He was well keyed in to the culture and traditions, speaking several of the local languages. The fact that a couple of them knew one of the captured (or killed) CIA agents made the mission all the more personal for the SBS soldiers. Although he wasn't a Brit, the lads still felt as if they were going in to rescue one of their own. And as for Sam, this had now become very personal. It was about saving the life of a fellow US warrior – a warrior who had either been captured by a fanatical enemy, or who had fallen on the field of battle.

The SBS soldiers headed up to the fort laden down with their weapons, ammo and other gear. The atmosphere in the vehicles was tense and silent, as each man mentally readied himself for the assault. Due to the woeful lack of intelligence, none of the men knew what they were up against now. This was the worst type of combat situation: basically, they were going to have to fight their way into that ancient fortress blind. Normally, the SBS prided itself on having as full an intelligence picture as possible, then planning and rehearsing a mission over several days. By contrast, the men were heading into Qala-i-Janghi with zero intelligence, no battle rehearsals and no concrete plans. There was an old saying in the SBS: 'Fail to plan – plan to fail.'

In the worst-case scenario there were some six hundred hard-core al-Qaeda and Taliban in that ancient and impregnable fort – so-called prisoners who had decided instead to fight. Against those six hundred battle-hardened terrorists they now had eight SBS soldiers, ten US 5th SOF operators and between fifty and a hundred Northern Alliance troops. At best, they were outnumbered some six to one. To cap it all, the men had been ordered to leave all their heavier weapons – grenade launchers, LAWs, machine guns – back at Bagram, so they could deploy into Mazar 'low profile'. And what sort of bollocks order had that been? Mat was thinking, angrily.

As they left Mazar city and hit the open road Mat glanced at his watch: it was 1.05 p.m. They had six hours of daylight left in which to fight their way into the fort. As the wheels hummed on the hot tarmac Mat found his mind drifting. What were their chances of coming out of this one alive? Every way he looked at it, they weren't too good. He thought about Suzie, and he wondered for a second if he'd ever get to see her again. Back in the Naka Valley he'd had a lot of time to himself to think, and the idea of kids with Suzie had become increasingly appealing. If it was a boy Mat had already decided to name him Gary, after his favourite footballer, Gary Lineker. If it was a girl, the naming was going to be Suzie's decision.

Catching himself daydreaming like this, Mat cursed himself and forced such thoughts to the back of his mind. Was he going soft or something? He had to remain focused on the mission. If he started getting all sentimental and loved-up in the midst of the coming battle, then he really would end up dead, of that he was certain. Two CIA officers were in that fort, somewhere, trapped and desperate. And they probably had a wife and kids back home, Mat told himself. It was their job – Mat and the others lads – to go in and rescue them. There was no choice now about what lay before them: they had to go in hard and take the fight to the enemy.

For a split second Mat tried to imagine the fate of those two CIA agents trapped in that fort. Mat thought about CIA Bob being one of them. What was it that he'd said to the little CIA spook on their parting, back at Commander Jim's fort? *You make sure you tell all your spooky mates: if they're ever in any real trouble – real trouble, that is – it's the SBS they should call for.* That's what he'd said. If it was CIA Bob trapped in that fort, he would be relying on his fellow soldiers to come fetch him. Well, it wasn't CIA Bob, but it *was* two of his spooky mates. And as far as Mat was concerned, he'd made a promise. So be it, he thought to himself, grimly. Let the fighting begin.

Mat was pulled away from such thoughts by the harsh clunk-clunk of Jamie checking and rechecking the GPMG on their vehicle. Since the two vehicle-mounted GPMGs were the only heavy machine guns that the SBS soldiers had between them, Jamie wanted to make damn sure that the gun was in perfect working order, just in case they needed it on arrival at the fort.

'What d'you reckon, mate?' Jamie asked, glancing up from the weapon at Mat.

'To the mission?' Mat replied. 'Suicide mate. Think about it. There's eight of us lot – let's say twenty with the 5th SOF boys – and six hundred of them. Factor the Alliance lot in as well, and there's about a hundred of us. Big deal. And they're inside a bloody great big fortress with towers and battlements and the works, and we're outside of it trying to get in.'

'We'll fuckin' well just have to fuckin' mallet the fuckers,' growled Ruff. Ruff was a man of few words, but he was a killing machine once he was behind a GPMG, or a 'Gimpy' as soldiers liked to call it.

'Yeah – thanks for that pearl of wisdom, Ruff mate,' Mat remarked. 'Then there's the weaponry: what've we got? Diemacos. And they've got AKs, RPGs, grenades, RPK and Degtyarev machine guns more 'n likely, and probably mortars too. Then there's the fact that we've got no element of surprise, no eyes on the ground, no comms on the ground, fuck-all useful intel and no back-up. You want me to continue, mate?'

'Nope. Shut the fuck up,' Jamie replied. 'You want to get off the truck? Never too late to bug out of the mission, mate.'

'What? I wouldn't miss it for the bloody world,' Mat said. 'Like Ruff there says, we'll fookin' well just have to fookin' mallet the fookers.'

'About as much of a plan as we have got though, isn't it, mate?' Jamie responded.

'Just have to wait see what happens when we get there,' Mat said. 'Make it up as we go along. Won't be the first time, will it, mate?'

'So what's fuckin' new?' Ruff interjected. 'Fuckin' SNAFU, again, ain't it?'

SNAFU is a commonly used abbreviation by the men of the SBS and SAS. It stands for 'Situation Normal – All Fucked Up'. Behind Ruff's grim humour lay the years of training that had prepared these men for all eventualities – even those that could never be foreseen, like the coming assault on Qala-i-Janghi. In fact, the letters SAS are often wryly said to stand for 'Suck it and See'.

As the Land-Rovers approached their destination, the sky above was thick with tracer rounds going in both directions. Every now and then there was the rocket trail of an RPG streaking across the fort, followed by the crump of the grenade's explosion. Added to this was the regular, thumping percussion of mortar rounds slamming into the fort grounds. Even at this distance, some half-mile away from the fort, the noise was deafening. As the SBS soldiers stared up at the fearsome battle that was raging all around the ancient site, it was like nothing they had ever seen, or even imagined, before. *Holy fuck*, Mat found himself thinking, *we're going into that?*

The two Land-Rovers turned right off the tarmac, taking the dirt track that led in towards the massive fortified entranceway. As they did so mortar rounds started slamming into the dirt all around them. One of the enemy gunners must have spotted their gleaming white vehicles, and was calling in fire on them. To Mat's trained ear the rounds sounded like 80mm mortars. One hit from one of those would flatten the Land-Rover and obliterate all its occupants. The driver of Mat's vehicle, the lead Land-Rover, put his foot to the floor and started weaving from left to right in an effort to avoid the enemy fire. With the vehicle's engine screaming and the driver red-lining it, they raced towards the towering entranceway, a massive arched doorway some forty feet high.

'Let's fookin' do it!' Mat yelled through the window of the cab, as the driver gunned the engine and the vehicle powered across the rough terrain.

The wooden gates were thrown open, but Mat could see that the last fifty yards ahead of them were just a wall of lead. After what seemed like an age – but could only have been a half-dozen seconds – the lead vehicle kangarooed through the open gates, locked its wheels up and came to an abrupt halt. The second Land-Rover was directly behind them, and the Humvees carrying the ten 5th SOF soldiers were just a few seconds behind the SBS vehicles. They careered to a stop just inside the fort entranceway tower in a cloud of diesel fumes and dust. The Land-Rovers and the Humvees were riddled with bullet and shrapnel holes, but miraculously no one had been hit.

'Am I fuckin' glad to see you guys,' Steve, one of the CIA officers based at the fort, started yelling. 'Fuckin' Mike's been set upon by the fuckin' ragheads, and Dave's gone missin' and we don't know where the fuck he is.'

The SBS and 5th SOF soldiers gathered round CIA Steve, as he briefed them on what he knew about the state of the uprising. He had to scream to make himself heard above the noise of the battle. As the CIA officer spoke, Captain Lancer squatted down in the dirt and scratched out a quick diagram of the fort in the sand, to try to get a better sense of the battle. Inside the hexagonal outer walls, the fort complex was split into a northern and southern half, with a dividing wall in between. In the centre of that wall there was a gateway, which provided the only passageway between the two ends of the fort. The entranceway through which the SBS and 5th SOF forces had driven into the fort was built into the eastern tower, at one end of the fort's central dividing wall. The entranceway tower overlooked both the southern and northern ends of the fort, making it a good vantage point from which to counter-attack.

Apart from that tower, CIA Steve was unsure which, if any, of the other parts of the fort were still in friendly hands. Although the prisoners had been held in the southern end, firefights now seemed to have broken out all over the fort complex. All he knew for sure was that small groups of NA fighters were stationed at points around the outside of the fort, trying to keep the prisoners bottled up inside it. But as none of the Afghan troops was equipped with a radio, the only way to maintain communications with them was by word of mouth. This was making it all but impossible to keep track of the battle from their side. As far as CIA Steve knew, there were eighty Northern Alliance troops at the fort, or at least that's what the Afghan commanders had told him.

The CIA officers had been visiting the fort for several days now, questioning prisoners, and returning to Boxer Base each evening. They'd not brought any long-range communication kit with them, which meant that they'd been unable to contact Boxer Base. This accounted for the lack of any definitive intel on the uprising. And things had started going badly wrong at Qala-i-Janghi some eighteen hours earlier. The previous evening the prisoners were being processed into the fort and searched for weapons. But suddenly, there had been an almighty explosion. One of the foreign Taliban had grabbed hold of Nazir Ali, a senior Northern Alliance commander, and held him in a death embrace, pulling the pin of a grenade hidden in his clothing. Both men had been killed instantly, and several other Northern Alliance soldiers had been injured.

The Northern Alliance guards had started yelling at the prisoners, as they cocked their weapons and prepared to open fire on them. With their hands above their heads, the captives had been herded below ground to the subterranean cells, to join the other prisoners being held there. In their rush to get them safely below ground the Northern Alliance soldiers failed to search the remaining captives. Later that evening another of the prisoners had pulled the same trick with a grenade, killing himself and NA Commander Saeed Asad. Since this was the second suicidal gesture of defiance, it should have acted as a powerful warning to the Northern Alliance soldiers and their CIA allies. But despite this, the size of the Northern Alliance guard had not been increased that night.

The following morning two CIA agents armed with pistols and AK47s had gone in to question the prisoners. They were Johnny Michael 'Mike' Spann and David 'Dave' Tyson. Their mission was to start screening the prisoners for any suspected al-Qaeda terrorists – in particular any that could be linked to the events of 9/11. At 9 a.m., the two CIA agents had gone into the courtyard area in front of the underground cells. They were in the company of Said Kamel, the Northern Alliance's local chief of intelligence. Prisoners were brought out of the makeshift underground prison for questioning and made to kneel in rows, segregated by nationality: the Arabs were first, then the Pakistanis and, finally, the Uzbeks. With a handful of Northern Alliance soldiers standing guard, the two CIA operatives had started to interrogate them.

Before joining the CIA, Mike Spann had been a captain in the United States Marine Corps. He was quiet, serious and totally unflappable, with a great sense of humour. He also believed that he could handle himself pretty well. The prisoners all had their arms tied at their elbows with their turbans and were largely incapacitated, so Mike Spann hadn't felt unduly threatened. At first, he had led the interrogations, while his colleague, Dave Tyson, stood by, filming the process on a small hand-held video camera. New groups of the 'foreign Taliban' were brought up to them one at a time. With each prisoner they tried to ascertain the same information: their names and their true national-ities, why they had come to Afghanistan and what they had been doing there.

'Why are you here in Afghanistan?' Mike had kept asking the sullen prisoners. 'What did you come here for?'

From most he had received no answers, just a dark, silent defiance. But one of the prisoners, a slightly built, dark-haired young man, had spoken good English and claimed to be from London. Another of the prisoners had claimed to be from Ireland, yet another from Germany. Around lunchtime, a further batch of prisoners had been brought up to face their interrogators. Most of these were from Uzbekistan. By now, Dave Tyson was doing the bulk of the questioning. CIA Dave was fluent in several of the local languages and was able to speak to the Uzbek prisoners in their own tongue.

Suddenly, there was the booming echo of a blast below ground, followed instantly by screams and cries of '*Allahu Akhbar!*' In a split second, all hell had let loose, with the rattle of small-arms fire echoing out of the basement where the remainder of the prisoners were being held, and the Northern Alliance troops opening fire from the fort battlements. Instantly, Mike Spann realised that the prisoners were trying to break out of their underground prison. Mike knew that he faced two choices: he could make a run for the fort entrance and get away to safety; or he could do what his training and his spirit compelled him to do, and advance and engage the enemy – in an effort to help put down the prisoner uprising. Mike Spann elected to step forward and make a stand.

With barely a moment's hesitation he started sprinting towards the basement entrance, some thirty yards away. As he did so, prisoners launched themselves off the ground at him, trying to snare his legs and wrestle him to the ground. Mike grabbed his AK47 and opened fire on the prisoners at the basement entrance, where they were surging out and attacking the Northern Alliance guards. Dozens of prisoners had grabbed rocks and knives and were fighting at close quarters. The Afghan guards were hugely outnumbered, and the prisoners wrested their weapons from their hands, killing several as they did so.

At the same time, one of the prisoners jumped CIA Dave, screaming out, as he did so: '*ALLAHU AKHBAR!* KILL THE AMERICANS!' CIA Dave immediately drew his pistol and shot his attacker. He jumped to his feet and started to put down covering fire, as his buddy, CIA Mike, advanced towards the basement entrance. But by now Mike was in serious trouble, with prisoners lunging at him, ramming him with their bodies. Mike opened up with his AK47 on the enemy that now surrounded him. As his weapon ran short of ammunition, the prisoners turned attackers closed in, and Mike Spann went down in a flurry of kicks and blows. Suddenly, the CIA agent – married and with three children – had become the first US victim of the uprising at Qala-i-Janghi fort, and the first US casualty of the war in Afghanistan.

A horrified CIA Dave had seen his buddy go down. He emptied his AK47 at the prisoners, but the courtyard was now a seething mass of enemy fighters. As confusion turned into chaos, CIA Dave was forced to turn on his heel and run. He'd had no choice but to leave his CIA buddy behind. If he'd remained there a second longer he would himself have been seized by the enemy. CIA Dave sprinted for a large building on the northern edge of the fort compound, which was General Dostum's headquarters. As he burst inside he'd yelled a warning at the first people he saw, two men from the International Committee of the Red Cross (ICRC). The ICRC workers had come to the fort to meet with the Northern Alliance commanders and negotiate access to the prisoners. Now they suddenly found themselves in the midst of an uprising, with the prisoners baying for 'infidel' blood.

'Get the hell out of here,' CIA Dave had cried. 'The goddam prisoners are takin' control of the fort and there's twenty dead Alliance guys out there. Get the hell out – unless you wanna join them.'

The terrified ICRC workers had headed for the basement of the building, searching for a way to escape. But they'd found themselves in a dead end. So they had climbed to the top floor of the fort headquarters and hoisted themselves over the wall. From there they had careered and tumbled down the sixty-foot outer rampart, bullets chasing after them. Once on the ground, they'd been intercepted by a group of Northern Alliance fighters and taken away to safety.

Within minutes of the uprising, CIA Dave was the only remaining Westerner in the HQ building. Although he was in a state of shock and knew that he was in grave danger, Dave had opted to stay behind in an attempt to keep eyes on his CIA buddy. It had looked as if Mike hadn't stood a chance as the mob had pounced on him, and Dave was almost certain he was dead. But none of the prisoners had had any guns at the moment that Mike had gone down, and there remained just a chance that he might still be alive. In which case, there was still hope.

In his last communication from the fort, CIA Dave had used a satphone to put an SOS call through to the American Embassy in Tashkent, the capital of Uzbekistan. This was the main base for US and British special forces operating in northern Afghanistan. In that satphone call, CIA Dave raised the alarm about the fort uprising. He reported that his fellow agent, Mike Spann, had gone down, and that Qala-i-Janghi fort was now completely out of control. CIA Dave was unsure if CIA Mike was dead or alive, and he stressed repeatedly that there should be 'no strikes by air' because there was an American still in there. Then the batteries on the satphone that CIA Dave was using had gone down and the line had gone silent.

The first that Ali and his brothers had known about the uprising was when the sudden noise of the explosion had reverberated through the fort's underground chambers. After processing the night before, the majority of the prisoners had been herded below ground, into a labyrinth of basements and tunnels that ran beneath the fort grounds. Here, they had waited out the night secured by little more than their own black turbans tying their arms. It had been a long night during which few of the brothers had slept. In addition to the dozen men in Ali's unit, he estimated that there had to be some four hundred other brothers down in the main basement building.

As the grenade had exploded at the entrance, Ali had realised that a group of the Uzbek brothers had started the breakout without him. One of them had thrown the grenade, injuring some of the brothers and their Afghan guards. The entrance to the basement was now seething with prisoners, as they fought hand-to-hand to over-power the guards. Ali felt a desperate urge to be free of his bounds and above ground now, joining the battle for the fort. Suddenly, he was forcing his way to the front of the prisoners. But there were still over a hundred of them down there, and Ali had to fight to get through them all. Finally, he raised his face to the stairwell leading out of the basement. Standing at the open entranceway and silhouetted against the bright midday sun were two of the former prisoners, a smoking AK47 in each of their hands.

'*Allahu Akhbar! Allahu Akhbar!*' Ali began yelling, over and over again, as he surged up the basement steps. 'Brother warriors! Come untie us, brothers, so we may join you in the jihad!'

'*Allahu Akhbar*, brothers!' the two men yelled back, brandishing their AKs above their heads. 'By the grace of the Most Merciful One, we are free. The Northern Alliance whores and the American dogs are running for their lives, brothers. By the grace of Allah, the Fort of War is ours.'

'*Allahu Akhbar!*' came the bellows from Ali and his brothers.

The crowd of prisoners gathered around the two brothers who had freed them, milling about excitedly, nervously. In the immediate aftermath of the initial attack it was eerily quiet in the fort. There was little fighting now, as the surviving enemy soldiers had all fled from their end of the fort. There were some wounded brothers gathered around the basement entrance, and they would need bandaging as best they could. Across the courtyard Ali could see the bodies of several brothers lying where they had fallen, and there was also a handful of the Afghan guards lying dead. Among them Ali spotted a man dressed in blue jeans and a dark jacket – the 'uniform' of a foreigner. As Ali laid eyes on him, his heart leapt. Could it be that the brothers had already killed one of the cursed infidels, one of the hated American dogs? If so, Ali wanted a weapon and a chance to find some more of the *kafir* to slaughter.

'What now, brothers?' Ali asked, excitedly. 'What now? What is the plan, brothers?'

'Make for the armoury,' the two men urged, pointing out a series of dome-roofed buildings clustered against the fort's central wall. 'Some of the brothers are there already, breaking out the weapons. Arm yourselves with whatever you can find. There are RPGs, machine guns, grenades, AK47s. And mortars, brothers. Bring mortars. The mother of all battles is upon us, brothers. This is what we came here for. Arm yourselves, brothers! *Jihad! This is jihad!*'

'Fetch me a weapon, Brother Ahmed,' Ali urged, grabbing hold of his deputy's arm. 'Get me an RPG and some rounds, and bring them back to me here. OK?'

'Of course, Brother Ali,' a grinning Ahmed replied, as he set off for the armoury.

'So where are the enemy, brothers?' Ali continued, turning back to speak to the two men who had just freed him. As he did so, he held out his arms so that his bounds could be cut. 'Where are the Northern Alliance whores? Where are the American dogs? Where are the cowardly infidels? By the grace of Allah let us hunt them down and slaughter them all.'

MISSION IMPOSSIBLE

WITH the SBS and 5th SOF vehicles now parked up inside the entranceway tower, they were positioned in the only part of the fort that was known to be in friendly hands. As the six hundred prisoners were in full revolt, the whole southern end of the fort had already fallen to the enemy. They had seized RPGs and mortars, which meant devastating fire could be put down on to any section of the fort. It would only take one lucky mortar shell, or a grenade lobbed over the wall, and the SBS Land-Rovers and 5th SOF Humvees would be blown to smithereens.

'Right, get the vehicles in close to the walls, to maximise cover,' Captain Lancer ordered, having to shout to make himself heard above the noise of battle. 'I want you lads,' he continued, indicating his SBS soldiers, 'to clear and secure this tower. That's both fire teams. This is our only known bridgehead into the fort, and it's crucial we hold it. Once we've done that, we set up fire positions up top – from where we should be able to cover both ends of the fort. Sergeant Major Trent, I want your fire team to take up positions on the tower's southern wall. From there you can put down fire on to the southern end of the fort. I'll take the northern wall. We've got to contain these bastards in here, inside this fort, OK? Worst-case scenario is they break out – then we've got a totally unknown threat on our hands.'

'Right,' the lads responded.

'OK, let's do it. On me.'

With that, Captain Lancer turned and scuttled in through the dark doorway leading into the tower. Ahead of him, a wide set of stone stairs led towards the top of the building. At ceiling level the staircase split, with one flight of stairs branching off towards the northern side of the tower and the other towards the southern end. Inside the massively thick stone walls the noise of the battle was eerily muted, yet every now and then what had to be much closer bursts of machine-gun fire echoed down the passageways. Clearly, there were some fighters on top of the tower who were still holding out against the enemy.

Using hand signals, Captain Lancer sent Sergeant Major Trent's fire team up the left-hand staircase, while his team took the right-hand fork. After climbing up three more flights of stairs, Captain Lancer's team reached a point where the staircase ended in the open air: the roof of the tower. Up above that there was just a wall of death, as a fearsome volume of fire was scything its way across the roof of the fort.

With barely a second's hesitation, the Captain dropped to his belly and crawled up the last few steps and out on to the roof. Mat, Jamie and Ruff followed close behind him. On each side of the tower, thick walls rose up to around chest height. Crouching behind the battlements which looked into the fort were eight Afghan fighters.

Day 1 of Fort Siege

N

General Dostum's H.Q. building

N.E. Tower and final location of Capt. Lancer's SBS team

Entrance to H.Q. and external ramp

Route taken by Major Martin, Tom, Sam, CIA, Steve plus Afghans on rescue mission

N.W. Tower and Dushka HMG location

Initial location of Capt. Lancer's SBS Forces plus Afghan Forces

Enemy attempt to rush Dostum's H.Q.

SBS fire by GPMG & assult rifle at enemy

Western Tower

Central dividing wall

Central Gateway of Fort

Fort ammunition and weapons store

SBS, 5th SOF plus Afghan forces fire onto enemy

Position from where Sam sees CIA agent Mike Spann's body

S.W. Tower

S.E. Tower

Initial location of Sgt. Mgr. Trent's SBS fire team, plus US 5th SOF and Afghan forces

Dostum's Stables. Enemy stronghold with underground basement

They were a group of Northern Alliance soldiers dressed in a motley collection of combats, and wearing the traditional Afghan flat woollen hats.

The Captain glanced over at the nearest fighter. As he did so the Afghan rose up on one knee, squeezed off half a dozen rounds with his AK47 and dived back down behind cover, as a barrage of answering fire smashed into the brickwork all around him. As he hunkered down behind the battlements waiting for the enemy fire to subside, the Afghan fighter turned and caught sight of the British soldiers. Immediately, his face broke into a broad grin, and he began gesturing to the SBS troops to come over to join him. It was an invitation that Captain Lancer and the rest of the team felt unable to refuse.

As they half ran and half crawled the twenty-odd yards across to the wall, there was a mind-blowing amount of enemy fire coming out of the fort. To Mat it seemed incomprehensible that this battle, any battle, could ever be so intense, so fearsome. Clearly, the six hundred enemy fighters must have got their hands on all the weaponry and ammo stored in the fort armoury. In which case, what on earth would their small number be able to do to stop them? But in a split second, his training had kicked in, and he'd banished such fears from his mind.

Suddenly, Mat flipped his body up over the battlements and was squeezing off three rounds with his Diemaco – Crack! Crack! Crack! Dozens of the enemy were bunched up at the base of the wall, some three hundred yards in front of him. As Mat dived back behind cover, he felt the wall shaking and juddering behind him as the enemy returned fire, and chunks of masonry spun off into the air. Six yards further down the battlements, Jamie followed suit now, forcing himself up on to his knees and pouring down fire on to the enemy positions. He was followed in quick succession by Ruff and Captain Lancer, each man squeezing off a few quick rounds before diving for cover.

As none of them could speak any of the local languages, they were unable to communicate directly with the Afghan soldiers. Even if they had been able to, the deafening noise of battle made it all but impossible to talk. Yet they were still able to appreciate the universal language of soldiers. As Mat glanced across at the nearest NA fighter, he realised that the guy was staring at him in complete amazement. *What is it, mate? You never seen the SBS in action before?* Catching the Afghan soldier's eye, Mat smiled, did a quick impression of shooting one of the enemy, and gave him a big thumbs up. The Afghan soldier broke into a grin and returned the thumbs up to Mat. Reaching across the roof, Mat grabbed the Afghan soldier's free hand and held it in a crude handclasp for a second.

From their side of the tower, Mat and the rest of the lads had a view down into the northern half of the fort, the dividing wall between north and south running directly across from them towards the far side. In the centre of that wall was the gateway linking the two halves of the fort, and it was here that the enemy were gathered in the greatest numbers. It looked to Mat as if there were a hundred or more of them down there, although he could only take snatched glances at their positions. The enemy fighters had taken cover in a series of domed buildings that clustered beneath the wall, and behind three white Toyota pickups that were parked up at one side of the gateway.

Suddenly, there were roars of '*Allahu Akhbar! Allahu Akhbar! Allahu Akhbar!*' coming from the opposite side of the wall. As Mat bobbed up to take a look he all but had his head taken off by a barrage of machine-gun fire that slammed into the masonry all around him.

In the split second before diving down again, Mat caught sight of some thirty enemy fighters sprinting out of the gateway towards the northern end of the fort. They were breaking out – making a charge for General Dostum's HQ building. If the enemy took this, it would give them a vantage point from which to control the whole of the northern end of the fort. Which would mean that practically all of Qala-i-Janghi would be in their hands. There was no way then that they could be prevented from breaking out. With a combined force of barely a hundred SBS, US 5th SOF and Northern Alliance troops, it would be impossible to encircle the whole fort.

Not only that, but Dostum's HQ building was the last known location of Dave Tyson. It was from there that his last communication had been received. Mat and the other lads were well aware that it was every jihadist's dream to be able to kill one of the cursed American, or British, 'infidels'. If they reached Dostum's HQ, CIA Dave was as good as dead.

Fired up by that thought, Mat swung his Diemaco up above the battlements and squeezed off a burst on automatic at the figures now charging across the fort compound. As he did so, he felt his SBS mates, and the Afghan fighters to either side of him, doing likewise. Just as he ducked back down again, he saw three of the enemy stumble, and then fall headlong on to the ground. *YES!* a voice was screaming inside his head with the exhilaration of the kill. *Fucking got the bastards!*

To the right of him the Afghan fighter he'd just befriended was putting down a whole magazine on to the running figures. But Mat just knew that he was holding the shot for far too long. As he turned to yell out a warning he saw the Afghan fighter's head jerk backwards and then his body slump to one side, coming to rest at a grotesquely twisted angle at the base of the battlements. Mat could see that he had taken a round through the forehead, and was already stone-cold dead. A second later, another of the Afghan fighters was writhing in agony on the roof of the fort, as a bullet had smashed through his right shoulder.

Holy fuck, Mat thought to himself, *two of the Afghans down and only six to go. If we keep losing blokes at this rate, then we're fucking finished.*

Crabbing his way across to the injured Afghan soldier, Mat grabbed an emergency dressing from one of his pouches and stuffed it as hard as he could into the gaping shoulder wound. Then he and Jamie together started dragging the fallen fighter back into the cover of the battlements.

'They're fucking breaking out,' Jamie yelled in Mat's ear. 'Dostum's HQ. We got to stop 'em. We're fucking dead if we don't, mate.'

'Yeah, but with fookin' what?' Mat yelled back.

'Wait one, I got me an idea.'

As soon as they had dumped the wounded Afghan soldier in the cover of the battlements, Jamie went crawling as fast as he could across the roof to Captain Lancer.

'Boss, the fuckers are breakin' out and we need some fucking firepower,' Jamie yelled into the Captain's ear. 'There's two GPMGs down on the trucks. I'm going to see if I can get 'em.'

'Fine. Do it,' the Captain yelled back. 'But hurry. They're going to make another run for it any time now.'

'Let's take as many of the fuckers with us as we can,

eh, boss?' a grinning Jamie said. 'Cos we ain't fucking getting out of this one alive.'

'We are if I can help it,' Captain Lancer replied. 'Fuck it, I'm coming with you.'

Dodging the enemy bullets as they ran, Jamie and the SBS Captain scurried back across the fort roof and dived down the stairway. The two men charged down to the base of the tower and out into the open, whereupon Jamie vaulted into the back of the nearest Land-Rover. A second later, he had his trusty Leatherman in his hand and had started working on the mounting that held the GPMG bolted on to the truck, Captain Lancer lending a hand.

As they were feverishly working on the gun, the Captain caught sight of Sergeant Major Trent and Tom Knight hurrying down the tower stairway towards him. They had a bunch of the US 5th SOF soldiers in tow, including the CO, Major Martin.

'Boss,' Sergeant Major Trent yelled over, 'you got a second?'

'Tell me,' Captain Lancer yelled back, as he jumped down from the vehicle and strode across to them.

'OK, we've got a couple hundred enemy down in the southern half of the fort,' the Sergeant Major began. 'They're holed up in a large pink building, the stables for Dostum's cavalry, under which there's a bunker network. There's a dozen NA soldiers up with us on the tower, plus the ten 5th SOF boys, so we're not doing too badly. But there's a shedload of incoming and we got our hands full. Couple of the Afghans have been hit already.'

'Same story our side. Tell me something I don't know,' the Captain replied.

'OK, buddy, like we gotta get us a rescue team

together,' Major Martin cut in. 'And mighty quick, too, cos our boys're in there somewhere –'

'I know that, Major,' Captain Lancer interrupted. 'So what d'you need?'

'Well, we got myself and one of the CIA officers, plus there's Sam, who's volunteerin' his services to rescue a fellow American –'

'And they need a fuckin' medic, boss,' Tom cut in. 'Stands to reason, cos either one of them CIA blokes could be injured bad in there, and as I'm the only fuckin' medic around –'

'Fine,' said Captain Lancer. 'What's the rescue plan?'

'Figure we gotta head for Dostum's HQ building,' Major Martin replied. 'That's the last known location of CIA Dave, so it's all we got to go on. If we can link up with him, maybe he can lead us to Mike Spann.'

'Sounds good to me,' said Captain Lancer. 'Have you got comms with CIA Dave?'

'Right now we got nothing,' said Major Martin. ''Bout an hour ago CIA Dave placed a call on a satphone. Said he was in Dostum's HQ, and all hell was breakin' loose. No one's been able to raise him since. Either his battery's dead, or the satphone's gone down.'

'Well, good luck then,' Captain Lancer said. 'We'll give you all the supporting fire we can.'

'You're welcome to it, lads,' Sergeant Major Trent added. 'Lucky madness trip that you're on and all.'

'We got us some air cover comin' over pretty fast, now,' said Major Martin, addressing his remark to the SBS Captain.

'Air strikes wouldn't go amiss, Major,' Captain Lancer replied. 'So who's doing the FAC?'

'We are, boss,' Sergeant Major Trent cut in. 'Seems the 5th SOF boys haven't got all their comms kit with them.'

'Fine,' said the SBS Captain. 'You familiar with the US FAC procedure?'

'No problem, boss,' the Sergeant Major replied. 'One thing though – the Americans want us to put up friendly coordinates to their pilots.'

'We don't put up friendly coordinates,' Captain Lancer said, turning to face the 5th SOF CO. 'It's against our SOPs.'

''Fraid that's the way it's gotta be,' the Major replied. 'Our fly boys won't put down any ordnance unless y'do.'

'We don't put up friendly coordinates because it's an invitation to the pilot to drop his bombs on us,' Captain Lancer said, acidly.

'They gotta have 'em or they won't do no air strikes,' Major Martin countered. 'An' you guys gotta do the FAC as you got the full kit and caboodle. Way I see it, ain't no way around it.'

'All right, Sergeant, put up the friendly coordinates,' the SBS Captain conceded. 'But relocate your FAC team to my side of the tower.'

'No problem, boss,' Sergeant Major Trent replied.

Just then there was an ecstatic yell from one of the Land-Rovers. 'GOT THE FUCKER!' It was Jamie and he was holding the GPMG aloft in his hands. 'Got the fucker!'

'Right, let's get the other,' Captain Lancer yelled back at him, 'and all the ammo we can carry.'

The one advantage of the GPMGs having been vehicle-mounted was that there was an almost unlimited supply of ammunition stacked up in the rear of the two Land-Rovers. Quick as they could, Jamie and Captain Lancer carried the two heavy machine guns and a couple of crates of ammo up on to the roof of the tower. But just as they were about to go back for some more ammo, frenzied cries of 'Allahu Akhbar!' went up from the far side of the wall. A second group of enemy fighters had broken cover and were charging towards the northern end of the fort.

Within seconds, Ruff Pouncer had grabbed one of the GPMGs and was standing braced at the battlements, the heavy weapon steadied against his thigh as he poured down fire on to the enemy. As the rounds tore into them half a dozen AQT fighters stumbled and fell. But at the same time Ruff was targeted by the enemy. In a split second he was faced with a wall of flying lead, the battlements being torn apart all around him. As Ruff dived back behind cover, Jamie was up on his feet, unleashing a further barrage of fire from the hip with the second GPMG. The hail of bullets tore into the running figures, and as it did so the enemy charge slowed, faltered and came to a stop. The survivors turned and went staggering back the way they had come. Jamie in turn dived for cover now, as the enemy fire tore into the section of wall where he'd just been standing.

'Fuck this for a game of soldiers,' Jamie yelled, as he lay prone on the roof cradling the still-smoking GPMG, the rounds slamming into the wall just behind him.

Jamie knew that the barrage of fire that he and Ruff were laying down was all that was stopping the enemy from breaking out en masse. If either of them got hit, or if one of the guns jammed, then the SBS soldiers were likely to get overrun. And Jamie and Ruff reckoned it was only so long before one or other of them would take a bullet. Either that, or the enemy rounds would start penetrating the mud-brick walls of the battlements, at which time it'd be pretty much game over for the small force holding out on the tower roof. The enemy were hiding in the mud-walled buildings at the base of the wall, and behind the Toyota pickups parked in the entranceway. If only they'd brought their 40mm grenade launchers with them, Jamie found himself thinking. If they had, they'd have been able to decimate the enemy with a few well-placed rounds.

Taking his GPMG with him, Jamie belly-crawled the short distance across the roof to Ruff.

'We got to mallet those fuckers in the gateway, mate,' Jamie yelled into Ruff's ear. 'Right now, they got us banged to rights. We need grenade launchers, LAWs, the whole how's your father, and we ain't got none.'

"Old on, I got me a fuckin' idea, mate,' Ruff yelled back, after a moment's silence. 'Use the fuckin' Gimpys to mallet the fuckin' pickups. Get the fuckin' fuel tanks to blow – one load of fried fuckin' ragheads coming right up.'

'Nice one, mate,' Jamie replied, with a grin. 'Now why the fuck didn't I think of that?'

Using hand signals, Jamie and Ruff indicated to Mat and Captain Lancer what they were about to do – and that the two of them, plus the Afghan fighters, should put down covering fire. Then they scuttled off to fetch a couple more crates of ammo for the GPMGs. Finally, they were ready.

'Right. Fuckin' on me – LET'S FUCKIN' GO!' Ruff yelled.

Simultaneously, the two men heaved the GPMGs over the battlements and opened fire, while Mat, Captain Lancer and the Afghan fighters started taking short, aimed bursts at the enemy positions. For three, four, five seconds, Jamie and Ruff poured fire into the three pickups parked up at the gateway, the heavy rounds from the GPMGs chewing into the vehicles. Suddenly, there was an almighty explosion, and one of the trucks burst into

a ball of orange flame. As debris from the fireball flew
into the air, there were two further detonations in quick
succession. In a split second all three vehicles had been
turned into a massive, blazing inferno. A thick mushroom cloud of oily black smoke rose above the twisted
wreckage at the gateway, and for the first time since the
battle had begun the enemy guns there had fallen silent.

Scattered around the burning vehicles were the blackened corpses of a dozen enemy soldiers, lying where
they'd fallen. But many of the fighters at the gateway
must have remained untouched by the blazing inferno.
Barely thirty seconds after the vehicles had exploded, a
series of RPGs streaked out of the gateway and flew the
three hundred yards across the fort compound, where
they slammed into Dostum's HQ. They were followed
by a barrage of machine-gun fire, as the enemy poured
rounds on to the building. Within seconds, the fighting
had resumed with renewed vigour, and a savage amount
of firepower was unleashed across the fort. Rounds were
going off everywhere and RPGs were repeatedly firing
off. It looked as if the enemy remained intent on seizing
the fort HQ.

Out of the corner of his eye, Mat caught a movement
down below him and off to his left. As he looked over,
he caught the movement again and spotted a figure with
an AK47 slung over his back, attempting to scale their
position. The enemy fighter was some sixty feet away,
where the tower met the fort dividing wall. He was
already three-quarters of the way up a wooden ladder
and climbing fast. In the shadowed crook of the corner
of the two walls he had been all but invisible. It was
only the flash of the fighter's movement, and some sort
of indefinable sixth sense, that had alerted Mat to his
presence. Below him, there was now a second figure

clambering up the ladder. A third followed. All had the same, fanatical look on their faces. Mat had no doubt that if they broke into the SBS positions they'd wipe out the British and US forces, or die in the process.

The angle was so oblique to the tower wall that Mat could get a bead on the enemy fighter while still remaining in the cover of the battlements. Carefully, he took aim with his Diemaco, the magnification sight bringing the enemy into sharp focus. They looked like Chechens, these fighters, as they had the telltale Mongoloid features, and wild hair unrestrained by the black Talib turbans. As the lead figure got to the top of the ladder and reached for the battlements above, Mat squeezed his trigger gently. He watched as the forehead of the enemy fighter caved in before his very eyes. The fighter threw back his arms and in slow motion tumbled from the ladder, landing with an inaudible thud on the ground below. Without needing to waste a second round, Mat dropped his weapon to the figure below and drilled a bullet into his brain, and then on to the next one.

It was the first time that Mat had ever definitely killed. Sure, he'd called in air strikes on enemy positions before, which would have accounted for scores of enemy dead. And in previous conflicts he'd exchanged fire with enemy soldiers. But he'd never shot someone at such close range, never watched himself end the life of a fellow human being so closely. Mat had been able to make out the features of these men, the lines on their faces, the hatred in their eyes. These were fanatical fighters, of that he had no doubt. They'd seen a lot of war. And they'd had their hearts set on killing Mat and the other lads, or being killed themselves. Now their fighting days were over, and Mat felt glad that it was so. In quick succession he put half a dozen rounds into the ladder's wooden uprights, whereupon it collapsed, toppling over on to the floor of the fort.

'Boss,' Mat yelled across to Captain Lancer, pointing out the fallen enemy fighters. As the Captain couldn't hear him, Mat crawled across to have a word in his ear. 'Boss, down there! They're trying to scale the fookin' tower. Get in among us.'

'Good shooting,' Captain Lancer yelled back at him, as he spotted the dead fighters lying at the base of the tower. 'Need eyes in the back of your head!'

'Boss, there's hundreds of them and only a handful of us. And we've no idea where the fookers are. I got lucky with them bastards. But at this rate we're going to get overrun. Where the fuck're those air strikes, boss? Without air power, we're fookin' finished.'

'Any moment now,' the Captain said. 'Just keep your eyes open. Keep the enemy pinned down in the fort.'

As Captain Lancer's fire team were trying to stop the enemy from breaking out of the fort, US 5th SOF Major Martin was getting the rescue mission underway. The 5th SOF forces had been stationed at Mazar far longer than the SBS soldiers, and the Major had visited the fort before, which was one of the main reasons he'd decided to lead the rescue mission. Of all the special forces soldiers, the Major figured that he had the best chance of navigating his way through the fort. His rescue team consisted of himself and CIA Steve, together with Sam and Tom, plus a dozen Northern Alliance soldiers. These Afghan fighters had served with General Dostum for many years, and they knew the layout of the fort well. It was their job to help guide the British and American soldiers to their objective: the two missing CIA agents.

The Major's plan was to advance some three hundred yards along the outside of the fort wall to the point where it met the north-eastern tower. Then they would climb over and advance through the fort's interior to the General's HQ building. The plan's biggest weakness was that on that last leg they would be totally exposed to enemy fire. But the only way the Major knew into the building was through a small entranceway on the inside of the fort – the very place that the charging enemy fighters were now trying to get to. This put the rescue party and their enemy on a direct collision course. None of the men had any illusions as to how dangerous, if not suicidal, their mission was. But the US military's *esprit de corps* has it that no man should be left behind. And so CIA Dave and Mike Spann had to be located and rescued, or if they were dead, their bodies recovered.

Creeping out of the fort entranceway the four special forces soldiers turned and headed north, keeping as close to the cover of the fort wall as possible. Moving stealthily and favouring the shadows, they aimed to advance as far as they could without being spotted. But the rescue team hadn't covered more than half the distance to the north-eastern tower when, suddenly, there was the scream of an incoming mortar round. Tom, Sam, CIA Steve and Major Martin threw themselves flat on the deck, as the shell went crashing into the earth some eighty yards behind them. Within seconds, there was the whoosh–crump! of further incoming mortars as the enemy began to zero in on their position. The rescue team had been spotted, and if they stayed where they were the enemy would soon be dropping mortars right on top of them.

'C'mon! MOVE!' Tom yelled, jumping to his feet and taking the initiative. He motioned for the Afghan fighters to do likewise and follow his lead. 'Get movin'. Move your fuckin' arses. NOW! MOVE!'

Tom waited until all the fighters were on their feet and running forward, before bringing up the rear. They charged towards the north of the fort caution thrown to the wind with the Afghan fighters in the lead. Behind them they could hear the mortar barrage creeping ever closer. Suddenly, up ahead of Tom, one of the Afghan fighters placed a foot on the ground and it just exploded. One moment he was running, the next there was a boom! and he was flying through the air, with his arms and legs flailing, before landing with a dull thump. As there had been no scream of an incoming shell, Tom knew that this was no mortar round. A second later, he realised what was happening.

Mines! he thought to himself, in horror. *We're running through the centre of a fucking minefield!*

Tom remained frozen to the spot, momentarily paralysed by fear. His shocked mind wondered what madness could have led the Afghan soldiers – who, on and off, had occupied this fort for decades – to allow them to route their rescue mission through the centre of a fucking minefield. Then he snapped himself back to the present, and as he did so his overriding concern was for his SBS mate, Sam, and the two US officers, who were racing ahead of him seemingly blind to the danger all around them.

'MINES!' he screamed, trying to get his voice to carry above the noise of the battle. 'It's a fuckin' MINEFIELD, Sam. FUCKIN' MINES!'

The pace of the action seemed to wind right down now, as Tom watched his three fellow soldiers come to a dead halt up ahead of him. As if in slow motion, they turned back to look at him, the shock and uncertainty writ large across their faces. Tom felt himself making a wide sweep of the area in front of him with his left hand

– as if to point out the minefield all around them. Then he was jabbing his finger repeatedly at the fallen Afghan fighter, whose right leg had been totally shredded in the explosion, and mouthing the word 'MINES!' again and again.

Sam, CIA Steve and Major Martin still looked confused. They hadn't seen the mine go off and it would make far more sense to them if a mortar round had taken out the fallen Afghan soldier. So Tom took a few fearful steps towards Sam, who was the nearest of the three to him.

'MINES!' he yelled in Sam's ear, and then over at the others: 'IT'S A FUCKIN' MINEFIELD.'

As the others suddenly understood, they glanced down in horror at their feet. At the same time Tom could hear the mortar rounds creeping ever closer. They were barely fifty yards away now, and the noise of their detonations kept getting steadily louder, as the mortar barrage came after them. For a few seconds they were all rooted to the spot, frozen with indecision. If they moved ahead, it was into a minefield. If they turned back, it was into that fearsome mortar barrage. But then there was the long, hollow hooowl! of another incoming shell, and as the noise drilled deep into their skulls it sounded as if the round was about to land right on top of them. Tom and Sam hit the deck and embraced as they waited for the impact – as this one clearly had their names written on it.

'This is it, bro!' Sam yelled.

'Nice knowing you!' Tom yelled back, just as the mortar round hit some half a dozen yards in front of them.

But rather than an ear-splitting, flesh-shredding blast of high explosives and razor-sharp shards of hot steel, there was just a dull, sucking flop! as the shell impacted with the soft ground and failed to go off. Either it was a blind or a dud, or the soft sand has prevented it from exploding. Or perhaps the enemy had forgotten to disarm the mortar's safety fuses. On either side of the special forces soldiers mortars started impacting now – but several more of them failed to explode. Even so, trapped in the midst of a minefield and with mortar shells raining down on them like this, the chances of survival didn't look too good for the two SBS soldiers and their US and Afghan allies.

Suddenly, with a wild-eyed look at his SBS mate, Sam leapt to his feet and started charging through the centre of the minefield up ahead of them. Forcing himself to overcome his fear, Tom jumped up and raced after him, and then the rest of the rescue team were following their lead, pounding their way across the minefield towards the north-eastern tower of the fort.

It seemed to take an age to cross the minefield, each step haunted by the dread of shredding flesh and bone. But in reality it could only have been a few seconds before Tom and Sam reached the shelter of the massive tower. They collapsed, breathless, in the cover of the wall – and for the first time since the assault began they risked a silent prayer. As their fellow soldiers charged in to the shelter to join them, Sam and Tom crouched there, staring at each other in wide-eyed fear. It was several seconds before they'd got their breathing under control, or stopped their hands from shaking. How was it that they were still alive? Behind them, there was the body of the Afghan fighter lying where he'd fallen, his lifeblood draining into the desert sand.

Once they'd caught their breath, the Major signalled for the rescue team to move forward. The Afghan fighters scrambled up the rampart to the top of the wall first. As soon as they made the battlements, they started taking incoming rounds from the enemy. Sam, Tom, Major Martin and CIA Steve followed them up the sloping earthen ramp, and as they reached the top, the Afghan fighters leaned down from the parapet so that the British and American soldiers could grab hold and get a helping hand up on to the wall.

As Sam and Tom went up, there were rounds buzzing past their heads like a swarm of giant, angry bees, and to either side of them the battlements were getting blasted apart. CIA Steve and the Major followed quickly. But as they did so there was the terrifying whoosh! of approaching RPGs. Suddenly, two grenades slammed into the wall just below them with a deafening blast. In a split second the wall was enveloped in a swirling mass of smoke and debris.

'*ALLAHU AKHBAR! ALLAHU AKHBAR!*' the brothers yelled in delight, as they saw the first RPG round smash into the wall just below where the enemy soldiers were trying to break into the fort.

'Die, you whores!' Ali roared, as he waited for his loader to fit the next grenade on to his weapon. This brother was good and quick and within seconds the next round was ready. Ali lined up the sights on the same spot. 'This fort is ours – so die like the whore dogs of the *kafir* . . .'

His last words were drowned out in the roar of the back-blast of the RPG firing. The rocket-propelled grenade streaked across the compound, leaving a smoky trace in the air like a vapour trail. Then a great gout of smoke and flame shot out from exactly the spot where the enemy were trying to breach the wall. There was a second round of delighted cheering as Ali and the brothers saw two matchstick figures falling from the wall head first into the fort.

Ali and the brothers were gathered at the central gateway, taking cover in the mud-walled buildings clustered at the base of the wall. It was a perfect vantage point from which to put down fire on to the northern section of the fort, and the positions of the Afghan, British and American soldiers. And it was from here that they had been launching their attacks across the compound to seize Dostum's HQ building. That was the key target of their assault now. The brothers knew that the American CIA agent – and maybe some foreign journalists and aid workers – were pinned down inside that building. *Kafir prey, ready for the killing.*

Behind the brothers, Ahmed had established a mortar-fire position, taking advantage of the shelter afforded by the thick mud wall. With one of the 80mm mortars from the arms store, he and a team of two other brothers were putting down sustained mortar fire on to the enemy. Not only was Ahmed a seasoned mortar operator, but he was one of the few brothers strong enough to manhandle the mortar and its base plate. He kept shifting it from one spot to another, continuously changing his position to avoid getting targeted by the enemy. It was a trick that he had learned during his years fighting with the Taliban, and he was putting it to excellent use now. Three rounds in quick succession dropped down the mortar tube, and Ahmed had the gun up on his shoulder and was running to the next position. Slam! The base plate was dropped on to the ground again, the trajectory checked and another three rounds fired – Boom! Boom! Boom! Then it was up again and on to the next position, before they were spotted.

Over at the gateway, Ali had a third RPG round ready now, but just as he was sighting the weapon on the same section of the fort wall and preparing to fire, a sustained burst of gunfire came back at him and he was forced to dive for cover into one of the buildings. The fire was coming from the enemy positions on the eastern entranceway tower, and it had them well and truly pinned down. By the sound of the weapon, the accuracy and the rate of fire – even the noise the rounds made as they whirred past his ears – Ali could tell that this was not an AK47, or any of the other Soviet weaponry with which he was familiar.

As he crouched in the darkness waiting for a chance to return fire, Ali exchanged glances with the brothers gathered around him. Instinctively, they knew that this was no group of Northern Alliance soldiers that they were up against now. The rounds coming at them were smaller than anything that the Northern Alliance whores used. These were 5.56mm rounds – the calibre used by the *kafir* American dogs and their allies. And the fire coming at them was well targeted and sustained – most likely a team of several gunners putting down short bursts and working in conjunction with each other. It was far too disciplined for Afghan soldiers, of that Ali was certain.

On two sides Ali was faced with the cursed, infidel enemy – the American and British dogs. And how he ached to kill more of them.

TWO WHITE DOVES

AT the same time as Major Martin's rescue team were fighting their way into the fort's interior, Captain Lancer's men were fighting for their very survival up on the roof of the entranceway tower. They were laying down a fierce barrage of fire on to the enemy trying to break out. But the enemy fighters were continuously counter-attacking: AK47 fire, heavier machine-gun fire, mortar rounds and RPGs were slamming into the battlements and pounding the tower walls. A continuous, deafening thunder of gunfire and explosions rolled around the tower roof, as Captain Lancer, Mat, Jamie and Ruff tried to return fire. The air was thick with smoke and cordite fumes. Without air strikes, there was little chance that this handful of SBS soldiers could hold their positions for much longer. Either they would be blown to pieces, or the enemy would overrun the tower and gun them down.

'FAST AIR ON ITS WAY!' Sergeant Major Trent yelled over. Even the burly Sergeant Major's voice was barely audible above the noise of battle. 'Mat, Jamie, Ruff, get your shit together.'

'Right,' the men yelled back, rolling away from the battlements.

Mat knew Sergeant Major Trent – or 'Trenty' as the lads called him – from previous missions, and he was a no-nonsense individual with many years' combat experience. No amount of enemy fire was going to break Trenty's nerve. Under his direction, Mat, Jamie and Ruff formed a FAC team, to talk the US aircraft down on to target. There was a real urgency to their actions now, as the fast air was just minutes away.

Scrabbling around in his bergen Jamie pulled out one of their laser target designators – a heavy, portable-TV-sized device used for 'painting' the target with a laser beam, so that a guided munition could home in on it. At the same time, Ruff was digging out the other LTD from his backpack. Dodging incoming fire as he crawled across the roof, Mat joined Trenty at the radio. Forward air control was Mat's second chosen SBS skill, after medic, and he would be doing the comms with the US pilots. The photography talents that he'd put to such good use in the Naka Valley just came naturally to him. He'd often wondered whether in another life he'd have made a good paparazzo, chasing after the stinking rich and the undeservedly famous.

'Right, I want you to concentrate on two target areas,' Captain Lancer yelled, as he gathered Trenty, Mat, Jamie and Ruff in the cover of the tower stairway. Down here they had some cover from the shrapnel and the bullets, but the noise of battle could be heard thundering down the stone steps and crashing off the walls. 'First, Target 1, here, the enemy at the gateway – the buildings they're hiding in.' The Captain jabbed his index finger at the map. 'After that, Target 2, the pink building at the southern end of the fort where the rest of 'em are holed up.'

As the Captain pointed out the targets, small shards of shrapnel from exploding RPG rounds and mortars was falling on to the map that they had spread out on the tower steps. Mat noticed that the red-hot shards of metal were burning black holes in the map's laminated surface, sending up little plumes of smoke as they did so.

'Jamie, you lase Target 1, the gateway,' the SBS Captain shouted. 'Hit that first cos that's where they're trying to break out from. Ruff, you lase the pink building, Target 2.'

'Got it,' Ruff and Jamie confirmed.

'And keep your GPMGs close to hand,' the Captain called after them, as the two men scurried back across to the battlements. 'In case they try another breakout.'

Captain Lancer turned back to Mat. 'We're danger-close to the targets, less than five hundred yards,' he yelled in his ear. 'At that distance five-hundred-pounders are a real threat. Be damn careful with those target co-ordinates.'

'We got solid walls between us and them,' Mat yelled back. 'Should be OK. But I'll be careful.'

Jamie and Ruff chose a vantage point behind the battlements from where they could get eyes on the targets. Incoming rounds were still ploughing into the tower roof, and both men were acutely aware of how much they needed those US air strikes to hit the enemy hard. They fired up the compressed air cylinders on the LTDs, which provided an all but silent means of operation, crucial for covert use of the LTDs. After shooting the lasers at their respective targets, the two men scribbled down the enemy coordinates. Then they made a note of their own, friendly coordinates, which they'd also be putting up to the US pilots. They didn't like doing so, but their need for the air strikes was far greater than their fear of one of the pilots targeting them by accident.

Up on the tower roof they were fortunately at a higher elevation than both the enemy targets. This meant that the laser beams would be pointing downwards when the air strikes went in and the laser-guided bombs homed in on the 'hot spot', the point where the laser beam hit the target. If the target happened to be higher than those operating the lasers, the laser beam would be tilted upwards. Then there was always a danger that the bomb would home in on the wrong hot spot – the source of the laser beam itself, targeting the LTD operator. This was one less thing to worry about now.

Over in the shelter of the tower stairwell Mat flipped up the eighteen-inch-long 'donkey dick' antennae for the VHF radio that they'd use to communicate with the US pilots. Somehow, he didn't find it hard to believe that the US 5th SOF soldiers had forgotten such a crucial piece of kit as their comms antennae. After seeing the way they'd been rushing around Boxer Base earlier, it didn't surprise him that they'd come in unprepared. As far as the SBS lads were concerned, there was a very good reason why the US military had a two-tier system for special forces. The US Tier 1 Special Forces – the SEALs and Delta Force – were every bit as good as the SBS and SAS. But their Tier 2 Special Forces were just that – second place in both training and combat experience.

As Mat finished setting up the comms kit, Jamie came crawling across the tower roof with the target coordinates. He pulled back one of the radio earphones so he could speak directly into Mat's ear.

'Here you go,' Jamie yelled above the noise of the battle, as he handed Mat the scrap of paper with the coordinates on it. 'Mallet the fuckers big time.'

Mat gave Jamie the thumbs up and then turned back to the radio set. After a few further comms checks, he put a call out to the US aircraft.

'Fast air, fast air, this is Romeo Zero Alpha,' Mat intoned into the radio set, calling up the F-18 Super Hornet high above him. The call sign that he was using had been specially designated as special forces, so any allied pilot hearing it would immediately know who he was dealing with.

'This is Red Fox Four, hearing you loud and clear, Romeo Zero Alpha,' the lead pilot's voice came back at him. 'Authenticate – Alpha PX.'

'Romeo Zero Alpha, authenticating: Alpha PX – Bravo ZX,' Mat replied, providing the pilot with the second half of the password that he'd been given during briefing for the Mazar mission.

'Authenticated, Romeo Zero Alpha,' the pilot responded. 'What can I do for ya?'

'What's your locstat and bearing you're coming in on?'

'Four-six-two-four. North-north-west.'

'OK, Red Fox Four, if you turn to your west you should see a mountain range,' Mat continued, looking over the map that he had spread out before him on the stairs. 'Then before that you'll see a small village to your front, centre. You got that?'

'Mountain range and a village. I got it.'

'OK, look beyond that village and to the north-east, about one kilometre, and you'll see an old fort. That's your target area.'

'I got the fort.'

'OK, Red Fox Four, what d'you have on board?'

'I have two-thousand-pound JDAMs and five-hundred pound laser-guided.'

'OK, we are danger-close, I repeat, danger-close to the targets. So, I want only your five-hundred-pound laser-guided.'

'Well copied. Five-hundred-pounders only on target.'

'OK, these are the first target coordinates: MGRS Foxtrot Echo 23849676. Repeat, coordinates are: 23849676.'

'Foxtrot Echo 23849676. Got it.'

'OK, I'm letting you see my laser,' Mat continued, pointing his laser torch into the air and executing a figure of eight with it. He waited for a few seconds. The pilot would need time to pick it up with his on-board camera: it would appear as a small dot of intense white light. 'You got it?'

'Yeah, I got it.'

'Right, I'm moving it down on to the mountain side.'

'Yeah, I got it.'

'OK, I'm moving it on to the target area now, the central wall of the fort.'

'Yeah. I have the target visual now.'

'OK, there's an LTD aimed at the centre point of that wall, the gateway. You see the hot spot?'

'I see it.'

'OK, that's where we want you to put the first five-hundred-pounder.'

'I got it,' the pilot responded. 'What's the friendly coordinates?'

'OK, friendly coordinates are Foxtrot Echo 23849675,' Mat replied. 'Like I said, we're danger-close.'

'OK, coming in now, west of your location: three miles out, two miles out . . .'

Mat glanced up into the sky and spotted the US aircraft. 'OK, Red Fox Four, I've got you visual now. If you look to your left front, you'll pick up on the sparkler on my helmet.' Mat was referring to the laser torch that he'd attached to his helmet, on pulse mode.

'OK, I got your sparkler . . .' the pilot began replying, but his words were lost in a confusion of yelling, as Jamie and Ruff spotted the enemy making another charge from the gateway.

'THEY'RE BREAKIN' OUT! THEY'RE BREAKIN' OUT!'

A split second later there was the roar of a GPMG kicking into life. Glancing over the lip of the stairwell Mat could see that Ruff had dropped his LTD and was back at the battlements, pouring down fire on to the enemy.

Fuck, Mat thought to himself, *which of them was lazing Target 1, Jamie or Ruff?*

'FUCKIN' GET THE FAST AIR IN,' Jamie screamed over, from where he was crouched behind his LTD. He had realised the source of Mat's confusion. 'I'm on Target 1. I'M ON TARGET 1. MALLET THE FUCKERS!'

'RED FOX FOUR, RED FOX FOUR, YOU HEAR ME?' Mat yelled into his radio.

'Yeah, buddy, I hear ya and I can see ya now,' came back the pilot's reply. 'There's around a dozen of ya on the battlements there, an' looks like you're in some trouble.'

'Yeah, that's us. We need that air strike now.'

'Right I'm starting my bombing run . . . I'm thirty secs to target . . . fifteen secs to target . . .'

Glancing up Mat was just in time to see a black, wheelie-bin-sized object streaking across the fort, homing in on the hot point of Jamie's laser beam. As it plummeted towards the central gateway it made a fearsome noise, like an express train screeching to a halt. The SBS soldiers and their Afghan brothers in arms threw themselves flat on the deck as the missile struck. For a moment their lungs emptied and eardrums imploded as the shock wave of the explosion rolled over them, chunks of shrapnel flying past overhead. And then a huge plume of smoke and dust was thrown into the air high above the enemy positions. That first five-hundred-pound bomb had smashed into the building on the nearside of the gateway, punching a massive hole in its domed roof. The explosion would have incinerated anyone inside, while shrapnel would have shredded those in the near vicinity of the blast.

In the seconds immediately following the aftershock of the bomb strike the enemy guns at the gateway had fallen silent. And suddenly Jamie and Ruff were back at the battlements, laying down long bursts of fire with their GPMGs, cutting down the enemy figures still making a run for Dostum's HQ building. The northern end of the fort was starting to look like a killing field now, with dozens of dead and injured AQT fighters littered across the sand. As the firing with the Gimpys ceased, an eerie quiet descended over the fort. Exhaustedly, the two men sank down behind the battlements, their backs to the wall and the smoking guns resting between their knees. But the respite was to be short-lived.

Barely thirty seconds after that first air strike had hit, the enemy guns opened up again. All of a sudden, wave upon wave of gunfire was coming up at the SBS soldiers hunkered down on the tower roof. The enemy must have reinforced their bombed-out positions at the gateway, and were hitting back against those who had called in the US air strikes. As they crouched down behind the battlements, Jamie and Ruff found themselves being targeted by massive amounts of incoming. At their backs the ramparts felt as if they were juddering with all the rounds ploughing into them, and dirt and chunks of masonry went falling down the necks of their combat jackets.

'Fuck! How many more of the fuckers are there?' Jamie yelled to Ruff.

'Fucked if I know, mate,' Ruff yelled back at him.

'How long before the wall gives out?' Jamie yelled again.

'Fucked if I know,' Ruff yelled back. 'Fancy a fuckin' smoke, mate?'

The previous summer, Ruff Pouncer had been in Sierra Leone, on Operation Barras, a do-or-die mission to rescue eleven British soldiers held hostage by murderous rebels in the jungle. The SAS had led the raid on the rebel base, but around a third of the force had been SBS. Then, as now, they had also been outnumbered five to one, and the men had nicknamed that mission 'Operation Certain Death'. The airborne raid on the rebel base to rescue the hostages had been scheduled to take an hour. But it had ended up lasting four, and it had been an awesome operation. Ruff and the seventy other SBS/SAS soldiers had had a hundred men of the Parachute Regiment in support. But they'd been up against a thousand drugged-up rebels and child soldiers who seemed to know no fear. Hundreds of the rebels had been killed, but they had just kept coming back at the British forces for more.

Yet the intensity of that firefight just didn't compare with what the SBS were facing now, here at Qala-i-Janghi, the Fort of War. While the rebels and child soldiers had been driven on by an evil cocktail of drugs, the enemy here were driven by a cold-hearted, diehard fanaticism. By a do-or-die need to kill British and American soldiers. If Ruff had to take his pick between fearless, drug-fuelled African rebels, or these crazy terrorists and religious fanatics, he knew who he would choose to fight. Repeatedly, the enemy here at Qala-i-Janghi were trying their suicidal charges. Sooner or later some of them were bound to succeed in breaking out. And in between those charges there was just a massive firestorm raging back and forth across the fort. No doubt about it, Sierra Leone had been a life-threatening mission; but here, several times already, Ruff had been convinced that he was about to die.

He and Jamie started chain-smoking to try to calm their nerves, sparking up one fag after another and passing it between them. As Jamie took the lighted cigarette from Ruff, he noticed that his own hands were shaking. For a second he felt a flush of embarrassment, in case Ruff had noticed. But as he passed the fag back again he saw that his mate's hands were shaking too. Jamie knew this wasn't from the fear: it was from the adrenalin rush of combat that was coursing through his veins. In fact, he felt oddly, weirdly calm. He was convinced that they were going to die. But he had reconciled himself to death during the first few minutes of the battle. If he caught a bullet he caught a bullet, and there was nothing he could do to prevent it. What he did fear was suffering the same fate as the two CIA agents – being captured alive. For if that happened Jamie had no illusions what would follow: the enemy would torture his very soul.

Jamie was torn away from his thoughts as a group of enemy fighters came bursting through the central gateway. Immediately, he and Ruff were up over the battlements with their Gimpys at the ready. They took it in turns to open up on the charging enemy fighters, each of them putting down sixty- to eighty-round bursts. They alternated their fire so that if either of them had a stoppage the other could take over, and to ensure that they didn't both run out of ammo at the same time. Giving the GPMGs a break also meant that the weapons had time to cool down a little – which would prevent rounds cooking off in the barrel. Even as they fought, Jamie and Ruff kept passing a lighted fag backwards and forwards between them, so that the guy not firing could take a few drags to calm his nerves. It would take just one fuck-up with one of the GPMGs, one stoppage, one fried gun barrel, and the enemy would be in among them.

Over in the tower stairwell, Mat glared at his watch. *Why the fuck did that second hand move so slowly!* He was waiting impatiently for the next warplane to be over target. It was 2.25 p.m., and they were barely an hour into the firefight. Yet it already felt like it had been a lifetime. Mat had few doubts about the seriousness of their situation. They were about to be overrun by hundreds of fanatical enemy fighters. If the fuckers came for them on the tower, Mat knew how he would react. He would stand shoulder to shoulder with his mates and fight to the last man. And if the bullets ran out, he would save the last round for himself. No way on earth was he letting himself get captured. Did he regret anything in his life? For a second Mat caught himself lamenting the fact that he'd had no kids with Suzie. And then he told himself to cut the crap. It was far better to be like this: his death would leave no young kid bereft of the father they needed.

Some three hundred yards to the north of Mat's position, Major Martin's rescue mission was starting to fight its way into the interior of the fort. The Major, CIA Steve, Sam and Tom had survived being caught by the RPG strikes as they climbed over the fort's outer wall. But only just. As the air had cleared of smoke and debris it turned out that the massive, mud-brick wall had absorbed most of the impact of the explosions. But two of the Afghan soldiers had been right on top of the RPG detonations: they had been blown off the battlements by the blast and were badly injured.

As soon as the dust had cleared, Sam pointed out the buildings clustered around the central gateway from where the enemy fighters had launched the RPG attacks. In a second, Tom had his Diemaco up over the battlements and had started putting down short, sustained bursts of fire on to the enemy positions at the gateway. He'd got off a magazine and a half on to the target when he turned round to check on Sam, some six yards down the wall from him. He was pleased to see that his fellow SBS soldier was pouring rounds on to the same target. It felt great to be taking the fight to the enemy at last.

Glancing around at the Afghan soldiers that were with them, Tom realised that they had gone all goggle-eyed as they watched Sam and himself in action. Tom had noticed that when he and his fellow SBS soldiers had first rocked up at the fort in their jeans, T-shirts and shamags, the Afghan soldiers had looked at them askance. It was as if they had been thinking; 'Who the fuck're you guys?' The Northern Alliance soldiers had a deep respect for uniforms, and it was clear that they hadn't thought much of the SBS's dress sense. In their minds, modern warriors wore smart military fatigues. Because the SBS soldiers were dressed in ragged, torn civvies, the Afghans had concluded that they couldn't be real soldiers and wouldn't know how to use a weapon.

But soldiers speak a universal language, and once the Afghans had seen Tom and Sam in action it had really broken the ice. Ultimately, if you were a warrior the Afghans would respect you, no matter how you might be dressed.

'You know what?' Sam shouted into Tom's ear, as they crouched down on the small ledge on the outside of the battlements. 'I've fucked my finger comin' over the goddam wall.'

'Which one, mate?' Tom yelled back at him.

'My trigger finger,' Sam yelled back, his face splitting into a wide grin.

'You fuckin' what?' Tom cracked up laughing. 'We're up here gettin' shot to fuck and you've fucked your trigger finger?'

'Yeah. Say, bro, you promise you won't tell the others?'

'Fat fuckin' chance. That's going' up on the notice-board back at Poole, mate.'

As Sam tried to massage his strained trigger finger back into life, the two SBS operators crouched behind the cover of the wall, pissing themselves laughing. The Afghan soldiers were staring at them now. They were clearly thinking that either these two foreign warriors were completely mad, or they were so at home in a fire-fight that they were quite happy to stop and have a laugh halfway through it all. Tom and Sam gave the Afghans a thumbs up, and got a grin and a thumbs up in return. But their merriment was, by necessity, short-lived. They knew that they had to get over the wall and push ahead pretty quickly now, if they were to have any chance of locating the two missing CIA officers.

Their destination, Dostum's HQ building, lay on the inside of the fort some 150 yards or so to the west of them. Once they were down the far side of the wall they planned to make a mad dash for that building. But as they did so they'd be sitting ducks for the enemy forces bunched up at the central gateway. As they psyched themselves up for the next stage of the assault, Tom decided to check if there might be any help on hand from the

US air power. They needed something to cover the next stage of their mission, and a nice big JDAM might just do the trick.

'Romeo Zero Alpha, this is Delta Zero Alpha, you got any fast air on its way?' Tom yelled into his radio.

'Romeo Zero Alpha, fast air inbound,' Mat responded, from his position on the entranceway tower. 'Expect five, repeat five, minutes to target.'

'Reckon you can hit those fuckers at the gateway?' Tom radioed back at him. 'Cos they've got us nailed somethin' chronic here, mate.'

'Give us five minutes and we'll mallet the fookers,' Mat replied. 'Wait out.'

Tom and Sam signalled to Major Martin, CIA Steve and the Afghan fighters to hold their position on the wall until the air strike went in. As soon as that US aircraft had hit the enemy at the gateway, they would be down the other side of the wall and heading for Dostum's HQ building as fast as they could. As they waited out the minutes, Tom and Sam took it in turns to lay down fire on to the enemy, taking a lot of incoming fire in return. The air was thick with the acrid stench of gunfire and burning, and the noise of the battle was building to a deafening crescendo. Finally, above the deafening battle roar there was the ear-splitting shriek of the missile going in over their heads. Tom and Sam gripped the battlements as the five-hundred-pound bomb smashed into the enemy positions, the blast wave rolling over the rescue team on the wall and all but bursting their eardrums.

'GO! GO! GO!' Tom yelled a split second after the missile had struck. Suddenly, he, Sam, CIA Steve, Major Martin and the Afghan fighters were piling over the wall and skidding down the rampart on the far side.

They hit the ground running and were immediately powering across the fort towards Dostum's HQ building. For the first few moments following the air strike a deathly quiet enveloped the battleground. But as the smoke and dust cleared from around the gateway, the guns that had fallen silent opened up with a vengeance, as the surviving enemy fighters spotted the rescue party sprinting across the inner grounds of the fort. Suddenly, there was a withering barrage of machine-gun fire cutting across the space in between. Tom, Sam, CIA Steve and the Major were caught in the open. Bullets started kicking up the dust and the dirt around their feet as they ran, the very ground dancing with the impact of the incoming rounds.

Sam and Tom hit the deck and started returning fire, 'pepper-potting' from one fire point to another – laying down short, three-second bursts and moving on before they could be targeted. It was only this movement that was keeping them alive. But around them the Afghan soldiers had taken up static fire points in the open ground, and were returning fire at the enemy with long bursts from their AK47s. Caught out in the open like this, the Afghan fighters were sitting ducks. Within seconds, one, then two, had fallen, as they were picked off by the enemy. They were all fighting for their very lives now. They knew that to continue on across the open ground in the face of this wall of fire would be pure suicide.

'MOVE!' Tom shouted at the Afghan fighters, as he dived on to his front and started belly-crawling forward. 'MOVE IT! ON ME!'

He had spotted the only piece of vaguely decent cover around, a crumbling mud-brick wall some dozen yards in front of them, and he started inching his way across the open ground towards it. As he pressed his body into the sandy earth, he heard rounds whirring past him barely inches from his flattened torso. More bullets kicked into the earth just ahead of him, throwing sand and dirt into his face and eyes. As soon as he reached the cover of the wall, Tom flipped over on to his back and checked behind him. With a surge of relief he found that the Afghan soldiers had followed his lead: they were down on their fronts and crawling as fast as they could towards cover. Sam was already beside him at the wall, and Major Martin and CIA Steve were just a couple of yards behind.

As far as the British and US soldiers were concerned, without more air strikes to take out the enemy guns, they were finished. The special forces soldiers and their Afghan fellow fighters put down short bursts of fire over the wall, but at the same time they could feel the enemy rounds tearing into the brickwork on the far side. If they were pinned down here much longer, the crumbling masonry would be shot to pieces and then they would be dead. Caught out in the midst of the open fort with next to no cover, their rescue mission was fast becoming a death trip. And while death trips appeared to be something that their fanatical enemy relished, the concept didn't fill Tom and Sam with any joyful anticipation. Paradise could wait, as far as they were concerned.

Tom rolled on to his side, ducked his head down and began yelling into his PRM radio. 'Romeo Zero Alpha, this is Delta Zero Alpha, where's the fuckin' fast air?'

'Romeo Zero Alpha, fast air inbound six, repeat six, minutes,' Mat responded, in a voice that he hoped sounded calm and reassuring.

'Mallet the fuckers at the fucking gateway!' Tom cried. 'We're fuckin' pinned down here and takin' fuckin' casualties.'

'You got it, mate,' Mat's voice came back at him.

'How about fuckin' covering fire from the GPMGs?' Tom yelled.

'Wait one, mate, I'll get the lads on to it.'

Seconds after that radio call, Tom and Sam heard the reassuring roar of the GPMGs opening up from the roof of the entranceway tower, as Jamie and Ruff put down bursts of suppressing fire on to the enemy positions. Immediately that they did so, the heavy rounds from the Gimpys began to take effect and the incoming enemy fire lessened considerably, taking some of the heat off the rescue team. This slight lull in the pace of the battle gave the soldiers a chance to catch their breath and consider their options. Tom, Sam, Major Martin and CIA Steve crawled across to each other for a hurried Chinese parliament in the cover of the wall.

'Once that air strike goes in, we gotta get goin', boys,' Major Martin yelled, 'cos they got us pinned down bad.'

'Sure thing, but which way're we goin'?' Sam yelled back at him. 'Cos we sure as hell ain't givin' up on this thing yet.'

'Too right, buddy, it's dead ahead,' the Major yelled back. 'We're pressin' on to the HQ building.'

'Ain't no way out of here but forward, mate,' Tom cut in. 'But I got an idea. This wall runs parallel to the main wall – in just the right fuckin' direction we want to go in. We got four minutes before that air strike hits – so let's move along it far as we can towards HQ.'

'What about puttin' down some return fire?' Major Martin asked.

'You're welcome to it,' Tom replied. 'You reckon you can hit those fuckers from here, under all this fire, be my guest, mate.'

'Ain't no time for talkin', guys,' Sam cut it. 'Like Tom said, let's just move it.'

With Sam leading the way, the three special forces soldiers and CIA Steve started to belly-crawl the length of the wall towards Dostum's HQ. As they did so, they motioned for the Afghan fighters to do likewise. The low wall stretched for some forty yards in the direction of the building, leaving some thirty yards of open ground to cover at the far end. Keeping as low as they could, the rescue team proceeded in this way until they reached a tumbledown section of the wall. Here, only three or four levels of brickwork survived above ground.

Sam went to move across this horribly exposed section, keeping his body pressed to the ground. But as he did so he heard a sound that made his blood run cold. It was the scream of a mortar round inbound towards them. The shell exploded about thirty yards away, throwing a great gout of sand and rocks into the air, and then the enemy mortar operator started to fire for effect, laying down a barrage of mortar rounds on their position.

'Someone get a bead on that motherfuckin' mortar operator and take the fucker out!' Tom screamed into his radio. 'We're getting fuckin' murdered down here!'

'Roger that, mate, we're trying to locate him,' came Mat's reply. He was trying to sound calm and reassured, but at the same time he knew what a bad, bad situation his mates were in.

'Well, fuckin' get him,' Tom yelled back at him. 'Or he's going to fuckin' get us.'

As Tom lay there, desperately trying to work his body lower into the soft earth, he found himself praying for that US air strike. And then, out of the corner of his eye, he caught sight of the weirdest thing that he'd ever seen in all his born days. For a second he wondered if he was hallucinating. In the midst of all this murder and mayhem, he could see two white doves slowly descending from the heavens. Down and down they fluttered, until they came to perch right on top of the wall where Tom and the others were hiding. And there the doves sat, as the bullets and mortar rounds slammed into the earth all around them, cooing at each other like a couple of love-birds or the universal doves of peace. For a second Tom just stared at them in disbelief. Then he caught Sam's eye. From his fellow soldier's expression he knew that Sam had also seen the two doves.

As the SBS soldiers continued to stare at the doves in amazement, the two birds turned and calmly gazed back at them. After what seemed like an age, the doves turned round again, spread their wings and took off gracefully, flying in a series of spirals ever higher into the air. While the bullets cracked and zipped all around them, the two white birds just seemed to be indestructible, untouch-able, immortal even, like they were leading the life of the charmed. As the doves rose higher and higher above the fort, the noise of the battle receded and Tom was filled with an unshakeable conviction that he would live through that day. He suddenly felt suffused with a deep and residing tranquillity, a pure sense of peace that coursed through his veins.

'Was I fuckin' dreamin', or what?' Tom said to Sam, as the doves finally disappeared over the fort's outer wall.

'That weren't no dream, bro. But it ain't like nothin' on this earth I ever seen before.'

'It's a sign, got to be. Like a miracle, mate.'

'Sure thing, bro. Like a message that we ain't gonna die.'

'We're going to fuckin' live, mate. And we're going to waste those fuckers.'

As if in response to Tom's last words, above the ear-splitting noise of the mortar barrage they heard the

Putting down fire with their Diemaco assault rifles from the fort battlements. 8 SBS soldiers were sent in to quell an uprising in the fort by hundreds of Al Qaeda and Taliban prisoners.

Northern Alliance soldiers shelter from the devastating incoming fire as they prepare their weapons for battle.

A Northern Alliance fighter takes aim on enemy positions from the fort battlements with his AK47.

(*Above left*) As SBS soldier Stevie 'Ruff' Pouncer pounds enemy position with his GPMG, fellow SB operator Jamie 'Bomber' Brian adds an extra belt of ammo. (*Left*) SBS soldier Stevie 'Ruff' Pouncer pours down fire from his 'Gimpy', as he and his SBS mates try to stop the Taliban and Al Qaeda enemy breaking out of fort.

(*Main picture*) SBS soldier runs across fort battlements, as smoke from the battle rises above the interior of the fort.

(*Above*) With SBS soldiers 'malleting' the enemy positions from the fort battlements, a Toyota pickup bursts into flames as its fuel tank explodes. (*Above right*) British SBS wore civvies, as opposed to the US special forces. A satellite comms device sits atop the fort battlements, to call in airstrikes. Just below the comms aerial is a white dove. When two of these birds flew into battle with the SBS rescue party, it was seen as a sign that they were going to live. (*Right*) Tracer rounds spark off the battlements as dusk descends over the fort and there is no sign of a let up in the ferocious battle.

At dawn on day two of the fort battle an errant US airstrike targets friendly forces with a 2000-pound JDAM. A T55 tank is blown in two, and dozens of SBS, US special forces and Northern Alliance troops are killed and wounded.

Northern Alliance soldiers survey the scene of devastation where a US airstrike hit friendly forces, blowing up a T55 tank and its crew and killing and wounding dozens of SBS, US and Afghan fighters.

The errant US airstrike by a 2000-pound JDAM reduced the northeastern tower of the fort to ruins, burying scores of SBS, US special forces and Afghan troops beneath the rubble.

As day three of the fort siege dawns, the bloated carcasses of dead horses litter the battlefield, alongside wrecked military equipment. Starving enemy resorted to eating the horse flesh to try to stay alive.

On the morning of day four of the fort siege Northern Alliance forces prepare to drive a Soviet-era T55 tank into the southern half of the fort, and assault the enemy stronghold.

At first light on Day 6 the SBS soldiers finally enter the southern end of the fort and the enemy stronghold – keeping to the cover of the trees as they do so.

The fort ammo store had been targeted by a US C130 Spectre gunship, the resulting explosion incinerating the machine guns and crates of ammo. (*Inset*) An SBS soldier inspects mortar rounds in the enemy stronghold. Luckily most were in bad condition and failed to explode when they hit British and US positions.

Blasted remains of the entrance to the enemy stronghold in the basement beneath the fort. Eighty-six enemy soldiers held out down there for seven days.

The fort basement immediately after the enemy have been forced to surrender. Discarded weaponry lies amongst the rubble of airstrikes.

scream of an incoming missile. Glancing up, they saw the flash of a spear-shaped projectile shooting across the sky above them, and then it slammed into the enemy positions in the southern end of the fort with a deafening roar. The very second that the five-hundred-pound bomb hit, Tom and Sam were on their feet, yelling, 'GO! GO! GO!' as they started pounding across towards the HQ building, barely thirty feet in front of them. As they dived into the shelter of the wall, Tom sank to his knees with relief. Somehow they had made it in there alive.

'Never run so fuckin' fast in all me life, mate,' he gasped, trying to catch his breath.

'Saved by the US Air Force, bro,' Sam panted, as he sucked air into his burning lungs.

'Saved by the fuckin' doves more like it,' Tom came back at him.

'Yeah . . . But you know somethin', bro? Them birds was made in the USA too, you know.'

'Fuck off. They were British,' Tom snorted. 'I saw the Union Jacks on their wings.'

A few seconds after the last of the Afghan fighters had dived into cover of the wall, Tom and Sam heard the enemy machine guns starting up again from the gateway. After the shock of the air strike, the enemy there must have regrouped and were coming back at them for more. So far four five-hundred-pound bombs had hit the enemy positions at the gateway, yet still they kept on fighting.

'Fuck me,' said Tom, shaking his head in disbelief. 'Don't they ever fuckin' give up? I mean, they fuckin' indestructible or something?'

'They came here to die, bro,' Sam replied, matter-of-factly. 'They ain't givin' up 'til the last of 'em is dead.'

'Fuckin' unbelievable,' Tom said, shaking his head in

bewilderment. 'I mean, they've got no fuckin' air power or nothin'. That sort of will to keep fighting . . .'

'You mean you don't kinda come across it that often? Like I said, they're fighting to the death, bro. Period.'

During Sam's eighteen months in the SBS he and Tom had never worked that closely, so they didn't really know each other before being thrown together on this rescue mission. But the intense pressure of battle meant that they'd formed an instinctive, natural partnership. Sam's dry, sarcastic humour helped enormously in his ability to fit in with the lads in the SBS. The piss-taking was universal and relentless within the SBS, and the SAS for that matter. If an operator proved incapable of taking it, he wouldn't survive in either unit. It was a way for each man to test out his fellow soldier, to push him as far as he would go, to prove that under pressure he would deliver.

As the rescue team were now in the cover of the massive mud walls of Dostum's HQ building they were pretty much invulnerable to the enemy fire. But in order to press on the last few yards to the entranceway, they would have to break cover and advance along the front of the building. This stretch of ground was completely exposed to enemy fire. After a short breather, Sam and Tom risked a quick look around the corner of the wall at their next objective. Along the front of the HQ building ran a shallow ramp at the far end of which was a raised doorway. Tom and Sam could see that the door frame was peppered with bullet holes and the blast marks of RPGs. In order to reach that doorway, they would have to run up that ramp in the full view of the enemy.

Just as they were about to duck back into cover, the two SBS soldiers heard frenzied chants of 'Allahu Akhbar!

Allahu Akhbar! Allahu Akhbar!' coming from across the fort compound. They turned in that direction and spotted a group of some thirty enemy fighters rushing towards them across the open ground, screaming at the tops of their voices as they did so. Dropping to one knee Tom and Sam started firing off on automatic, spraying the charging fighters with rounds. As they surged forward the enemy soldiers opened fire in return with their AK47s levelled at the hip. The bullets went zipping and whining past Tom and Sam, ricocheting off the walls.

Tom and Sam were taking aimed shots and dropping the fighters as fast as they could, but still they kept charging forwards. Suddenly, there was the throaty roar of Ruff's Gimpy opening up from the eastern tower. Tom and Sam saw the heavy GPMG rounds tearing into the enemy figures, but still they kept on coming. As they got closer and closer, the two SBS soldiers realised that the surviving fighters were clutching grenades. Repeatedly, Tom and Sam fired and re-aimed, fired and re-aimed with their Diemacos, as the enemy bore down on them. Tom got the lead fighter nailed in his sights, and for a split second he saw a crazed figure rushing towards him brandishing a grenade in either hand, his mouth set in an animal snarl, an undying scream of hatred on his lips.

At the same time that Tom squeezed his trigger, the enemy fighter must have pulled the pin in his grenade. He was barely thirty yards from Tom's position as he did so, and suddenly there was a blinding flash and the roar of the explosion. As Tom and Sam dived back behind cover, four other blasts rang out, as the first grenade set off the others that the fighter had been carrying. As the smoke cleared, Tom saw the bottom half of the man's body toppling slowly to the ground. The top half of his torso had been completely obliterated in the blast. He and Sam searched with their weapons for any remaining enemy among the drifting smoke. But all they could see was the sandy earth littered with shattered human remains and soaked in blood and gore. Severed arms, legs and heads were lying scattered across the ground in front of them.

The two SBS soldiers sank back exhaustedly into the cover of the wall and buried their heads in their hands. There seemed to be no end to the slaughter and the bloodshed that would be required of them that day. The enemy weren't fighting like soldiers any more, or conforming to any rules of combat. They were making no attempt to preserve their own lives and survive. They were rushing towards death, embracing it like a long-lost friend. And it was falling to Sam, Tom and the rest of them to deliver their final death sentence. But this was no moment for reflection or for battle nerves to kick in: it was already time to prepare for the next round of killing.

Major Martin took advantage of the temporary lull in the fighting to check in with Boxer Base. He needed to know if they'd got comms going with Dave Tyson, supposedly holed up in the HQ building. But even the Major's comms back to Boxer Base were intermittent and kept breaking up. The intel situation seemed as confused as ever, and he was left unsure as to whether CIA Dave was still inside the HQ building. In fact, no one seemed to have any definitive information on the whereabouts of the missing CIA officers, or what state they were in.

CIA Steve had remained pretty quiet throughout the whole of the rescue mission. He'd had the honesty to admit from the start that he was out of his depth on this one. It was a full-on combat mission, hard-nosed fighting all the way, and that's not something for which the CIA trained its officers. The Agency trained them to shoot straight and in explosives use. It trained them in espionage, intelligence gathering and black operations. It trained them to operate behind enemy lines. But it didn't train them for full-on, chaotic, relentless war-fighting.

'Steve, you reckon your buddies might still be in there, right?' Major Martin asked.

'There's been no intel so far that says they're not,' CIA Steve replied.

'OK, then, I guess we leave no man behind,' Major Martin announced. 'We press on with the mission. Which means we gotta get a couple of guys inside Dostum's HQ building.'

After seeing the US and British soldiers in action, the Afghan fighters had realised that they more than knew their stuff. Two of the bravest now offered to join Tom and Sam as they made the dash up the HQ's ramp and into the entranceway. But first, Tom called up Mat on the radio to ask if there were any more air strikes expected any time soon. Just one more hit on the enemy positions at the gateway and it should buy them enough time to rush the building. By now, five strikes had gone down. One was a JDAM dumped about a half-mile out in the desert; the others were the five-hundred-pounders dropped on the enemy positions in the fort. Mat radioed Tom that he had another air strike some ten minutes away, and so they should wait it out.

After what seemed like an age, there was the scream of the incoming missile and the five-hundred-pounder slammed into the enemy positions. As it did so, Tom, Sam and the two Afghan fighters broke cover and made a mad dash for the doorway. The wiry Afghans were faster and lighter than the bulkier SBS soldiers, and they leapt ahead. But just as they reached the doorway there was a sudden burst of gunfire and the first of the Afghans was cut down in a hail of bullets, his legs being shot out from under him. The second was so close behind that he ran headlong into the wall of machine-gun fire, his bloodied body being blasted in though the doorway of the fort.

Sam and Tom were bringing up the rear and they just managed to stop themselves in time. They dived back behind cover again. They had been that close to both getting blown away. The enemy had to have a machine gun zeroed in on the HQ doorway, which had been turned into a killing zone. Major Martin's rescue team had finally succeeded in getting one of their men into the HQ building. But they had little doubt that the Afghan fighter had been dead on arrival.

'It ain't happenin', bro,' said Sam, turning to face Tom. 'No matter now many goddam air strikes we put down, they tryin' to stop us reaching those boys alive.'

'There's got to be a way, mate,' Tom replied, racking his brains for an answer. There was only one doorway into the HQ building, of that he was certain, but maybe there were some windows that they could try for. 'Let's take a look, mate, just in case we missed something. We're so close.'

'Well, I ain't giving up, either way,' said Sam, quietly. 'I ain't leaving those CIA boys behind. No way am I abandoning them in a place like this. No way, bro – not even if it kills me.'

'The brothers are getting wiped out, Ali!' one of the younger men announced, screaming to make himself heard above the noise of the battle. 'The *kafir* soldiers are calling in air strikes. Five buildings have been hit along the line of the wall. The brothers are getting massacred.'

'You think I haven't noticed?' Ali barked in reply. He was staring out of the blasted gateway in the fort's central wall, across to Dostum's HQ building.

Over the last few hours Ali had started to assume a leadership role among the surviving brothers. As their spontaneous revolt had developed into a savage fight to the death, he had found himself acting as a tactical and spiritual guide to his fellow fighters. He knew his Muslim theology better than almost any other brother. He could quote extensively from the Koran. And with Ahmed's help he could plan their defence of the fort. Or so he had thought, until the air strikes started pounding their positions and shredding the brothers before they had a chance to stand and fight.

'Maybe this is how Allah wills it, brother,' Ali continued, quietly. 'That we all die here in this fort. Do the other brothers not want to be glorious *shouhada'a*? To taste the fruits of Paradise?'

'Not this way, Brother Ali,' answered the young fighter. 'Not cut down by a *kafir* bomb dropped from the air. They want to die fighting, brother. Fighting for the glory of Allah. With honour in their hearts.'

'Fine, then the brothers have got two choices. They either stick with us here and we try another counter-attack, or they retreat and get down in the basement, where the *kafir* bombs can't reach them. And for those that do that, they must put brothers on the windows, so they can return fire from there. If anyone gets hit, they must pull more brothers up from the basement to replace them. As for me, I know where my duty lies and where I'm staying.'

Ali lifted the armed RPG up on to his shoulder and gazed out into the northern half of the fort, searching for a target. 'By the grace of Allah, I've got infidels to fight and to kill.'

12

BEHIND ENEMY LINES

IT was 3.45 p.m. by now and the SBS soldiers were some two and a half hours into the battle for Qala-i-Janghi fort, but the firefight showed no signs of abating. Captain Lancer, Mat, Jamie and Ruff were still in the full flow of battle up on the tower roof. The enemy positions at the gateway had been transformed into a mass of blasted debris – the scorched and twisted remains of the Toyota pickups and piles of smoking rubble. The air was thick with the stench of burning, of cordite and of charred human flesh. At times the smell was so strong that it made the SBS soldiers at the battlements gag.

In the next thirty minutes, Mat called in four more air strikes. Two hit the enemy positions at the gateway, and two further strikes went in on the southern end of the fort. The laser-guided bombs rocketed in over the forty-foot-high diving wall to target the pink building, General Dostum's stables, where the bulk of the enemy were holed up. At all times Mat was coordinating the bombing runs with Tom and Sam, as they tried to push ahead with their rescue mission inside the fort.

As each of the bombs slammed into the fort there was an ear-splitting explosion, and a thick plume of smoke and dust was thrown into the sky. During the short after-shock following each air strike the battlefield fell silent. But then the enemy would come back at the SBS soldiers as strongly as ever before, and no amount of five-hundred-pound bombs seemed to break their will to fight.

Unless the enemy were immortal, which Mat somehow doubted, they had to be reinforcing their positions from places where the air strikes couldn't hit them. Mat had a sneaking suspicion that each time an air strike hit the enemy at the gateway, they were drawing fresh fighters from the cellars and passageways that ran beneath the fort. Even five-hundred-pound laser-guided bombs would have trouble taking out enemy fighters sheltered deep in those underground chambers – especially as Mat had no way of knowing where they were, or of directing the air strikes on to them. Mat racked his brain for some way of hitting the enemy below ground, but for the moment he was lost for ideas.

As the sun began drifting towards the distant horizon, it lit up the thick pall of smoke hanging above the ancient fortress an angry blood red. Fires were burning fiercely at the gateway in the fort's central wall, where the air strikes had ignited ammunition supplies. Every now and then a magazine would cook off in the heat, throwing up a series of staccato rifle-crack explosions. And in the silence between the detonations, the cries of the wounded lifted eerily above the fort. There were dozens, perhaps hundreds, of corpses strewn across the northern end of the fort – scattered on the ground in the grotesque, twisted shapes that the human body only ever seems to assume in death. Some of the enemy soldiers lying there were yet to die. They had come here seeking Paradise, and had found instead a slow, agonising lingering death. No one was coming to help them.

For half an hour or more there had been no further suicide charges by the enemy at the gateway. But there were still sustained bursts of gunfire coming from the enemy positioned there. And one of the enemy fighters had now got a mortar zeroed in on the SBS's position up on the tower roof. The accuracy of the rounds meant that he must have placed someone high up on one of the walls, spotting where his shells were falling and correcting his aim. But as much as Mat, Jamie and Ruff searched for that 'spotter', they still failed to locate him.

The enemy mortar operator had been seen firing from several positions in the southern compound. But he was very good and never allowed himself to fire from the same position twice – which prevented him from being targeted. He'd come running out of a building, plonk the mortar baseplate down, lob off a salvo of mortars and get back into cover again – doing it all so quickly that it was impossible to get him. And while the fire wasn't exactly 100 per cent accurate it was good enough to cause the British forces some problems. With the mortar rounds creeping ever closer to their positions, Captain Lancer decided to act. He ordered his men to relocate to the tower on the north-eastern corner of the fort, some halfway across to the HQ building.

On the way up there, the SBS soldiers picked up a dozen Afghan fighters who had just arrived on the scene. They were the first re-inforcements and had been sent over by General Dostum. Once they had reached their new positions, Jamie and Ruff set up the GPMGs facing south towards the gateway in the fort dividing wall. Although the enemy seemed to have given up trying to break out en masse, they might still try to do so in smaller

numbers as darkness began to fall. Jamie zeroed in his
weapon on the killing box in front of the gateway, and
settled down behind the cover of the battlements. As he
did so, he felt someone dragging at the Diemaco assault
rifle that he had slung across his shoulder. Turning round,
he saw that it was one of the newly arrived Afghan
soldiers.

'Ta-li-ban,' Jamie said, pointing at the enemy positions and grinning. Then he passed the Afghan fighter
the assault rifle, and motioned that he should take a few
potshots at the enemy.

'Taliban,' the Afghan soldier replied, bringing the
weapon to his shoulder and aiming in the direction of
the gateway. 'Bang. Bang. Taliban.'

But as the Afghan went to pull the trigger, nothing
happened, and try as he might he couldn't get the weapon
to fire. Finally, Jamie could help himself no longer and
he cracked up laughing. From where he was standing he
could see that the Diemaco's safety catch was still on,
and that was why the Afghan soldier couldn't get it to
fire. As he gave up trying to shoot and handed the weapon
back to Jamie, the Afghan fighter must have recognised
the humour of the moment. Suddenly, he too started
pissing himself laughing, and the two men did a broth-
erly handclasp.

Then the Afghan soldier motioned skywards and
performed a rotating movement with his finger in the
air. While he did so he made the noise of a helicopter's
rotors, then ran his finger across his throat like a knife
cut. 'Taliban,' he said, grinning. The meaning was clear
– the air power would help them finish off the enemy
forces in the fort. Suddenly all the British and Afghan
fighters were grinning and backslapping each other at
the thought of an end to all the fighting. It was the first,

truly light moment that the soldiers had experienced since the siege of Qala-i-Janghi had begun. It was the first time that they had felt they could start to relax a little.

'Take it easy, lads,' Captain Lancer remarked, as he gazed over the battlements into the darkening fort. 'If I were those fuckers, I'd see dusk as my chance to break out. Just keep your eyes peeled.'

'What's the score on the rescue party, boss?' Mat asked.

'I've no idea, Mat,' said the Captain. 'Since the last call about the air strikes, we've not heard from them.'

'It's gone pretty quiet in there. A bit worrying, ain't it?'

'I guess they'd call us if they needed us.'

Down in the fort next to General Dostum's HQ building, Major Martin's rescue party were just considering calling off the search. The US Major had finally received a radio call from Boxer Base, informing him that CIA Dave had escaped the fort of his own accord and been found safe and alive. Apparently he had made his way back to Mazar city in a local vehicle. CIA Dave had been able to confirm that things looked bad for his missing buddy, Mike Spann, who had been surrounded and attacked by the enemy at the start of the uprising. But as the intel on CIA Mike was all third-hand, it wasn't totally convincing. Until someone found Mike Spann's body, no one could be certain that the CIA officer had been killed. In which case there remained just a chance that he might be lying somewhere in that fort, badly injured but still alive.

Tom, CIA Steve and Major Martin gathered around in the cover beneath the HQ wall, and tried to decide what to do. Sam was still sniping at the enemy from the corner of the building. He'd put down more rounds than any of the rest of them, and just seemed hell-bent on spending his time fighting. Sam seemed to have an unshakeable conviction that their mission would succeed. With all the air strikes that had gone in on the enemy positions, Tom and Major Martin reckoned that the uprising had to be pretty much under control by now. And with the approach of dusk, it would soon become impossible to distinguish friend from foe. In addition to which, more Northern Alliance reinforcements were arriving on the scene to secure the fort.

But the men were also aware of their acute shortage of ammo. They were each down to three or four mags, and Sam had even less than that. And they knew how desperately the enemy wanted to get an American or British soldier. If they stayed at the fort for very much longer they would be the first to be targeted by the enemy in the darkness, that much was for sure. And none of them fancied fighting off any midnight suicide attacks. Eventually, Tom and Major Martin decided that they had to abandon the fort for the rest of the night to the care of the NA forces. It was time to return to Boxer Base for an ammo resupply, a debrief and some rest.

But Sam still appeared torn: on the one hand he knew the others were right, and that they should withdraw from the fort. On the other, he hated abandoning CIA Mike to his fate. As the rescue team carefully retraced their steps to the point where they'd first crossed over the wall into the fort, Sam was wrestling with his conscience. The men climbed back over and started getting their kit together in preparation for leaving. But then Sam came over to have a quiet word with Tom.

'This just ain't right, bro,' Sam announced, quietly. 'I can't just leave him in there. I wanna go find Mike.'

'What the fuck, Sam? It's dark, mate, we got to get

out of here and you don't know where the fuck he is. Don't be fucking crazy, mate.'

'I'm headin' for the western tower, bro,' Sam replied. 'That's where I reckon I'll find him.'

With that he turned round, scaled the parapet and climbed back on to the top of the wall. Without a backward glance he jumped down into the darkened fort and headed off into the unknown. Tom immediately felt compelled to follow his fellow SBS soldier, but at the same time he felt he had to inform Major Martin what the hell was happening. The US 5th SOF Major had just got off the radio to Boxer Base and he was unaware that Sam had gone back into the fort.

'Right, we're out of here guys, we're leaving,' the Major announced.

'Sorry, mate, but we can't,' Tom replied. 'Sam's just gone off to find Mike.'

'Jesus Christ! What the hell for, buddy? It's gettin' dark and we just gotta get the hell outta here.'

'Yeah, I know, mate, but it's Sam,' Tom replied. 'Hang on – I'll try raise him on the radio.'

As Tom tried to reach Sam on his PRM radio, the commander of the recently arrived Afghan forces started remonstrating with Major Martin that he needed all of his men out of the fort. With darkness descending, the Afghan commander wanted to shut the fort complex down and make any no man's land a killing ground. Which meant that anyone seen there after dark would be shot on sight. Clearly, he'd be unable to do so if there were any SBS soldiers still wandering around the fort. Finally, Tom gave up trying to raise Sam on the radio. Either he was out of range or he wasn't answering his calls.

'Look, buddy, we gotta get out of here,' said Major Martin, as soon as Tom got off the radio.

'What about Sam?' Tom asked.

'We're out of here,' CIA Steve interjected. 'There's no way we can wait for Sam, or anyone else, buddy.'

Tom knew that he couldn't openly try to overrule a CIA officer and a US 5th SOF major. In any case, he doubted that they'd listen to him, even if he tried. But he couldn't leave Sam behind.

'Well I'm going back to look for Sam,' Tom replied. 'He's a fellow SBS operator, which makes him my responsibility. And I ain't fuckin' leavin' without him.'

'What's that gonna achieve?' CIA Steve countered.

'Look, wherever Sam is I'm going to find him and bring him in,' Tom explained. 'I'm not fuckin' leavin' him behind.'

'Goddammit,' Major Martin snapped, dropping his grab bag on the ground. 'If you're goin' in to find your buddy, you ain't goin' in alone. We may as well go with ya, search for the other CIA officer, Dave.'

'I thought he was already outta here?' CIA Steve queried.

'Yeah, but the comms are all to fuck,' Major Martin replied. 'And if we're fuckin' around looking for Mike, then may as well double-check that Dave ain't still in there while we're at it.'

Together, the three men vaulted back over the wall and began to retrace their steps towards the HQ buildings, hugging the shadows of the wall and any cover that they could find. There were still sporadic bursts of gunfire ringing out in the fort, but for now at least none of it seemed directed at them. As soon as they reached the HQ building, CIA Steve and Major Martin dived in through the doorway and disappeared into the shadows to search for CIA Dave. Tom was left alone on the outside.

The rescue team was now split up into three groups,

and it suddenly dawned on Tom just how badly things were going. Sam had disappeared alone into completely uncharted enemy territory, looking for a CIA officer already believed dead, and with no idea where to find him. Major Martin and CIA Steve had disappeared into the fort HQ – again, potentially hostile territory – looking for Dave, the other CIA officer. But he was believed to be back at Boxer Base already, shocked and shaken but pretty much all right. And as for Tom, he couldn't see either party, had no comms with Sam and didn't know what to do next. It crossed his mind that if he stayed where he was he could at least act as a rendezvous point for all elements of the rescue team. But his instincts told him to press on and look for Sam.

Tom set off at a crouching run for the western side of the fort, disappearing into the dark unknown. Hugging the fort's outer wall he headed for the north-western tower. There, the wall would turn south, Tom told himself, and he should be able to follow it all the way to the western tower, which was where Sam had said he was heading. As he hurried forward Tom couldn't help but admire the bravery of his fellow special forces soldier. But at the same time he wondered why on earth he had decided to head for the western side of the fort – which was completely unknown territory.

The western tower was the furthest point possible from friendly forces, from the SBS and 5th SOF positions on the eastern side of the fort. And then it suddenly dawned on Tom that that was probably the very reason that Sam had chosen this route in. As there were no British or American troops positioned on this side of the fort, the enemy were more likely to have left it unde-fended. If there was one vantage point from where Sam might be able to locate Mike Spann without being detected by the enemy, then his intended destination, the western tower, might just be it.

Suddenly, Tom's attention snapped back to the present. One hundred yards up ahead of him there was a fierce outbreak of gunfire. It sounded like a heavy machine gun of some sort, and he could hear the sharp reports of an AK47 returning fire. Instantly, Tom knew for certain that Sam was involved and that he had hit trouble. He hurried ahead. As the dark bulk of the north-western tower loomed ahead of him he could just make out a figure hunched behind the corner of a nearby wall. It was Sam all right, and he was putting down fire on to the enemy to his front.

'Sam, you crazy bastard,' Tom said, speaking softly into his radio. 'I'm right behind you, mate.'

Tom figured that Sam had ignored the earlier radio calls when he'd first set off on his lone mission of madness, but that he might react differently now. Sure enough, there was a faint crackle of radio static and then Sam replied.

'I hear you, bro. Come on in.'

At that, Tom scurried across to join him in the cover of the wall. It was one in a long row of single-storey buildings that clustered at the base of the fort's outer wall.

'Say, bro, you just couldn't keep away?' Sam said, as soon as he caught sight of Tom.

'You crazy fucker . . . Where d'you get the weapon from, mate?' Tom asked, pointing to the battered AK47 that Sam was using.

'Picked it up from a dead Afghan on the way over,' Sam replied. 'Figured he didn't need it and as I was all out of ammo . . .'

'So, you got a plan, mate?' Tom asked, as he stole a

glance around the corner of the building. It was getting dark now, and the north-western tower was some 150 yards further down the wall from them.

'Up ahead on the tower, reckon there's three or four of 'em, bro. They got somethin' large calibre up there, maybe a Dushka, plus they got some small stuff. But I reckon in this light they can barely see us. So if we can just get around this corner without bein' spotted . . . I reckon we could make it to the tower if we stick close to the base of the wall. What d'you think, bro?'

'Sounds good to me, mate – specially if we belly-crawl it. Once we're round the corner, we can do the rest at a run.'

'OK, bro, let's do it,' Sam said, dropping on to his hands and knees.

'Say, mate, those doves,' Tom began, just as they were about to set off at a crawl, 'they were real, weren't they?'

'Sure they were, bro,' Sam replied. 'You doubtin'? Don't ever doubt the power of bein' on the side of right.'

With that the two special forces soldiers began edging their way around the corner of the building. As they inched forwards, Tom found himself wondering what the hell they were risking their lives for in such a crazed venture as this – searching a darkened fort infested by a fanatical enemy for a US officer that they'd never met before and who was more than likely dead. But as he did so, he remembered the calm and the sense of peace that had descended upon him as he'd seen those two white doves flying into the air above the battlefield. With it had come the overwhelming conviction that somehow they were being protected. They had already fought their way through more danger and bloodshed than ever seemed humanly possible. And if they had cheated death so far, there was no reason why they shouldn't make it through this final battle.

They had barely advanced fifteen yards at a crawl, when all hell broke loose. The heavy machine gun up ahead opened up again, large-calibre rounds chewing into the wall behind them. Glancing back, Tom could see that the incoming fire was tearing into the corner of the building where he and Sam had just been standing. Perhaps the enemy gunner hadn't spotted them and was just laying down some suppressing fire. In which case, they needed to get the hell out of there. Jumping to his feet Tom set off at a crouching run along the base of the wall, with Sam close on his heels. The taller American was faster than Tom and soon overtook him. As they approached the tower, they could hear the enemy gunner laying down further, probing, bursts of fire. Any second now they feared that they were going to be hit.

At last they made the cover of the tower itself. Flattening themselves against the wall, they stood there in the shadows gasping for breath. Up above them was the enemy machine-gun nest. Each man knew what he had to do next, as they had rehearsed and prepared for it so many times during training. They exchanged a few brief hand signals, and then they moved in through the tower entranceway, their weapons held at the ready. Taking it in turns to cover each other, they advanced towards the stairway and began to mount the steps leading up on to the roof. The interior of the tower appeared deserted. But up above there was the inter-mittent roar of the heavy machine gun, as the enemy kept squirting off bursts of fire into the semi-darkness.

They reached the last flight of stairs, hearts pounding, and prepared to break out on to the roof. With their weapons at the shoulder and on the aim, they crept up the last few steps. Each soldier stayed as light on his feet as possible. As their heads emerged from the stairwell, Tom and Sam were already searching for the enemy. Simultaneously, both men opened fire on the positions right in front of them. They took the three enemy soldiers by complete surprise and cut them down in a hail of bullets. For a split second the Dushka operator tried to spin his heavy machine gun around, but then he took a bullet in the head and slumped over on top of his weapon. His two fellow fighters were already lying dead or dying at the feet of the tripod that supported the giant gun.

Not a word had been spoken between Tom and Sam as they moved forward to secure the rest of the tower roof. They did a quick body-check. All the enemy fighters were dead. Tom reached down and picked up one of their AK47s, pulling several full magazines out of the dead man's clothing. He knew that his Diemaco was down to the last few rounds. Slinging the AK47 over his shoulder he continued checking over the tower roof for any more of the enemy.

'I'm movin' forward, bro,' Sam called over, softly, once they'd finished securing the position. Using hand signals again, he indicated to Tom that he was advancing along the parapet that ran along the outer wall towards the western tower. 'I'm going to look for Mike. Cover me, bro.'

Giving the thumbs up, Tom heaved the corpse of the dead gunner off of the heavy machine gun, and gave it the once-over. It was undamaged, and would certainly give him a far greater firepower and range than the AK47 that he had slung over his shoulder. Lowering himself into the gunner's 'seat', he spun the weapon around and pointed the barrel in the direction of the southern end of the fort. If the enemy were to counter-attack, it was from there that they'd be coming. Out of the corner of his eye Tom saw Sam set off at a crouching run along the parapet in the direction of the western tower. Soon, his lone figure was lost in the gathering darkness. Tom knew that the life of this brave and selfless American soldier now depended, in part, upon him.

As his eyes adjusted to the gloom, Tom tried to make out what movements, if any, the enemy were making up ahead of him. For a second, he caught what he thought were crouched figures running along the base of the fort's dividing wall, some four hundred yards away from him, moving as if to cut off Sam's advance. But then he wasn't certain that he'd seen them at all. In the half-light of dusk, he was struggling to make things out clearly. And at this distance a film of evening mist seemed to have settled between himself and the distant walls of the fort, obscuring any detail.

'*Cover me*,' Sam had told him. *Well, how the fuck could he cover him if he couldn't see properly?* Tom thought to himself, frustratedly.

But what the hell. If he opened fire in the general direction of those shadowy figures, it would at least create a diversion. And that might mean that Sam would get a clear run at things. By doing so, Tom reasoned, he'd be sure to draw down fire on to his position, so diverting any attention away from Sam. Sighting the heavy weapon on the base of the distant wall, Tom squeezed the trigger. Suddenly the Dushka roared into life, an ear-splitting percussion shattering the evening stillness. It was dark enough for Tom to follow the giant tracer rounds as they arced across the fort and hit the distant wall. Adjusting his fire, he dropped the target point six feet or so to the base of the wall, and began to fire for effect. If any of the enemy were trying to move across to intercept Sam, they'd now have to walk through a wall of fire to get to him.

Almost immediately, rounds started cracking back across the fort in Tom's direction. The enemy had woken up to the fact that one of their 'own' guns was being turned on them. But at such range, most of the incoming fire was pretty inaccurate, and rounds were slamming into the tower well wide of their target. In any case, Tom had other things to worry about. As the Dushka kicked back with the powerful force of the rounds firing off, Tom felt his feet being forced off the floor. The weapon was obviously adjusted to suit a much taller operator than Tom, who was somewhat on the short side, and he was in danger of losing control of it. Calming his nerves, Tom leaned back, braced himself by getting his boots wedged up on to the weapon's carriage, and settled into a position where he could continue operating the gun.

After a sustained burst Tom ceased firing and hunched over the Dushka, searching for any signs of enemy movement out there in the shadowy no man's land of the fort. As he did so, sporadic bursts of enemy fire kept coming back at him. Then Tom heard the crack-crack-crack of several well-placed shots coming from the direction of the western tower. *Fuck it*, he cursed to himself, *Sam must've run into trouble*. Somehow, the enemy must have got through to him. Tom was expecting a fully-fledged firefight to break out on the western tower, and if it did then his only option would be to advance and try to go to his fellow soldier's aid. But after those well-placed shots, all seemed to go quiet again.

As he sat there alone on the roof of the tower, Tom listened to the odd, sporadic burst of gunfire drifting across from the more distant sections of the fort complex. The newly arrived Northern Alliance forces would have a long night ahead of them keeping the enemy bottled up here, that much was for certain. A couple of minutes had passed since that isolated burst of shots, and Tom decided it was time to lay down some more suppressing fire. But he had to conserve the big gun's ammunition. He allowed himself to squeeze off a few short bursts in the general direction of the enemy, and then ceased firing.

In the deafening silence that followed, Tom thought he caught the sound of a voice up ahead of him in the shadows. But then he thought he must have imagined it. Yet as he strained his ears in the echoing darkness he caught the voice again, calling to him out of the night.

'Tom! Buddy! You hear me?' came the voice. It was Sam, coming back along the parapet from the western tower. 'What's up, bro?' he added, as soon as he caught sight of Tom. 'What you got your legs up in the air for? You firin' that gun or you ridin' it?'

'Fuck off, you lanky git,' Tom replied. 'Am I fuckin' glad to see you, mate.'

As Sam appeared from the darkness, Tom was shocked by his appearance. He was ashen-faced, and looked completely drained and shaken.

'You look like death, mate,' Tom said, as he extricated himself from the machine gun. 'What the fuck happened out there?'

'I'm OK, bro,' Sam sounded exhausted. 'I just wanna get outta here. You know, it was pretty dark down there, but I saw this guy, lying there, face down, in jeans and a black shirt. I guess it had to be him . . . Hell, I don't wanna talk about it – not now, anyways. Let's just get the fuck outta here, bro.'

'Fuckin' fine by me, mate,' Tom replied, trying to make light of things. 'It was your fuckin' crazy idea to come out here in the first place.'

As far as Tom was concerned Sam was right – it was high time they got the hell out of the fort. They began to retrace their steps. As they did so, Tom was busy trying to figure out what on earth had happened to Sam, out there alone on the western tower. He looked like he had gone through something that had shocked and sickened him – something that had affected him far more deeply than anything that had happened during the whole of that day's bloody fighting, something that had forced him to face one of the worst decisions of his life. Or at least that was the only way that Tom could make any sense out of things now.

Twenty minutes later and all members of the rescue team had rendezvoused at the main entrance to the fort. Not surprisingly, Major Martin and CIA Steve had failed to find any signs of CIA Dave in the HQ building. The rescue party met up with Captain Lancer's team and the rest of the 5th SOF boys, and everyone declared themselves more than ready to head back to Boxer Base.

As the SBS Land-Rovers pulled away from Qala-i-Janghi and hit the high road back to Mazar, every single man on those vehicles felt a massive adrenalin rush surging through his exhausted body, a burning sense of exhilaration. At some stage during the last six hours of combat operations, each and every one of them had faced the certainty that they were not going to live through that day. Yet somehow, they had cheated death and made it out alive from the Fort of War.

By the time they got back to Boxer Base it was dark. The first day of the battle for Qala-i-Janghi was over – and the SBS soldiers were wondering just how long the bitter siege would last. The first thing they did was a major ammo resupply. If anything major kicked off at the fort again that night, they'd be heading back up there to lend a hand, of that they were certain. So, before anyone could even think about a good feed and a kip, they had to get themselves battle-ready again.

'The fookers,' Mat remarked to no one in particular, as he slotted new rounds into his magazine. On the one hand he was feeling utterly exhausted, while on the other he was still on the adrenalin rush of combat. '"Prisoners" be fooked. They weren't bloody prisoners and they never bloody well intended to be. They went to that fort to fight. They'd never stopped being bloody combatants.'

'You can say that again, mate,' said Jamie.

'Tell you another thing, mate, they're fuckin' evil, even by our standards,' Tom observed, as he cleaned his weapon. 'I'd say they're the most hard core of the lot of 'em. You know, the fuckin' "Arab Afghans". Bunch of foreigners – Saudis, Chechens, whatever. You saw the way they fought? They'd break cover, take a couple of well-aimed shots – then dive back into cover again before you could even get a fuckin' bead on 'em. Not bad for a bunch of ragheads.'

'They were good all right,' said Jamie. 'I reckon we're lucky we made it out of there without taking casualties.'

'In a way you got to fuckin' admire them, mate – a grim admiration,' said Tom. 'Fighting to the death they were, and fearless –'

'I don't bloody admire them,' Mat interrupted. 'And I wouldn't bloody say they were fearless, either. Driven insane for a cause, I'll grant you. But I can't see that they was brave. They was bloody fanatical, and I don't admire them nowt for seeking death. Even the local Afghans, the local Muslims, even they don't understand it. I mean, those bloody suicide charges. How can you blow yourself up for a senseless cause? It's crazy, downright mad.'

'Yeah, all right, mate,' said Tom. 'But this fort housed all the foreign fighters. These people come from all over the fuckin' world to fight, to seek death in this cause. So, call it whatever you fuckin' want to, mate – bravery, an attitude, madness, suicide, whatever – it ain't like nothin' else you've ever seen before. And the question is, how do you fight against fuckers like that?'

'Fuckin' simple, mate,' Ruff interjected. 'You just fuckin' get your Gimpy and fuckin' mallet the fuckers.'

'It ain't no different from what we trained for back at home,' Mat added. 'How long we been training for it – counter-terrorism, close-quarter battle, room-to-room combat – call it what you bloody well like? Years mate, that's what. And it don't matter where you are – in Bosnia, Sierra Leone, East Timor or bloody Afghanistan, this is what we trained for. And it don't matter who the enemy is, we're still doing what we bloody trained for. Killing the fookers. Every time you train, you do it like it's for real, and every time it's for real you're relying on your bloody training.'

There were a few seconds where no one spoke, as they were all contemplating what Mat had just been saying. The sound of metal scraping on metal, of rounds being slotted into magazines, filled the room.

'So, it's just a fuckin' test for all the trainin', is that it?' Tom countered, finally. 'Is that what you're sayin'? Is that all it is? Don't get me wrong, mate. I still think we should put a bullet in every last one of the fuckers. I'm just trying to work out how best we do that, that's all.'

'You know why we're operating so bloody well in there, mate, despite all the madness?' Mat answered. 'Cos that's what we trained for back at home – for it all going to rat shit, for it all going totally bloody pear-shaped. That fort is a fuck-up but not of our making, and it's one we've been sent in to sort out.'

'Fair enough, mate,' Tom conceded, after a slight pause. 'But I'll tell you another fuckin' thing – I reckon there's a good number of 'em will get away tonight, under cover of darkness.'

'How d'you figure that?' asked Jamie.

'Tom's got a point there, mate,' Mat cut in. 'Stands to reason. There's no way the Afghans will be able to keep all those fookers in there – in that fort – overnight. It's dark. You seen the bloody size of the place. Like three bloody great big football pitches laid side to side. There's hundreds of them left in there, got to be. Stands to bloody reason some of them are going to get away, don't it?'

'Yeah, and what with the way the fuckin' Afghans police the place and all,' Tom added, shaking his head, 'it'll be a quick leg-up over the wall and they'll scarper. What is it, a few guys wandering about on the outside of the fuckin' fort and the rest of 'em crouchin' around their fires to keep warm. I mean, there's no formal sentry system or nothing, is there? Yeah, a good number of the fuckers'll sneak away tonight.'

'But we aren't exactly expecting them to come back for any more, are we?' said Jamie. 'There's a lot of people have died in there today. And they must know that a fuck sight more of 'em are going to get malleted, before this thing is over.'

'Did someone say it was called the Fort of War?' said Mat. 'More like the Fort of bloody Death, I reckon.'

'Reckon I must've malleted dozens of the fuckers while I was on the Gimpy,' Jamie remarked. 'Just mowing 'em down I was. So was Ruff there. It was like they were all just looking to die, like they wanted nothing more than to get it over with, to get slotted. Fucking weird it was. Young kiddies a lot of them, too.'

'Fuckin' Gimpy's too fuckin' good for the fuckers,' Ruff growled.

There was an interruption as one of the 5th SOF soldiers put his head around the door. 'Heads up on the top floor, guys,' he announced. 'Say, you know, that Tom guy of yours – he's got balls made of brass from what I been hearin'.'

'Yeah, well, you had to be there, mate,' Mat replied, with a forced grin.

'Well, all right, I'll see you up on the top floor, buddy,' the US soldier added.

'Balls of brass?' said Mat, once the US soldier had gone. 'Reckon your missus will be shocked when she hears that, mate.'

'Fuck off, mate,' Tom retorted, with a grin. 'She fuckin' knows already, don't she.'

Once the SBS soldiers had finished rearming themselves, they headed up to the top floor of the building. After fixing a brew, they settled down for the debrief and to plan the next day's operations. First off, CIA Dave stood up to give an account of what had happened in the fort from his side of things. He covered the period from the start of the uprising and seeing Mike Spann go down under a pile of enemy prisoners, to the moment of his final escape from the fort. CIA Dave had eventually taken the same route out to safety as the ICRC workers had done before him. He'd climbed out a window at the rear of the HQ building, scaled the outer parapet of the fort and run down the sloping buttress on the far side. Once there, he'd jumped in a local taxi that had just ferried a news crew to the battle scene, and headed back to Boxer Base.

CIA Dave said that he'd only decided to abandon the fort at the last possible moment, when darkness was coming down and he was convinced that there was no rescuing Mike Spann. The general consensus in the room seemed to be that Mike was unlikely to have survived the initial attack on him by the prisoners. And it was clear that he was even less likely to survive a night alone in the fort. This being the case then, the following day's battle plan could be very different. If there were no allied personnel left alive in the fort, they could go in hard and just obliterate the enemy positions from the air. The gloves would be off. A plan for the following morning was drawn up which involved the same SBS/5th SOF teams going into action. But now the teams would be tasked almost exclusively with calling in air strikes.

'All around the walls of that place there's rooms stuffed full of ammo and weapons,' Tom remarked. 'OK, a lot of it might be World War II vintage, but it still goes bang if you point it in the right fuckin' direction. It's a fuckin' stupid place to put your prisoners –'

'Yeah, an' they got kinda irrigation channels running beneath the walls,' one of the 5th SOF soldiers interjected, 'which, you know, bring in the water.'

'So, they've got weapons and they got water,' Tom continued. 'The point being they could hold out in there for fuckin' weeks, if they wanted to. But I reckon their real aim is to break out and cause as much havoc and mayhem as possible.'

'No two ways about it, we gotta break that siege,' said Major Martin. In spite of the earlier friction between the 5th SOF commanding officer and one or two of the SBS soldiers, the US Major was more than rising to the challenge of the fort uprising. 'An' the only way I can see to do that is with the air power. That's unless, you know, anyone else can think of a better way.'

'Well, consider the options,' said Tom. 'We can't fuckin' storm the place, that's for sure. We're outnumbered and the enemy are well armed and well dug in. We can't just wait it out as a siege tactic, cos there's still enough of 'em in there to try and break out. There's only one option that makes any sense: we got to locate their strongholds and fuckin' mallet 'em from the air.'

'We got fast air on standby all day tomorrow,' Major Martin enthused. 'Way I see it, they ain't never gonna give it up unless we break their hold on the place, that's for sure.'

'Tell you one thing, mate,' Jamie remarked. 'Without them air strikes today we'd have been in real trouble. We had some real angels on our shoulders.'

'Appreciate you sayin' it, buddy,' the Major replied. 'Question is, where do we best place our FAC teams tomorrow?'

'Best place is the western tower, mate,' said Tom. 'End of today, Sam was there and I wasn't far behind him. You got the best vantage point to see into the southern end of the fort. Plus they won't be expectin' us to be over that way, as we concentrated on the eastern side today.'

'All right, then my team – that's Tom, Sam and a couple of the 5th SOF boys – we'll take the western tower. Captain Lancer, you OK with your guys taking up positions on the eastern side of the fort? You know that area well, n'all.'

'That's fine by me, Major,' the SBS Captain replied. 'That way we can have FAC teams covering both sides of the fort. But one thing, Major,' he added, with a grin, 'your boys will remember their comms antennae this time, won't they?'

'Well, you know, you Brits did such a good job n'all in there today, so maybe we'd be best off forgettin' it,' the Major retorted.

At that, the soldiers in the room fell about laughing. The mission planning was coming to an end, and they began to talk more freely about the events that had taken place that day in the fort.

'So, do any of you lot have any idea what they're fighting for?' Mat asked. 'Like, do they have any sort of strategy? Any grand plan that we're not aware of?'

'Grand plan? Yeah, like they all want to fuckin' die,' Tom answered. 'You saw those suicide charges, mate. Fanatical fuckin' death wish or what?'

'Well, we just might have a take on that,' one of the CIA officers volunteered, from the corner of the room. He was one of the Agency's intel experts and had remained at Boxer Base all that day. 'Seems like at the time those six hundred AQT surrendered, Dostum was undecided as to what they was up to. He reckoned there were three options: the first, that it was a trap; the second, they were surrenderin' to see how they'd be treated; the third, that it was a genuine surrender. But he didn't know which it was. So, think about the trap scenario. Right now there are some 6,000 AQT holed up in Kunduz, with heavy armour. And Kandahar – that's the AQT stronghold in the south – hasn't been taken yet. So, if the AQT forces could successfully counter-attack out of Kunduz and hit Mazar, you'd then have the Northern Alliance sandwiched in the middle, with the 6,000 AQT in the north and the rest of the AQT forces in the south. We reckon that was their overall game plan.'

'But how does that relate to the six hundred prisoners, mate?' Mat asked.

'Like, how does getting yourself thrown in the

slammer contribute to your grand strategy?' Tom added.

'Think if it wasn't never a genuine surrender – the six hundred prisoners real aim bein' to get their hands on the weapons in the fort and start a counter-attack from the west of Mazar. See what I'm drivin' at? Then you got AQT breakin' out of the fort and hittin' Mazar from the west, and AQT breakin' out of Kunduz and hittin' Mazar from the east. So Mazar gets hit in a pincer movement. And then the whole NA forces get hit in a second pincer movement. And that, maybe, was their game plan.'

'But we've got no proof on that,' said Mat. 'It's just a theory, right?'

'Yeah, it's still just a theory,' the CIA agent answered. 'But it's one a lot of the local Afghans are talkin' about right now.'

'What's the score on Mike Spann, then?' Mat asked, changing the subject. 'We are confirmed he's dead, right?'

'There was a guy lyin' in the southern end of the fort,' said Sam, quietly. 'I saw him from the western tower. He was dressed in jeans and a shirt. That ain't the sort of garb the AQT wear. And it's the right place to have seen him, according to Dave. He wasn't movin', that's all I can say.'

'How's the finger, mate?' said Tom, deliberately trying to change the subject. He knew that Sam was still troubled by whatever he'd seen from the western tower at the end of that day's fighting.

'Which one, bro?' Sam replied, with a tired grin. 'Anyhow, thought you promised never to mention it?'

'Promised? Fuck off, mate. You know, the one you fucked going over the wall – your trigger finger, mate.'

'You what?' Mat asked, incredulously. 'He buggered his trigger finger? Who the hell was doing all the fighting in there, then?'

'Who d'you fuckin' think, mate?' Tom replied. 'Tom "Balls of Brass" Knight, mate, that's who.'

For several minutes the SBS lads ripped the piss mercilessly out of Sam over his strained trigger finger, each of them using it as an excuse to relieve some of the stress and tension of the day. As the meeting broke up, Major Martin quietly drew Tom to one side.

'Say, buddy – you guys always, you know, dress this way, kinda informal, like?' he remarked, as he put an arm around Tom's shoulder. 'An' you always kinda call your officers "mate" and "boss", an' they don't object or nothin'?'

'That's just the way we do things, mate,' Tom replied. 'It's the ethos behind UK special forces – everyone is respected and has their say, pretty much regardless of rank. No one stands on fuckin' ceremony. That's just the way we go about gettin' things done.'

'I mean, no offence intended, buddy, you guys did a great job in there today. It's just, you know, from where I'm standin' it all seems pretty kinda strange is all.'

'Well, I reckon you must be gettin' used to it by now, eh? Cos I tell you one thing, mate, it won't be no fuckin' different tomorrow.'

After the debrief had ended, Mat and Jamie went for a smoke and a stroll around the Boxer Base compound. Jamie handed out the Marlboro to his friend, and they lit up. He still wanted to talk about the events back in the fort.

'You scared in there today, mate?' Jamie asked.

'Didn't have time to think about it,' Mat replied. 'I'm bloody petrified now, though, mate.'

The two men laughed. Then Jamie spoke again.

'I killed a lot of people in there today.'

'Me too,' said Mat.

'Yeah, but on the Gimpy, I was just murdering them.'

'How many d'you reckon?' asked Mat.

'Dozens,' Jamie answered, quietly. 'Maybe hundreds. Who the fuck knows? I reckon I saw white faces in there, too. You know, like Europeans. Maybe there was Brits in among them, like Muslim converts.'

'Can't be helped, can it, mate? If they're Taliban or al-Qaeda it doesn't matter where they're from. Just got to take 'em out.'

'Just fuckin' call me the "Executioner",' Jamie said, ignoring Mat's last remark. 'Just fuckin' call me the "Executioner" –'

'Look, mate, way I see it is this,' said Mat, trying to get Jamie's attention again. 'Back in the Naka Valley I saved a lot of people that needed saving. And I killed a load of people in that fort today that needed killing. Simple as that. And I ain't troubled by it.'

Jamie took a long drag on his Marlboro and as he did so Mat stole a quick glance over at him. In the glow from the cigarette he could see that Jamie's face was looking haggard and exhausted. Jamie was one of Mat's closest mates and he knew that the big man was a tough and fearless warrior, with hidden strengths. But he was also a sensitive soul. And Mat could tell that Jamie was troubled by today's killing – the wholesale slaughter that had taken place in that fort. It was all so different from their image of how war should be fought. They'd expected tough and bloody combat, and that they'd found today. But they'd also encountered a senseless, numbing, mindless slaughter.

Yes, Mat knew that he too had killed that day, but only a fraction of the numbers accounted for by the two GPMG gunners. He didn't exactly expect Ruff to be disturbed by the killing – it wasn't in his nature. But he

made a mental note that when they got back to Poole
he'd get Jamie out on the lash. They'd have a proper
talk over a few beers, and probably both get all emotional.
Which was about the nearest any of the SBS lads ever
got to analysing and dealing with the trauma of their
job.

As the men retired to their beds, Sam Brown found
himself unable to sleep. He was deeply troubled by the
day's events. At the end of their rescue mission, he had
spotted a figure that he was convinced was CIA Agent
Mike Spann. None of the Afghan soldiers, or the enemy
for that matter, wore jeans and a dark Western shirt.
They wore combats and djellabas. So it had to be CIA
Mike. He was lying in the courtyard outside the enemy
stronghold, face down and unmoving, and Sam had been
unable to tell if he was dead or alive. So the soldier had
proceeded to put two bullets into the ground, as close
to the CIA agent's head as he dared, to see if the figure
moved or flinched. Both times he squeezed the trigger
there had been no sign of life from the CIA agent. But
Sam still didn't know for sure that Mike Spann was dead.
He could conceivably have been unconscious and badly
injured, but still breathing.

Sam had known that it was impossible for him and
Tom to fight their way any further into the fort alone.
As it was, they had taken their lives in their hands even
to get this far. But it was the thought of abandoning CIA
Agent Mike Spann – when there was just the chance that
he could still be alive – that troubled him so very, very
deeply.

'Brother Ali, Brother Ali.' It was Ahmed speaking, as he
gently tried to shake Ali's comatose form awake. 'Brother
Ali, it's me, Ahmed.'

'What is it?' Ali replied, groggily. After the day's vicious and bloody action he'd been sleeping the sleep of the dead. 'What time is it, brother?'

'A little after four thirty,' Ahmed answered. 'Brother, during the night several of the brothers broke out of the fort via the drainage channels. They said they were going to seek help in the village. I could do nothing to stop them. We've just heard an outbreak of fighting. A fire-fight, mainly AK47s, down in the village. It's all gone quiet now. I think the brothers were intercepted.'

'As sure as Allah is the All Merciful One, anyone who tries to escape now is a fool,' Ali replied, angrily. 'We should expect no quarter from the *kafir*, and give none in return. If they catch you they will kill you and that's one more brother who has died in vain. We stay here and fight. To the death. Until the last drop of *kafir* blood that can be shed has been shed.'

'*Al-hamdu Lillah*, brother, I am with you,' Ahmed replied, quietly. In the faint light of the coming dawn Ali could see just how drawn and haggard his giant warrior friend was looking. 'But some of the brothers are still talking of surrender. They do not want to face another day of the *kafir* bombing. How can we fight them, they ask, when they just use their air power to massacre us? How many brothers have we lost like that already, Brother Ali? One hundred? Two hundred? Maybe more? Brother Ali, the fort grounds are littered with the bodies of the *shouhada'a*.'

'Is this truly the other brothers speaking, Brother Ahmed, or is it you?' Ali asked, softly. 'Do you agree with them, brother, that this is no way to die, to be *shaheed*? If so, do you really think the *kafir* would accept our surrender, after all that we have now done? After "surrendering" and then betraying them? After killing

the American CIA dogs? After killing the Northern
Alliance whore commanders? After taking the alcohol-
drinking and pig-flesh-eating Dostum's fort and
destroying it? After all that, do you really think they
would accept our surrender?'

'I don't know, brother. I doubt it,' Ahmed replied,
looking at the ground. 'If it were only me, brother, I
would fight back to back with you until either the last
kafir had his throat cut or we were both *shouhada'a*.
And then, *insh'Allah*, we would be together in Paradise.
But some of the brothers are young and scared and tired,
and their hearts are not firm, brother. What do we tell
them? What do we say to them to make them stand and
fight?'

'We tell them the truth, Brother Ahmed,' Ali replied.
'We tell them what the forces of *kofr* have done to this
beautiful, pure Islamic country. What these dirty infidel
dogs have done to the Muslim sisters, the Muslim children, the young babies and the grandparents. How they
have bombed our villages, our towns, our mountains and
our fields. Call the brothers together, Brother Ahmed. I
will speak to them. And I will put fire back into their
hearts. And I will make them yearn to kill the *kafir* like
never before.'

Some thirty minutes later, the surviving brothers were
gathered together in the darkness of the largest of the
underground bunkers. Ali stood up to speak to them.

'Brothers, remember the words of the Holy Koran,
chapter nine, verse fourteen: "Fight against them so that
Allah will punish them by your hands and disgrace them
and give you victory over them and heal the breasts of
a believing people." Brothers, from the four corners of
the world we came to the jihad, to Afghanistan and now
to this fort to heal the breasts of a believing people. And

how the believing people have suffered, brothers, under the murderous hand of the *kafir*. That is why we are here, brothers. Remember, the All Merciful One never promised that the path we have chosen, the path of the jihad, would be easy. And now is not the time to lose heart, brothers. Now is not the time to lose heart.'

'He's right, brothers, he's right,' said Ahmed, as Ali paused for breath. 'Listen to the wise words and reflect on the path of the jihad.'

'This war is, in the infidel leader Bush's own words, a "crusade", brothers. It is a war of *kofr* – disbelief – against the one true faith, Islam. The history of this conflict does not go back only to the glorious day of 11 September, when the Nineteen Lions roared and changed the course of history. It goes back to the time when the Jewish tribes gathered against the Prophet, peace be upon Him, and the Christians launched the Crusades against the Muslims. It goes back to the American government's murderous policies on Iraq, Palestine, Bosnia, Kashmir and the Sudan, to name but a few. Like Bush himself said, you are either with the forces of *kofr*, the disbelievers, the forces of Zionist-controlled America, or against them. Did the Prophet – peace be upon Him – not say, "A Muslim is the brother of a Muslim, he does not forsake him or betray him"?'

'Brother Ali speaks the truth, brothers,' one of the young men in the group shouted out. 'And what if we do die? There lies the path to Paradise.'

'As soon as the first hostile disbelievers entered this land, this Holy Land of Afghanistan, defensive jihad became obligatory on all Muslims,' Ali continued. He could tell that he was winning the brothers round. 'Those who have not answered that call and were able to do so, brothers, will be punished by Allah in the hereafter. Have no doubt about that. And those who *have* answered the call, as we have, brothers, they will be lifted up in the hearts of green birds into Paradise itself. Remember the words of the Holy Koran, chapter three, verse 140: "Allah may distinguish between those who believe so that He may take from your ranks the Martyrs. And Allah does not take the wrongdoers."

'And do not think the path of the jihad is without pain, without sacrifice, without blood, without fatigue, without torture.' Ali was growing in confidence as he spoke. 'For it says in the Holy Koran, chapter two, verse 214: "Do you really think that you will enter Paradise without such trials as came to those who passed before you? They were afflicted with severe poverty and ailments and were so shaken that even the Prophet and those others who believed said: 'When will come the help of Allah?' Yet, certainly, the help of Allah was near!" The path to victory is long and arduous and full of challenges, brothers. Brothers, without suffering, where is the test of the true believers? And when the suffering is at its greatest, believe then that the help of Allah is nearest at hand.'

'Hear him, brothers,' Ahmed interjected. '*Al-hamdu Lillah*, those are fine words.'

'Now is not the time to turn aside from our path, brothers. For it says in the Holy Koran, chapter nine, verse 111: "They fight in Allah's cause, so they kill and are killed . . . Then rejoice in the bargain you have concluded. That is the supreme success." Can we give up the path of jihad now, brothers? Can we break the bargain that we have made with the All Merciful One? Can we desert our duty to the jihad, to kill the *kafir* or be killed in the process? We cannot turn away from the true path now, brothers. The gates to Paradise lie before us, brothers. Those gates are open for us, ready to welcome each and every one of us in.'

'Death to the *kafir*!' Ahmed started to chant. 'Death to the *kafir*!'

The call was quickly taken up by the other brothers, growing in power and volume as more and more joined in.

'I know you are with me, brothers,' Ali shouted, raising his hands to silence them. 'I know I can count on every single one of you to do your duty to Islam. This war in Afghanistan is the start of a war that will last for decades, and after much suffering it will end in victory for the believers. For it says in the Holy Koran, chapter sixty-one, verse nine: "It is He who has sent His Messenger with guidance and the religion of truth, that He may make it prevail over all other religions, no matter how much the disbelievers detest it."'

'*Al-hamdu Lillah!*' several of the brothers shouted, excitedly.

'Now, today, brothers we will fight differently,' Ali continued. 'Listen to me carefully. Unless absolutely necessary, no one is to go outside and expose himself to the *kafir* bombings. We will stick to the underground chambers and we will fight from the cover of the windows and doorways. In that way, brothers, we will force the *kafir* to come into the fort and fight us. And then – by the grace of Allah – we will massacre them and wipe them out. We have water to drink from the irrigation channels, brothers, and the meat of Dostum's horses to eat. We can survive here as long as it takes, brothers, until the *kafir* are forced to come and fight us here, on our own terms.'

'*Allahu Akhbar!*' several of the brothers chanted.

'I promise you, brothers, that this morning you will

see a sign that the help of Allah is near at hand. A great and magical blow will be struck against the *kafir*, and you will witness the wondrous power of the All Mighty One. This morning, brothers. This very morning. *Allahu Akhbar!*'

As the brothers took up brother Ali's war cry, their cries of *Allahu Akhbar* echoed thunderously around the underground basement, their clenched fists punching the air in time with the chanting.

13

DAWN AWAKENING

'DID you hear, mate? Report's just come in' Tom said to Mat, early the next morning, as he was pulling on his boots in preparation for a second day's action at the fort. 'Half a dozen of the fuckers broke out overnight and busted into some houses in a nearby village. They just slaughtered people left, right and centre – men, women, children, the lot. The alarm was raised in the village, every man grabbed a gun and went on the hunt, tracked the fuckers down and killed 'em all. Apparently, they've hung the bodies from the trees at the edge of the village.'

'Nice,' Mat replied.

'*Pour encourager les autres*,' Jamie added.

'What?' said Tom.

'French, mate,' Jamie said. 'Means "to encourage the others". Like a warning not to try the same trick again.'

'Yeah, I guess,' said Tom, trying to stifle a yawn.

At 5.10 a.m. the SBS and 5th SOF soldiers left Boxer Base and headed out of Mazar city to the fort. On arrival they would filter into their positions without being detected. Once inside the fort they would go quiet on

the mission, which meant no talking or radio communications unless absolutely necessary. And then they
would call in the US air strikes as an early-morning
surprise for the enemy. Some twenty minutes later they
reached Qala-i-Janghi, just as the pre-dawn light had
started to paint the skies to the east of them a brilliant
blue red. The Land-Rovers and Humvees pulled to a halt
several hundred yards from the fort's walls and out of
range of the enemy weaponry. Major Martin's team set
off on foot in the semi-darkness heading for the western
tower, while Captain Lancer's men headed for the eastern
entranceway tower.

As the Captain's team approached their position, they
were spotted by a group of Northern Alliance soldiers
who were crouching around their fire to keep warm. The
Afghans started waving their arms around and gesturing
wildly. It turned out that the enemy mortar operator who
had caused so much trouble the previous day was still
in operation, and he had his weapon zeroed in on the
eastern entranceway tower. So Captain Lancer opted to
relocate his men to the north-eastern tower – the position where they had seen out the last of the previous
day's fighting. The men skirted around the outside of the
fort giving a wide berth to the minefields. But as the
north-eastern tower hove into view Mat had to do a
double take, just to make sure that he wasn't dreaming.

'Holy fuck,' he said, pointing to the top of the squat
tower. 'Will you take a look at that?'

'How the fuck did they get that up there?' Jamie said,
letting out a long, low whistle.

Perched atop the squat structure and silhouetted
against the light of dawn was a massive T-55 Soviet-era
battle tank, its main gun pointing ominously towards
the southern end of the fort.

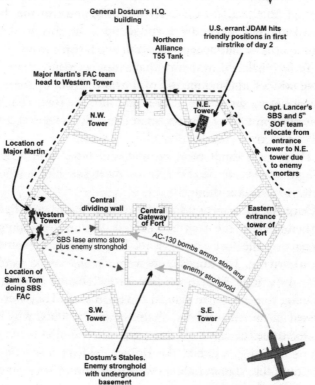

Day 2 of Fort Siege

N

General Dostum's H.Q. building

Northern Alliance T55 Tank

U.S. errant JDAM hits friendly positions in first airstrike of day 2

Major Martin's FAC team head to Western Tower

N.W. Tower

N.E. Tower

Capt. Lancer's SBS and 5th SOF team relocate from entrance tower to N.E. tower due to enemy mortars

Location of Major Martin

Central dividing wall

Central Gateway of Fort

Eastern entrance tower of fort

Western Tower

SBS lase ammo store plus enemy stronghold

AC-130 bombs ammo store and enemy stronghold

Location of Sam & Tom doing SBS FAC

S.W. Tower

S.E. Tower

Dostum's Stables. Enemy stronghold with underground basement

US AC-130 Spectre gunship hits enemy on second night of fort battle

'Now unless I'm going nuts, that wasn't there yesterday when we left,' said Mat.

'Like fuck it was, mate,' said Jamie, trying to stifle a chuckle.

'You can just imagine some Northern Alliance bloke trying to explain it all to General Dostum, can't you? "Just popped out for an early-morning drive in me T-55, I did, and somehow I ended up atop this tower. Dunno how it happened, General Sir, I really don't."'

'Yeah, well, I'd warrant that's no accident, mate.' Jamie nodded in the direction of the tank 'From up there, it must have a direct line of fire right into the fort. That's been put there for a reason, mate, and I'd wager it's to mallet any of the enemy left alive in there.'

'These guys don't mess around, do they?' said Mat. 'Tell you what, mate, I'd like to meet the bloke who drove it up there, though.'

Once the men were up on the roof of the tower, they worked out that the T-55 had been driven up the sloping rampart of the fort's outer wall. It was certainly some feat of driving. The tank's crew were already awake, and there were four Afghan soldiers crouching on its hull, huddling to keep warm against the night chill. They were dressed in mixed combats, shamags and sandals, which seemed to be the standard uniform for General Dostum's troops. As they watched the British soldiers inspecting their tank the Afghan fighters were all smiles. Using hand gestures and doing impersonations of a straining tank engine, they gave a short demonstration of how they had driven the machine up on to the tower.

'Nice to have some firepower on hand, ain't it, mate?' Mat whispered to Jamie, once the Afghans had finished. 'I mean, who needs the US Air Force when you've got General Dostum's flying tanks?'

'Yeah, just as long as the walls are strong enough,' Jamie whispered back.

'What d'you mean?'

'Well, that's no Nissan Micra, is it?' said Jamie, eyeing the T-55 suspiciously. 'I mean, what's a T-55 weigh – several tons, got to be. And then there's the recoil when it starts firing. Put it another way, when they built this fort d'you think they did so with tanks in mind? Unlikely, mate. More like foot soldiers and cavalry.'

'Who gives a flying fuck, as long as it can fucking mallet the fuckers,' growled Ruff. He wasn't at his best in the mornings.

'Keep your voice down, Ruff mate,' hissed Mat.

'You can have the position nearest it when it starts firing then, mate,' Jamie added.

Some twenty yards in front of the T-55 tank the US 5th SOF soldiers were already setting up a FAC position overlooking the fort. Unfortunately, it was difficult to get a direct line of sight from the tower on to the enemy positions in the southern end of the fort. But with H-hour for the air strikes set at 0601 hours and fast approaching, they'd have to make do. In any case, Major Martin, Tom and Sam would soon be taking up their positions on the opposite side of the fort, on the western tower. From there they could provide eyes on the target and laser coordinates, while the FAC team concentrated on liaising with the US pilots and talking them down on to target.

By 5.45 a.m., Jamie and Ruff were manning the GPMGs at the tower battlements and covering the gateway in the central wall, while Mat was lending a hand with the 5th SOF as they set up the comms equipment. It was still fairly dark within the fort and deathly quiet, and there hadn't been any sign yet that the enemy had spotted them. Once the US FAC team had got their comms up and running they made contact with the lead pilot. In sixteen minutes the aircraft would be over the fort – and all being well the air strikes would tear into the enemy positions.

Mat kept his eyes glued to the southern end of the fort, searching for enemy movement. As he did so, he started counting down the minutes to the air strikes. He could just imagine the scene inside the cockpit of the lead US warplane as it streaked across the dawn skies inbound towards the fort. In addition to flying the F-18 Hornet fighter-attack aircraft, the pilot would be talking to the FAC team on the ground. He'd be scribbling their instructions on to a pad strapped to his leg, and then punching the target coordinates into his on-board computer system so that the plane could home in on the enemy positions to be hit. And he'd also be taking note of the friendly coordinates, so that he could avoid any potential confusion over where the nearest US and British forces were positioned. This is known as 'deconfliction' in military speak. There was no doubt about it in Mat's mind, the pilot had one hell of a lot to do as he prepared for that bombing run.

Over on the opposite side of the fort Sam and Tom were just settling into their positions on the western tower. As they nuzzled up against the battlements they had an unobstructed view into the southern end of the fort. Not a soul appeared to be moving down there, although they had little doubt that some of the enemy would be awake, keeping watch from their positions in the basement. Sam and Tom had brought one of the Northern Alliance soldiers with them. The Afghan soldier had been stationed in Qala-i-Janghi before, when General Dostum was last in control of it, so he knew the fort complex like the back of his hand. He pointed out the two target buildings that they wanted to hit: the pink stable block, below which the majority of the enemy were supposedly sheltering, and the main ammo stores situated on the far side of the fort's dividing wall.

Sam lased the two targets using their LTD and recorded the coordinates. Then Tom ducked his head down to speak into the PRM he had attached to his shoulder webbing – relaying the target coordinates back to Major Martin. The Major had brought a 5th SOF signals officer with him this morning, to help with the FAC comms, and the two of them were positioned towards the rear of the tower some thirty yards back from Tom and Sam's positions.

'Target 1, pink building in middle of southern half of fort,' Tom whispered into his radio. 'Coordinates are MGRS Foxtrot Echo 23849678.'

'MGRS Foxtrot Echo 23849678,' the Major confirmed back to him.

'Target 2, row of metal shipping containers – ammo stores, located on southern side of dividing wall of fort,' Tom continued. 'Coordinates are MGRS Foxtrot Echo 23849667.'

Again, Major Martin confirmed the coordinates. Once he'd done so, he began calculating the distance the targets were from their own positions. Unfortunately, both targets were in extreme danger-close proximity to the western tower: the pink building was about 250 yards distant, while the ammo store was barely 150 yards. With the first F-18 Hornet inbound and some ten minutes away, the Major knew that he needed to put up some target coordinates to the pilots, and fast. But by anyone's reckoning, these targets were too close for comfort.

Keeping his voice low, the Major spoke into his radio set: 'Sam, Tom, on me – need a heads-up, guys.'

'You got any alternative targets?' the Major whispered to them, once Tom and Sam had crawled over to join him. 'Those two are extreme danger-close. Like, they're on top of us.'

'It's the stronghold and ammo store, mate,' Tom whispered back at him. 'There's nothin' else that makes any sense to hit.'

'Well, we gotta get some good-to-go targets up to the fast air, cos they're inbound now, buddy.'

'So give them those goddam targets,' Sam cut in, impatiently.

'Listen, buddy, a five-hundred-pounder is danger-close at five hundred yards,' the Major countered. 'Those two targets are less 'n half that distance. You tellin' me you wanna be here when they get hit?'

'They're all we've got that's good to go,' Sam retorted.

'All right, but they're too damn close for comfort, that's for sure,' the Major replied. 'You got the friendly coordinates too, right?'

'Got 'em, mate,' Tom confirmed.

'Well, OK. Wait one.'

Turning back to the radio, Major Martin began to relay both the target coordinates and those of their friendly positions back to the 5th SOF team, who would in turn put them up to the US pilots. But once he'd finished doing so, a message came back to him that the lead aircraft had to first deploy a 2,000-pound JDAM munition, before any of its five-hundred-pounders could be activated. Apparently, the avionics of the aircraft meant that the laser-guided bombs couldn't be dropped until the JDAM had gone down.

'Jesus! Now they got a goddam JDAM that's gotta

go down first,' Major Martin snapped, as he came off the radio.

'Make a big bang,' Sam commented under his breath. 'Sure will be one hell of a wake-up call.'

'Will be when it fries our arses all to toast,' Tom added. 'Only joking, mate. Get the fucker in here. JDAMs are GPS-guided, aren't they? Accurate to ten metres. We'll be all right.'

'If I give the green light, that bomb's on its way and we're underneath it,' said the Major, deliberately looking at both Tom and Sam. 'That's a two-thousand-pound munition. You guy's OK with that? I'm just makin' certain –'

'Listen, mate, you're right – we're too fuckin' close for comfort,' Tom replied. 'But the JDAM's got to go, ain't it? And we ain't got no fuckin' option other than using the air power, have we? There's no other way we're goin' to take those fuckers out, is there? We'll just have to be careful as fuck with the targeting and get our fuckin' heads down as the big one goes in.'

'JDAMs at dawn,' said Sam, with a grin.

'I love the smell of JDAMs in the mornin',' Tom added.

Major Martin nodded at each of them in turn, making doubly certain that they were happy for the air strike to go in, and then grasped his radio.

'This is Major Michael E. Martin, of the US 5th SOF,' he announced, 'and I'm givin' permission to go in and hit those targets, but my forces are danger-close, I repeat, extreme danger-close to those coordinates . . .'

Sam and Tom left the Major to liaise with the FAC team and crawled back to their positions overlooking the southern half of the fort. As soon as that first muni-tion hit, they wanted to be up at the battlements and laying down some fire on to the enemy. They kept their eyes glued to the enemy positions. It was ominously quiet down there. The Northern Alliance had kept the enemy bottled up in the fort all night long, so they had to be in there somewhere. And once those air strikes went in, all hell was going to break loose. The F-18 aircraft now had several target coordinates programmed into their on-board computerised attack systems. Once that JDAM hit they would be coming in to strike a series of pre-planned targets in quick succession.

Bang on H-hour, Tom and Sam detected the faint whirr of a munition coming in from behind them at a great distance. It was barely audible in the still, early-morning air. Within seconds the whirr had increased to a whine and then to a deafening scream. Tom and Sam threw themselves flat behind the battlements just as an almighty explosion rocked the fort. They clasped their hands over their heads as the angry blast wave rolled over them, sucking up the air and creating a momentary vacuum. But both men had expected a far greater impact, considering the target was at such close range.

A split second after the JDAM hit, Tom and Sam jumped up from behind the battlements and opened fire with their Diemacos on the enemy positions. But almost immediately, they were confronted by a fierce barrage of return fire. The enemy had started counter-attacking from the windows of the stable-block building. The two special forces soldiers searched the ground in front of them for the plume of dust and debris from the JDAM strike. But suddenly they realised with a shock that there was no sign of any air strike on either of the pre-designated targets.

What the fuck is going on? both of them were thinking. *Where the hell is that air strike?*

Ducking back behind the parapet, Tom and Sam

looked at each other in bewilderment. As they did so, their PRMs just started going haywire. For a moment they couldn't make any sense of what they were hearing on the radio net – it sounded like a confusion of shouting mixed in with a horrible yelling and screaming. But then there was the unmistakable sound of English voices mixed in with the cacophony of crying and panicked Afghan voices.

'Fuck! Fuck! We've been hit!'

'Holy fuck! Get a fuckin' medic!'

'That's Mat!' Tom yelled, above the uproar on the radio. 'That's Mat!'

'Jesus Christ,' said Sam, the colour draining from his face. 'How the fuck . . .'

'The fuckin' Yank pilot must've hit the wrong fuckin' target!'

'Oh my God, we've taken casualties!' Major Martin started yelling from behind them. 'We've taken casualties!'

As Tom and Sam turned in horror, they caught sight of a massive plume of smoke rising into the dawn sky up above the northern end of the fort. With his heart in his mouth Tom grabbed his binoculars and focused in on the devastation. Through all the smoke and dust, he could just make out that a missile had ploughed into the tower on the opposite side of the fort from them. The squat structure had been almost completely destroyed. Tom's shocked mind struggled to make sense of the scene that he was seeing through his binoculars, and the cries that they were hearing over the radio. There was only one thing that he was certain of – that his mates had been hit real bad.

'WE GOT TO ABORT THE AIR STRIKES,' Sam suddenly started screaming.

Amid all the confusion, Sam had suddenly remembered that the F-18s were inbound on their second bombing run. Jumping up from his position he pounded across the tower roof to Major Martin.

'ABORT THE FUCKIN' AIR STRIKES! ABORT! ABORT!' Sam was yelling as he ran.

The Major and Sam dived for the radio piece and started screaming into it: 'ABORT! ABORT! ABORT! ABORT!'

A split second later an F-18 pulled up from its attacking run and went tearing across the fort. They had stopped the second air strike just in the nick of time.

'Where's the fuckin' casualties?' Tom yelled in bewilderment, as he came racing across the roof to join them. 'It's the wrong fuckin' tower.'

'JDAM's hit the north-eastern tower,' Major Martin roared a reply. 'Gotta be our boys hit there.'

'But it's the wrong fuckin' tower,' Tom repeated. 'Our boys're on the entrance tower. It's the wrong tower –'

'We've taken casualties bad!' Major Martin started yelling.

'I'm the only fuckin' medic left alive, for all I know,' Tom yelled back. 'And my mates are over there in a world of pain and hurt.'

'So get the hell outta here,' the Major roared. 'Go help your buddies. We'll be right behind ya.'

'BUT WHICH FUCKIN' TOWER?' Tom screamed.

'Tom, Tom, let's go find 'em,' Sam cut in, grabbing his arm. 'Let's go find 'em, buddy. Let's go find 'em.'

Jumping to their feet, Tom and Sam vaulted over the wall. As fast as they could they began retracing their steps towards the eastern side of the fort. Obviously, the air strike had gone horribly wrong, and somehow their own men had been hit. But what their shocked and confused minds couldn't get to grips with was the fact that the JDAM had hit the north-eastern tower, and not one of their men should have been positioned there. In the battle plan agreed at Boxer Base the previous night, Captain Lancer's team were supposed to take up positions on the eastern tower, over the main gateway to the fort. In which case, how could their SBS mates have been hit?

'Imagine, brothers, the look on the faces of your mothers and sisters when they learn the glorious news – that their son or brother has made the ultimate sacrifice in the jihad,' Ali announced. He was speaking softly to a group of brothers down in the basement. 'Imagine the joy, brothers. Imagine a Muslim sister or wife back in Yemen, Somalia or Chechnya and the pride she will feel when she learns that her Muslim brother has become *shaheed* and has gone to join the Nineteen Lions in Paradise. Imagine how she will then long to join you, brothers, and bless you for smoothing her own path to Paradise. Imagine the fate that now awaits us, brothers.'

Ali led the brothers in the first prayers of the morning. Despite the carnage of the previous day's fighting, Qala-i-Janghi was quiet and almost peaceful in the pre-dawn stillness. Ali and the brothers turned east, to face the direction of the Holy Shrines, and started the Arabic incantation of the dawn prayers. From their standing position the brothers dropped to their knees and then bowed low, placing their foreheads upon the earthen floor of the basement in obeisance to their God, the All Merciful One. Then they rose to their feet again in unison. But as they did so the sonorous chanting of their prayers was drowned out by the scream of an incoming missile.

Instinctively, the brothers flung themselves back down

on to the basement floor. Suddenly there was a loud
explosion up above them. Even though the impact
sounded distant, the noise of the air strike echoed around
the fort, striking fear into the hearts of the assembled
men, and instantly bringing back the memories of the
terror of yesterday's bombing. Ali caught himself listening
out for the screams of the wounded brothers – the first
to be hit by this cowardly bombing on their second day
of battle. But while he strained his ears for the cries of
the dying, no such sounds reached him.

'Calm yourselves, brothers, calm yourselves,' Ali urged,
as he glanced around at the fearful faces before him.
'Brother Ahmed, how far was that air strike from us?'

'When you compare it to those of yesterday, Brother
Ali,' Ahmed replied, 'it must be five hundred yards away,
at least.'

'Listen, brothers!' Ali cried, excitedly. 'Listen! Perhaps
this is the great miracle that we have been waiting for,
to show that Allah's help is near at hand. Come, brothers,
follow me. Let us hope and pray that the *kafir* dogs have
suffered a terrible blow.'

The brothers rushed forth from the basement and gathered at the gate in the fort's central wall. There they
caught sight of a giant plume of smoke rising from the
north-eastern tower of the fort.

'Look, brothers! LOOK!' Ali yelled, stretching his arm
out in the direction of the bombed-out tower. 'By the
grace of Almighty Allah, the *kafir* dogs have been struck
down with their own weapons. Look – they have bombed
themselves. *ALLAHU AKHBAR! ALLAHU AKHBAR!*'

'*ALLAHU AKHBAR! ALLAHU AKHBAR!*' the
brothers yelled, taking up Ali's thunderous cry as they
danced around the wrecked gateway.

'Didn't I tell you, brothers?' Ali cried. 'Didn't I promise

that this morning you would witness the wondrous power
of the All Mighty One? With all their weapons and technology, the *kafir* are no more than puny ants before the
Almighty Allah. He has taken their bombs and thrown
them back on themselves and now the *kafir* suffer like
the infidel dogs they are. Come, brothers, now is the
time to counter-attack. The *kafir* hate to see death,
because they have no belief. No faith in the afterlife. But
death does not touch us. Here we are, surrounded by
the sights and the smell of death, by hundreds of the
brothers who are *shouhada'a*, yet we carry on fighting.
Come, brothers, after me, we will hit the infidel dogs
hard while they are still reeling.'

Quickly, Ali led a group of some thirty fighters in a
scuttling, crouching run out of the gateway and into their
attacking positions, in the shattered remnants of the
buildings to either side of the gateway. Taking cover in
the bombed-out ruins Ali instructed them to set up three
of the Degtyarev 7.62mm machine guns, so they could
pour a wall of concentrated fire on to the shattered tower.

'Hurry, brothers!' Ali urged. 'I can see the infidels
searching for their injured among the rubble. By the grace
of Allah, put the guns to good use on them. And Ahmed,
get your mortar zeroed in on them. Let's massacre these
kafir dogs before they have a chance to recover.'

14

TEN MEN DOWN

Mat, Jamie, Ruff, and Captain Lancer had all felt a
surge of exhilaration as they'd heard the US FAC team
doing the countdown to that first surprise air strike of
the morning: 'One minute to target, forty-five seconds,
thirty seconds . . .' As the fifteen-seconds-to-target mark
had been reached, they'd thrown themselves flat on the
tower roof to take cover. At the same time they were
poised to leap to their feet as soon as the JDAM hit and
open fire on the enemy positions. There had been the
ear-splitting scream of the incoming missile to their rear,
and the SBS soldiers had turned round – only to see the
arrow-shaped projectile hurtling directly towards them.
And in that split second they had known that the JDAM
targeting had gone haywire, and that they were all dead.

A millisecond later exhilaration had been transformed
into a nightmare of pain and trauma, as the tower had
been engulfed in a roaring firestorm of high explosives
and fractured, razor-sharp steel. As the JDAM had
slammed into their position and exploded, a massive
blast wave plucked the soldiers off the tower roof, hurling

them into the air and then smashing them into the ground at the base of the tower. Somehow, Mat had still been conscious as the battlements had disintegrated. He had flown in a slow-motion arc across the fort, his life flashing before his eyes. And then his body had hit the ground and the earthen brick wall had collapsed on top of him, the lights had gone out.

The 2,000-pound JDAM had 'scored' a direct hit on the T-55 tank, blowing the turret clean off and vaporising the four Afghan soldiers who'd been sitting astride it. Twenty or so Afghan fighters had also been clustered around the tank, and as the missile exploded it had torn them limb from limb. The US 5th SOF FAC team had been positioned on the far side of the T-55, some thirty yards away, and while the sheer mass and armour of the tank had shielded them from the worst of the explosion, they had been among the first to be hit by the crushing blast wave that engulfed the tower. The SBS soldiers lying prone at the battlements had been the furthest from the epicentre of the explosion. They had been the last of the allied forces to be hurled into the air by the impact like so many rag dolls.

Some three minutes after the errant JDAM strike, Tom and Sam came tearing around the outer wall of the fort and arrived at the point of the bomb blast. A terrible sight met their eyes. A vast pall of smoke and dust hung over the scene of the wrecked tower. To Tom and Sam it seemed impossible that anyone could have survived a direct hit by a JDAM. They could feel the anger and rage welling up inside them against whoever was responsible for this mother of all fuck-ups. Whether it was pilot error, a mistake by the FAC team, or some sort of confusion over the enemy versus friendly coordinates, neither Sam nor Tom could be certain. But they knew that some of their finest fellow soldiers and closest friends must have perished as a result of it.

As they rushed towards the confusion of shattered walls, floors and stairways, they thought that they could just make out the faint cries of the wounded coming from somewhere within the devastated tower. But they couldn't be certain. The first thing Tom noticed was the grisly remains of a severed arm, lying atop a pile of crushed masonry. But then, like a scene from some biblical parable, he caught sight of a lone figure stumbling out of the curtain of smoke and debris that hung before the ancient fortress. By a complete miracle someone at least had survived.

Tom and Sam were staring straight into the rising sun and so the lone figure remained little more than a silhouette among the dust and the golden light. They could just make out that he was plastered in mud and sand, but they were unable to identify him. Was it one of the Afghan soldiers? A 5th SOF operative? Or one of their own, SBS men? As the two special forces soldiers rushed across to him Tom let out a cry of recognition. He grabbed the survivor and gave him a massive bear hug. It was Jamie – cut and bruised and badly concussed, but still very much alive.

'Who's left . . . Loads of dead . . . Alive . . .' Jamie started mumbling, incoherently, as Tom and Sam half carried him away from the immediate area of the bomb blast.

'LISTEN, MATE, STAY PUT, ALL RIGHT?' Tom yelled into Jamie's ear, not knowing whether he could hear or not. 'WE'RE GETTIN' THE VEHICLES. JUST STAY HERE.'

Tom stared into Jamie's face and it was as if he was looking into the eyes of a sleepwalker. Then there was a faint flash of recognition, and Jamie seemed to acknowledge what had been said with a faint nod.

Tom and Sam set off at a run to fetch the Land-Rovers, which were parked at a safe distance from the fort in open ground. As they did so, they realised there was unexploded ordnance (UXO), dud mortar rounds and mines littered all over the place. But they just closed their minds to the danger and hammered their way across towards the two vehicles. Without any transport in which to get the worst of the wounded back to Boxer Base and proper medical facilities, they would stand far less chance of saving any of them. They gunned the engines of the Land-Rovers and headed back at breakneck speed weaving a path towards the centre of the bomb strike.

As the vehicles skidded to a halt Tom let out another whoop of joy. He'd just caught sight of their OC, Captain Lancer, crouched over a figure lying prone on the ground. The Captain looked like he was trying to give the injured soldier first aid. Tom rushed across to him. He could tell immediately that the SBS Captain was badly disorientated and suffering from shock. His speech was slurred, his movements sluggish and he was unsteady on his feet. Tom wasn't sure if he had even recognised him. Captain Lancer just seemed to be acting on autopilot: he was kneeling down at the injured soldier's side pressing a field dressing into his bloody wound.

'Boss, let me take over, BOSS,' Tom yelled into the Captain's ear. He placed his hand over the field dressing and applied pressure, gently removing the OC's hands as he did so. 'Come on, boss, just take it easy.'

The Captain looked across at Tom with a glazed expression, finally seemed to recognise the thrust of what he was saying if not the actual words, and relinquished his hold over the bloodied dressings. The injured man

was one of the 5th SOF soldiers. Tom and Sam took
over treating him and they could tell that the US soldier
was in a bad way. As Tom turned to grab another field
dressing, he caught sight of the SBS Captain and Jamie
heading back in among the ruins of the tower. He could
only presume they were going in to search for more of
the wounded. They were some of the toughest, bravest
soldiers that he'd ever had the honour to serve alongside. And he knew that there was no stopping them.

'He's pretty serious, ain't he, bro?' Sam remarked, as
Tom turned back to the wounded American soldier.

'He's got internal injuries, and that's what's really
worryin' me,' said Tom. 'We got to get him to a fuckin'
hospital.'

Like Mat, one of Tom's specialist SBS skills was medic,
and he could tell that the soldier had suffered organ
damage. He wasn't surprised: the JDAM's shock wave
would have ripped through anyone caught in the blast.
The body is made up mainly of water, and the JDAM
blast would have had a similar effect to a rock dropped
in a pond. The shock waves would have rippled outwards
from the point of impact, like waves in a pool of water.
And while body armour could prevent damage from
flying shrapnel, it did little to stop internal injuries from
such a blast.

The US soldier started coughing up blood, confirming
that he was bleeding internally. Tom loosened the
wounded operator's body armour – which must have
been acting like a straitjacket – and immediately the
unconscious soldier let out an agonised groan. Tom
passed his hands down along the man's torso, and as he
did so he could feel massive swelling and bruising on
the right side. That must've been the side that had taken
the brunt of the JDAM's blast, and Tom hated to think

what havoc it had wreaked on the soldier's delicate organs.

'We got to get him back to Boxer and get him air-evacuated,' Tom said. 'Fast as fuckin' possible.'

'Sure thing, bro,' Sam replied. 'I'll just –'

But Sam's last words were drowned out by a long burst of heavy machine-gun fire. Suddenly, rounds started slamming into the ruined tower, as the enemy forces opened up on them – trying to pick off any survivors of the errant JDAM strike or those attempting to rescue them. But Tom and Sam hardly missed a beat, as they tried to get a drip into the wounded soldier's veins. As they did so, Tom had images flashing through his head of his SBS mates lying beneath the rubble of the blasted tower with their skulls caved in. Where were Trenty, Ruff and Mat? he wondered. Had they survived the JDAM's blast? And if they had done, how badly wounded were they?

From having been poised to launch the mother of all wake-up calls on the enemy – a series of precision-guided air strikes on pre-programmed targets – the tables had now been completely turned on the British, US and Afghan forces. As Jamie and Captain Lancer stumbled about amid the debris of the collapsed tower searching for survivors, enemy rounds went ricocheting all around them. Scattered among the piles of shattered masonry were the grisly remains of the Afghans who'd been gathered around the tank and taken the brunt of the blast. Severed arms and legs were sticking out of the rubble at grotesque angles. Scorched bodies lay in the rubble, half obscured by the smoke and dust that hung like a dark pall over the wreckage of the tower.

Having finally got the US soldier's condition stabilised, Tom and Sam headed into the rubble to help with the search. It was like a nightmare in there. The stench of burned human flesh was sickening in their nostrils. With every rock that they overturned the two men expected to discover the worst: a face staring upwards, crushed, bloodied and broken amid the shattered masonry, but still clearly recognisable as one of their own. Miraculously, Tom, Sam, Jamie and Captain Lancer managed to locate all of the 5th SOF soldiers. And while four of them were in a very serious condition, the remaining six were walking wounded and not in need of urgent medical assistance.

Jamie eventually spotted a civvy pair of boots, and pulled Ruff out from under a huge pile of rubble. The big SBS gunner had been all but buried alive, but he appeared largely unscathed. Ruff kept on mumbling on about losing his Gimpy, and Jamie told him to shut the fuck up, as they'd both lost their GPMGs. But as both men's eardrums had been blown in the explosion, neither could make out much of what the other said. Ruff joined Jamie in the search of the ruined tower, and they pulled out six Afghan soldiers who'd survived. And then they discovered Trenty, covered in dust and unable to stand, but still very much alive.

Quickly, the priority of the rescue moved from treatment at the scene of the attack to getting the wounded the hell out of there. They needed urgent casevac to the nearest military hospital, and the ruined tower was fast becoming a dangerous place to be. The enemy poured down fire on to their positions, but few of the SBS and 5th SOF soldiers had escaped the blast unscathed, and they were in no fit state to fight back. More importantly, they had no weapons with which to return fire. As the JDAM's shock wave had engulfed the tower and the soldiers had been blasted into the air, their guns had been blown out of their hands. A dozen or more Diemacos were now buried beneath the rubble of the tower, along with the GPMGs.

Fortunately, help was now on its way. Back at Boxer Base the previous day, the US 10th Mountain troops had formed an ad hoc QRF. Shortly after the JDAM had hit the friendly forces that morning, the 10th Mountain QRF had been called in. Thirty minutes after the errant air strike the troops roared up to the fort and, in the absence of any better instructions, headed for the main entranceway. Jamie was the first to spot them, and he knew that they needed those 10th Mountain boys over at the wrecked tower fast. At any moment now he was convinced the enemy were going to try and rush them. And if they did they'd surely overrun their positions – which meant they'd be able to finish off the American, British and Afghan wounded.

Jamie set off at a run to intercept the 10th Mountain boys, accompanied by a still shell-shocked Ruff. As he did so, he was well aware that Mat was still unaccounted for. Jamie and Ruff arrived in the entranceway to the fort, battered and bloodied and covered from head to toe in dust and debris. As the two men tried to catch their breath, they coughed up thick clods of dirt from their lungs. To the newly arrived US troops it looked as if the two British special forces soldiers had just crawled out of the grave.

'Where d'you need us . . . buddy?' the 10th Mountain commander shouted over at them, trying to recover from the shock of their ghostly appearance.

'WHAT D'YOU SAY, MATE?' Jamie yelled at maximum volume, as he was still deafened from the bomb blast.

'WHERE D'YOU NEED MY GUYS?' the 10th

Mountain commander yelled back, realising that the British soldiers must've lost their hearing.

'DON'T PARK THERE,' Jamie yelled, as he still couldn't hear. 'YOU'LL GET MORTARED. MOVE YOUR VEHICLES – THERE.'

'OK, BUDDY,' the commander yelled right into Jamie's ear. 'NOW WHERE D'YOU NEED MY MEN?'

'NO NEED TO SHOUT,' Jamie yelled back, his face breaking into a grin. 'JUST FOLLOW US, MATE. BRING ALL THE FIREPOWER AND AMMO YOU'VE GOT. AND KEEP YOUR BLOODY HEADS DOWN.'

Jamie and Ruff led the twenty-odd 10th Mountain boys in a crouching run along the parapet that ran from the entrance tower towards the northern end of the fort. It was the quickest route across to the bombsite. Within seconds they were spotted by the enemy and almost immediately started taking incoming rounds. They managed to reach their destination without anyone being hit, and Jamie instructed the troops to set up their heavy machine guns atop the wrecked remnants of the tower. From there they would be able to lay down a wall of covering fire on to the enemy positions at the gateway. At the same time they'd act as a protection force for the ongoing rescue operation that was taking place just outside the ruins of the fort walls.

'YOU GOT A SHITLOAD OF ENEMY ACROSS THERE,' Jamie yelled, pointing to the positions around the gateway. 'BE APPRECIATED IF YOU COULD MALLET THE FUCKERS.'

'YOU GOT IT, BUDDY,' the 10th Mountain commander yelled back. While he wasn't completely familiar with Jamie's phraseology, he'd got the gist of what he wanted, and pretty quickly his men swung into action to 'mallet the fuckers'.

Jamie slid down the bank of shattered masonry, which was all that remained of the tower wall, to rejoin the rescue party at ground level. But as he did so he ran straight into a familiar figure – one who was wandering about among the ruins at the base of the tower.

'MAT!' he yelled, as he grabbed the confused figure and embraced him. 'MAT! THANK FUCK – YOU'RE ALIVE!'

'Where are the *kafir* soldiers now?' Ali asked, sneeringly. He was crouched over a smoking Degtyarev machine gun, and searching with his eyes for enemy targets amid the shattered ruins of the tower. 'Where are the cowardly infidels? By the grace of Allah, they drop just one of their own bombs on their puny selves, and run to cower beneath their mothers' skirts. We own this fort now, brothers. No one comes in here now unless we want them to. And, *insh'Allah*, it will remain that way.'

'*Al-hamdu Lillah*, brother,' Ahmed said, with a tired grin.

'Put the word out, Brother Ahmed,' Ali continued. 'Let the brothers know that we have witnessed a wondrous miracle. By the grace of the All Merciful One, we have won a great victory. We must tell the brothers to strengthen themselves, for now is the time to look for an even greater victory. We must take this opportunity to counter-attack, while the *kafir* are still reeling from the air attack, from the wrath of Allah who hurled their own weapons against them. We keep attacking this morning, brother, we keep attacking. And we hit the enemy at every possible opportunity.'

'What did you have in mind, Brother Ali?' Ahmed asked.

'We must ask for volunteers, Brother Ahmed,' Ali

replied, excitedly. 'Men with courage and conviction to walk the path of the true jihad. We must charge down the enemy positions while they are undefended. We must take them by surprise and cut out their infidel hearts. In that way, brother, we show Allah that we are worthy of this miracle, worthy of the jihad.'

15

NIGHT STALKERS

As more and more dead and wounded soldiers were brought into the makeshift triage area at the base of the wrecked tower, the extent of the losses from the errant JDAM strike were becoming increasingly clear. In addition to the four, badly wounded US soldiers, it seemed that the Northern Alliance had taken the brunt of the casualties. A five-man crew had been inside the T-55 tank when the JDAM had hit and they had died immediately, as had the four Afghan soldiers who had been perched atop its turret, and it was feared that as many as twenty other Afghan soldiers had been buried alive as the massive wall supporting the tank had collapsed.

Mat had been one of the lucky ones. He'd been knocked unconscious by falling masonry and lain beneath a half-collapsed beam for the best part of half an hour. When he'd finally come to, his last memory was of the arrow-like JDAM heading right for him. After regaining consciousness, Mat had peered around in the darkness of the wrecked tower and wondered if he was alive or dead. Then he'd spotted the light from a nearby doorway filtering in through the dust and smoke. Painfully, he had crawled towards it. He had emerged from the rubble bruised and battered and badly concussed. But as soon as he'd spotted Jamie he'd known that he had to be alive – for they'd always told each other that while Jamie was going to heaven Mat was going to hell. So there was no way they could be together in the same place if they were dead.

Up on the ruined parapet the 10th Mountain troops had finished setting up their M240 heavy machine guns, with arcs of fire covering every approach to the tower. The M240 is a 7.62mm weapon, the US equivalent of the GPMG. It is almost identical to the British weapon, and it is equally devastating. As the 10th Mountain boys settled down to engage the enemy, a group of some thirty raggedy figures broke cover from the fort's central gateway and began charging towards the ruined tower. Screams of '*Allahu Akhbar!*' reached the troops on the acrid wind, but they were ready. Suddenly, half a dozen M240s barked into life, and it was as if the enemy fighters had run into a wall of bullets, their charge quickly faltering.

Jamie, Mat and Ruff headed back into the chaos to help dig for the wounded and dead. As they did so, they heard the roar of the M240s opening up on the tower ruins above them. It was a mightily reassuring sound. They joined the Afghans combing the rubble for bodies. But the SBS soldiers could tell that the Northern Alliance troops were angry. The SBS lads were well aware of the fact that the Afghans had taken the brunt of the casualties, and while they couldn't understand what the soldiers were saying, they could read the emotions and the resentment that was written across their faces. *What the fuck have you done here?* the Afghans were clearly thinking. *What the hell's going on? And why the fuck did you do that?*

With the 10th Mountain boys providing covering fire, the evacuation of the wounded got underway in earnest. Some of the less serious cases were moved along the parapet to the eastern tower. But the worst cases had to be carried down the outer parapet of the fort and lifted across to the waiting vehicles. The 5th SOF soldier with the extensive internal injuries was the most serious of the American wounded. Tom and Sam had managed to stabilise his condition, but he required an urgent medevac. And they needed some form of usable transport in which to carry his prone form away from the fort. So Jamie got hold of the rear door of one of the four-wheel drives and ripped it clean off its hinges. Then he fetched an old carpet out of the wrecked tower, and made a makeshift, padded stretcher.

When the evacuation convoy finally set off for Boxer Base, they had eleven seriously wounded American and Afghan troops laid out on old rugs and improvised stretchers in the back of the vehicles. As they drove away from the fort, Major Martin got the comms going in the lead vehicle and started trying to call in a medevac chopper. He had one US casualty with blast burns all over his face, two with flesh wounds and bad concussion, and the one with the internal injuries. A mile or so out from the fort, the Major got a reply on his radio telling him to pull over on the roadside and wait where he was. Within five minutes a medevac chopper would be putting down right there to collect all of the casualties.

They stopped the vehicles and began debussing the worst of the wounded. But as they did so a silver minivan passed by in the opposite direction. A few yards further on it drew to a halt, and out of it stepped a news crew. They immediately started to film the scene. Within seconds, Major Martin had run across to them and placed his hand over the cameraman's lens.

'Will ya stop filming, guys?' he said. 'You all hear me? This ain't to be filmed.'

The cameraman appeared to agree to the Major's request without complaint, and lifted his camera off his shoulder and put it down. But Mat was keeping a close eye on him. He could tell that the camera lens was still surreptitiously pointing directly at them and that the cameraman had kept his camera rolling. Mat pulled his shamag up to cover the lower half of his face and took a few steps across the road to the film crew. As he did so he grabbed his Sig Sauer pistol and flipped the weapon off safety, making sure that the cameraman had noticed him doing so.

'FOOKIN' WANKER!' Mat snarled, as he placed himself bang in front of the cameraman's lens. 'You're fookin' dead if you keep doing that.'

As the cameraman stared back at him feigning ignorance, Mat felt rather than heard Jamie and Ruff taking up positions directly behind him. His two fellow operators towered over the news crew, and they just stared down at the cameraman with cold, unblinking fury in their eyes. There'd been a lot of people killed already during the last forty-eight hours, and Jamie and Ruff had done more than their fair share of the killing. They were pretty daunting at the best of times, but right now the essence of so much death clung to them like the dark shroud of the executioner.

'OK. OK. I – I – I am stopping,' the cameraman finally stammered, as he reached down to switch off his camera. He had some foreign-sounding accent that Mat couldn't place.

'You want your fookin' brains spattered all over the fookin' sand?' Mat said icily, as he gripped the butt of his Sig Sauer pistol. 'Or you want to get the fuck out of here?'

'OK, OK. I fuck off,' the cameraman answered, hurriedly, holding up his hands in a gesture of submission.

'NOW! You fuck off NOW.'

'OK, OK. Now I fuck off. But where is it you want me to fuck off to?'

'Anywhere. JUST FUCK OFF. We don't fookin' want you around. So fuck off. NOW.'

As the terrified cameraman and his crew grabbed their kit and made a dash for their vehicle, Mat turned and watched them go, his eyes like murder as he did so. He'd just had some of his best friends pounded in that errant JDAM strike; several of his newly made American buddies were badly wounded and one or two might not make it through; and dozens of their Afghan fellow warriors were injured or lying dead in the rubble of the fort. What fucking right did that cameraman have to stick his camera in their faces and film all their pain and hurt, without even asking anyone if they minded? And then, as if to add insult to injury, the fucker had kept on filming even after the Major's request to stop doing so.

'Would you really have slotted him, mate?' Jamie asked, as they watched the silver minivan accelerate away from the scene.

''Course not, mate,' Mat replied. 'I'd have marched the cunt out into the desert, made him kneel behind the bushes and put a few rounds through his fookin' camera, just to make him really shit his load.'

'He looked as if he was about to burst into tears,' Jamie added, with a grin. 'Were you the school bully, mate? Cos if you weren't, your talents were seriously wasted.'

There was a practical side to Mat's aggression that he didn't need to explain to his fellow special forces soldiers. As SBS operatives, they could and did end up operating in some highly sensitive environments. The last thing they needed while they were up against hardened terrorists, drug dealers or warlords was to have their faces all over the media. That would be asking for trouble. Just occasionally, an SBS operative did get himself photographed by accident. On those rare occasions, the operator would be removed from all sensitive missions for some considerable time. But the worst-case scenario was one in which the media broadcast their images without Poole realising it – in which case their mugshots could unknowingly fall into enemy hands. Which was why Mat would have taken all necessary measures to stop that film crew on that roadside.

After several minutes waiting the promised medevac chopper had still not materialised, so they loaded the wounded back on to the vehicles and headed for Boxer Base. Upon arrival they laid out the wounded on the tables on the ground floor. Tom struggled to get a new drip into the arm of the seriously wounded 5th SOF soldier, but he couldn't find a vein that would take it. Eventually, he was forced to get the soldier aboard the helicopter, which had finally turned up, without the drip being inserted. As the medevac chopper clawed its way into the sky, laden down with the American and Afghan wounded, Tom hoped and prayed that he had managed to do enough to keep the US soldier alive for as long as it took to get him to the nearest hospital.

As soon as the wounded had been evacuated the relentless urgency went out of the situation. The SBS soldiers sat around at Boxer Base in a stunned silence, lost in their own thoughts. Somehow, they had just survived a direct hit on their positions from a 2,000-pound JDAM. That alone beggared belief. In that one hit, half of the 5th SOF force had been put out of action, and scores of the Afghans had been killed. But somehow, the eight SBS lads had just walked away. By some miracle of chance none of the eight SBS soldiers had been seriously hurt. The worst injuries that any of them had suffered were Jamie's and Ruff's busted eardrums.

'Fuck me, we should be dead,' Jamie muttered, voicing the thought that was on everyone's mind.

'Two-thousand-pound bloody JDAM,' said Mat, quietly. 'Us lot were, what, thirty metres away when it hit? No way should anyone've survived.'

'Someone was looking after us, that's for sure,' Jamie added.

'Reckon it was the two white doves, mate,' said Tom, the remark slipping out before he'd even realised it.

'The two *what*?' Mat asked.

'The two fuckin' *doves*, mate,' Tom replied. He'd said it now, and he knew from experience what was coming. To deny it would only make matters worse. 'Two white doves. Birds. The feathered kind, mate.'

'Funny, I didn't know you blokes was hit by that JDAM,' Mat snorted. 'Cos you sure must have some bad concussion. "Two white doves." Sounds like you been hallucinatin', mate.'

'You reckon?' Tom retorted. 'Should've left your sad arse in the rubble when we had the fuckin' chance. Anyhow, Sam saw 'em too.'

'So there's two of you blokes been hallucinatin',' said Mat. 'It's a wonder you can bloody shoot straight, if you keep seeing shit like that in that fort.'

'Bro, let's just not go there,' said Sam, as he and Tom exchanged glances. 'Guys like my bitch Mat there, there's just no tellin' 'em.'

An hour later and the SBS soldiers gathered together with their remaining 5th SOF colleagues in one of the meeting rooms. The mood was sombre, as Major Martin stood up to begin a debrief on the disastrous events at the fort. The US Major wanted to get all the facts down as quickly as possible. There was sure to be an inquiry into what had gone wrong and it was his duty to investigate as quickly and thoroughly as possible. An officer with the US military police had arrived to direct the debrief. As Mat wrapped his bruised and battered hands around a mug of hot, sweet tea, he glanced across at his fellow SBS soldiers and realised what a complete and total mess they were in. They were sat there covered in dust and dirt, with their cuts and flesh wounds freshly bandaged, looking for all the world as if they had just walked away from World War III.

'You guys sure you're all OK?' the US military policeman (MP) asked, directing his comments at the SBS contingent. 'I mean, I wanna do this now, while it's fresh in your minds. But only if we can. You all aren't indestructible or something, now are you?'

'A nice cuppa and we'll be right as rain,' Mat replied, forcing a grin.

'After a good brew we'll be back out there again,' Jamie added.

'Tell you one thing, though,' volunteered Tom. 'Could easily have been a second friendly-fire incident up there – in which case we'd be needing more than a fuckin' cup of tea to put us right.'

'Buddy, I'd like to hear all about it,' the MP announced, pulling a notebook from his chest pocket.

'Well, it could all have been a fuck sight worse than it was,' said Tom. 'If we'd not called off the fuckin' air strikes when we did there was a one-in-three chance that we'd've been the next to be malleted. Four sets of co-ordinates were put up to the fast air – two of which were enemy targets and two of which were friendlies. The first set he hit was the friendlies on the north-eastern tower. So, chances are pretty good it would've been us got hit next, on the western tower.'

'Go figure,' remarked the US policeman. 'So what did happen, bud?'

'Well, we aborted the fuckin' air strikes, didn't we?' Tom replied. 'Just kept screaming "ABORT, ABORT, ABORT" into the radio until the pilot pulled up and out of the attack. But that's how fuckin' close it was.'

It took over two hours to go through the events of the last night and early morning in detail. The men were at ease and allowed to smoke and get their brews in, but they had to persevere and get through it. There was some conflict in the various recollections of the events surrounding the friendly-fire incident, but no violent disagreement. Many of the facts were not in dispute. Both the friendly and enemy coordinates had been put up to the pilot in the correct format used by the US military. And while the JDAM had been going in danger-close, that had been a calculated risk that the soldiers on the ground had agreed to take. The main point of contention seemed to be that those doing the FAC had not had eyes on the enemy target, or so Tom and Mat argued.

'In my book, if you're doing FAC you need to see the target that's being hit,' Mat remarked. 'It's a golden rule that you should have eyes on target.'

'Too right,' said Tom. 'I mean, you can go down there

and recce it and then take the coordinates away with you, and make it a pre-recorded target. But even then the fuckin' FAC guys have still *had* eyes on target and have a mental picture of it in their minds. So they can describe it to the pilot. In a live situation like we was in, it's simple: the FAC guys should've had eyes on target.'

'Fair point,' Jamie said. 'But the FAC boys aren't here to explain it from their end, are they, mate? Cos they was underneath that JDAM. Anyway, whether they had eyes on target or not it still doesn't account for how the pilot managed to drop a two-thousand-pound JDAM on friendly coordinates.'

'Well, let's say the JDAM was buggered,' said Mat. 'A faulty GPS or something. It's still got the whole of the Afghan desert where it could have landed. The chances of it scoring a direct hit on the friendly coordinates are just about zero. The only way I can see it doing that is if the JDAM had been programmed to hit those friendly coordinates. So, got to be human error, ain't it?'

There were only two things that seemed as if they could account for the friendly-fire incident. The first was simple pilot error – the lead pilot mistakenly punching in the friendly coordinates as the first target to be hit. The second was human error on the ground – the FAC team mistakenly putting up the friendly co-ordinates as if they were the enemy target. And none of the men in that room knew which was the correct explanation for the errant JDAM strike. What they *did* know was that things could so easily have been so much worse. It was the armoured mass of the T-55 tank combined with the thick mud walls of the tower that had taken the brunt of the JDAM's impact. Without those two factors it was highly likely that all of them would now be dead.

The soldiers spent the rest of the day at Boxer Base tending to their injuries and recovering. There were bruises, flesh wounds and sprained limbs to be dealt with. And even for those like Ruff who were impatient to get back and resume the fighting there was little chance that they might do so. Few of the SBS and 5th SOF soldiers had managed to recover their weapons from the rubble of the bombed-out tower. The plan for the remainder of the day was to recover their fighting fitness and get battle-ready. For now, there were more than enough Northern Alliance soldiers up at Qala-i-Janghi to keep the enemy bottled up in the fort.

That afternoon, the CIA officers at Boxer Base presented the SBS with a sizeable lump sum in cash: $40,000 as expenses to cover their trashed gear, and another $200,000 to pay for a new laser target designator. The LTD that the lads had been using was buried in the debris of the JDAM blast. The CIA officers had also entered into negotiations with the Northern Alliance commanders over how much compensation was to be paid to them, to make up for their deaths and the destruction to equipment (including the T-55 tank). One of the stumbling blocks to a deal being struck was that the CIA suspected the Afghan commanders of inflating the estimates of their dead, in order to extract a larger payment. Once a compensation deal was reached, the Afghan soldiers started returning the Diemacos and other missing bits of kit to the SBS at Boxer Base.

As the afternoon wore on there were sporadic bursts of gunfire up at the fort, and bitter exchanges of mortar fire. But there seemed little chance of dislodging the enemy any time soon. Their forces numbered in the hundreds still, and they were well entrenched in the southern end of the fort. They had ample supplies of water via the irrigation channels, and they had been eating the flesh of some of General Dostum's horses that had been caught in the crossfire. Most importantly, they had an almost unlimited supply of weaponry, as the fort's capacious arms stores had been stuffed to capacity. For now at least, the battle for Qala-i-Janghi seemed to have reached a stalemate.

But that night, a blow would be struck to break that impasse. At 2200 hours Major Martin, Jamie, Ruff and Mat headed up to the fort to oversee a night attack on the enemy. Around midnight there was the faint drone of an aircraft overhead, as a US AC-130 Spectre gunship began to circle lazily above the fort. As the watching special forces soldiers donned their NVGs, an extraordinary scene became visible to them. The Spectre gunship was using an infrared searchlight to comb the whole of the southern end of the fort for targets. The powerful ray of eerie green illumination that was beaming down from the night sky was only visible to those using NVGs, and it was an awesome sight to the watching British and American soldiers.

As it flew a series of search transects back and forth above the fort, the gunship was preparing to unleash its terrifying firepower, which would rip through the enemy positions. Coordinates were being fed into a state-of-the-art on-board computer system that pre-planned the strikes on the enemy targets. The AC-130 Spectre carried a powerful array of side-mounted, trainable weaponry, including two M61 20mm Vulcan cannons, one L60 40mm Bofors cannon and one M102 105mm howitzer. The $70 million aircraft also carried a crew of fourteen, including a low-light TV (LLTV) operator, an infrared detection set operator and five aerial gunners. As the

Spectre flew over Qala-i-Janghi at an altitude of 10,000 feet, all of its human and technological know-how was focused on detecting and targeting enemy movement in the darkness below.

Mat, Jamie and Ruff waited with bated breath for the aircraft to open up on the enemy positions from the night-dark skies. As they did so, it occurred to Mat that the aircraft truly was living up to its name – *the Spectre, a ghostly presence or apparition.* The giant, four-engined aircraft was invisible in the darkness and all but inaudible to those on the ground. That morning's surprise air strike had gone horribly wrong, the dawn wake-up call for the enemy turning into a nightmare for the allied forces. But now the Spectre was preparing to give the sleeping AQT fighters a midnight alarm call – after which many of them would never be waking again.

Suddenly, there was what looked like a golden stream of fire arcing down from the night sky, and the Spectre began pounding the southern end of the fort with its weaponry. As thousands of large-calibre rounds slammed into the enemy positions, interspersed with the giant shells from the howitzer, a series of thunderous explosions rolled across the fort. Repeatedly, the Spectre gunship made silent passes over the fort, and on the fourth pass the infrared detection set operator spotted three enemy figures grouped around a mortar. Even as they had dropped a round down the mortar tube, the Spectre's crew were feeding their target coordinates into the aircraft's on-board computer system. Now, as the Spectre started spewing fire into the fort, the M61 operators opened up on the mortar crew, spraying a deadly barrage of 20mm rounds into their position.

As the gunship completed its attacking pass over the

fort, a huge ball of flame lifted up from one of the buildings, followed by a series of enormous explosions. They
in turn kicked off a dramatic firework display, as rounds,
ammo belts, grenades and mortar shells went firing off
into the air. As the night sky above the fort was lit up
a burning white, Mat, Jamie, Ruff and the Major broke
into a round of spontaneous applause. The Spectre had
just hit the fort's main arms dump, and much of the
weaponry and ammo that the enemy had been relying
on to sustain their uprising had just been blown sky-
high. The AC-130 flew away from the scene and the
pilot reported back on a job well done. As far as he was
concerned, now that his AC-130 Spectre had been
allowed to do its work the ground forces should expect
little further trouble from the enemy.

'Aaaahhhh!' The unearthly screaming pierced the gloom
of the underground basement, again and again and again.
'Aaaaahhhhhh!'

'By the grace of Allah, get us out of here!' one of the
brothers was crying. 'Help us! We're trapped! Allah have
mercy.'

'Has it gone? Can you still hear it?' Ali asked fear-
fully, as he crouched in the darkness beneath the basement stairs, nursing a shrapnel wound to his right thigh.

'It may have gone, brother,' Ahmed answered wearily,
from out of the darkness. 'I can't hear it any more. But
that doesn't mean a thing. I didn't hear it the first time
it hit us.'

'The *kafir* strike the brothers silently, from the air, in
the dark of the night, like the cowardly dogs that they
are.' Ali spat out the words, his voiced laced with fear
and a wild, bitter fury. 'May Allah punish them with all
His wrath for what they have done this night. May they

burn in eternal hell for what they have done to us, secretly, as we slept.'

'It is not so bad, brother,' Ahmed tried to reassure him, placing a giant hand on Ali's arm. As he did so he winced with pain, the fresh wound to his shoulder pulsating with agony. 'Most of the brothers were deep in the basement when the *kafir* gunship fired. Only those near the doorway were hit. Many have survived.'

'It is not so bad, brother?' Ali shook his head in despair. 'We have no bandages, no dressings and no morphine and the brothers are bleeding to death and calling for their mothers in this stinking basement. We are using our turbans to patch up their wounds, brother. *Our sacred turbans.*'

For a second Ali and Ahmed squatted there in silence, listening to the cries of the wounded echoing around the dark walls.

'Just look at what they did to you, brother,' Ali continued, with vehemence. 'Over these past two days none of the *kafir* soldiers could get your mortar team. By the grace of All Merciful Allah you were so quick, so deadly. So, what did they do, brother? They targeted you under the cloak of darkness, silently, without warning, from the air. And yet you say it is not so bad. Look at your wounds, brother. You didn't even see the aircraft that did that to you. You didn't even hear it. You didn't even know it was there. How can we fight such things? *How can we fight such things, brother?* They are breaking us, Brother Ahmed. Slowly, bit by bit, hour by hour, they are tearing us apart and breaking us down with their cursed technology, their cowardly, secret weapons of war.'

'But by the grace of Allah, we are still alive,' Ahmed replied, forcibly. 'We knew it would not be easy. Yet we have endured, brother. And while we still have breath in our bodies we can fight.'

'But for how much longer, brother?' Ali asked, despairingly. 'And to what purpose? Great and glorious it is to die in the jihad, brother, but not to suffer and bleed to death like pigs, like dogs in a pit, while the *kafir* pick us off at their will. How can we fight them, brother? *How can we fight them?* Maybe we should finish it here and now, brother – a quick, honourable death at our own hands? Is that not a better way to go to meet the Holy Prophet, peace and blessings be upon Him?'

'Brother Ali, it is not yet over,' Ahmed urged, taking his friend's face between his giant hands and staring into his eyes. 'Remember, brother, they still have to take this ground that we control, this fort. And we have shelter, brother: even their cursed gunship cannot hit us deep in the basement like this. We have water. We have weapons. If you give up, Brother Ali, truly all the brothers will lose heart. Imagine when the *kafir* are forced to come in here, brother, to fight their way into this fort, on foot, clearing it building by building. Then we shall be waiting for them, brother. We shall wait for them like death itself lurking in the basements, and we shall strike the *kafir* down.'

'But do you really think they will come, Brother Ahmed?'

'They will come. They have to,' Ahmed answered, quietly, matter-of-factly. His years of experience in combat meant that he knew how this battle had to end. There was no way that he could see for the enemy to dislodge them from the fort, unless they came in on foot and cleared every room, every underground passageway. And that would mean hand-to-hand fighting – at which stage all the *kafir*'s technology and air power would be of little help to them. 'Hold on, Brother Ali. Hold on. Be strong. By the grace of Allah, we shall have our day of glory. And then the *kafir* will know our anger as it rages like a storm upon them. We cannot do that, brother, if we take our own lives.'

16

FIRE AND WATER

ON the morning of day three of the siege, the bandaged and aching SBS soldiers and their 5th SOF colleagues headed back to the fort. As they arrived at the scene of the previous day's errant JDAM strike, they were shocked at the scale of the destruction that lay before them. As the 2,000-pound missile had struck, the T-55 tank had been blown into the air. It had come crashing down to earth in two pieces, with the body of the tank landing upside down and the turret next to it the right way up. Even now, there was still a severed human arm sticking out of the rubble next to the disembowelled machine. Parked up at the base of the tower there had been two Soviet-era armoured personnel carriers. As the JDAM's blast wave had rolled over them it had torn them to pieces. It was like a giant tin-opener had ripped them apart.

Twenty-four hours earlier, the Northern Alliance soldiers and their British and American comrades had been pulling each other out of the smoke and the debris of the bomb strike. Now, they were hugging each other and embracing, as they discovered who exactly had made it out of there alive. As Mat, Jamie, Tom, Sam and Ruff stood around surveying the scene, the Afghans started handing around smokes and some local sweetmeats. There was a spirit of genuine camaraderie between the NA soldiers and their foreign friends now. Jamie felt himself being grabbed by one of the Afghans and smothered in a bear hug. It was the same Afghan soldier who had tried, and failed, to fire Jamie's Diemaco on the first day of the siege. He seemed overjoyed that he'd found Jamie alive.

The soldier then proceeded to do a repeat performance of his charade from that first afternoon: helicopter rotor blades done with a twirling finger, the sound effects of the turbines to accompany it, and then a finger across the throat like a knife cut to signify death. And then the Afghan said simply: 'Americans.' Suddenly the SBS lads were cracking up laughing. The Afghan soldier was taking the piss out of the US warplanes having bombed their own forces. It was just the sort of grim humour that they appreciated. Once the merriment had died down a little, the grinning Afghan soldier asked for Jamie's address back in the UK, so he could write to him.

Strangely enough, it was a great feeling to be back at the scene of the errant bomb strike and to have survived. The SBS soldiers had expected to get a hostile reception from the Afghans. But instead the reverse was turning out to be true. Somehow, it felt as if the British and American special forces and their fellow Afghan soldiers had been blooded together and were now true brothers in arms. Some of the American soldiers started handing out grenades to the Afghans – as if they would help make up for the errant air strike. Barely a minute later there were a series of loud explosions as the Afghans hurled the grenades over the wall in the general direction of the enemy, all for a bit of fun and games.

'Will you tell your American buddies to stop handing out the grenades?' Jamie remarked to one of the CIA officers. 'They're not sweets, mate.'

Jamie didn't want to be a killjoy exactly. But sooner or later one of the Afghans was going to end up injuring himself, or someone else. And as far as Jamie was concerned there'd already been more than enough deaths from friendly fire at the fort.

Once the party atmosphere had started to die down a little, Captain Lancer took his men up to their former positions on the devastated ramparts. Now they faced the grisly task of digging in the rubble for any remaining bits of kit, and for any Afghan bodies that had not yet been recovered. One of the SBS's LTDs had been completely buried in the air strike. As it was such an expensive piece of kit, the lads were keen to recover it – despite the compensation money already paid by the CIA. But as they commenced digging in the shattered brickwork and bomb-blast debris, they started coming under sporadic fire from the enemy positions in the southern end of the fort.

'Fuckin' get behind the wall before we all get fuckin' shot,' Tom yelled out, as rounds cracked into the dirt right next to him. 'It's only a fuckin' LTD and not worth getting slotted for.'

Mat, Sam, Jamie, Tom and Ruff got down behind some cover and started to do a bit of shooting in return. The Diemaco made for a good sniping weapon, being fitted with a x4 magnification sight with cross hairs and accurate up to four hundred metres. It was a damn sight more effective than the AK47s that the enemy were using, that much was for sure. But few of the enemy soldiers were making themselves easy targets. They were hunkered down in their subterranean stronghold, and only popping up occasionally to crack off a few rounds, before disappearing again. There was little chance of the SBS soldiers being able to get a clear shot at them and pick them off this way.

Whatever the Spectre gunship might have achieved in terms of destroying the ammo stores, it had not done nearly as much as had been expected in terms of taking out the enemy. The Northern Alliance commanders were trying to argue that there were less than a dozen enemy fighters left alive in the fort. But the SBS lads just knew that they had to be wrong. There were clearly more than enough enemy fighters with the energy and will to organise themselves properly and carry on fighting. While the NA forces did seem to be well in control of the situation from the outside of the fort, there was one big unanswered question that they would all have to face sooner or later. And that was how they were going to dislodge the enemy from the fort?

The previous night, General Dostum had left the siege at Kunduz and travelled back to Qala-i-Janghi. Upon arrival he had made it clear to his Afghan commanders that he was not a happy man. Apart from the devastation visited on the ancient fortress by the 'prisoners', he was painfully aware that he had personally negotiated the terms under which the six hundred fighters had supposedly surrendered. Sure, war was a nasty business and he didn't exactly have a spotless reputation himself. But as far as the General was concerned, he had tried to hold out an olive branch to the prisoners and this is what they had done in return. Like most Afghans, the General viewed all soldiers as fighting men with a code of honour and conduct. Yet that code had been abrogated by the foreign fighters now occupying the fort, and he felt they had betrayed him.

Even so, the General appeared to want to give the enemy one last chance to lay down their weapons. He had brought with him two captured Taliban commanders. These were the same two Taliban leaders with whom he had negotiated the terms of the original surrender deal. Those terms had enabled any Afghan Taliban to lay down their arms and get safe passage back home to their villages. But as for the foreign Taliban – the Pakistanis, Chechens, Saudis, Sudanese, Yemenis, Algerians, Egyptians and assorted Europeans and Americans who had answered the call to jihad – they were to be given over to General Dostum's custody.

The two Taliban leaders had been brought to the fort to try to re-establish the currency of that original cease-fire deal, to use their good offices to convince those still holding out in the fort to surrender once and for all. But with the battle now locked into a bitter and bloody stale-mate, with each side giving no quarter, there was no way in which the Taliban leaders could get to speak to the besieged fighters. And even if they had been able to do so, there was little guarantee that they would have received a sympathetic hearing.

In addition to the betrayal by the six hundred pris-oners, General Dostum's other main worry seemed to be his horses. The mounts that the General had kept stabled at the fort were his finest, the cream of the Northern Alliance's cavalry. The fact that so many had been caught in the crossfire of the previous two days' fighting – and that some had even been eaten by the prisoners – added insult to injury, as far as he was concerned. Whatever else happened over the next few days, the General had made it clear that no more of his horses were to be harmed. In particular, there were two of his favourite steeds still tethered next to the central wall of the fort. At the end of the fighting those two horses had to be brought out alive.

'Whatever you do, don't hit those two little bastard nags tethered near the wall,' Tom announced to the others, once he'd heard of the General's concerns. 'Cos if you do, Dostum's going to have you for dinner.'

After a quick lunch break in the cover of the ruined tower, Jamie and Ruff got the GPMGs zeroed in on the windows of the pink building in the southern end of the fort. This had by now become the enemy's redoubt. As the Gimpys roared into life, Jamie and Ruff pounded the enemy stronghold. But however many rounds they kept pumping into the target, more of the enemy kept coming back at them. As soon as the GPMGs stopped firing, enemy fighters would pop up from below ground and return fire. It was obvious that the bulk of the enemy fighters had survived the Spectre gunship attack. In the basement that ran beneath the stronghold building, even the Spectre's big guns had been unable to reach them.

By the eve of the third day of fighting, the battle for Qala-i-Janghi seemed to have reached a no-win situation on both sides. Back at Boxer Base that night the SBS lads were racking their brains, trying to see if there was some way of breaking into the southern end of the fort and lifting the siege.

'We got to think about this differently,' Mat said to the others. 'We ain't going to break this siege otherwise. Whatever the idea, let's hear it. For starters, those bloody irrigation channels, any ideas how they work and where they go to? They run beneath the walls, don't they? Why don't we use those – or the sewers if the place has them – to get in there and attack?'

'They're drainage channels,' Tom responded. 'And it's been tried already, mate, only the other way round. First few hours of the siege, several of the fuckers tried to escape through them. They was met by the Afghans on the outside of the fort, who malleted 'em good n'proper, and that was that.'

'OK, but that's them coming out,' Mat countered. 'What about us nutters going in?'

'If those fuckers've tried to use 'em to escape, they'll be well on to the fact we could use 'em to try to get in,' Tom replied. 'Fuckin' certain they will be, mate.'

'But in theory it could bloody work,' Mat persisted. 'Cos we got to think of something, mate. All the fire-power of us lot, plus the tanks, plus a squadron of F-18s, plus the Spectre gunship, and the fookers are still holding out. So let's not write off any idea 'til we're bloody certain about it.'

'All right then, you go first, and come back and tell us all about it,' Tom said. 'Then we'll consider coming after you.'

'All I'm saying is, mate, we shouldn't rule anything out,' Mat said. 'Cos it's going to take something we haven't thought of to break this bloody siege.'

'Mat's got a point, mate,' Jamie interjected. 'No way are bloody air strikes going to do it, not with them taking shelter down in the basements.'

'An' don't I fuckin' know it,' Tom retorted. 'Eventually, mate, we're just going to have to fuckin' go in there on foot and root the fuckers out. Nasty. Like rats down a fuckin' drain. Like evil. I mean, do you fancy fighting your way into them fuckin' basements? Cos I know I fuckin' don't. It'll be like Custer's Last Stand for 'em. But I don't see any other way of fuckin' ending it.'

'If we do that, we're going to lose a lot of blokes,'

Mat said. 'Like I said, there's got to be another way.'

'Well, there might fuckin' not be, mate,' Tom replied. 'Just got to face up to it. Might not be any other way of going about it.'

The lads discussed options for breaking the siege long into the evening, but by the time they hit the sack they were none the wiser as to how they would go about doing it. On the morning of day four of the battle, they returned to Qala-i-Janghi with no clearer sense of a battle plan. Upon arrival at the fort they had a quick heads-up with the Northern Alliance commanders. But they were still trying to re-assure the SBS soldiers that there were less than a dozen enemy holding out in the southern half of the fortress. Which, as all the lads knew, was a load of total bollocks.

'Hey, there's only bloody six of 'em left,' Mat sang out, as they climbed up on to the walls of the fort to take up their fire positions on the ruined tower.

'S'all right then,' Tom responded.

'Be over in a jiffy,' Jamie added.

'Have to be hard as fuckin' nails, though, eh?' Tom said. 'I mean, if it's the same half-dozen of 'em have survived all this time.'

As soon as they had resumed their sniping duties, the SBS soldiers could tell what was happening, and it was a repeat performance of the previous day's action. Once again, they targeted a window in the pink building where four of the enemy were positioned, returning fire with their AK47s. When eventually they did see one of the enemy go down, seconds later there'd be a replacement fighter who'd popped up from below ground and taken up the same fire position.

'Six of 'em?' Tom snorted, as he took careful aim with his Diemaco. 'More like six fuckin' hundred, I reckon.'

By mid-morning it was clear that the battle was going nowhere. Finally, General Dostum decided that it was time to fight their way into the southern end of the fort. But the General wanted none of the British or US special forces soldiers going in on the ground. They were to remain in their positions and provide top cover as his Afghan fighters went in on foot. As soon as the SBS lads heard of the General's plan, they knew that it was going to be a bloodbath. The enemy had perfect cover, and the Afghans would be going in there with none. The SBS lads had fought alongside these Afghan soldiers for several days now. They'd dug each other out of the rubble of the JDAM strike. They'd built up a strong sense of cama- raderie with them. They had a deep respect for the Afghans as soldiers. They didn't want to see these Afghan warriors get mown down in a futile attempt to recap- ture the fort.

'What does the General think his men are – bloody bulletproof?' Mat asked, incredulously. 'They'll be no more than cannon fodder when those fookers catch sight of 'em.'

'It'll be a massacre, pure and simple,' Jamie added. 'As if there hasn't been enough death here already.'

'Why doesn't the General send a couple of his fuckin' tanks in with 'em – a T-55 or even a T-64?' said Tom. 'I mean, send the armour in first and use it to blast the stronghold from close range.'

'Bloody cracking idea, mate,' Mat enthused.

'Well, it ain't fuckin' rocket science, is it, mate?' said Tom. 'At least that way the Afghans'll have some fuckin' cover to advance behind.'

'Come on, Einstein,' Mat replied, enthusiastically, 'let's put your plan to the bloody General then.'

With the help of one of the CIA officers acting as a

translator, Tom and Mat went and presented their idea for the plan of attack to General Dostum. At first the General was less than enthusiastic. He argued that he'd already lost one tank to the errant US air strike, so why should he risk any more. But then Tom outlined in graphic detail what was likely to happen if the tank wasn't used, and how many of the General's soldiers would get massacred. And Mat pointed out that the only weapon the enemy had with which they might conceivably take out a T-55 was the RPG – and it would take an extremely lucky shot to penetrate the tank's armour. If the tank kept itself front on to the enemy positions and held back a good distance, it would be able to pour shells into the stronghold pretty much with impunity. So what did the General have to lose?

Pretty quickly the General found himself warming to their plan. And he decided that if they were going to do it this way, then they would do it well. He ordered one of his crack T-55 tank crews to prepare to lead the ground forces into the southern compound. As the tank manoeuvred its way into position at the entranceway to the fort, some sixty Afghan soldiers clustered behind it, clutching their AK47s. From their vantage point on the battlements, Mat, Tom, Jamie, Sam and Ruff readied themselves to provide top cover. They heard the bellow of the tank's engines as the crew prepared for the advance, and then there was a belch of thick, oily smoke as the T-55 lurched forward into the fort. Finally, the British, American and Afghan forces trying to lift the siege of Qala-i-Janghi were taking the fight into the heart of the enemy's heartland.

The SBS soldiers watched through their sniping scopes as the tank clattered forward, the Afghan troops following in its wake at a crouching run. As he followed the

T-55's halting progress, Mat felt certain that this was a signal moment in the siege of the fort – that the enemy's iron grip on the southern half of the complex was finally about to be broken. He hugged the butt of his Diemaco close to his shoulder, as he trained his sight on the main window of the enemy stronghold. As soon as the T-55 entered the enemy field of fire, machine-gun rounds started slamming into the tank's armour, but with little effect. First one and then another RPG round streaked across the compound towards the lumbering machine, but both impacted well wide of the target.

Momentarily, Mat caught an enemy gunman at the window in his sniping scope. In that split second he squeezed his trigger and three rounds went tearing into the fighter. Mat watched as his bloodied body slumped forward over the shattered sill of the window. But within seconds a second enemy gunman had taken his place, taking cover behind the body of his dead comrade. More enemy fighters appeared at other windows of the stronghold now, drawn to the battle by the clatter of the approaching tank. They started putting down a wall of fire on to the approaching T-55, and the Afghan soldiers sheltering at its rear. And from their sniping positions on the battlements Mat, Jamie, Sam, Tom and Ruff started pumping rounds into the enemy figures.

The tank advanced some sixty yards into the southern compound, as the SBS sniping kept the enemy's heads down. By the time the T-55 ground to a halt, the enemy fighters had still failed to score a direct hit with an RPG. There were some further belches of black exhaust fumes followed by the whine of its turret motor, and slowly the tank's cannon swung around and was brought to bear on the target. After a few seconds' inactivity, a gout of smoke and flame shot forth from the barrel, and the first round from the tank's main battle gun slammed into the enemy stronghold. For a moment there was an ominous silence, as the T-55's crew hurried to reload and the enemy reeled from the shock of the explosion. And then there was the menacing death rattle of machine-gun fire rising above the fort walls, as the enemy launched a desperate counter-attack.

As the Northern Alliance soldiers had advanced for the first time into their end of the fort, Ali and Ahmed had rallied the brothers for one last, decisive battle.

'This is our chance to fight and kill the *kafir* dogs,' Ali had urged them. He was exhausted and injured and his voice was weak, but he tried to hide all this from the brothers. 'Use every window and every door. Prepare to massacre them, to tear their throats out, to cut out their infidel hearts.'

But then, the first of the T-55 shells had slammed into the stronghold, tearing it – and those brothers inside it – apart. After a salvo of six further rounds, the giant tank churned its way further into the compound, crushing the corpses of the martyred brothers under its tracks as it went. Further high-explosive shells punched huge holes in the walls of their redoubt, shrapnel ripping into the brothers and lacerating their bodies. They brought about a sudden end to Ali and Ahmed's dreams of a glorious last battle. Within seconds, their plans to spread death and destruction among the besieging enemy forces, their hopes of waging a victorious jihad, had been torn to pieces.

The smell of acrid smoke and the stench of burning flesh filled the brothers' holdout. Down below in the basement, there was complete chaos and mayhem where the iron girders keeping up the ceiling had collapsed and the walls had come tumbling in, crushing the brothers and pinning them to the floor. The subterranean passageways had been transformed into a terrifying, shadowed, charnel house – a place reeking of the stench of death, and ringing with the screams of the injured and the dying. Rather than finding the Paradise that they had been promised, many of the brothers were at this moment trapped in a terrible, agonising hell on earth.

Among the two dozen wounded lying in the shattered remains of the stronghold at ground level there was a giant, bearded figure with a smaller, darker figure at his side. Ali and Ahmed, leading the resistance from above ground, had been among the first of the brothers to be hit by the T-55 shelling. Their bodies were lacerated by shrapnel, and they had suffered terrible internal injuries from the shell's blast. As they lay there amid the smashed walls and the broken bodies of their fallen brothers, both men knew that they were dying and that with death would come an end to the suffering and the killing and the hatred and the bitter, endless bloodshed.

'I see a bright light . . . my beloved Brother Ahmed,' Ali murmured, through cracked and bloodied lips. 'It is . . . the light . . . of Paradise, brother . . . Paradise . . . awaits . . .'

'Praise be . . . to Allah . . . brother . . .' Ahmed replied, his words choking on the blood that he was coughing up from his lungs.

'Help . . . me . . . to stand, brother,' Ali whispered, his arm gripping Ahmed's with a sudden, vice-like strength. 'Let us . . . stand . . . Let us walk . . . together . . . into Paradise.'

Agonisingly slowly, the two wounded brothers staggered to their feet. Still clutching their AK47s they stumbled to the nearest window – which had been blasted into a gaping hole the size of a garage door. They reached the opening and it was full of thick, choking fumes that swirled around the ruined building. Obscured by the smoke, each brother held the other steady as they raised their weapons and opened fire. But as soon as they did so, the SBS soldiers up on the fort's battlements spotted the muzzle flashes among the shadows. In a split second, Mat, Jamie, Sam, Tom and Ruff had readjusted their aim, and half a dozen bullets riddled Ali and Ahmed full of holes. By the time their bloodied bodies hit the floor of the building, Ali, the self-appointed leader of the brothers, and his loyal lieutenant, Ahmed, were dead.

As Ali and Ahmed's weapons stopped firing, an eerie silence settled over the enemy stronghold. Smoke poured forth from the ruptured building and the bodies of the enemy dead lay where they had fallen among the shattered rubble. As they watched over the ruins through their sniping scopes, the SBS soldiers presumed that the battle for the fort was finally over. But little did they know that down below in the basement there were still scores of surviving brothers. Brothers who had vowed to continue the fight to the last, to kill or be killed, to find their path to Paradise.

17

FORT OF WAR

THE T-55 continued pounding the superstructure of the enemy stronghold until it had been reduced to blasted walls and heaps of rubble. But even so, the tank's shells were unable to penetrate below ground. As the Northern Alliance fighters advanced towards the shattered ruins, they were confident of a final victory. But immediately they started taking casualties. Amazingly, there were still surviving enemy fighters in that building and they were counter-attacking against the Afghan soldiers. As the General's men tried to rush the entranceway to the basement, they ran into a wall of bullets, which cut down several of their bravest men. In a split second they had learned a costly lesson: anyone who tried to fight their way into that basement would be instantly shot dead.

The SBS soldiers were powerless to help: from their positions on the battlements they could not target an enemy out of sight and sheltering in the basement. As the Afghan soldiers withdrew to the cover of the T-55, they took stock of their casualties. A dozen of their men had been hit, and they had to get the wounded out of there as quickly as possible. After witnessing the fanatical resistance of the enemy, none of them were keen to battle their way into the labyrinth of tunnels and passageways that ran beneath the complex. And so the fourth day of the battle for Qala-i-Janghi drew to a close with the tank and the General's foot soldiers withdrawing from the fort.

By nightfall on day four of the fort siege, one-third of the ancient fortress still remained in enemy hands. And at Boxer Base that evening, none of the men had any fresh ideas how to flush the enemy out of their underground lair.

Just after dawn on day five of the fort siege, the SBS soldiers were back at their positions on the battlements, as the Northern Alliance forces did a second sweep into the southern end of the fort. This time, they were searching for the body of CIA Agent Mike Spann. As the Afghan soldiers advanced on foot through the fort they started taking fire. Several smaller groups of enemy fighters were discovered holding out in separate underground chambers, some distance from the main enemy stronghold. It seemed as if a warren of passageways ran beneath the whole of the southern end of the fort.

General Dostum's soldiers started hurling down grenades through the tiny ventilation windows above ground, followed by long bursts of machine-gun fire. But no one knew for sure how many of the enemy still remained alive in this subterranean labyrinth.

'They've started to get real medieval on the fuckers,' Tom announced, as he and Mat returned from a midmorning discussion with General Dostum and his commanders.

'Like how, mate?' Jamie asked.

'Remember them castle sieges of old, when they poured

boiling oil down on top of the enemy?' said Mat. 'And
they used catapults to hurl burning rocks over the walls?
Well, mate, Dostum's lads figure that if GPS-guided
JDAMs and laser-guided bombs won't do the trick, then
it's time to take a little lesson from history.'

'They've burnt the fuckers out,' Tom added. 'Poured
a few drums of diesel oil down into the basement, chucked
in a couple of grenades, and bingo – one load of fried
ragheads.'

The Northern Alliance forces had come up with an
ingenious, yet brutal, plan to escalate the subterranean
assault – one designed to break the enemy's resistance
once and for all. A truckload of fuel drums had been
driven in through the gateway of the fort, and the Afghan
soldiers had rolled the drums over to the stronghold
where the enemy was holding out. Getting the diesel
down into the basement had proved tougher than
expected though, as the enemy had kept firing on anyone
who tried to pour it in through the windows. But the
Afghans had soon realised that anyone standing or lying
to either side of the basement's main doorway was largely
invisible to the enemy forces below ground. So General
Dostum's men had taken up their positions and used
pipes to start feeding the contents of the fuel drums below
into the dark basement.

The thick fuel oil had gushed down the stone steps.
When a dozen of the drums had been emptied, the Afghan
soldiers had stood back and thrown white phosphorous
incendiary grenades into the darkness below. The
exploding grenades threw off a thousand balls of burning
white phosphor, some of which shot back up the steps
of the entranceway. Almost immediately, flames started
licking out of the doorway and windows of the basement, as a pall of greasy black smoke billowed over the

building. For several seconds the stench of burning had enveloped the ancient castle, as conditions below ground became impossible for humans to bear. The flames and fumes would have quickly taken effect, burning and asphyxiating the enemy fighters – were it not for the fact that the heavy diesel oil proved almost impossible to ignite. Once the fire from the phosphorous grenades had died down the oil-soaked basement stubbornly refused to burn.

It was plain for all to see now that the battle for control of this ancient fortress had descended into a brute barbarity. In spite of the T-55 tanks and the high-tech warplanes and the modern weapons of war, the battle for Qala-i-Janghi had begun to resemble a scene from some castle siege set in the Dark Ages. As Mat watched over the battleground, it crossed his mind that it was like a classic scene of hell. A thick cloud of choking smoke hung over the southern end of the fortress. Scattered across the fort grounds were the bloated carcasses of General Dostum's cavalry. Some of the limbs had been lopped off, where the ravenous enemy fighters had feasted on the raw horseflesh – the only food available since the battle began.

Hundreds of decomposing human corpses lay where they had fallen. While the bodies of the Afghan soldiers were covered in shamags, as a mark of respect, many of the enemy dead had been left where they had fallen. Several had been crushed under the tracks of the T-55 tank, as it had lumbered into the fort. As far as General Dostum's men were concerned, through their betrayal the enemy fighters had lost any claims to honour and dignity even in death, and despite the fact that they were supposedly fellow Muslims.

As the smoke drifted away from the fort sporadic

bursts of defiant gunfire still came echoing up from the basement. General Dostum's men finally withdrew to the outer reaches of the fort with the body of CIA agent Mike Spann. They were more than happy to do so, as the Afghan soldiers remained spooked by the enemy's suicidal bravery. They seemed indestructible, as if nothing were ever going to kill them or force them to give up their hold over the southern end of the fort.

A convoy of US and British vehicles was drawn up at the fort entranceway to receive the CIA agent's body. Mat, Jamie, Sam, Tom, Ruff and the other SBS soldiers came down from the battlements to pay their last respects to the dead man. Over the previous weeks they had built up close working relationships with several of the CIA agents stationed at Mazar and elsewhere. As far as they were concerned they were all part of one team with a shared mission – to defeat the terrorist threat now emanating out of Afghanistan and menacing the wider world.

The Afghan soldiers carried Mike Spann's body out of the fort on a stretcher, whereupon a sombre mood settled over the US and British soldiers gathered at the gates. His fellow CIA officers then took over and they draped his prone form in a US flag. A short prayer was said over the body, and then it was placed in one of the vehicles. On the first day of the fort uprising, the SBS soldiers had fought heroically either to save Mike Spann's life, or to prove that he was killed in action. From the moment of the uprising itself, it had taken five days to prove conclusively that CIA Agent Johnny Michael Spann was dead.

That evening, back at the Old Schoolhouse, Mike Spann's coffin was loaded on board a US helicopter to begin the first leg of the long flight back to the USA. He was given a guard of honour send-off with all the SBS troops in attendance. After the ceremony was over, an American agent drew Jamie to one side for a private conversation. It was the evening of day five of the fort siege now, and the agent was trying to find out exactly how Mike Spann had died on that first day of battle.

'Listen, buddy, we kinda know each other pretty well by now and I wanna ask you a real private question,' the agent said. 'Like, d'you reckon Dave did enough to save Mike Spann in there? I mean, like, just your own personal opinion, you know.'

'God, I can't say, mate,' Jamie answered. 'I mean, how the hell do I answer a question like that? You're asking me to move into the realms of speculation, mate.'

'Hey, buddy, come on. You was there – when it all went down. You Brits are awesome, I mean like goddam indestructible. And I'm just asking your opinion on what went down in there.'

''Fraid I can't say, mate. Best I can do is stick to the facts of what I know. We killed a lot of people in there. It's not over yet – so we'll probably do the same tomorrow and kill a lot more of the fuckers. And one of your blokes died too. I'm sorry for him. But that's life, mate. I mean, shit happens.'

'Well, all right, buddy, no worries. I mean, I was just sort of noodling over whether Mike may have killed himself, you know.'

'Now why the fuck would he have done that?' Jamie asked, sharply.

'Cos like, maybe he was still alive, in the fort, buddy. Cos like, maybe the fuckin' ragheads hadn't managed to finish him off. Cos like, he sure as hell knew what was coming. So, he ended it all, before the motherfuckers could rape his soul. Rather that than face what those evil fuckers would do to him if they came back and got him that first day when the darkness came down.'

'What, you saying he still had his weapon and turned it on himself?'

'Something like that, buddy, yeah. I mean, if the body had just the one shot to the head, you'd think it kinda pretty likely, wouldn't you?'

'I might do. Yeah, I probably would do, mate. That's what it had then, was it, just the one shot to the head?'

'That's what I heard, buddy. But I ain't never seen it. And I can't vouch for what I only heard.'

'Then you don't know shit, mate,' Jamie said, with finality. He didn't really appreciate such speculation, and thought the agent's line of questioning had been well out of order.

The following morning, day six of the fort siege, was the moment when the SBS soldiers finally ventured into the interior of the fort. They advanced into the grounds following a rutted dirt track, the ground to either side being covered in tree branches that had been scythed off by the firepower unleashed during the previous days' fighting. The twisted skeleton of a burned-out pickup lay by the side of the track. Further on, the ground was littered with the blackened detritus of war: a discarded boot, a smouldering rifle butt, a machine gun cut in two. Unexploded RPG rounds and mortar shells were embedded in the earth and all up the ramparts of the fort walls.

As they entered the southern end of the fort, the sight that met the SBS soldiers' eyes was one of complete devastation. Scores of dead and decomposing bodies littered the grounds. Two Northern Alliance soldiers were piling corpses on to a trailer – but whether they were their Afghan comrades or the enemy dead no one was certain.

One of the Afghans was perched atop a layer of dead bodies in the trailer, as his fellow soldier hauled another towards him. Stiffened, bloated limbs stuck out from the pile of corpses, forming odd, grotesque shapes. Tattered shreds of clothing and equipment hung down from the trailer, and littered the bloodied ground.

A handful of the enemy dead still had their hands tied behind their backs: clearly, they had failed to get themselves untied and join the uprising proper before they had been gunned down. Wherever the enemy fighters had launched their suicide attacks, they had either been cut to pieces by machine-gun fire and air strikes or they had blown themselves up intentionally. Consequently, there were eviscerated bodies, dismembered limbs and scraps of human flesh scattered around the blood-dried grass and the scorched, pockmarked walls. The stench of burning and of the decomposing dead was unbearable – and the SBS soldiers pulled their shamags over their faces to try to block out the sickening smell. As Mat walked on he stumbled over the blackened, charred stump of a hand. He glanced down at it momentarily, but it barely appeared human any more.

While the SBS soldiers wandered past the total carnage that lay all around them, the Northern Alliance fighters started to loot the dead. They searched for money, cigarettes and even pulled the shoes off the stiff, grey bodies. It had to be a sign that the fighting was nearing an end, Mat reasoned. The carcasses of some thirty dead horses – General Dostum's finest – added a putrescent stench to the acrid reek of cordite still hanging in the air. The occasional explosion from the smouldering arms dump sent soldiers running in panic, jumping over dead bodies and diving for cover. No one could quite believe that the fighting was really over. Which in a way it wasn't. Even in death, the enemy fighters still sought their revenge. Scores of the corpses had been booby-trapped with grenades in an attempt to kill anyone who tried to move them.

More worryingly still, the Afghan soldiers tasked with removing the bodies and securing the fort kept hearing muffled voices coming from below ground level. Suddenly, there was a burst of fire from an underground position, and two of the Afghan stretcher-bearers were cut down in a hail of AK47 fire. Angry Northern Alliance soldiers rushed forward and hurled grenades in through the nearest ventilation shafts. There were a series of powerful detonations that shook the earth, and gouts of smoke and flame shot up from the entranceway and windows of the enemy bunker.

To Mat and the other SBS troops it was hard to imagine how anyone below ground could have survived those explosions – let alone what had gone before. But suddenly, there was a long burst of answering fire from the enemy, and the SBS soldiers were forced to dive for cover, along with their allies. The two Afghan fighters nearest the enemy bunker emptied a magazine each from their AK47s through the ventilation shafts. More grenades were thrown into the smoky gloom below, but it was hard to say with what effect. No one was keen to go down into that basement and check.

'Maybe we should go have a chat with them,' Mat announced to Jamie. The SBS soldiers had taken cover behind a brick-built wall. 'Like get a brew on. Two sugars or three? And talk 'em into surrender.'

There was a ripple of laughter among the men.

'There's got to be a way to finish it,' Jamie remarked. 'What're the options, mate?'

'Options?' said Mat. 'Well, we can enter the bunker

and die, or enter the bunker and die, or enter the bunker from another direction and still bloody die. Or just die. Take your bloody pick, mate.'

'After you, mate,' Jamie replied, with a grin.

'Well, we've tried fire, haven't we, mate?' said Mat, after a pause. 'So how's about we try water. What about flooding the fookers out?'

'Like how exactly, mate?' Jamie asked.

'Simple. Water runs downhill, don't it?' said Mat. 'So get the Afghans to hose a load of water down there from the irrigation channels. They got to have water pumps somewhere. Pump the water down the ventilation shafts.'

'Fuckin' awesome idea, mate,' Tom cut in.

'We'll freeze the fookers out,' Mat announced. 'It'll take a while, but I ain't in no hurry to go down there and die.'

The SBS and Afghan soldiers went into a huddle as Mat outlined his plan for drowning the enemy out of their holes. Eventually, he explained, the water level would rise to dangerous levels and the enemy would be forced to give themselves up. And so it was that the Afghan soldiers, aided by their special forces colleagues, diverted the water from one of the main irrigation channels and sent it pouring down into the basement. The siege for the fort had now become a war of attrition, as the allied forces waited for the enemy's will to crack.

It was the night of day six down in their subterranean holdout and the brothers' existence had become a living hell. All evening long the freezing cold waters had poured into the basement, rising higher and higher. Dozens of corpses lay floating on the dark waters, adrift in a scum of blood, human faeces and diesel oil. The walls of the basement were scorched and blackened with explosions and burn marks, and pockmarked with bullet holes. Over everything hung the reek of death. For those who were still holding out down here, these last few hours had been distinguished only by a leaderless, brute survival.

There had been nothing glorious or noble or uplifting about the last hours of the jihad at Qala-i-Janghi. There had been nothing that might suggest that Paradise was near at hand. But there had been an abundance of terror, despair, defiance and fear – and madness and insanity by the bucketload. Over the previous two days many had died slow, brutal deaths from their wounds; others had burned to death in agony, as the diesel fuel had ignited and turned into a raging inferno; yet more had died the numbing death of hypothermia, as the freezing waters had sapped their strength and their will to live; still more had died from nothing more tangible than simply giving up the will to go on.

The surviving brothers had spent a night entombed below ground, chest-deep in the stinking, icy-cold waters. As the last hours of the fort siege ground agonisingly slowly towards dawn, one of the brothers had spoken up – was it for sanity, a vague sense of compromise, for survival? Or simply because this living pain could be endured no longer and so someone had to call a halt. The brother was shaking uncontrollably and he knew that he was close to collapse. If he went down in the freezing waters the brothers could not save him and he would die a horrible death. He had heard the frantic, thrashing, choking deaths of others, as they had drowned in the shadows.

'If we don't give up we'll all die,' the brother had announced, matter-of-factly, voicing the thought that was on several of their minds. 'If we do give up they might kill us but it can't be worse than this.'

There were muted murmurs of agreement from the darkness all around him, where half-crazed, animal eyes gazed out of sunken sockets, sickly white in the cloying blackness. Without another word that 'brother' had turned and waded through the chest-deep waters towards the steps that led out of the basement, and prepared himself to surrender to the enemy forces.

18

ENDGAME

BY 6.30 a.m. on the morning of day seven of the fort siege the SBS soldiers and their Afghan allies were back inside the southern end of the fort. Conditions in that basement had to be horrific by now. The surviving enemy had spent hours in the freezing water that had been pouring down on top of them all night long. Overnight, an old fire truck had been brought in to help pump gallons of water into the enemy's lair. None of the soldiers had any idea how many survivors were holding out down there. And none of them were tempted to go take a look, either. Although they figured it could be no more than a handful, they'd already learned the hard way that to fight their way into the basement would mean all but certain death.

At 7 a.m., Mat thought he spotted movement in the entrance to the basement. Instinctively, he raised his Diemaco and prepared to fire. Slowly, painfully slowly, a lone figure came crawling up the steps. Mat kept his finger poised on the trigger as he followed the enemy fighter. He tracked his every move as the figure emerged

above ground, blinking, from the darkness into the harsh
sunlight. He was a pathetic sight. He was drenched to
the skin, shivering uncontrollably and looked utterly
exhausted. Yet after what they had witnessed over the
last seven days, Mat knew what these men were capable
of. Maybe this one was on a last-ditch suicide mission,
with grenades hidden under his clothing. Mat held his
fire, but kept the enemy covered.

As he reached the top of the steps, the figure paused
and looked around himself confusedly. Two of the Afghan
soldiers moved forward, grabbed the enemy fighter and
shoved him roughly to his knees. They barked commands
at the man, and then began frisking him, removing all
of his weapons. Finally, his boots were taken and his
hands cuffed tightly behind his back. Clearly, the
Northern Alliance weren't taking any chances with the
survivors. One by one, twelve further fighters stumbled
out of the basement, several still clutching their AK47
assault rifles. The thirteen emaciated survivors were black
with diesel oil and looked like the walking dead.

Each fighter was quickly disarmed and taken away,
being made to walk barefoot down the dirt track leading
towards the fort entrance. There, a red container lorry
was waiting for them. Several of the enemy were in such
a bad way that they were unable to walk even the short
distance to the container lorry. They were loaded on to
the same stretchers that the Northern Alliance soldiers
had been using to remove the dead from the fort, and
carried across to the waiting truck. The enemy survivors
were suffering from dehydration, exhaustion, blood loss,
hypothermia and asphyxiation – not to mention the
wounds they had received during the days and days of
fighting.

As the Afghan soldiers stood guard, several members

of the International Committee of the Red Cross arrived. The ICRC workers had come to tend to the prisoners' injuries. One of the prisoners couldn't stop shaking. Another had stopped moving, and appeared to have fallen unconscious. The ICRC staff tried feeding the men apples and bananas, but most of them were too weak to eat. One Chechen fighter was rocking back and forth, as he stared at an ugly shrapnel wound in his leg. He was mouthing off in Russian, still spouting extremist rhetoric about killing the *kafir*. He didn't realise that some of the Northern Alliance soldiers could understand him. One of them answered him sharply in Russian, ordering him to shut up or face the consequences. He immediately changed his tone and began begging for first aid, food and water.

One of the Red Cross workers gave the Chechen an apple. As he munched on it, he started rambling on about how terrible it had been down in that dark basement, surrounded by the dying and the dead. As the Red Cross proceeded to tend to the prisoners' wounds, and tried to get some food and water into them, the Afghan soldiers became increasingly restless and angry. They couldn't understand why these foreign aid workers were treating the enemy in such a humane way. These men were fanatics, terrorists, suicide bombers, unreasoning killers. Surely they didn't deserve anyone's kindness? Had they captured any of these ICRC workers within the fort, they would have treated them as just one more group of infidels that they could kill. So why were these foreigners now doing so much to help them, to save their lives?

Finally, one of the younger Afghan soldiers cracked. He began yelling at the nearest Red Cross worker: 'They'll eat your apples and bananas today, and then they'll blow you to smithereens tomorrow!' Apparently, this was exactly what the Taliban had done to this man's home. One of the older Afghan soldiers was itching to smash the prisoners' heads in. 'You bastards killed my son!' he kept roaring, as he swung a rock around in his hand, waiting for his chance to strike. His fellow soldiers had to hold him back to prevent him from rushing in and using it. There was an ugly, bitter menace to the scene, as if it could so easily explode at any moment into yet more hatred and bloodshed.

After the thirteen enemy fighters had emerged, there was a quick debate among the SBS soldiers and their Afghan allies as to whether there were others left in that basement. The Afghan commanders found it hard to believe that any more could have survived down there. But no one was sure. At 10 a.m., Mat spotted further movement on the steps. One by one more enemy fighters came staggering and crawling up the basement steps and into the daylight. Ten, twenty, thirty, forty of them – the stream of survivors seemed never-ending. Many had horrific injuries. One fighter came hopping up the steps on his one good leg, the other hanging smashed and useless. But despite their terrible condition, the eyes of these men were still burning with hatred for those who had denied them what they sought most in life – death in jihad.

'Amazing stuff, water, ain't it?' Mat remarked to Jamie, as he kept his weapon trained on the silent figures emerging, ghostlike, from the basement.

Some fifty fighters had given themselves up when a young, emaciated man with a leg wound stopped in front of his captors. As the pale, scraggy, bearded figure was placed on to a stretcher, he mumbled something to his captors in English.

'I'm an American,' the young man whispered, through cracked and bloodied lips.

At first, the man refused to give his name, but maintained that he was from Washington State. Then he began explaining that he was a US convert to Islam who had studied at an Islamic school in Pakistan, before deciding to join the jihad in Afghanistan. He said that he had come to fight the jihad and help build 'a perfect Islamic state in Afghanistan'. It turned out that this man was John Walker Lindh, the so-called 'American Taliban'. He was a twenty-year-old citizen of the United States who had spent his childhood in a liberal community in northern California.

As the SBS soldiers kept watch over the surrendering enemy forces, one of the 5th SOF operators came across to have a word.

'You guys ain't gonna believe this,' the operator announced. 'But there's a goddam American.'

''Course there is, mate – there's bloody loads of you,' Mat retorted.

'No. *Not us.* There's a goddam American *enemy*, buddy,' the 5th SOF soldier replied, as he pointed out the pale figure lying on the stretcher. 'A fuckin' prisoner. An *American Taliban.*'

Holy fuck. How the hell did he end up here? Mat wondered. He watched the 'American Taliban' being stretchered away towards the waiting truck. The SBS counted a total of eighty-six enemy fighters who emerged alive from the basement of Qala-i-Janghi. Once the last one had supposedly given himself up, the Afghan soldiers finally went in to check out that basement. They trod carefully on the steps, advancing cautiously, feeling their way foot by foot down into the darkness. Mat decided that he had to take a look himself, and that he was going with them.

He descended the steps holding his weapon ready at

the shoulder. He checked for booby traps along the walls and floor, and for any enemy fighters that might still be holding out down there. At the base of the stairway a cold, foul air wrapped him in its embrace. He could immediately sense the death and the terror that had gripped this place just hours earlier – the enemy trapped in the darkness, freezing, soaked to the skin, starving, wounded perhaps, and with corpses afloat among the oily scum. At the foot of the stairs a body was floating face upwards. Water stretched away into the darkness – a flooded corridor leading into a cavernous, shadowed room.

How many men had died here? Mat wondered. How many corpses were entombed in this watery grave? They had come to this fort seeking death, of that Mat was certain. And with the help of Mat, Jamie, Tom, Sam, Ruff and the other SBS lads, many of them had found it.

EPILOGUE

When you think of how it played out in the press I suppose the news of five hundred prisoners being shot dead sounds sensational, it sounds like it might be a war crime. Then you look at the facts – that they had an endless supply of weapons, that every room was stuffed full of the stuff, and all of them were actively seeking to die. What choice did we have but to take them out?

– SBS soldier, on the battle for Qala-i-Janghi

AT the time of the uprising at Qala-i-Janghi the world's media was massed around Kunduz to report on the battle for that city. But once the prisoner revolt got underway, large sections of them relocated to the scene of the fort siege. It quickly became the focus of the media's war in Afghanistan: from the relative safety of the fort's exterior news crews had a perfect vantage point from which to witness the drama as it unfolded. Footage of the air bombardment of the fort was broadcast around the world, as were the bloody scenes after the fighting was over. Because of its accessibility, the battle for Qala-i-

Janghi received more coverage than just about any other event of the Afghan war. It also became one of the most controversial episodes in the whole of that conflict, with sections of the media claiming that British, US and Afghan forces carried out a massacre.

Indeed, the very first day of action by the SBS at Qala-i-Janghi was filmed by an Afghan, using a small, hand-held video camera. As he was positioned on the entranceway tower along with the Northern Alliance soldiers, the SBS operators presumed that he was somehow part of the NA forces. In fact, he was an independent Afghan video journalist. The footage that he filmed of the SBS in action quickly made its way into the hands of the international media. Among other things, it clearly showed Jamie and Ruff in action using the GPMGs from the fort battlements. 'Amnesty International has called for an inquiry into the death of so many Taliban prisoners,' a Channel 4 news report stated over the footage. 'Now it's clear that British special forces were closely involved in the fighting, attempts may be made to draw them into the investigation. But it's equally clear that they were operating in a very hostile environment.'

But, despite the media accusations of a massacre, no one knows for certain how many enemy were killed at Qala-i-Janghi. Approximately 150 bodies were recovered from the fort grounds, though many were unrecognisable due to the heavy bombardment. With eighty-six survivors coming out alive and 150 bodies recovered, the majority of the six hundred prisoners reportedly held at the fort remain un-accounted for. Doubtless, many of the bodies were never found because they had been obliterated during the bombing. But it also seems highly likely that some of the prisoners managed to escape, especially during the initial twenty-four hours of the uprising and prior to the fort being sealed off by Northern Alliance troops. That is certainly what I have been told by my sources from the AQT side of the story. And there were, of course, significant casualties on both sides of the fighting – reflecting the fact that this was a fierce and prolonged firefight, as opposed to a massacre.

The Northern Alliance lost some fifty soldiers in the fort siege – a number of whom were killed by the errant JDAM strike. The five US 5th SOF soldiers who were injured in that errant air strike were air-evacuated via Uzbekistan to a US military hospital at Landstuhl, Germany. The only Western operative to be killed at Qala-i-Janghi was CIA Agent Johnny Michael Spann. Mike Spann was part of the CIA's elite and secretive Special Activities Division (SAD). This serves as the Agency's knifepoint in its cloak-and-dagger work to provide security to the USA around the globe. Members of SAD are drawn from the Navy SEALs, the Army Special Operations Forces and, as in Mike Spann's case, the US Marines. The unit is skilled in the dark arts of paramilitary warfare, including assassinations, advanced demolitions, high-tech surveillance and behind-enemy-lines combat. CIA SAD operatives were some of the first forces deployed on the ground in the war in Afghanistan.

Some controversy surrounds the death of Mike Spann. The US military supposedly has an ethos to 'leave no man behind'. This means that no combat operative should ever be abandoned by his fellow men. The father of Johnny Mike Spann, Johnny Spann Sr, is deeply troubled by events surrounding his son's death. He raises several questions. First, at what stage exactly did the US and allied forces trying to lift the siege conclude that his son was dead? How did they reach that conclusion, as no one had been able to get to his son and check if he was still alive? The nearest that anyone had reached was Sam Brown, the US SEAL on secondment to the SBS, who thinks he spotted Mike Spann's body from the western tower of the fort. Johnny Spann Sr believes that a serious rescue attempt carried out by scores of US and British special forces might have succeeded in reaching his son before nightfall of the first day, at which time he might have been injured and unconscious, but still alive. So why were no US or British reinforcements rushed in to the fort during those first hours of fighting, to help suppress the uprising and rescue his son?

Another question Johnny Spann Sr asks is why air strikes were used on the fort, when there was an American operative still inside who might have been alive? He believes that at some stage a decision must have been reached by those in allied high command that his son was dead. Otherwise, he can't account for the rescue mission being abandoned at the end of day one of the uprising, in favour of the policy of using air strikes against the enemy holed up in the fort. Of course, none of this detracts from the heroic efforts made by the SBS team of Sam Brown and Tom Knight to locate and rescue CIA Agent Mike Spann. Johnny Spann Sr is full of gratitude for the way in which the whole SBS contingent fought ferociously and against all odds to put down the uprising and locate and rescue his son. But he still has questions to which he's seeking answers, and most of those questions relate to the bigger picture and those in high command making the decisions.

However, Johnny Spann Sr does not believe that his son died in vain. 'Mike went to Afghanistan for one reason only – to find and deal with al-Qaeda and Osama bin Laden because of what they had done to us, because we were attacked by al-Qaeda and bin Laden on 9/11,' he says. 'It's important we remember that, along with Mike, others died fighting al-Qaeda and the terrorists. My son gave his life fighting al-Qaeda, and the terrorists are still out there, they haven't changed. People mustn't lose sight of that and why we were in Afghanistan. Mike could have run away and got out to safety. The day he died at Qala-i-Janghi he gave his life capturing and punishing al-Qaeda and saving the lives of good people. He could have turned and run, but he elected to step forward and take a stand. It's good Mike had the fortitude and courage to do what he did, what he was trained to do. If he'd run that day he'd not have been able to live with himself.'

The friendly-fire incident involving the errant JDAM strike has since been investigated by the relevant US authorities. The US CENTCOM's initial findings were that the accident was a result of 'procedural errors in the transmission and application of friendly and enemy coordinates'. In other words, it was human error. US forces have now changed their standard operating procedures for forward air control so that forces calling in air strikes do not put up friendly coordinates to the pilots. This is the UK military's standard operating procedure for calling in air strikes, and it was the procedure that the SBS forces argued should have been used at Qala-i-Janghi. Clearly, if pilots are not given friendly co-ordinates this makes it far harder for them to accidentally target friendly forces.

The friendly-fire incident at Qala-i-Janghi was not the only such incident in the Afghan war. In April 2002, four Canadian soldiers were killed and eight wounded when a US F-16 aircraft dropped two five-hundred-pound bombs on them. The Canadian troops had been engaged in a live fire exercise around Kandahar, and the US warplane mistook their actions for hostile fire. This was one of a dozen or more friendly-fire incidents in which Western personnel and Afghan soldiers were killed or wounded. On 5 December 2001, a US B-52 providing close air support dropped a JDAM, which killed three US troops and five allied Afghans and injured forty others. On 1 July 2002, US aircraft misinterpreted celebratory gunshots at a wedding in the region of Oruzgan for hostile fire and targeted the wedding party, killing forty-four of the wedding guests.

The siege of Qala-i-Janghi is known in the US as a US-led mission in which UK special forces played a significant part. In fact, it was very much a British-led operation. After the fort siege, there were articles that appeared in the press stating that all the SBS troops would be awarded the CGM (Conspicuous Gallantry Medal) in the USA. The SBS soldiers were told that grateful CIA officers had planted these articles in the media. They believed that the British troops deserved to be honoured in the US for their actions at the fort trying to rescue the two CIA officers. The CIA also sent a telegram to the British government praising several of the SBS soldiers involved in the lifting of the fort siege and urging that they be given the recognition they deserved. Despite their best efforts, no SBS soldiers have received decorations in the USA for their actions at Qala-i-Janghi.

In the US, 5th SOF Major Michael E. Martin was awarded the Distinguished Service Cross (DSC) for his actions at Qala-i-Janghi. His medal citation states that he showed 'unparalleled courage under fire, decisive leadership and personal sacrifice which were directly responsible for the success of the rescue operation and were further responsible in ensuring the city of Mazar-e-Sharif did not fall back into enemy hands'. Major Martin himself stated of the award: 'It is a tremendous honour. But I don't consider myself a hero. I am not personally convinced that my actions warranted more than a pat on the back. I was just doing my job and our mission was accomplished.'

For his actions at Qala-i-Janghi, Sam Brown was duly awarded the US Navy Cross, second only to the CGM, for bravery in combat (his full citation is quoted at the start of this book). Only a handful of Navy Crosses have been awarded since the Vietnam War. Sam Brown also received the Military Cross (MC) from the Queen, making him one of only a few US servicemen ever to have been decorated by Her Majesty. Tom Knight, the SBS soldier who fought alongside him in the rescue mission, was awarded a high gallantry medal.

SBS Captain Lancer was also awarded a high gallantry medal for his actions at the fort. Stevie 'Ruff' Pouncer was awarded a mention in dispatches, although originally he had been nominated for an MC, and Sergeant Major Trent also received a mention in dispatches. Surprisingly, the other SBS soldiers received no British (or US) decorations for their actions at Qala-i-Janghi, though the siege of the fort remains one of the most highly decorated SBS missions, and one of the most extensively decorated missions in British special forces history.

By the time the siege came to an end, the battle for Northern Afghanistan had already been won. Immediately afterwards, the SBS team around Mazar went back to providing security for the rebuilding of villages and schools in the region. But the fort battle had been the turning point for the UK special forces in Afghanistan. Just weeks earlier, they had received a hostile reception from the Afghan resistance. After Qala-i-Janghi, General Dostum sent a letter of thanks to Her Majesty's Government for the SBS actions, and SBS units started getting the choicest missions. As one SBS soldier expresses it: 'Qala-i-Janghi really put the SBS (and SAS) on the map in Afghanistan. It meant that UK special forces had arrived and been seen to arrive, and had been seen to mean business.'

Several SBS soldiers question why they were left to deal with the Qala-i-Janghi uprising largely alone. Why were no UK or US special forces called in to reinforce the tiny group of soldiers trying to put down the uprising? Certainly, allied forces were overstretched in Afghanistan and many were deployed on far-distant operations. But to have had eight SBS soldiers deployed as the QRF for the whole of the Mazar region was certainly a risk-laden strategy.

The battle for Qala-i-Janghi remains one of the most controversial events of the Afghan war. At the time of the uprising, sections of the media questioned how the putting down of the revolt could have resulted in the majority of the prisoners being killed. It led to an outcry in the newsrooms, accusations of a 'massacre', and calls for an inquiry. Under the headline THE CASTLE OF DEATH, this is how the UK's *Independent* newspaper reported the uprising: 'How did US and British special forces come to be involved in the massacre of at least 150 prisoners of war – and maybe as many as 400 – who should have been protected under the Geneva Convention? In terms of numbers, Qala-i-Janghi could be the worst massacre to have come to light since the US bombing began.'

Months after the siege, the media continued to speculate as to the scale of the alleged war crimes that took place there. This is how the Globalvision News Network described the events. 'After a couple of phone calls to the special forces, the "unlawfuls" [the prisoners] were shot with mortars, machine guns, tanks and, finally, aerial bombardment. Just to make sure no "unlawfuls" would get out of what was left of the ruins, grenades were thrown into the basement of the fort. Diesel fuel was poured into the basement and ignited.' *Frontline*, an Indian news magazine, concluded: 'The massacre of prisoners of war at the Qala-i-Janghi fort may be the incident that exposes the inflated claims being made for a war by the richest nation against the poorest in the world.'

There are certainly several possible explanations as to why the six hundred fighters surrendered at Mazar, and then broke that surrender agreement at Qala-i-Janghi. But none of them support accusations of a massacre or war crimes. I have argued that the prisoners launched their uprising as part of a strategy aimed at attacking US, British and allied Afghan forces. This conclusion is based on extensive research and first-hand testimony from those who were there. Carrying out such a mock surrender is treachery, and goes against the rules of modern warfare. It was certainly not the first time such tactics had been tried by the 'foreign Taliban' in this war.

In the case of the Qala-i-Janghi uprising, it may have been part of a wider, but ultimately abortive, strategy to counter-attack against allied forces across the whole of northern Afghanistan. At the time of the six hundred fighters' initial surrender, some 6,000 enemy combatants were holed up in Kunduz, to the east of Mazar, reportedly planning to withdraw from Kunduz, loop northwards overland and launch a lightning counter-attack against Mazar. The six hundred fighters could reasonably have presumed that they would be held at

Mazar airport after their surrender. Had that been the case, they would then have been in position to launch an uprising and attack from the south. This would have trapped Mazar – defended at that time by only a handful of British and American troops – in a pincer movement, and it may well have fallen back into enemy hands.

Some commentators have suggested that the six hundred prisoners had offered a genuine surrender, and that it was only their subsequent treatment by the CIA agents Dave Tyson and Mike Spann that provoked the prisoners into launching the uprising. For example, Alex Perry, of *Time* magazine: 'The threats that they [the two CIA officers] made to the Taliban could quite plausibly have set off the revolt.' Others have claimed that the six hundred prisoners were faced by American and Afghan forces who threatened to kill them, and thus they were forced to launch the uprising and fight for their survival. Some have even suggested that it was the high-profile presence of the Western – 'infidel' – media that provoked the prisoners into launching the uprising.

However, a number of facts run contrary to such theories. First, the enemy combatants who had supposedly surrendered had actually hidden grenades and other weapons under their clothing. This is not the behaviour of those offering genuine surrender. Second, prisoners had launched two previous suicide attacks at the fort in the days prior to the uprising. Again, these are not the actions of genuinely surrendering forces. Third, the fact that concealed weapons were used to launch the uprising strongly suggests that those weapons were hidden with intent. Once they had taken up those weapons that changed their status from prisoners of war to armed combatants. Fourth, at no stage of the battle did any of the fighters offer to surrender, or indeed have that offer turned down. Those who did finally give up did so in part because they had run out of ammunition and to avoid being drowned.

Certainly, both Afghan parties to the war – Taliban and Northern Alliance – had an extensive record of mistreatment of prisoners of war prior to 9/11. The Taliban had mistreated Northern Alliance prisoners and vice versa. Following the fall of Kunduz and the surrender of 6,000 Taliban prisoners there, reports of greater horrors started to emerge. Some 3,000 prisoners from Kunduz were crammed into a facility built for 800, at Sheberghan prison, in appalling conditions. But they were the lucky ones. Many hundreds of their comrades had reportedly perished on the journey from Kunduz to that prison. Crammed into airless and baking container trucks, they had been driven through the burning hot desert and suffocated in huge numbers. Many of the dead were reportedly buried in mass graves in the desert around Dasht-e-Leili.

This event has become known as the 'Convoy of Death'. It is still being investigated by human rights experts, aid workers, the UN and related officials. The US-based Physicians for Human Rights has been particularly rigorous in pursuing such investigations. They maintain that 'death by container' has been a cheap means of mass murder utilised by both Afghan forces – Taliban and Northern Alliance – for a decade or more. There now seems little doubt that the Afghan forces who fought alongside British and US special forces were involved in serious abuses in the war. This is one of the problems with fighting 'proxy wars' – using small numbers of special forces to direct and assist local forces on the ground. It can be argued that in the Afghan war, UK and US special forces worked alongside allies who committed what could well qualify as war crimes.

Criticism has been levelled at US and British special forces that they are somehow culpable for such war crimes, alongside their Afghan allies. Those forces have denied such allegations. In February 2002, US CENTCOM was given copies of a Physicians for Human Rights report into the Convoy of Death. CENTCOM subsequently investigated whether US special forces were involved. 'Central Command looked into it and found no evidence of participation or knowledge or presence [of US forces],' said Lt. Col. Dave Lapan, a Department of Defense spokesperson. 'Our guys weren't there, didn't watch and didn't know about it – if indeed anything like this did happen.' CENTCOM concluded that: 'No US troops were present anywhere near that site. US troops were present in . . . the time frame, when the first mass graves were first discovered.'

In all the research that I have carried out for this book, I have come across little to suggest that such abuses took place during the siege of Qala-i-Janghi. In fact, quite the reverse appears to be true. The 'surrender' of the six hundred prisoners was taken as genuine by the Afghan forces; no proper search of the prisoners was carried out because their surrender was treated as authentic; their imprisonment in Qala-i-Janghi took place with repre-sentatives of the International Committee of the Red Cross being present; the prisoners were constrained by having their hands tied only in response to the suicide grenade attacks. The eventual surrender by the survivors of the revolt was accepted.

On the evening of 1 December a truck arrived at Sheberghan prison bearing the eighty-six surviving pris-oners from the siege of Qala-i-Janghi, including the

American Taliban, John Walker Lindh. Upon arrival, it was a medic from the US 5th SOF who first treated Lindh for his wounds. By 2 December representatives of the ICRC were negotiating access to visit the eighty-six prisoners and check on their welfare. At the same time some sections of the press got a chance to interview the survivors. The prisoners included Pakistanis, Sudanese and Somalis, and fighters from the Caucasus.

'It was our commander who began the fighting,' Abdul Jabar, a defiant 26-year-old Uzbek told a reporter from Britain's *Observer* newspaper. 'It is better to be a martyr than to go to prison. Prison is painful. Our commander said we would fight to the last bit of blood. But we gave up because we had nothing left. We had no ammunition and weapons and they cut the water. Only God knows what will happen to us now.' Most of the eighty-six survivors from the Qala-i-Janghi uprising ended up as prisoners in the US detention centre at Guantánamo Bay. Guantánamo was set up to hold what the White House terms as 'unlawful enemy combatants'. Their fate is yet to be decided.

John Walker Lindh had been amongst the last to give themselves up at the fort siege. It subsequently turned out that he was one of the prisoners interrogated by CIA Agent Mike Spann, just before the start of the uprising. That interrogation was videotaped and it shows Lindh refusing to respond to the CIA agent's questions. But once he had given himself up, he did talk to the press. From a hospital bed at Sheberghan prison he told a CNN reporter that the uprising was 'all the mistake of a handful of people. This was against what we had agreed upon and against Islam. It is a major sin to break a contract, especially in military situations.' But Lindh also demonstrated ongoing commitment to jihad. Asked if jihad was the right cause, he answered: 'Definitely.' He claimed to be a member of Ansar – 'the helpers' – a group of Arabic-speaking fighters funded by Osama bin Laden and fighting in Afghanistan.

After Sheberghan, he was moved to the USS *Bataan*, a navy warship sailing in the north Arabian Sea. After being questioned there, he was brought back to the US on 23 January 2002. He was subsequently tried in the US courts, but agreed a plea bargain whereby he would cooperate with US intelligence officials, telling them all he knew about the Taliban and al-Qaeda. He was sentenced to twenty years in prison for supplying services to the Taliban and carrying a rifle and grenades while fighting against Northern Alliance forces. If John Walker Lindh ever associates with terrorists again, he will be tried in the US courts as an enemy combatant.

'He was a soldier in the Taliban,' his attorney, James Brosnahan, commented. 'He did it for religious reasons. He did it as a Muslim, and history overcame him.'

John Walker Lindh's story shocked America. That there could have been a white American Taliban rocked the nation. But there were countless other Western nationals fighting alongside the AQT forces in Afghanistan at the time. The only difference is that most did not get caught, or if they did they did not surrender under the glare of the world's media. By the summer of 2002, British intelligence had identified some 3,000–4,000 British or British-based Islamists who had trained in al-Qaeda and Taliban training camps in Afghanistan. Intelligence officials reached this figure using documents recovered from the camps, and after interviewing those captured during the fighting. This shocking figure represents the total numbers that have travelled to attend the camps during the last decade.

All recruits undertook basic military training and religious instruction. A smaller number went on to receive 'advanced' training on how to select terrorist targets. A 'small minority' then went on to undertake full terrorist training, learning bomb-making and assassination techniques. From this minority the al-Qaeda leadership drew volunteers for specialist 'martyrdom' operations. One of those Britons thus recruited was Richard Reid, the so-called 'shoe bomber' who was caught while trying to blow up a passenger airliner in December 2001. For every American Taliban that waged jihad in Afghanistan, there were as many British and other European-based Islamic extremists willing and able to fight alongside them. Scores of these British-based extremists fought against the Northern Alliance and US and UK special forces troops in the war in Afghanistan.

By March 2002 the war had been largely won by the US, British and allied Afghan troops. Operation Anaconda was then launched, spearheaded by US special forces, a mission to flush out al-Qaeda elements from eastern Afghanistan, once again around the infamous Shah-i-Khot Valley. During Anaconda, US SOF took heavy casualties. One of those killed would have special meaning for Sam Brown, the US SEAL who distinguished himself with such heroism in the battle for Qala-i-Janghi. Neil Roberts, a fellow SEAL, was captured and killed by AQT forces in shocking circumstances. He had survived a fall from an MH47 Chinook helicopter that was hit by an RPG round, but had then been surrounded by al-Qaeda fighters. The SEAL operator had fought them off for thirty minutes, as his colleagues desperately tried to mount a rescue mission. But finally, his machine gun had jammed, and the enemy had closed in on him. He was subsequently tortured and then executed by the mob, the whole grisly scene being captured on video by a US Predator UAV. A six-man rescue team sent in to retrieve the body came under fire, and a second US soldier was killed. A further rescue attempt resulted in five more US deaths, and the area was only declared clear of enemy forces after US gunships destroyed the enemy mortar and machine-gun positions. The seven American bodies, including that of Neil Roberts, were then retrieved. The US military gave the battle location the name 'Roberts' Ridge', in memory of their fallen comrade.

After the tragedy of Operation Anaconda, Delta Force mounted a payback mission and invited several men from the SEALs to join them, as it was one of their guys who had died. The team flown in on this payback mission included one SBS soldier, on secondment to the SEALs. They were taken into an area where they knew that an al-Qaeda convoy was passing through – because the convoy was unknowingly being tailed by a UAV. The ambush team were dropped on the ridgeline, and when they spotted the five-vehicle convoy in the valley below them they opened up with everything they had. Those enemy who managed to get out of the vehicles were hardly able to raise their weapons and return fire, before they too were taken out.

Once the firefight was over, the Delta and SEAL (and SBS) ambush force descended to the valley floor. As they searched through the twenty-odd bodies, they noticed that most were Arabs or Chechens, with few Afghans among them. Several of the dead were sporting captured US Army webbing kits. One of the enemy lying on the ground was still just alive, and as a US soldier turned him over he released a grenade. Luckily, his body took the brunt of the blast, and it caused few injuries to the ambush force. In addition to the military webbing, a US

Army GPS and NVGs were retrieved from the dead. The serial numbers were subsequently traced, and these pieces of kit turned out to be from US soldiers originally killed or captured in Somalia, during the US military intervention there (immortalised in the book and then movie *Black Hawk Down*).

Since Afghanistan, the SBS has been through a major rebranding exercise, in part to try to get out from under the shadow of the SAS. The cap badge has been redesigned and the original motto – 'Not by strength, by guile' – has been changed to 'By strength and by guile'. During the rebranding, one of the options considered was whether the SBS should adopt a sandy-coloured beret, akin to that worn by the SAS. Requests went out to all serving – and some past – members of the SBS for cap badge redesign suggestions. Inevitably, one of the lads put in a design showing a big boot kicking a pair of balls. As most of the men agreed, it was a cracking cap badge – showing how the SBS would kick 'em in the balls every time. But when the final shortlist of ten designs was drawn up, the 'kick 'em in the balls' cap badge hadn't made it on to the list.

There were several designs utilising the dagger theme, but it was argued that the dagger was too much of an SAS symbol. However, once SBS archives were consulted it was discovered that one of the original forebear units of the SBS, the No. 2 Special Boat Section, had utilised a dagger and sea waves as its original insignia. The No. 2 Special Boat Section – whose motto was 'United we conquer' – had launched the very first canoe demolition raid, when, at the end of June 1941, they landed on the Sicilian coast via the submarine HMS *Urge* to attack a railway tunnel. The final SBS badge redesign sports a dagger pointing upwards through waves.

And what of the MV *Nisha*, the ship that was seized by the SBS in December 2001? A three-day search of the ship reportedly found no evidence of terrorist activity. 'A full security search of the ship has been completed,' a Scotland Yard spokesperson said. 'No noxious or dangerous substances have been found aboard the vessel.' The ship's owners, the British company Great Eastern Shipping, a subsidiary of the highly reputable East India Shipping Company, objected to the ship's seizure. The company pointed out that the British authorities could have contacted any one of three parties involved in the ship's chartering – the East India Shipping Company, the Mauritius Sugar Syndicate or Tate & Lyle – to investigate her cargo prior to seizing the ship.

However, the UK's counter-terrorism authorities maintain that the perceived threat from the ship was too great to have risked doing so. In the immediate aftermath of 9/11, concern over terrorism was at an all-time high. Governments and intelligence agencies were desperate to stop a repeat of the horrors that hit New York and Washington, when passenger aircraft had been turned into massive bombs. With all the available evidence to hand at the time, the MV *Nishu* was believed to constitute a major threat. Any chemical bomb the ship might have been carrying could conceivably have caused more death and destruction in central London than even the attack on the Twin Towers in New York.

At the time of the MV *Nisha* assault, politicians in Mauritius had made statements to the press about a home-grown terrorism threat. These led to headlines like: 'MAURITIUS ISLAMISTS STOCKPILE POISON FOR TERROR ATTACKS' (Agence France Presse). The Deputy Prime Minister of Mauritius, Paul Berenger, warned that an Islamist party in Mauritius was stockpiling insecticides

for terrorist purposes. 'All precautions have been taken,'
Berenger said, 'and the people have nothing to worry
about.' Opposition parties in Mauritius have since
accused their government of inflating the scare over
Lannate (methomyl) and the MV *Nisha*'s sugar cargo,
to gain political advantage. Others maintain that there
is still a serious threat of Islamist terrorism in Mauritius.

Could the MV *Nisha* have posed a serious danger to
the UK if it had deployed a 'methomyl bomb' in densely
populated central London? In a report entitled 'Deliberate
release of biological and chemical agents in Scotland',
the Scottish Executive lists chemical agents most likely
to be used in such an attack. Methomyl is listed as one
of those agents. In personal correspondence, Julian Perry-
Robinson, an expert on chemical and biological warfare
at Brighton University's Science Policy Research Unit,
states that 'Methomyl is described as a carbamate, having
a high anticholinesterase activity conferring use as a pesticide. It has a parallel with nerve gases, although, in terms
of animal lethal dosage, some orders of magnitude less
potent.' A lethal dose of methomyl is in the order of
12–15 milligrams per kilogram. A poor man's chemical
bomb made from methomyl could pose serious dangers
to humans.

A report in the *First Responder*, a US-based magazine
aimed at emergency services personnel, poses the question: 'Can a terrorist disperse pesticides to get the same
effects as nerve agents?' It continues: 'Pesticides which
inhibit cholinesterase [like methomyl] have very low
vapor pressures and are much less toxic than nerve agents.
Other toxic chemicals (ammonia, chlorine) may be more
attractive to terrorists. This is not to say that pesticides
would not be used as a terrorist weapon . . . The same
technologies used in the pesticide industry . . . to ease

dispersal can potentially be used by terrorists to disperse a toxic chemical into a crowd.' In short, pesticides may offer terrorists the potential to make a poor man's chemical weapon.

The MV *Nisha*'s cargo of sugar would need to be mixed with other chemicals, like ammonium nitrate, to make an explosive device. But such improvised explosive devices are incredibly simple to make and largely safe until detonated. Believing the MV *Nisha* to be carrying such an explosive device, the UK authorities decided at the time that they had no alternative but to act as they did and stop the ship. Despite the lack of terrorist paraphernalia found on board, British authorities still describe the MV *Nisha* assault as 'a successful run-out of the counter-terrorism machinery'.

The assault on the MV *Nisha* remains a textbook special forces seizure of a ship at sea, and the threat from terrorists deploying such dirty bombs remains high. In the spring of 2004, British authorities arrested several terror suspects who were planning to make a poor man's chemical weapon, using a highly toxic, easily obtainable chemical called osmium tetroxide. Used primarily in laboratory research, osmium tetroxide attacks soft human tissue and can kill anyone who breathes its fumes. Terrorist suspects have also been arrested in the UK while attempting to manufacture a poor man's biological weapon using ricin, a naturally occurring, but potentially lethal, toxin. Fears concerning a 'terror fleet' of merchant ships controlled by al-Qaeda remain very real. A report by RAND, a European policy think tank, concludes: 'The marine sector – and specifically the container transport sector – remains wide open to the terrorist threat.'

With the capture in November 2002 of al-Qaeda's maritime strategist, Abd al-Rahim al-Nashiri, US offi-

cials began tracking fifteen cargo ships allegedly operated by terrorists under flags of convenience. In August
2002, the captain of the *Sara* merchant ship sent an SOS
message to Italian authorities, as fifteen Pakistani men
were threatening his crew with guns. All fifteen had links
to al-Qaeda and were arrested on terror conspiracy
charges. They were found to be carrying maps of Italian
cities, false documents and tens of thousands of dollars
in cash. In the spring of 2004, Israeli commandos seized
the 4,000-ton *Karine A*, flying the flag of convenience
of the Pacific Islands of Tonga. They discovered fifty tons
of weapons on board, mostly manufactured in Iran and
bound for the Palestinian conflict.

And what of the Afghan conflict now? Military forces
from the International Security Assistance Force have
been largely restricted to operating in the north of the
country and Kabul – as powerful warlords and the
Taliban try to reassert control in the south of Afghanistan.
In the winter of 2004, the UK military deployed some
5,000 fresh troops to Afghanistan, to counter the
perceived threat of a resurgent al-Qaeda and Taliban.
These forces have been spearheaded by the men of the
Parachute Regiment. Some 18,000 US and British troops
are continuing to hunt for Osama bin Laden and rene-
gade al-Qaeda elements in the hills that border Pakistan.
They are being aided in their efforts by British special
forces troops – the Special Boat Service and the Special
Air Service.

Osama bin Laden – still believed to be at large –
succeeded in creating the world's foremost terrorism
university in Afghanistan. He was able to do so because
of a unique set of factors: chaos in Afghanistan; a weak
set of neighbours; violent Islamist ideology backed by
affluent Middle East factions; and a profound lack of

interest or engagement in the region by the West. Bin Laden – or any number of bin Laden wannabes – will be able to do so again should the same set of factors reassert themselves. This demonstrates the importance of reconstructing Afghanistan, and building a stable, democratic, accountable regime. A young university student in this region has really only two choices. He can aspire to the so-called glamour and material affluence of the West, while accepting the squalor, lack of jobs and freedoms at home. Or he can embrace the extreme, but empowering, ideology of 'fascist' Islam. Destroying bin Laden's terror university did not destroy the supply of potential students. Only democracy and development has any chance of doing that.

GLOSSARY

AK47 Soviet-designed 7.62mm Kalashnikov assault rifle

APC armoured personnel carrier

AQT al-Qaeda and Taliban forces

AWOL absent without leave, but also used as slang for someone going crazy

bergen army backpack containing mess kit, sleeping bag, etc.

casevac casualty evacuation (by air)

CENTCOM US Central Command, primarily based at MacDill Airforce Base, Tampa, Florida.

Chaff radar-reflecting tinsel and heat-seeking missile confusing flares used by aircraft to deter homing missiles

Chinook CH47 a large, twin-rotor transport helicopter with a lifting capability of ten tons, with door-mounted machine guns

CSMR chemical and biological warfare specialists attached to the SBS/SAS

CO Commanding Officer

COBR Cabinet Office Briefing Room, the national crisis centre from which the British government responds to all types of major crises

CSM Company Sergeant Major

CT Counter-Terrorism

CTR close-target recce

CQB close-quarter battle

danger-close when friendly forces are in dangerous proximity to target

Delta Force supposedly ultra-secret US Special Forces with very similar functions to the SAS

Dushka DShK 12.7mm (50-cal) Soviet heavy machine gun

E&E escape and evasion

EP evacuation point

ERV emergency rendezvous

exfil short for exfiltration, leaving battle scene or area of operations at end of mission

FAC forward air control, the ability to call in air strikes to specific enemy targets

FMB forward mounting base, a forward position from which to prepare for deployment into action

kafir Arabic word meaning an unbeliever

kofr Arabic word meaning disbelief

LTD laser target designators, devices for guiding in airstrikes

Green Slime British soldiers' slang for British intelligence (MI6)

GPMG general purpose machine gun

HE heavy explosives

heads British military slang for urinals

Hercules (C-130) American-built C-130 transport aircraft, used by British military, commonly known as a 'Herc'

hexy stove a tiny, collapsible metal stove, which burns solid, paraffin-based fuel blocks

HMG heavy machine gun

humint human intelligence sources

infil short for infiltration

JDAM joint direct attack munition, a 2,000-pound GPS-guided bomb

JSOC Joint Special Operations Command, the US headquarters element in control of US Special Forces

lase military slang for firing a laser at a target to be hit by laser-guided bombs, as in 'to lase'

LAW light anti-armour weapon, an American-made 66mm or 94mm disposable, one-man-portable rocket system with a 500-metre range

loadie slang for the loadmaster of an aircraft

LOE limit of exploitation, the agreed extent to which a military unit will advance on the battlefield

LTD laser target designator, for guiding laser-guided munitions on to target

Lynx British-built attack helicopter

LZ landing zone

malleting slang for shooting or blowing up the enemy, as in 'give them a good malleting'

MGRS Military Grid Reference System, a system for identifying targets on a map grid

MH47 a Chinook helicopter extensively modified for special forces use

Mi-17 Soviet bloc transport helicopter

Mi-24 Soviet bloc helicopter gunship

Minimi SAW (squad assault weapon) 5.56mm light machine gun

MP military policeman

MRE meals ready to eat, US Army ration packs

MP5 a Heckler & Koch short machine gun, ideal for special forces use

NAPS nerve agent pre-treatment set

NCO non-commissioned officer

NVG night-vision goggles

OC Officer Commanding

OP observation position, a hidden position from where to spy on enemy movements

op short for operation

Operation Enduring Freedom 2001 US military intervention in Afghanistan

Operation Veritas 2001 British military operations in Afghanistan

opsec short for operational security

Paras the men of the Parachute Regiment

PE plastic explosives

PJHQ Permanent Joint Headquarters, the UK military tri-service command centre

plasticuffs strips of tough plastic with a simple ratchet device used for handcuffing prisoners

Predator the RQ-1 Predator unmanned aerial vehicle, a low-flying aircraft armed with missiles

prepped prepared for a mission

PRM personal radio mike

psyops psychological operations

PT physical training

QRF Quick Reaction Force

RPG rocket-propelled grenade

RPK Soviet-era light calibre 7.62mm machine gun

SAM surface-to-air missile

SAS Special Air Service, the UK's foremost special forces unit

SBS Special Boat Service, the UK's smaller, sister special forces unit to the SAS

Sea King Naval anti-submarine helicopter, capable of carrying 20 men

SEAL Sea Air Land Team, US special forces recruited from within the Navy and Marine Corps

SF special forces

shaheed Arabic for a martyr

shihada Arabic word for martyrdom

shouhada'a Arabic word for the martyrs

Shakyboats slang for the men of the Special Boat Service

sigint signals intelligence

sitrep short for situation report

SOF Special Operations Forces, US Tier 2 special forces

SOP standard operating procedure, the normal way of doing things in any given military situation

SOCOM Special Operations Command, the US special forces headquarters

STASS short-term air-supply system, an emergency air bottle for underwater operations

TACBE tactical beacon, used by troops for emergency surface-to-air communications

TOW tube-launched, optically tracked, wire-guided anti-tank missiles

UAV unmanned aerial vehicle

UKSF United Kingdom Special Forces (the SAS and the SBS)

USAF United States Air Force

UXO unexploded ordnance

warned off British military phrase meaning to be given first warning of an impending deployment

WMD weapon of mass destruction

WP white phosphorous, an incendiary shell

X-ray code name for an enemy combatant

Yankee code name for friendly forces